PAINT VARNISH SOLVENTS AND COATING TECHNOLOGY

PAINT VARNISH SOLVENTS AND COATING TECHNOLOGY

Written By :

EIRI Consultants and Engineers

ENGINEERS INDIA RESEARCH INSTITUTE

4449, Nai Sarak, Main Road, Delhi-110 006 (India)

Ph. : 91-11-23918117, 23916431, 45120361, 45626431

✶ **E-Mail :** eiribooks@yahoo.com

✶ **Website :** www.eiriindia.org & www.eiri.in
www.eiribooksandprojectreports.com

Sole Distributor :

EIRI PROJECT CONSULTANTS & PUBLISHERS

4/54, Roop Nagar, Delhi-110007

Printed and Published by :

ENGINEERS INDIA RESEARCH INSTITUTE

4449, Nai Sarak, Main Road, Delhi-110 006 (India)
Ph. : 91-11-23918117, 23916431, 45120361, 45626431
★ **E-Mail :** eiribooks@yahoo.com
★ **Website :** www.eiriindia.org & www.eiri.in
www.eiribooksandprojectreports.com

Distributed by :

EIRI PROJECT CONSULTANTS & PUBLISHERS
4/54, Roop Nagar, Delhi-110007

Second Edition

ISBN : 9788186732441
Printed in New Delhi (India)

Rs. 800

Printed and Published by Sudhir Gupta for
"Engineers India Research Institute", 4449, Nai Sarak, Main Road,
New Delhi-110 006 and Printed at Swastik Offset, Delhi

Preface

Preface

The Book 'Paint Varnish Solvents and Coating Technology' covers Introduction, General Pigments Physical Properties, Pigments Processing, Plasticizers and Solvents, Synthetic Resins, Cellulose Ester and Ether Products, Varnishes, Pigmentation, Paints (Decorative & Building), Coatings (Water Borne), Methods of Applications, Industrial Paints and Coatings, Industrial Finishes, Miscellaneous Coatings and Ancillary Materials, Testing and Evaluation, Miscellaneous Formulae, Project Profiles of Aluminium Paints, Cement Paints, Acrylic Emulsion Paints, Insulating Varnish, Powder Coating, Primer Paints and many others. Suppliers of Raw Materials, Suppliers of Plant and Machinery, Present Manufacturers, Packaging Material Addresses.

Hope, the book will undoubtedly help the new entrepreneurs as well as well established industrialists.

Director

ENGINEERS INDIA RESEARCH INSTITUTE

4449 Nai Sarak, New Delhi (India)

Contents and Subject Index

Chapters	Page No.

Chapter - 1

INTRODUCTION

Paint Ingredients

A liquid paint contains three major ingredients together with smaller quantities of 'additives' which play an essential role. The major ingredients are pigments (including extenders), binder (or film former) and solvent or thinner. A dispersion of the pigment in the binder constitutes the paint film the properties of which depend, to a large degree, on the nature of the binder, but the nature and quantity of pigment are also important. The solvent or thinner is used to render the pigment/binder mixture sufficiently fluid for application as a thin film after which it is lost by evaporation and plays no part in the performance of the dry paint film. The additives employed comprise materials such as driers, antiskinning and anti-settling agents, fungicides of bactericides and surface active agents used to assist pigment dispersion.

The following is a brief summary of the general nature and functions of the major paint ingredients.

Pigments

These are finely divided solids, the average particle size of which can vary from 0.2 to 10 μm (micrometres). They may be inorganic or organic in constitution. The general classification of pigments can be illustrated by the following scheme.

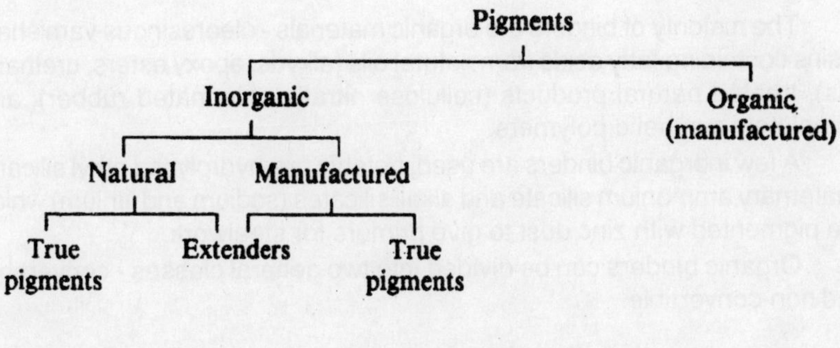

Extenders have been included with the inorganic pigments since they are all inorganic solids. They differ from 'true' pigments in their behaviour when dispersed in organic media. True pigments exhibit opacity or hiding power in varying degree, whereas extenders are practically transparent. Extenders are used in certain types of paints (notably undercoats, primers and some low-gloss finishes) to modify or control physical properties. They make no contribution to colour (unless they are very impure) or to opacity.

True, pigments are used to provide colour and opacity or hiding power. In finishes they contribute to durability. A pigmented film is more weather resistant than an unpigmented film of the same binder. In primers for metals, specific pigments are used to check or inhibit corrosion of the metal.

The majority of natural pigments are oxides or hydroxides of iron but may contain appreciable quantities of clay or siliceous matter. The colours are less bright than the corresponding manufactured oxides and hydroxides.

The manufactured inorganic pigments contain the whites and a wide range of colours, including yellows, reds, oranges, greens and blues. Carbon black, consisting essentially of elementary carbon, is usually included in the inorganic pigments.

The organic pigments cover the entire spectrum range, but the brilliance and opacity vary considerably. There are no white organic pigments and organic blacks find only limited use; carbon black satisfies most paint requirements.

In general, organic pigments are brighter than the inorganic counterparts but show much greater variation in opacity and in lightfastness, the latter particularly when mixed with white. Organic pigments derived from plant and animal sources are no longer employed in paint manufacture. Although some possess bright self-colours, they lack permanence.

Binder (or film former)

This is the continuous phase in a paint film and is largely responsible for the protective and general mechanical properties of the film. Film properties depend also on the nature of the pigment, the degree to which the pigment is dispersed in the binder,"and the volume of film occupied by the pigment.

The majority of binders are organic materials - oleoresinous varnishes, resins containing fatty acids from natural oils (alkyds, epoxy esters, urethane oils), treated natural products (cellulose nitrate, chlorinated rubber), and completely synthetic polymers.

A few inorganic binders are used, notably pre-hydrolysed ethyl silicate, quaternary ammonium silicate and alkali silicates (sodium and lithium) which are pigmented with zinc dust to give primers for steelwork.

Organic binders can be divided into two general classes - convertible and non-convertible.

Convertible binders These undergo a chemical reaction in the film. In the conventional oxidizing binders, oxygen is absorbed and the film slowly sets and then dries to a product which is no longer soluble in the solvents used in the liquid paint. The drying and hardening of the film is catalysed by 'driers' and since oxygen absorption is involved, there is a limit to the thickness of film which will dry through.

The two-pack materials, notably epoxies and polyurethanes, cure by chemical reaction between two components in the film. Absorption of oxygen is not involved and thicker coatings can be applied. By the use of low molecular weight resins and hardeners; 'solventless'. epoxy systems can be produced and very thick films can be applied and cured.

Thermosetting binders These are also known as 'thermohardening' and as 'stoving' types. As in other convertible coatings, film hardening is the result of three-dimensional linking of the polymer molecules, but in this case it is brought about by the action of heat. The film is cured much more rapidly and attains the full resistance to reagents and solvents in a fraction of the time required by the air-drying types.

Stoving of the films is carried out in either hot-air convection ovens or in infra-red ovens heated by either electricity or gas. Certain types of coating, especially those which cure by a free radical mechanism, can be cured in seconds only, by either an electron beam or ultraviolet radiation. Since no heat is involved, this process is suited to finishes on sensitive substrates such as wood or card:.

Non-convertible binders These do not depend on chemical reaction of any sort for film formation, the process consisting solely of evaporation of solvents. The film remains soluble in the parent solvent blend and is therefore classed as 'non-convertible'. Such materials are often designated 'lacquers' and are usually applied.by spray (especially' a second coat) since the solvents present tend to dissolve the previously applied coat. This would be disturbed or 'lifted' if brushing were employed. Typical examples of non-convertible binders are chlorinated rubber and cellulose nitrate.

The familiar vinyl emulsion paints contain a non-convertible polymer dispersed in water in which the pigment also is dispersed. Film formation results from evaporation of the water followed by coalescence of the binder in which the pigment becomes embodied.

Solvents (or thinners)

These are usually volatile organic liquids in which the binder or film former is soluble. When the paint film is deposited on a surface the solvent should evaporate completely. It plays no part in film formation and is used solely as a means of conveying the pigment/binder mixture to the surface as a thin uniform film.

Classes of materials used as solvents include aliphatic hydrocarbons (white spirit and the SBP solvents), aromatic hydrocarbons (toluene, xylene and the trimethyl benzenes), alcohols, esters, ketones, esters and ether-esters of propylene glycol. Water is the solvent in water-borne and emulsion paints.

The fact that these materials are volatile, flammable and possess a degree of toxicity has raised a number of serious problems. Atmospheric pollution by solvents can be appreciable in areas containing a number of paint-consuming industries.

Organic solvents can be taken into the human body by swallowing (this is uncommon), by the respiratory system, or by absorption through the skin. The effects can vary from skin irritation to damage to internal organs.

CLASSIFICATION OF PAINTS

As mentioned above, paints can be divided into two general types, convertible and non-convertible. Further subdivisions are possible - particularly with convertible coatings - into types of curing mechanism (air-dry, stoving, etc,) and performance characteristics (heat-resisting, corrosion-resisting, etc.).

A further, very general classification is based on the order of application, a method familiar to professional decorators, industrial finishers and the general public. In brief, the types are the following.

Primers are, with a few exceptions, the first coats applied and are formulated to meet the requirements of the surface. Primers for steel, for instance, are required to meet an entirely different set of conditions from primers for wood, and the formulations differ considerably.

Sealers Where surfaces are porous, absorption of paint medium can upset the pigment/binder ratio of the paints applied and sealers are therefore used to. eliminate the suction. In some cases the formulation of the primer can be modified to enable it to function -as a sealer also.

Stoppers and fillers When surfaces contain holes or deep indentations they are treated with paste stopper after application and drying of the primer. Stoppers are very highly pigmented so that they dry hard without shrinking and can be rubbed down to a smooth surface before application of further coats of paint.

If the surface contains merely shallow indentations or irregularities, these are corrected by the application of filler. This is liquid and can be applied by spray or brush. Like the stopper, it dries hard and can be rubbed down to a smooth finish. Both stoppers and fillers are porous when dry and require treatment with sealer before further painting.

Undercoats are applied over the primer or filler. They are fairly highly pigmented to give good obliterating power and to give build or thickness-to the paint film. They usually dry to an eggshell finish which is suitable for good adhesion by the finishing coat.

Finishing coats can be designed to dry to films which exhibit a high gloss, semi-gloss, eggshell or matt finish.

High build, high solids and solventless paints

The protection afforded by a paint film is, in general, proportional to the thickness and the purpose of these paints is to provide a means of achieving a desired film build or thickness in the minimum number of coats.

High build paints contain a structuring or gelling agent which allows thick films to be applied without risk of sagging or forming 'curtains' on vertical surfaces.

High solids paints contain only a small quantity of solvent so that shrinkage of the film on drying is minimal: These paints are environmentally attractive as the low solvent content means less atmospheric pollution than is caused by traditional types of paint.

Solventless paints are based on liquid resins of low viscosity and are used where the presence of solvent is undesirable as, for example, in tank interiors and other enclosed spaces. They are used also in the underwater painting of steel and concrete structures.

These high build paints are formulated to cure either by chemical reaction (two pack types such as epoxies or polyurethanes) or are non-convertible types (high build vinyls or chlorinated rubber) which dry solely by solvent evaporation.

With oxidizable media, such as alkyds or oleoresinous types, there is a limit to the film thickness which can be applied in one operation. Oxygen is required for cure and must be available throughout the film until it is dry and hard. With thick films oxidation of the surface layers produces a 'skin' which reduces the rate of oxygen. penetration to the lower layers. These can remain soft for a considerable time.

Very thick films should contain a minimum of solvent. Films of normal thickness can retain small amounts of solvent for a considerable time - and this is more pronounced with thick films since migration of solvent molecules to the surface is retarded by increasing rigidity of the film. This must be borne in mind when multicoat systems are applied; recoating intervals must be adequate.

APPLICATION OF PAINTS

Whilst decorative paints continue to be applied by brush or roller, newer methods have been introduced in the maintenance and industrial fields. Among these are (a) electro-deposition, both anodic and cathodic, used .mainly for primers for metals and made possible by the introduction of water-soluble resins, and (b) airless and air-assisted spray which permits the rapid coating of large areas and is capable of applying 'highbuild' or thixotropic paints to give greater film build than is possible with conventional paints.

The demand from a number of industries for shorter drying or curing times has been met by the use of new and modified resins; industrial air-drying primers and undercoats with drying times of 10-20 minutes and over-coating times-of 1-2 hours are now common.

Films which cure by a free radical mechanism are cured very rapidly by irradiation with either electron beams or ultraviolet. The electron beam method has been applied to metal strip (coil coating) whilst ultraviolet irradiation is suited to wood finishes.

The paint film

The loss of solvent by evaporation from a freshly applied paint film results in a shrinkage or decrease in thickness of the film. The ratio of the thickness of the dry film to that of the wet film is controlled -by the volume of thinner used or, conversely, by the volume of solid material in the paint. This is known as the 'volume solids' or 'solids by volume' and is expressed as a percentage:

$$\%\ \text{Volume solids} = \frac{\text{Dry film thickness x 100}}{\text{Wet film thickness}}$$

The figure is generally quoted on manufacturers' data sheets. It can also be calculated from the paint formula (using specific gravities) or can be determined practically by the method of BS 3900, Part A 10. Painting specifications usually require a minimum dry film thickness for each coat of paint and for the thickness of the complete system. Film thickness is usually expressed in micrometres symbol μm) but the terms 'thou' and the US 'mil' (both of which equal 25.4 μm) are often encountered.

In order to apply a given dry film, thickness an operater requires to know the corresponding wet film thickness which can be readily checked on the wet film The required wet film thickness is calculated by the equation

$$\text{Wet film thickness} = \frac{\textit{Dry film thickness x 100}}{\textit{\% Volume solids}}$$

Coverage rate

This **can be defined as the area covered** by unit volume of paint when applied at a specified film thickness. It is usually expressed in square metres per litre and can be calculated from the **dry- film** thickness and the volume solids using the equation

$$\text{Coverage } (\text{m}^2/\text{litre}) = \frac{\%\text{Volume solids x 10}}{\text{Dry film thickness } (\mu\text{m})}$$

The figure derived is the ideal or theoretical coverage. Practical coverage rates are always lower since they are influenced by design of structure, method and technique of application and general losses. The site engineer or painting contractor is best qualified to assess practical coverage rates which can vary from 50 to 80 percent of the theoretical value.

Pigment Volume Concentration

A number of the properties of a paint film are determined by the volume of the film occupied by the pigment - the 'Pigment Volume Concentration' (PVC). This is defined by the expression

$$\textbf{Pigment Volume Concentration} = \frac{\textbf{Volume of pigment x 100}}{\textbf{Volume of pigment + volume of non-volatile binder}}$$

Glossy films- are characterized- by a low PVC, but with increasing PVC a point is reached where the gloss falls rapidly and radical changes occur in the film properties. This is illustrated in Fig. 1.1, in which film properties (in arbitrary units) are plotted against PVC. Other film properties such as moisture permeability and tendency to blister also change radically at about the same point. This point of rapid change in film properties is known as the 'Critical Pigment Volume Concentration' (CPVC). It represents the situation where just sufficient binder is present to coat the particles of pigment and to fill the interstices between them. An increase in pigment content will result in a film containing voids (an underbound film), whereas an increase in binder will become evident by an increase in gloss. The value of the CPVC is characteristic of a given system and varies from one system to another.

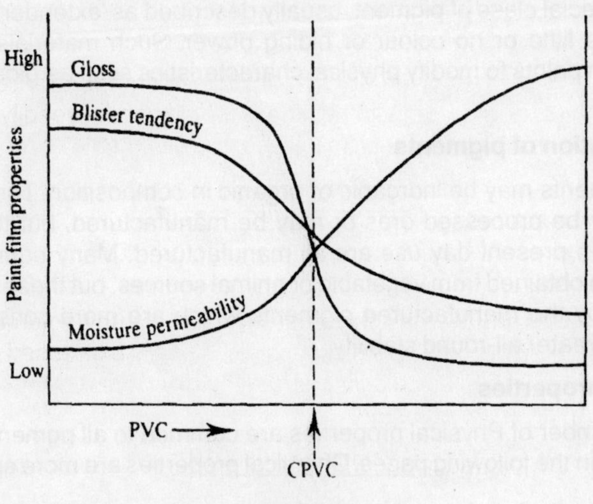

Fig. 1.1

Chapter - 2

GENERAL PIGMENTS PHYSICAL PROPERTIES

A pigment can be defined as a finely divided powder which can be dispersed in media of various types to produce paints or inks. It is insoluble in the medium and confers the following properties on the mixture.

1 Colour, for decorative effect or aesthetic appeal.

2 Obliteration or hiding power It should obliterate the surface, whether it is metal, wood, stone, or an earlier coat of paint. As will appear later, pigments differ considerably in their hiding power and, in some instances, several coats of paint may be necessary to effect complete obliteration of the surface.

3 Protective properties These are important in paints on exposed wood and certain types of metals, particularly iron and steel. A suitably pigmented varnish is more weather-resistant and therefore more protective than the unpigmented material.

4 Corrosion repression Primers for iron and steelwork contain special pigments chosen for their corrosion-repressing properties.

A special class of pigment, usually described as 'extender', generally possesses little or no colour or hiding power. Such materials are often included in paints to modify physical characteristics such as.gloss and flow properties.

Classification of pigments

Pigments may be inorganic or organic in composition. The inorganic types may be processed ores or may be manufactured, but the organic pigments in present day use are all manufactured. Many earlier organic types were obtained from vegetable or animal sources, but these have been replaced by the manufactured pigments which are more consistent and possess greater all-round stability.

Physical properties

A number of Physical properties are common to all pgments and are described in the following pages. Chemical properties are more specific and will be considered under the pigment classes or individual pigments.

COLOUR

Colour can be defined as a sensation resulting from activation of the retina of the eye by electromagnetic vibrations which we describe as light-waves. These light-waves differ in wavelength and each wavelength produces a specific sensation. Thus the longest waves produce the sensation which we describe as red and the shortest give the sensation of blue. The range of sensations between red and blue, which we call colours, is known as the visible spectrum. The fact that daylight contains the whole visible spectrum is shown by the simple experiment of passing a narrow beam of white light through a glass prism. The beam is opened out and a spectrum is produced.

The relationship **between colour and** wavelength is illustrated in the following diagram.

Relationship between colour and wavelength

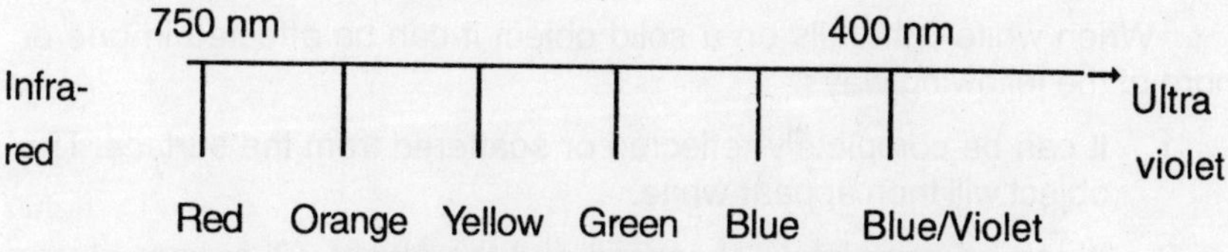

(One nanometre (nm) =10^{-6} mm)

The visible spectrum consists of only a part of the whole electromagnetic range of wavelengths or vibrations. Beyond the red are the infra-red (heat) rays and the much longer radio waves. Wavelengths shorter than the blue/violet are the invisible but intensely reactive ultraviolet, X-rays, and gamma rays.

Primary colours

By the use of mixtures of narrow wavebands of three spectrum colours - red, green and blue - it is possible to produce white light as well as a very close approximation to the range of spectrum colours. The three spectrum colours are known as the 'light primaries' (or, sometimes, 'additive primaries') and correspond approximately to wavelengths, of 650 nm, 530 nm and 460 nm.

Additive colour mixing

The light primaries can be combined by directing the light from three lanterns, each fitted with the appropriate filter to transmit the desired wavelength, on to a white surface. The reflected colour is a mixture of the three incident beams and no appreciable energy is lost; the mixing is therefore said to be 'additive'. The matching or measurement of colours by mixtures of light primaries is the basis of colorimetry.

Complementary colours

When the three primary colours.are mixed in pairs, red and blue give magenta, red and green give yellow, green and blue give cyan. If each of these resulting colours is mixed with the remaining primary, the result is white light, i.e. magenta + green, yellow + blue, red + cyan are pairs of colours which can produce white light on mixing. Such pairs are known as complementary colours or, sometimes, as complementaries.

Another, more practical, way of describing complementary colours is by considering a coloured material such as a pigment. When illuminated by white light, the reflected wavelengths (the observed colour) are complementary to those absorbed.

Magenta, yellow and cyan are sometimes known as 'subtractive primaries'.

Colour of objects

When white light falls on a solid object it can be affected in one or more of the following ways.

1 It can be completely reflected or scattered from the surface. The object will then appear white.

2 It can be completely absorbed and the object will appear black. Complete reflectance or absorption are not achieved in practice, although certain surfaces such as magnesium oxide and high-quality carbon black, respectively, are close approximations.

3 Some of the wavelengths can be absorbed and some reflected. The object will then appear coloured, the colour being determined by the nature of the reflected wavelengths.

In practice, 3 is often accompanied by a certain amount of 1 or 2. If accompanied by 1, that is, by some reflectance over the whole spectrum (white), the colour will appear lighter. When accompanied by 2 or absorption over the whole spectrum (black), the colour will appear darker or often dirtier.

Subtractive colour mixing

When a mixture of coloured pigments is exposed to white light, the colour observed depends on the absorption and reflectance characteristics of the individual pigments. Consider, for example, a mixture of yellow and blue pigments. The blue absorbs the red, orange and yellow wavelengths whilst the yellow absorbs the blue and violet. The mixture absorbs all the spectrum colours except green, which is the resulting colour. The green is produced by subtractive colour-mixing. (This is an ideal condition - in practice the absorption bands are not clearly differentiated and overlap occurs. There are, for instance, 'reddish' and 'greenish' blues, 'reddish' and 'greenish' yellows; and a range of greens will be produced from the combinations.)

Again, a mixture of red and green pigments, unlike the light primaries, will not produce yellow on account of absorption. Yellow is therefore introduced as a primary in pigment mixing, and the pigment primaries are red, yellow and blue. However, it is not possible to produce white by any combination of these, but, as a result of absorption effects, a range of greys is obtained.

Colour perception

On entering the eye, rays of light pass through the transparent lens and are focused on the interior surface at the back of the eye. This surface comprises the sensitive ends of the optic nerve and is known as the 'retina'. The wavelengths of the incident light produce characteristic impulses which pass to the brain by the optic nerve and produce the sensations associated with colour.

The ends of the optic nerve form a large number of rods and cones which have distinct functions. The rods do not react to colour but are sensitive to differences in intensity. They are responsible for night vision, when objects appear as different intensities of dark grey or black.

The cones are sensitive to colour but do not function efficiently in poor light. There is an old theory, put forward in the nineteenth century by Young and Helmholtz, in which cones are classified in three types, i.e. (i) those sensitive to long wavelengths which, produce the sensation of red, (ii) those sensitive to medium wavelengths which produce the sensation of green, and (iii) those sensitive to short wavelengths which produce the sensation of violet. This theory has been difficult to prove but fits in with modern ideas of colourblindness.

The sensitivity of the average human eye varies with the wavelength of the light. It is greatest in the green waveband (about 560 nm) and decreases rapidly on each side (Fig. 2.1).

Colour-blindness

A person with normal colour vision can match any colour of the visible spectrum by using red, green, and blue lights in the correct proportions. Such a normal person is known as a *trichromat.*

Colour-blindness in females is comparatively rare, but with men a common type involves difficulty with one of the primaries, so that the colour match produced will be different from that of a trichromat. About 1 percent of males have difficulty with red and about 4 -6 percent with green. Difficulty with blue is uncommon. Persons suffering from this defect are known as anomalous trichromats:

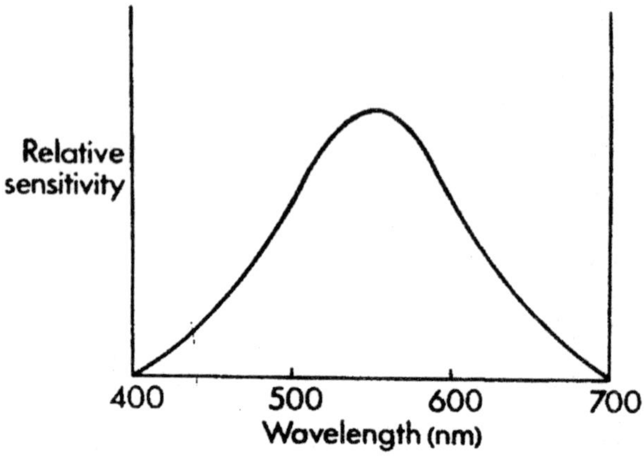

Fig. 2.1 Sensitivity of the human eye

Dichromats are completely blind to one of the primaries and would use only two for a colour matching. The most common forms are blindness to red or green. Blindness to blue is very rare.

Totally colour-blind people, monochromats, are extremely rare. They can distinguish only light and dark, and their world, therefore, is one of varying shades of grey.

It is possible to diagnose deficiencies in colour vision by the use of the Ishihara Colour Chart, or the Colour Matching Aptitude Test.

Colour matching

This involves the mixing of suitable pigments (or paints) to match a given standard and requires (i) an operator who has normal colour vision, and (ii) a standard source of illumination. The latter is important for comparison of the standard and the matching; and whenever possible, in the Northern hemisphere, a north light is used. In the absence of a north light it is possible to use a source of illumination in which the wavelengths in white light have been simulated by blending the light of fluorescent and tungsten lamps. These are often called daylight lamps.

The colour of an object illuminated with white light can be different when viewed in, for example, tungsten light since the latter is deficient in the blue/violet wavelengths and richer in the red wavelengths, compared with white light. Two colours can be matched in daylight but may not match under other types of illumination unless identical pigments have been used. This phenomenon is known as 'metamerism'.

A colour which matches a standard under all types of illumination is known as a 'spectral' match and can be obtained only if identical pigments are used in both.

illuminant standards

Standard light-sources are specified in the CIE system (see below) and called 'Standard Illuminants'. They refer to 'colour temperature' which is the temperature to which a black-body radiator is heated to emit light which matches the light in question. The standards generally adopted are the following.

illuminant A colour temperature 2850°K, corresponds to the light from a tungsten filament lamp.

illuminant B colour temperature 4800°K, corresponds to noon sunlight.

illuminant C colour temperature 6740°K, corresponds to north sky light or average daylight. This is the most frequently used.

illuminant D_{65} colour. temperature 6500°K, is a more, recent addition to the range. It includes more ultra-violet radiation than does Illuminant C , and covers all wavelengths between 300 and 830 nm. Like Illuminant C, it is a close approximation to average daylight.

COLOUR MEASUREMENT

Instruments for the measurement of colour fall into two general classes.

1 Colorimeters, in which the colour is measured in terms of three primaries. **2** Spectrophotometers, which measure the reflectance at a number of wavelengths over the entire spectrum.

Colorimeters

The basic principle of these instruments is evaluation of a coloured surface either by matching with an additive mixture of the three primaries or by measuring the reflectance of the three primaries from the surface by photoelectric methods. The former method is embodied in visual colorimeters which, although the least expensive, have been largely replaced by photoelectric instruments in which the human factor is eliminated.

Photo-electric colorimeters

These operate on one of two basic principles.

1 The coloured surface is illuminated by each of the three primaries in turn, the intensity of the reflected beam being measured by photoelectric cell and galvanometer. A matt white surface is used as a reference standard.

2 The coloured surface is illuminated by a standard source, and the reflected beam is passed through red, green and blue filters in turn. The intensities of the transmitted beams are measured as in 1 and the results recorded as tristimulus values.

Although the optical and electrical systems in 2 are more complex than in 1, the majority of commercial instruments operate on this principle. It is not possible, within the confines of this text, to describe the many tristimulus colorimeters available today. They vary from relatively simple instruments which measure tristimulus values only to sophisticated types which either embody-a computer or to which a computer can be attached. These are capable of calculating CIE x, y, Y and CIELAB co-ordinates as well as small colour differences ΔE.

Colorimeters which perform the functions described are available from a number of manufacturers some of whom are listed [3] in the References at the end of this chapter.

Some colorimeters employ a portable sensing head which enables colour measurements to be made on surfaces which cannot be placed in or brought to the instrument. The principle was first employed by the Paint Research Association in the Fibre Optics Colorimeter [4]. The sensing head and detector are connected by a flexible lead consisting of a bundle of glass fibres. Light is conducted along the fibres which, in order to prevent loss of light energy, are surrounded by a protective material of lower refractive index.

Reflectance spectrophotometers

If, instead of measuring reflectance values at three narrow wave-bands as in colorimetry, a large number of reflectance values can be determined covering the entire spectrum, then a more complete picture of the reflectance characteristics of a colour can be obtained. If these reflectance values are plotted against wavelength a 'spectral reflectance curve' (Fig. 2.2) is obtained which is a permanent record of the reflectance characteristics of a coloured surface or pigment.

The general principle of a spectrophotometer is illustrated in Fig. 2.3, but commercial instruments can vary appreciably in design: A narrow beam of white light is split into a spectrum by a prism or diffraction grating and the spectrum thrown on to a screen. The screen embodies a movable slit by means of which a very narrow band of wavelengths is allowed to illuminate the standard white surface and the colour to be measured. The intensity of the reflected beams is measured by photocell and a special type galvanometer.

The figure obtained is the reflectance of the particular waveband from the coloured surface in relation to the reflectance from the white surface. Any number of measurements over the spectrum can be made in this way, and modern spectrophotometers can present the results in tabulated form or as a spectral reflectance curve. With computer attachment they will also furnish tristimulus values as well as CIE x,y, Y and CIELAB co-ordinates.

Abridged spectrophotometers are simpler and less sophisticated instruments and produce a spectral reflectance curve'for a limited number of measurements. Although less accurate than the full spectrophotometer, they are often adequate for a number of control and routine measurements.

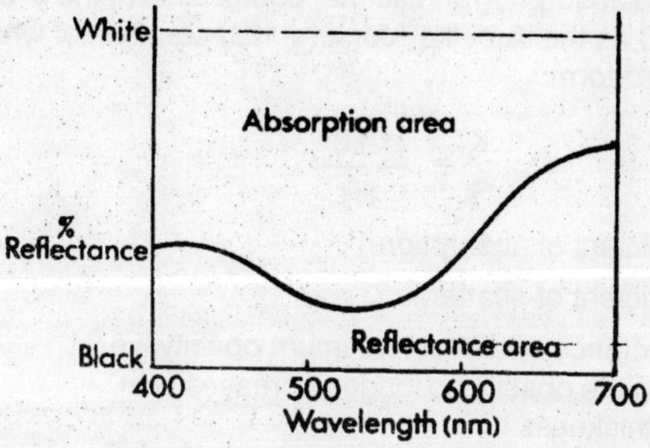

Fig 2.2 Spectral reflectance curve

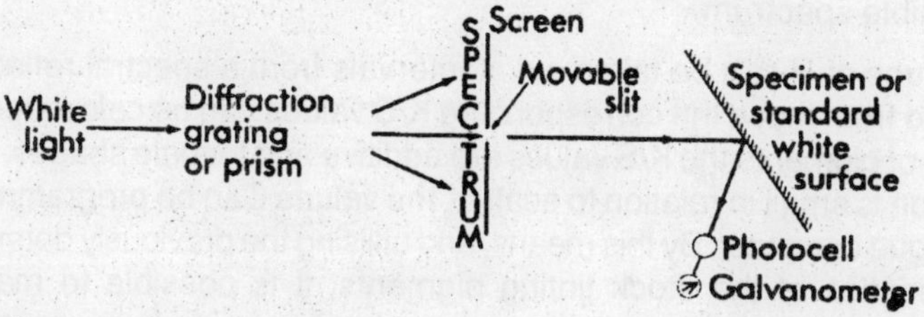

Fig 2.3 Principles of the spectrophotometer

They incorporate nine to sixteen narrow-band filters mounted round a wheel through which the sample and the standard magnesium carbonate can be illuminated. The filters are used in turn to illuminate the magnesium carbonate and then the specimen. The reflected beams are directed to a photoelectric cell and galvanometer. The figures obtained give the percentage of the particular wavelength reflected from the specimen relative to that reflected from the white surface. Filters can be fitted also to enable X, Y and Z values to be determined. Instruments of this type are the EEL Reflectance Spectrophotometer and the Sheen Miniature Colorimeter.

Spectral reflectance curves

These provide much more information on the reflectance characteristics of a coloured surface than do tristimulus values. They are particularly useful in colour matching in the avoidance of metamerism. Spectral colour matches will give identical spectral reflectance curves but if metamerism is present the curves usually cross each other, often more than once. Another important use of these curves is in calculation of absorption and scatter coefficients (below) used in colour-mixture formulation and control.

Use of spectral reflectance curves in colour-matching

Kubelka and Munk , as a result of their studies on the optical properties of dispersed powders, derived a relationship between the reflectance of a pigmented film and the absorption and scatter coefficients of the pigments. This is now referred to as the Kubelka-Munk (or KB) equation of which the following is a simplified form:

$$\frac{K}{S} = \frac{(1-R)^2}{2R}$$

where K = coefficient of absorption,

S = coefficient of scatter,

R = reflectance of film at maximum opacity, i.e. when the opacity no longer increases with the thickness.

For opaque pigmented films the expression is valid at any wavelength in the visible spectrum.

Values of R can be taken out at intervals from a spectral reflectance curve and from these the corresponding K/S values can be calculated. With mixtures of pigments the K/S values are additive and for pale shades; where absorption is small in relation to scatter, the values Can be programmed for an analogue computer. By this means, and utilising the previously determined characteristics of the stock tinting pigments, it is possible to match or correct a shade. The calculations are more involved with deep or saturated colours and the original Kubelka-Munk equation may be required.

Assessment of whiteness

There is no agreed standard of whiteness but several formulae have been suggested using red, green and blue reflectance values. Of these the following form is widely used:

$$\text{Colour index (of whiteness)} = \frac{100(R - B)}{G}$$

where R, G and B are percentage reflectances compared with magnesium oxide in red, green, and blue light. The formula is useful in assessing the degree of yellowing of white paint films as well as for comparisons. Positive values indicate yellowness and negative values blueness. A value of zero indicates neutrality.

Chapter - 3

PIGMENTS PROCESSING

MINERAL PIGMENTS AND EXTENDERS

These materials are either mined or quarried and are obtained in the form of coarse lumps. The lumps are broken down to a coarse powder which is subjected to further grinding in one of the mills described below.

Grinding

Ball mills

Ball mills used for pigment grinding are similar in construction to those used in paint production and consist of a horizontal steel cylinder which is rotated on its axis. The mill contains a charge of steel balls; and the grinding action arises from the cascading of these balls when the mill is rotated (Fig. 3.1). For each size of mill there is a critical speed which ensures optimum cascading. Very low speeds give little cascading, whilst high speeds will result in the balls and charge being carried round by centrifugal action.

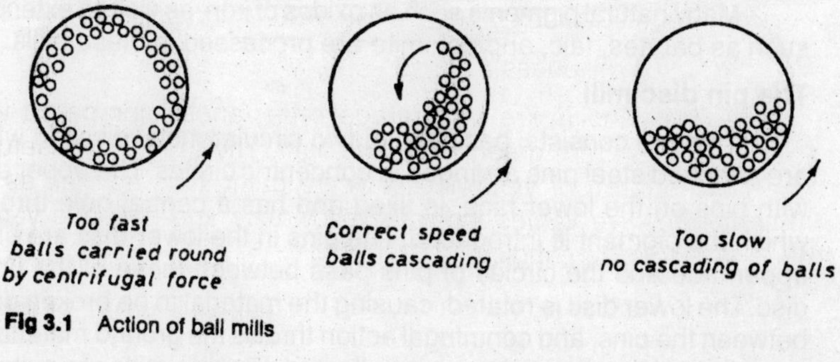

Fig 3.1 Action of ball mills

The gross volume occupied by the balls should be about 40 to 45 percent of the total' volume of the mill, and for maximum efficiency the material to be ground should just fill the voids in the ball charge.

These mills are used for both dry and wet grinding and, for the former purpose are often fitted with. an exterior dust casing. They are batch mills and in dry grinding suffer considerable wear on the balls and steel lining. When white pigments are ground the mill is lined with silica. or porcelain blocks, and the steel balls are replaced by steatite or high-density alumina balls. However, the lower specific gravity of these materials results in much longer grinding times than when steel balls are used.

The micronizer

Size reduction in this mill takes place as a result of inter-particle attrition. The mill contains no moving parts and the energy required is derived from highvelocity compressed fluids entering the grinding chamber through tangential jets. For this reason it is classed as a fluid energy mill.

The mill, shown in Fig. 3.2, consists of aflat cylindrical grinding chamber fitted with inlet and outlet nozzles: The former are arranged tangentially round the outside and the compressed fluid - compressed air or superheated steam -creates a violent turbulence in the mill. The material to be ground is introduced by a venturi through which the compressed air or superheated steam is passed.

The violent turbulence and high velocities result in rapid size reduction by attrition. The fine particles are taken off in a stream of exhaust fluid and enter a collector. Uniformity of particle size is controlled by regulating the rate, of feed and/or the pressure of the grinding fluid. The micronizer is used mainly to produce powders with an average particle size of about five microns or less, but it can be used, if necessary, to produce coarser products.

Many natural pigments such as oxides of iron, as well as extenders such as barytes, talc, and dolomite are processed in these mills.

The pin disc mill

This mill consists, basically, of two circular metal discs to which are attached steel pins arranged in concentric circles. The upper disc, with pins on the lower face, is fixed and has a central hole through which the pigment is introduced. The pins in the lower-disc are on its upper face and the circles of pins pass between those of the upper disc. The lower disc is rotated, causing the material to be broken down between the pins, and centrifugal action throws the ground material off the edges of the discs where it is collected. Pin disc mills are suited to the softer types of pigment as they are pulverizing rather than grinding mills.

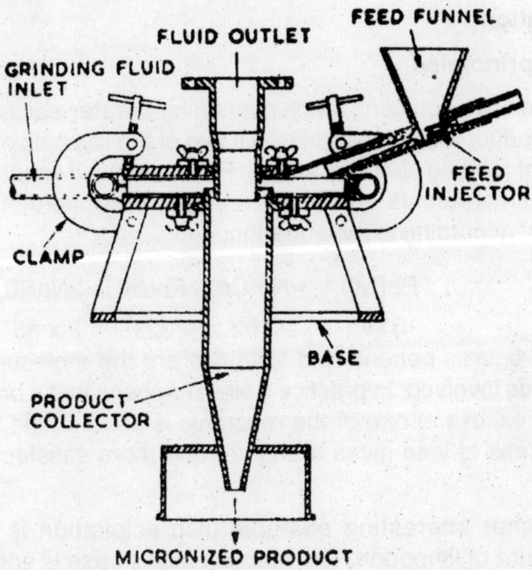

Fig 3.2 The micronizer

Levigation

If a suspension of a pigment or extender in water is allowed to overflow from one to another of a series of vats of increasing diameter, the particles which settle out will be progressively smaller. The rate of flow of the liquid is reduced by the increasing diameter of the vats, so that the smaller particles are given the longer time required to settle out. In this way a material can be separated into a series of fractions of decreasing mean particle size, but there is no sharp line of demarcation between the fractions. Each will comprise a particle size range which will be determined by the size of the vats and the initial rate of flow of the liquid. There will be a degree of overlap with fractions above and below.

This process, known as levigation, is employed to remove oversize particles and grit from several natural extenders where there is a plentiful supply of water near the source of the powder. It is generally preceded by a grinding operation. The deposit in each vat is filtered, dried, and finally reground.

MANUFACTURED PIGMENTS

The processes employed in the manufacture of pigments can be divided into the following types: (i) precipitation, (ii) precipitation followed by calcination, (iii) calcination, (iv) vapour-phase oxidation. A few pigments are prepared by methods not within this classification and these will be described under the pigments concerned.

Precipitation

General principles

When two solutions, each containing a water-soluble salt, are mixed, a solid product will be precipitated if two of the radicals or ions present are capable of forming such a material. For example, if solutions of lead nitrate and sodium chromate are mixed, a yellow precipitate of lead chromate is produced,' according to the equation:

$$Pb(NO_3)_2 + Na_2Cr0_4 \text{-} PbCr0_4 + 2NaN0_3$$

331 162 323 2 x 85

The figures beneath the formulae are the molecular masses of the compounds involved. In practice it often happens that a product is improved if a slight excess of one of the reactants is used. In the above instance a slight excess of lead gives a brighter and more satisfactory product (Mid Chrome).

Another interesting example of precipitation is afforded by the manufacture of lithopone. The reaction in this case is somewhat unique in that both products of the reaction are insoluble. The process consists of mixing solutions of barium sulphide and zinc sulphate, when zinc sulphide and barium sulphate are precipitated:

$$BaS + ZnSO_4 \rightarrow ZnS + BaSO_4$$

Again, a slight excess of zinc produces a more stable product. The precipitated mixture is filtered, dried, and calcined.

Reduced pigments

If an insoluble base such as barytes is-present-when precipitation occurs, the precipitate will form on the particles of the base. Such pigments are known as reduced, and their tinting strength will vary with the amount of base present. Reduced pigments can also be made by dry-grinding the components.

Co-precipitated pigments

Some pigments contain more than one salt of a metal. For example, Lemon Chrome contains both lead chromate and lead sulphate. It is possible to make a pigment of this nature by mixing the two salts, but a far superior product is obtained if the two compounds are precipitated simultaneously. In this case a mixed solution of sodium chromate and sodium sulphate can be added to a solution of lead nitrate:

$$2Pb(N0_3)_2 + Na_2Cr0_4 + Na_2SO_4 \rightarrow PbCrO_4PbSO_4 + 4NaN0_3$$

This produces a very intimate mixture of the two products and the process is known as coprecipitation. It is used to produce a number of pigments.

Conditions of precipitation

It is a well-known fact that the physical characteristics of a precipitate depend largely on conditions such as the concentration and temperature of the reacting solutions. This applies particularly to pigment manufacture, many of the properties of the pigment being influenced by the conditions of precipitation, of which the following are important.

Concentration *of solutions*

In general, fine precipitates are formed from dilute solutions, and coarser precipitates from more concentrated solutions. In practice, a compromise is often used. Whilst a fine particle size may be desirable for the end use, it can be difficult to filter. In a few cases the latter difficulty can be overcome by boiling the pigment suspension and so causing the particles to flocculate. Ten percent solutions have been found to be a very suitable compromise for a number of pigments, but there are several exceptions.

Temperature

High temperatures usually result in coarse precipitates, whilst finer precipitates are : formed at lower temperatures. In most cases precipitation is carried out at 10°C to 20°C (50° to 68°F) unless the precipitate formed is too fine to filter. Prussian Blue is a pigment of this type and is therefore precipitated from boiling or near-boiling solutions.

Uniformity *of stirring*

The rate of stirring should be directly related to the rate at which the solutions are mixed. Considerable variation in particle size can result if these are not uniform.

pH value

For many pigments this is critical and the optimum value has, in most cases, been derived by experience. Variations-from the critical value can affect colour and crystal form, as, for example, in the scarlet chromes.

Precipitation plant

This is comparatively simple, the basic unit consisting of a precipitation vat holding up to 5000 gallons (22700 litres), flanked by smaller dissolving vats.

The vats are constructed of oak or pitch pine and, when necessary, are lined with lead, rubber, or other. acid-resisting material. In special cases, stainless steel vats are used, but these are very expensive. Stirrers are of wood or coated metal and the vats are also fitted with open or closed steam pipes for heating, a cold water supply, and a bottom outlet to the filtration plant.

Filtration

The filtration of the pigment suspension from the precipitation vat can be carried out by either a filter press or a vacuum filter.

Filter presses

In these the suspension is pumped into chambers lined with filter cloths. The aqueous solution passes through the cloths to waste, and the pigment, in the form of a paste, remains in the chambers. Clean water is then passed through the paste to remove soluble byproducts and the paste is 'dewatered' by blowing air through the press. Some water remains and the product is then ready for drying or flushing.

Vacuum filters

Vacuum filters are of two general types which can be designated as the rotary vacuum filter and the leaf type filter.

Rotary vacuum filter

The general principle of the machine is illustrated by Fig. 3.3. A large drum is rotated on a horizontal axis and is partly submerged in a trough of the pigment slurry. The ends of the drum are solid, but the curved surface is constructed of perforated plate to which filter cloth is attached. Vacuum is applied to the interior of the drum. As the latter rotates, the water is drawn into it and the pigment collects as a paste on the outside, from which it is removed by a scraper. In some cases the drum is designed so that the adherent pigment is washed and partially dried by air-blowing before reaching the scraper.

It is necessary for the level of the pigment slurry in the trough to be kept constant, and the rotary vacuum filter is therefore admirably suited to continuous process filtration.

Leaf type vacuum filter

in this type of filter **rectangular frames are made up** of a number of leaves and attached to a vacuum line. The leaves are then covered with filter cloths. When the frames are lowered into a pigment slurry and vacuum applied, the liquid passes through the cloths and a layer of pigment paste builds up on the outside. When the layers are sufficiently thick the frames are lifted from the 'slurry and lowered into tanks of water for washing and the filtration repeated. After washing, the pigment cakes are removed and transferred to the drying ovens. This type of filter can be used for batch or continuous production.

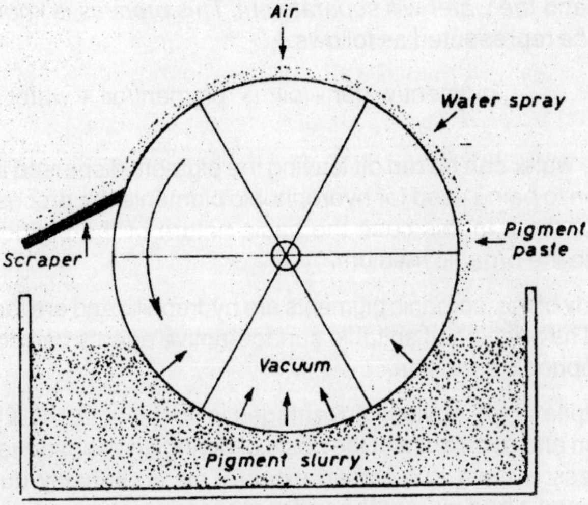

Fig 3.3 Principle of the rotary vacuum filter

Drying

The conditions of drying can influence the texture and colour of many pigments. It is essential that the temperature be kept as low as possible otherwise hard clusters or aggregates of pigment particles can be formed and these can prove difficult to break down in subsequent operations. Ideally, the pigment when dry should be in the same physical condition as when filtered, but this is difficult to attain. Again, some organic pigments are very heat-sensitive when in the water-wet state and these must be dried at a low temperature.

The filter-press cakes are usually passed through an extruder in order to expose as large a surface as possible and spread in trays. These are either passed through a conveyor oven, where they meet a counter current of warm air, or placed in a low-temperature vacuum oven.

After drying, the pigment aggregates .are reduced to their final size.by grinding (for the harder aggre ~ates) in mills of the type described earlier. For the softer aggregates, such as the organic and some inorganic pigments, the pin disc mill is used.

Flushing [1]

Pigments can be divided into hydrophilic (water attracting) and hydrophobic(water repelling) types. If the wet filter-press cake of a hydrophobic pigment

such as Hansa Yellow G is mixed with linseed oil or other organic

medium in a suitable mixer, the pigment will pass into the organic medium and *the water will separate out. This process is known as* flushing *and can be* represented as follows:

$$\text{pigment/water + oil} \rightarrow \text{pigment/oil + water}$$

The water can be run off leaving the pigment dispersed in the medium. In addition to being used for hydrophobic pigments the process is also used with white lead. In this case the basic nature of the pigment assists the transfer to the organic medium.

Many of the inorganic pigments are hydrophilic and are therefore difficult to flush. The addition of suitable surface-active agents can convert them to the hydrophobic condition.

In spite of the obvious advantages in flushing, such as good pigment dispersion and avoidance of the costs of drying and subsequent dispersion, the process is used to a limited extent. This is probably due to the wide range of media and pigments used in modern paint manufacture.

Calcination

This term is applied to the process of roasting or heating to a high temperature in a suitable furnace. It is used as a process in itself or as further treatment for materials which have been precipitated, such as titanium dioxide.

The rotary furnace is the most widely used type of calciner for bulk production. It consists of a long steel cylinder mounted on trunnions. It is inclined at a slight angle to the horizontal so that material introduced at the top rolls round slowly and is discharged at the bottom. Heating is provided by combustion of a mixture of gas and air injected at the lower end. This 'type of furnace -is employed in the manufacture of titanium dioxide.

Other types of calciners include the muffle furnace, the reverberatory furnace, and earthenware or silica crucibles.

Subsequent processing

During the process of calcination a certain amount of sintering of the pigment often takes place, resulting in the formation of clinker. To assist in breaking this up, the hot mass is discharged into cold water, when the clinker disintegrates. The pigment is then filtered, washed, dried, ground and graded.

Examples of pigments produced by direct calcination are red lead and Ultramarine Blue. Lithopone and titanium dioxide are produced by precipitation followed by calcination. Among the natural pigments, calcination is employed to convert Raw Sienna and Umber to the Burnt varieties

Vapour-phase oxidation

The metals zinc and antimony can be volatilized if heated to a sufficiently high temperature, and the vapours combine with oxygen by admixture with air to produce pigments of fine particle size.

In the case of zinc, the volatilized metal is mixed with air and the non-volatile zinc oxide precipitates. The zinc oxide is carried by the airstream to a classifier. (If the metallic zinc is volatilized in absence of air and then cooled rapidly, zinc dust is produced

Antimony oxide is produced by vapour-phase oxidation of the metal, but the oxide is volatile at the temperature of reaction. It is removed to cooling chambers and cooled as rapidly as possible to produce a fine particle-size pigment.

There is also a vapour-phase oxidation method for the production of basic lead sulphate from galena.

The formation of carbon black by the controlled combustion of petroleum gases is also an example of this type of process.

Chapter - 4

PLASTICIZERS AND SOLVENTS

Solvents are used in paints and lacquers to reduce the viscosity or consistency of the material and so facilitate the application of a uniform coating. They must be solvents that are suitable for the oil or resin present. After application the solvent is no longer required and should evaporate completely from the film.

The resins used in lacquers frequently form hard and brittle films and require plasticizers to confer the necessary elasticity and adhesion. These are usually liquids which must have a minimum tendency to volatilize so that they will remain in the film. It is essential that the plasticizer should be completely miscible with the resin, and to this extent it can be regarded as a solvent.

SOLVENTS

Paint and lacquer solvents, with the exception of water, are volatile organic liquids which can be classified into well-defined chemical groups. The solvent power and general physical properties vary over a wide range. A useful but arbitrary classification of solvents is by boiling point (though these are not necessarily related to evaporation rates), thus:

Solvents	*Boiling point*
Low boiling point	Below 100°C (212°F)
Medium boiling point	Between 100° and 150°C (212° and 302°F)
High boiling point	Between 150° and 250°C (302° and 482°F)
Plasticizers	Above 250°C (482°F)

The important properties of paint solvents are the following:

1 Solvent power
2 Rate of evaporation
3 Boiling point and distillation range
4 Flash point and inflammability
5 Toxicity.

The following properties are also of importance as indicators of purity-specific gravity, colour, moisture content, acidity or alkalinity, and non-volatile matter.

General properties of solvents

Solvent power

The film-forming materials used in paints and lacquers are, with a few exceptions, organic in nature and possess no crystalline structure. When treated with suitable solvents they dissolve to give solutions the viscosity of which increases with increasing concentration. There is no solubility limit, as in inorganic solutions, but problems of application limit the concentrations used. These solutions produce continuous films on evaporation of the solvent.

It is well known that certain types of resin or polymer dissolve only in certain types of solvent ('like dissolves like') and it was early realized that the polarity of the molecules of each was an important factor. Polar compounds are unsymmetrical in molecular structure and can contain groups which cause changes in the electron distribution. Typical examples are the nitro ($-NO_2$), carbonyl (= CO) and hydroxyl (- OH) groups. Molecules containing such groups exhibit a permanent dipole moment, indicating the presence of separated charges.

One result of this polarity is the tendency of such molecules to form associated groups by attraction of opposite poles. A consequence of this association is the fact that the viscosity of polar liquids is generally greater than that of non-polar liquids of similar molecular weight.

The effect of polarity in the solute is illustrated by cellulose nitrate which dissolves readily in polar solvents such as esters and ketones but is insoluble in non-polar hydrocarbons. On the other hand, some of the weakly polar drying oils are insoluble in polar alcohols but soluble in non-polar hydrocarbons.

In both polar and non-polar solvents there are variations in solvent power or strength between individual types. Thus in the non-polar solvents, the aromatics give solution of resins of lower viscosity (at the same concentration) than those in aliphatic hydrocarbons.

Miscibility of solvents

When two liquids, A and B, are brought into contact, mixing will occur only if the molecules of species A are able to move freely among those of species B. If, however, the attractive forces between A and -A or B and B are greater than those of A for B, then the two liquids will be immiscible.

The attractive forces between the molecules in a liquid are responsible for the internal cohesion of the liquid, and the intensity of this is known as the 'cohesive energy density' It can be defined as the energy required to separate the molecules in unit volume of liquid or the cohesive energy per unit volume. It is related to the latent heat of vaporization in the following way:

$$\text{Cohesive energy density} = \frac{\Delta H\text{-}RT}{M / D}$$

where ΔH -latent heat of vaporization

R = gas *constant*

T = absolute temperature

M =molecular weight

D = density

It can also be defined as the energy required to separate the molecules in 1 cm^3 of liquid, i.e.

$$\text{Cohesive energy density} = \frac{\Delta H_v}{V}$$

where ΔH_v = molar *heat of vaporization in calories*

V = molar volume in cm^3

Solubility parameter

This term was suggested by Hildebrand and Scott for the square root of the cohesive energy density, i.e. $(\Delta H_v / V)^{½}$, and has been assigned the symbol δ.

Solvents which possess similar solubility parameters possess similar internal cohesions and, in the majority of cases, solvents are miscible, provided the solubility parameters do hot differ by more than one unit. Similarly, polymers dissolve in solvents of similar solubility parameters, but, as in the case of solvents, exceptions to this general rule are encountered.

This problem was investigated by Burrell who suggested that hydrogen bonding played an important part in cohesive energy density, and also that solubility parameter values should be a range rather than single figures. However, difficulties were encountered initially in assigning quantitative values to the hydrogen bonding factor, as explained by Burrell The idea that three types of intermolecular forces - dispersion, hydrogen bonding and dipole moment - should be included in solubility figures was suggested by Hansen *and by Crowley* et al. They proposed a 'three dimensional' solubility parameter. The parameters originally suggested have been modified into the present day 'Hansen Solubility Parameter' which comprises a.hydrogen bonding component ∂h), a polar component (∂p) and a non-polar component (∂d). This method of defining solvent power is widely accepted.

Hydrogen bonding is low in aliphatic and aromatic hydrocarbons (which are also non polar), moderate in ethers, esters and ketones (which contain polar and non-polar groups) and high in alcohols, acids and amines (where the polar component predominates-).

Solubility of polymers

Figures for amorphous polymers are determined experimentally by ascertaining the solvent 'or solvent mixture in which the polymer exhibits maximum solubility. The figure assigned to the polymer is that of the solvent or solvent mixture used. Vales for solvent mixtures are calculated on a volume basis. Graphical analysis of resin solubilities has been employed by Teas.

'Crystalline' polymers, e.g. PTFE (polytetrafluoroethylene) or polyethylene, are not. amenable to the treatment described above since they are insoluble in normal solvents at ambient temperature. If they are heated above their melting points in the presence of certain solvents they will dissolve, but separate on cooling.

Measurement of solvent power (traditional method)

Kauri-butanol value

This test is applied to solvents to be used in varnishes and paints. The solvent to be tested is put into a burette and added slowly to 20 g of a solution of Kauri gum in butanol (100 g Kauri to 500 g butanol). The solution is contained in a flatbottom flask which is placed on a printed sheet of paper. The end-point is reached when the precipitated gums causes the outline of the print to appear blurred. The volume of solvent added (in millilitres) is the Kauri-butanol (KB) value. A good solvent is indicated by a high KB value.

Dilution ratio

This is important with solvents for cellulose nitrate which are divided into three classes.

1 True solvents.

2 Latent solvents which are not solvents for cellulose nitrate but which increase the solvent power of the main solvent.

3 Diluents which are not solvents for cellulose nitrate but which are added to reduce cost or to assist the solution of other ingredients.

The dilution ratio can be defined as the tolerance of a solution of cellulose nitrate in a given solvent for a given diluent and is determined in the following way.

A solution of cellulose nitrate is made up in the given solvent and titrated with the diluent in question until a permanent slight precipitate is formed. The titration can be repeated after addition of a further quantity of solvent, but the concentration of cellulose nitrate at the end should not be-less than 8 percent. The dilution ratio is the volume of diluent added divided by the volume of solvent used.

The concept of latent solvent applies also in systems other than cellulose nitrate lacquers. A mixture of xylol and n-butanol is a much more effective solvent than xylol alone for stowing finishes, especially for the alkyd-amino type.

Rate of evaporation

This is of fundamental importance in the choice of a solvent for a particular use, and with solvents of the same type, e.g. the petroleum distillates, it is roughly proportional to the distillation range. This does not hold, however, with,solvents of different classes. The fundamental factors which control evaporation are the specific heat of the material and the latent heat of evaporation, and these can differ considerably in different classes of solvents. As an example, the evaporation rate of tetrachlorethane with a boiling point of 147°C (296.6°F) is considerably higher than that of water with a boiling point of 100°C (212°F).

A simple and rapid method for evaluation of evaporation rate is to place 0.5 ml of the solvent on a No. 1 Whatman filter paper. This is suspended from the edge, away from direct draughts, and the time noted for complete evaporation.. Ethyl ether is frequently taken as a standard for fast evaporating solvents, but other standards, e.g. 2° xylol, can be used.

This test is known as the filter-paper spot method and is useful also for detecting the presence of oil or other non-volatile (or less volatile) contaminant. Oils and greases form a permanent spot on the paper.

It is often desirable to measure the rate of loss of solvent under conditions similar to those in a drying paint film. For this purpose a suitable instrument is the Shell Liquid Film Evaporometer in which the rate of solvent loss from resins or plasticizers can be measured. The instrument also enables an analysis to be made of the solvent mixture present at various stages during the evaporation.

Distillation range

The boiling points of pure liquids at a specific pressure are constant and can be used as a method of identification. If 100 ml of such a liquid is distilled in the standard apparatus the whole of the sample will distil at a constant temperature.

Commercial solvents, however, are seldom pure and when distilled by the previous method, the temperature indicated by the thermometer will risethroughout the distillation. The range of temperature shown is known as the 'distillation range' and is used both as a method of identification and as an indication of the purity of a given solvent. A small piece of copper foil is usually placed in the distillation flask. The degree of staining of the foil is an indication of the amount of corrosive sulphur compounds present.

In the determination of distillation range, the temperatures taken are (i) at the appearance of the first drop of distillate, (ii) at the completion of. 95 ml,. of distillate.

Flash point and flammability

With the exception of the chlorinated hydrocarbons, organic solvents are flammable, and a fire risk is therefore associated with their use. When these liquids are heated, the concentration of vapour in the air above will increase until it will flash on application of a flame. The lowest temperature at which this occurs is known as the flash point.

The determination of flash point is carried out by one of two standard methods. The Abel (closed cup) apparatus is used for liquids which flash below 49°C (120°F) .

A flash tester is used for the rapid determination of flash point using small quantities (2 cm^3) of material and is described in BS 3900, Parts A13 and A14.

For liquids with flash points above 49°C (120°F), the Pensky-Martens apparatus is used.

The flash points of mixtures of two solvents of differing flash point can lie between the two or can be below either of the individual flash points.

This is exhibited by mixtures of xylol and n-butanol. Flash points of solvents can be raised by mixing them with small quantities of the non-flammable chlorinated solvents.

If the temperature is high enough, a mixture of flammable vapour and air can ignite without application of a flame or spark. The temperature at which this takes place is known as the auto-ignition temperature.

Explosive limits

Mixtures of flammable-vapours and air are capable of exploding on ignition if the concentration of vapour lies within certain limits. These are known as the Lower (LEL) and Upper (or Higher) Explosive Limits and are expressed as a percentage, by volume, of the vapour in air. Below the LEL there is insufficient solvent vapour and above the upper figure there is insufficient oxygen for an explosion to occur. In practice the concentration of flammable vapour should be kept below the LEL.

Toxicity of solvents

The majority of solvents can dissolve and so remove the natural oils from the skin leaving the latter prone to dermatitis and other infection. The skin should be protected when solvents are handled; barrier cream should be applied or gloves should be worn. On prolonged contact some solvents can be absorbed into the system causing internal disorders of various types.

It is extremely difficult to prevent inhalation of solvent vapour by paint makers and applicators. Although the common paint solvents such as white spirit and xylol are not considered to be highly toxic, inhaling the vapours even in low concentration over a prolonged period can result in headache and/or nausea. Limits have therefore been laid down for the maximum permissible concentration of vapours to which an operative can safely be exposed over an 8-hour working period. These concentrations are always well below the LEL and are expressed as Occupational Exposure Limits (OEL). These are timeweighted average figures and vary from one class of solvent to another and among individual members within a group.

Other solvent properties

Specific gravity

This can be determined by several methods. For rough determinations, a hydrometer can be used. In this case it is essential to note the temperature and to use a wide vessel to avoid wall effects. More accurate measurements can be made with the specific gravity bottle or the Westphal balance.

Colour

With the exception of the heavy naphthas, solvents have very little colour. Any intensification of colour (or appearance of colour) in solvent which is normally water-white is an indication of contamination.

Moisture

An indication of the presence of moisture can be obtained by shaking the solvent with anhydrous copper sulphate, which turns blue in the presence of moisture, or by the addition of a miscible solvent which has no tolerance for water. Examples of the latter are benzene and petroleum ether. In this test the presence of moisture is shown by the separation of droplets.

Moisture can be determined quantitatively using the Karl Fischer method.

Acidity or alkalinity

If the solvent is miscible with water or industrial methylated spirit, a solution in one of these is titrated with standard acid or alkali using phenolphthalein as indicator. Other solvents are shaken with neutral distilled water and the aqueous extract titrated.

Non-volatile matter

The presence of non-volatile matter is often indicated in the filter-paper spot test for evaporation rate. It is determined quantitatively by placing a known quantity of solvent in an open dish and evaporating in a steam bath or in a steam-heated oven. Any non-volatile residue can then be weighed after cooling.

CLASSES OF SOLVENTS

Petroleum hydrocarbons

A considerable number of very useful and widely used solvents are obtained either by distillation of crude petroleums or by thermal cracking of petroleum gases. The products obtained by distillation are mainly paraffin hydrocarbons containing small amounts of aromatics. The thermal cracking processes are designed to give solvents with high aromatic contents.

Low-boiling petroleum fractions

Petroleum ethers *(ligroins)*

These are marketed in several grades according to boiling range. The three most common ranges are 40° to 60°C (104° to 140°F), 60° to 80°C (140° to 176°F), and 80° to 120°C (176° to 248°F). The specific gravities range from 0.645 to 0.676 and the aromatic contents from 1 to 5 percent.

Special *boiling* point solvents

These are produced in six or more boiling ranges between about 30° and 160°C (86° and 320°F). They are generally referred to as SBP 1,2,3, etc. and can vary considerably in aromatic content. The solvent power generally increases with aromatic content, and members of this range are used as rubber solvents as well as for lacquer formulation.

Flash points below 23°C (73°F):Highly Flammable Liquids.

White spirit

This solvent was introduced as a paint thinner in about 1885 and for many years it was regarded as a substitute for turpentine. The term 'turpentine substitute' persists in some quarters, but the term 'white spirit' is universally accepted

White spirit is produced from the petroleum fraction distilling between the low boiling fractions (the SBPs and petrols) and the burning oils. The boiling range is mainly between 150° and 190°C (302° and 374°F), although a small percentage may boil up to 210°C (410°F). This high-boiling fraction evaporates slowly at room temperature and should therefore be as small as possible. The actual composition and especially the aromatic content varies with the process and source of petroleum

In addition the material must be neutral, free from objectionable sulphur compounds, and the residue on evaporation must not exceed 0.005 percent.

The characteristic odour of white spirit is due mainly to impurities and aromatics. A special grade of odourless white spirit with a higher flash point (46°C, 115°F) is available, but due to the removal of aromatics the solvent power is not as good as the normal grade.

White spirit possesses moderate solvent power and is miscible with most organic solvents. It dissolves raw and refined vegetable oils as well as light and medium stand oils. It is not, however, a good solvent for highly polymerized stand oils and blown oils. In this case the-addition-of a proportion of a stronger solvent such as an aromatic or dipentene is necessary to prevent separation on standing.

Generally white spirit is a poor solvent for resins, and its use as the sole solvent in oil/resin combinations such as oleoresinous varnishes or alkyd resins is limited to the long-oil types of media. As the proportion of oil decreases, stronger solvents have to be introduced, and the short-oil types of alkyd will tolerate little, if any, white spirit. Comparatively few resins are soluble in white spirit; examples that are soluble are rosin, ester gum, soft and modified phenolic resins, and Damar resin. White spirit also dissolves asphaltic bitumen and petroleum pitch.

In addition to the extensive use of white spirit as a paint thinner, large quantities are consumed in ,the manufacture of polishes, and for cleaning purposes.

Flash point of commercial white spirit: 41°C (105°F).

Distillate

This can be regarded as a type of white spirit containing a higher proportion of highboiling hydrocarbons. The boiling range is about 150° to 275°C (302° to 527°F) and consequently the material contains an appreciable tail. When used in paints this tail holds the film open much longer than normal white spirit does, and distillate is sometimes used to lengthen the wet-edge time of brushing finishes and undercoats.

VM & P naphtha (Varnish Makers' and Painters' naphtha)

This is a petroleum fraction marketed in the United States. It is somewhat similar to white spirit.

Aromatic hydrocarbons

Toluol (commercial toluene), $C_6H_5CH_3$

This is the most extensively used diluent for cellulose nitrate lacquers. It is not a solvent for cellulose nitrate, but solutions in true solvent will tolerate greater additions of toluol than of other hydrocarbons. This has an important bearing on the cost of the lacquer. Toluol is a solvent for a large number of resins and is miscible with drying oils and most other solvents. It does not dissolve PVC, copals, or shellac.

The range of commercially available toluols is described in BS 805 (Toluenes):. 1977.

Flash point 4°C (39.2°F). Class 1. Highly flammable liquid.

Xylol (commercial xylene)

This is a mixture of the three isomers in which the meta-isomer predominates:

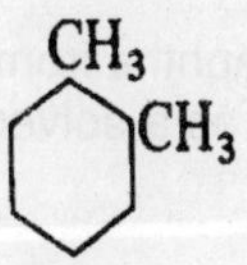

o-xylene
b.p. 144·2 C (291·6 F)

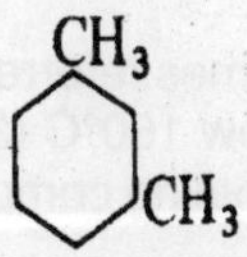

m-xylene
b.p. 139·1 C (282·4 F)

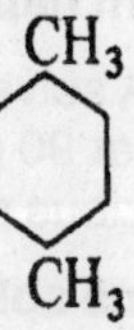

p-xylene
b.p. 138·3 C (280·9 F)

In some grades small quantities of other aromatic solvents are also present.

Xylol is now one of the most important solvents used in the paint industry. This is the result of its high solvent power for a very wide range of resins used in both stoving and rapid air-drying coatings, together with a convenient rate of evaporation. The solvent power is increased appreciably on addition of 10 to 20 percent n-butanol, and this mixture is very widely used in stoving finishes. The rate of evaporation is too great for use in brushing finishes.

Xylol is used as a diluent in cellulose nitrate lacquers and as the main solvent in lacquers based on polystyrene, polymethylmethacrylate and chlorinated rubber. It is also an excellent solvent for asphaltic bitumen and petroleum pitch.

In BS 458:1977 (Xylenes) there are three principal grades based on boiling range, i.e. the difference in temperature between 5 percent and 95 percent distillation. Thus for 3° xylene the range is 3°C lying between 137.5° and 144.5°C. For 5° and 10° xylenes the boiling ranges lie between 137° and 145.5°C, and between 135° and 148°C, respectively. The specific gravity range for 3° xylene is 0.860 to 0.875, but in this and the other grades the specification includes lowgravity material:

The flash point of 3° xylene is 24.4°C (76°F), but mixtures with n-butanol (flash point 36.7°C, 98°F) can-flash below 22.8°C (73°F) and are then subject to the restrictions on highly flammable solvents laid down in the Petroleum Act. Xylol is classed as a highly flammable liquid.

High aromatic solvents from petroleum

These range in specific gravity from 0.833 to 0.895 and contain high percentages (80 to 93) of aromatics, principally the isomers of trimethyl benzene. They are supplied in graded boiling ranges between 100° and 210°C. (212° and 410°F) and have flash points above 32°C (89°F).

They possess high solvent power and the odour is faint and not unpleasant. These solvents are marketed under proprietary names and have largely replaced the coal-tar solvents.

Solvent naphtha

A solvent which is sometimes referred to as 90/ 160 naphtha from the fact that 90 percent distils below 160°C (320°F). It is used as a solvent in bituminous paints and in anti fouling compositions.

Terpene solvents

Turpentines

These solvents are obtained from the resinous Materials present in pine and other coniferous trees. If a. cut is made in the trunk of one of these trees a gummy material is exuded and can be collected by cups attached to the trunk. Distillation of this material yields the volatile 'gum' turpentine. Steam distillation of the wood or of the stumps of pine trees yields 'wood' or 'stump' turpentine.

Another variety known as sulphate turpentine is obtained as a by-product in the wood pulp industry and is obtained chiefly from Sweden.

For many years turpentine was the standard thinner for paints and varnishes, but since the introduction of alkyds and other synthetic resins together with supply difficulties during World War II, it has been replaced by other solvents.

The composition of turpentine is related to that of dipentene and pine oil and for this reason a survey of its properties is included.

Composition and properties The turpentines consist of mixtures of members of the terpene group of unsaturated cyclic hydrocarbons. The mixtures consist chiefly of α-pinene, β-pinene, carene, sylvestrene, and dipentene and the properties vary with the source of the turpentine. a-pinene is the-main constituent of gum turpentine, whilst the wood turpentines consist mainly of dipentene.

The turpentines are clear colourless liquids with a characteristic pungent odour. Long exposure to the vapour can cause headache and nausea.

They evaporate uniformly but, due to the unsaturation, a degree of oxidation and polymerization takes place at the same time. The product (linalool) so formed is non volatile but miscible with drying oils and resins and therefore becomes part of the film.

The physical characteristics of the turpentines are as follows:

The turpentines are good solvents, and the Kauri-butanol value ranges from 50 to 90. In this respect wood turpentine, which consists largely of dipentene with small amounts of pinene, is a better solvent than the gum variety.

	Gum turpentine	Wood turpentine
Specific gravity	0·862–0·872	0·859–0:875
Distillation range	150°–180°C (302°–356°F)	150°–170°C (302°–338°F)
Refractive index ($D_{20°C}$)	1·469–1·478	1·463–1·483
Flash point	30°–37°C (86°–99°F)	34°–36°C (93°–96°F)
Non-polymerizable material	Not more than 11%	Not more than 16%

Dipentene

This solvent is prepared by a modification of the distillation process for wood turpentine. It has a higher distillation range (175° to 195°C, 347° to 383°F) and an appreciably lower rate of evaporation. It is an excellent solvent for many synthetic resins and is often used to improve the wet-edge time of decorative undercoats and finishes. It also possesses some anti-skinning properties. The physical characteristics of dipentene are:

Specific gravity	0.844-0.850
Boiling range	175°-195°C(347°-383°F)
Refractive index ($D_{20°C}$)	1.472
Flash point	54°C (130°F)
Kauri-butanol value	105

Dipentene forms coloured complexes with some metals, and the green coloration resulting from its, reaction with cobalt is sometimes apparent in white enamels.

Pine oil

Pine oil is usually obtained with turpentine and is separated by fractional distillation. The chief constituent is terpineol. It has a higher boiling range (200° to 230°C, 392° to 446°F) than turpentine and a very much lower rate of evaporation. The specific gravity ranges from 0.932 to 0.945 and the refractive index (($D_{20°C}$) *from 1.475 to 1.483.*

Pine oil has an agreeable odour. and is used as a re-odorant in paints and disinfectants. It also possesses some germicidal properties.

Alcohols

Methyl alcohol (methanol), CH_3OH

Large quantities of methyl alcohol are produced by reacting carbon monoxide and hydrogen at high pressures and in presence of a catalyst. The reaction temperature is about 300°C (572°F).

$$CO + 2H_2 \rightarrow CH_3OH$$

The mixture of carbon monoxide and hydrogen is obtained from methane present in petroleum gases. The methane is reacted with oxygen at high temperature (about 1400°C, 2552°F):

$$CH_4 + \frac{1}{2}O_2 \rightarrow CO + 2H_2$$

An alternative method utilizes a high-temperature reaction between carbon dioxide and hydrogen:

$$CO_2 + 3H_2 \rightarrow CH_3OH + H_2O$$

In both these processes the methyl alcohol is condensed out of the system.

Methanol is readily oxidized to formaldehyde and this constitutes one of its. principal uses. It has a limited use in varnishes and stains. The physical properties are :

Specific gravity (20°C)	0.792
Boiling range	95% between 64° and 67°C (147° and 153°F)
Flash point	6°C (42°F)

Methyl alcohol has pronounced toxic properties and is used as a denaturant for the ethyl alcohol in methylated spirit. It is a cumulative poison and can lead to giddiness, unconsciousness and in extreme cases to impaired sight or permanent blindness.

Ethyl alcohol (ethanol), C_2H_5OH

Two general methods are used for the production of ethyl alcohol, the choice being determined by economic considerations.

Where there is an ample supply of fermentable material such as potato starch or molasses the fermentation process is employed. Enzymes contained in malt convert the starch into sugars, and these are converted to ethyl alcohol and carbon dioxide by the yeast enzymes. The alcohol is removed from the final liquor by distillation.

The second general method uses ethylene as the raw material and is widely used in the USA. There are two methods by which ethylene can be converted to ethyl alcohol.

In the older method ethylene is dissolved in 95 percent sulphuric acid under pressure and forms a mixture of mono- and diethyl sulphates. On hydrolysis, ethyl alcohol is produced and is separated by distillation.

The more modern method is to. pass a mixture of ethylene and steam over a catalyst at 300°C(572°F) and at high pressure. The reaction is a reversible one:

$$CH_2 = CH_2 + H_2O \rightleftarrows C_2H_5OH$$

and the alcohol is condensed out of the system.

Properties and uses Pure anhydrous ethyl alcohol has the following characteristics:

Specific gravity (20°C)	0.7937
Refractive index	1.3619
Boiling point	78.3°C(172.9°F)
Flash point	14°C (57°F)

Anhydrous alcohol is not usually encountered outside the research laboratory. The material used as a solvent is known as Industrial Methylated Spirit (IMS) and consists of ethyl alcohol (95 percent by volume) denatured with 5 percent methyl alcohol. Grades of IMS are available ranging from 61° overproof (91.84 percent by volume) to 74° overproof (99.24 percent by volume).

The sale and use of Industrial Methylated Spirit is very tightly controlled by the Customs and Excise Authorities.

Ethyl alcohol forms azeotropic (constant boiling point) mixtures with a number of other solvents and with water. The mixture with water boils at 78.15 ° C(172.67°F) and contains 95.57 percent ethyl alcohol and 4.43 percent water.

Industrial Methylated Spirit dissolves a number of natural resins including shellac, with which it forms several spirit varnishes. It also dissolves some synthetic resins such as polyvinyl acetate and cyclohexanone resin. It is completely miscible with water, hydrocarbons and castor oil.

n-propyl alcohol (n-propanol), $CH_3CH_2CH_20H$

This is obtained as a by-product in the American Hydrocol process for production of hydrocarbons by the interaction of carbon monoxide and hydrogen in presence of a catalyst. It can also be obtained by the hydration of propylene.

The physical constants of the pure-alcohol are:

Specific gravity (20°C)	0.8052
Refractive index	1.3860
Boiling point	97.2°C (207°F)
Flash point	22°C (71.6°F)

It forms azeotropic (constant boiling point) mixtures with a number of other solvents and with water. The latter mixture boils at 87.7°C(189.9°F) and contains 71.7 percent npropyl alcohol and 28.3 percent water.

n-propanol dissolves rosin, shellac, ester gum and castor oil. It is sometimes used as a substitute for ethyl alcohol.

Isopropyl alcohol (isopropanol), $(CH_3)_2CHOH$

Isopropanol is prepared by the hydration of propylene, $CH_2CH = CH_2$ The latter is dissolved in strong sulphuric acid under pressure to give a mixture of isopropyl sulphates. The mixture is then hydrolysed to give isopropyl alcohol. The overall reaction can be represented by the equation

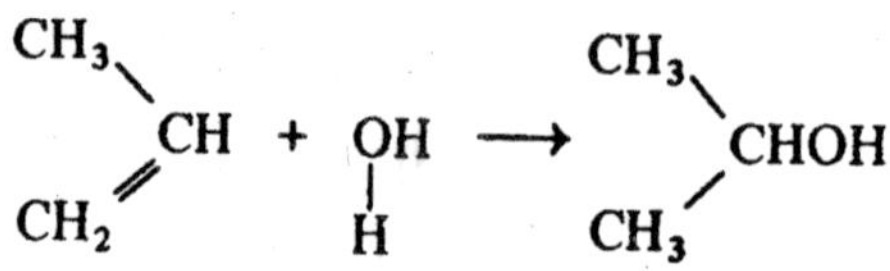

The crude alcohol obtained in this way is purified by azeotropic distillation.

Pure isopropyl alcohol has the following physical constants:

Specific gravity (20° C)	0.7925 (commercial isopropanol 0.787)
Refractive index	1.3776
Boiling point	82.4°C (180.3 °F)
Flash point	12°C (53°F)

Isopropanol has a somewhat stronger odour than ethyl alcohol and, like the latter, is miscible with water in all proportions. It is very similar to ethyl alcohol in solvent properties and has been used extensively as a substitute for ethanol. It is not a solvent for cellulose esters but possesses latent solvent properties, in that small additions increase the. solvent power of the true solvents. In admixture with small quantities of esters it dissolves cellulose nitrate.

n-butyl alcohol (n-butanol), $CH_3(CH_2)_2)CH_2OH$

The older process of manufacture is dependent upon the fermentation of maize starch and molasses by a special enzyme. Some acetone and other alcohols are produced at the same time. Distillation then yields a product containing about 98 percent n-butyl alcohol, the balance being small amounts of acetone and other (chiefly ethyl) alcohol.

There are two modern processes for the production of n-butanol. One of these is based on the 'Oxo' process in which carbon monoxide and hydrogen are added to olefines in the presence of a cobalt catalyst to give aldehydes. Under these conditions propylene yields n-butyraldehyde together with some isobutyraldehyde:

$$CH_3CH = CH_2 + CO + H_2 - CH_3CH_2CH_2CHO$$
$$(+ \text{some } CH_3CH(CH_3)CHO)$$

High-pressure hydrogenation of the aldehydes, using a cobalt catalyst, then yields the alcohol:

$$CH_3CH_2CH_2CHO + H_2 \rightarrow CH_3CH_2CH_2CH_2OH$$

(+ some $CH_3CH(CH_3)CH_2OH$)

The n-butanol is then purified by distillation.

The alcohol can also be obtained by hydrogenation of crotonaldehyde, which is itself prepared from acetaldehyde. The reaction is carried out at 180°C (356°F) using a nickel-chromium catalyst:

$$CH_3CH = CH.CHO + 2H_2 \rightarrow CH_3CH_2CH_2CH_2OH$$

n-butanol possesses the following physical constants:

Specific gravity (20°C)	0.811
Boiling point	118°C (244.4°F)
Refractive index	1.3992
Flash point	37°C (98°F)

It dissolves a number of natural resins and the following synthetics: ureaformaldehyde, melamine-formaldehyde, polyvinyl acetate. It is miscible with hydrocarbon solvents and linseed oil.

n-butanol is used extensively in conjunction with xylol in stoving finishes, where it appears to act as a very efficient latent solvent. It is also used as a damping agent for cellulose nitrate and is used in high-flash and brushing lacquers where it also increases the blush resistance.

Secondary butyl alcohol (methylethylcarbinol), $CH_3CHOH.C_2H_5$

This is prepared from butylene, $C_2H_5CH = CH_2$ by a method similar to that used for isopropyl alcohol (q.v.). It has the following physical constants:

Specific gravity (20°C)	0.806
Refractive index	1.397
Boiling point	99.0°C (210°F)
Flash point	21°C (70°F)

It is extensively used as a medium boiling-point solvent in lacquers and is a latent solvent for cellulose nitrate.

Diacetone alcohol, $CH_3COCH_2C(OH)(CH_3)_2$

A colourless, odourless liquid with the following physical properties:

Specific gravity (20°C)	0.942
Refractive index	1.424
Boiling point	167°C (333°F)
Flash point	67°C (153°F)

Diacetone alcohol tends to decompose slowly on heating or long storage, especially in the presence of alkali. The main product is acetone. It is a good solvent for cellulose nitrate and is a useful high-boiling solvent for cellulose acetate lacquers.

Esters

Esters are produced by the general reaction between an alcohol and an acid according to the equation

$$R.COOH + R'.OH \rightleftarrows R.COOR' + H_2O$$

The reaction is a reversible one and ultimately a state of equilibrium is reached. If however the water is removed by the use of a small quantity of concentrated sulphuric acid or other powerful dehydrating agent, the esterification will proceed to completion.

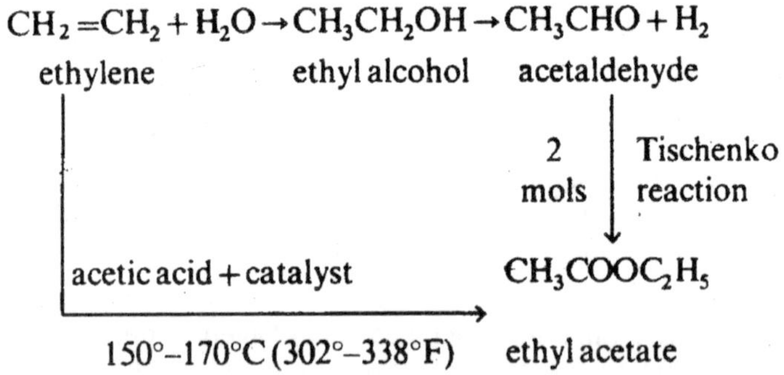

Some esters can be synthesized from unsaturated hydrocarbons in petroleum gases; for example, ethyl acetate can be synthesized according to the following scheme:

The esters prepared from the lower alcohols are volatile liquids, some of which are used in cellulose ester lacquers. They have high solvent power and the different esters are generally similar in properties, the main difference being in the distillation range and rate of evaporation. For a given alcohol, the boiling point of the ester increases with increasing size and complexity of the molecule of acid used. The same general rule holds for a given acid with increase in the alcohol molecule.

The lower esters possess characteristic fruity smells which in some cases can be very pungent. Their main use is in cellulose ester lacquer, and the following esters are among the most widely used.

Ethyl acetate, $CH_3COOC_2H_5$

A low boiling solvent of high solvent power, which is now being replaced gradually by methylethyl ketone which is appreciably cheaper. The British Standard Specification for ethyl acetate specifies specific gravity (20°C, 68°F) 0.901 to 0.904. Boiling range-a minimum of 95 percent between 76° and 78°C (169° and 172°F).

n-butyl acetate, $CH_3COOC_4H_9$

This is the most widely used medium-boiling solvent for cellulose nitrate lacquers. It is sufficiently volatile to leave the film readily but does not cause chilling of the film with consequent blushing. It is an excellent solvent for many other resins and oils but is not used to any degree outside cellulose nitrate lacquers. In these it is gradually being replaced by methyl isobutyl ketone which is cheaper and possesses greater solvent power. The specific gravity at 20°C (68°F) is 0.879 to 0.882 and the boiling range from 124° to 128°C (255° to 262°F).

Oxo-acetates

These are hexyl and heptyl acetates marketed under the trade names Exxate 600 and Exxate 700 respectively They are powerful high boiling solvents suited particularly to use in high solids paints

Ethyl lactate, $CH3{\cdot}CH(OH)COOC_2H_5$

This is a very efficient high-boiling solvent for cellulose ester lacquers. It has high solvent power for other resins and will tolerate the addition of considerable amounts of diluent. It imparts good flow to the lacquer and high gloss to the film, but the slow evaporation rate causes the film to remain soft for some time.

Ethyl lactate is also used in small quantities in stoving lacquers where it assists secondary flow in the stove and eliminates any film imperfections. The specific gravity at 20°C (68°F) is 1.032 to 1.038; boiling range, 95 percent between 135° and 160°C (275° and 320°F).

Ethers

Ethers are produced by the elimination of a molecule of water from two molecules of alcohol by the use of a powerful dehydrating agent such as concentrated sulphuric acid. The two alcohol molecules may be identical or different.

$$R.OH + HO.R' \rightarrow R\text{-}O\text{-}R' + H_20$$

The lowest member of the group is dimethyl ether, $CH_3.O.CH_3$ which is a gas. Diethyl ether, $C_2H_5.O.C_2H_5$ (ordinary ether) is a very volatile liquid with a boiling point of 34.5°C (94.1°F), and is highly flammable. It is used in laboratories as an extraction solvent.

As the size of the alkyl group or groups increases, the ethers become less volatile. They are generally inert (apart from flammability) toward the majority of chemicals and are useful solvents for oils and a number of natural resins.

$$\text{Di-isopropyl ether, } (CH_3)_2CH.O.CH(CH_3)_2$$

Used industrially for low-temperature and other extractions. It is less volatile than diethyl ether and is a solvent for rosin and ester gum, oils, hydrocarbons and rubber. It is not a solvent for synthetic resins.

Di-isopropyl ether is a dangerous material as it forms very unstable peroxides on exposure to the air and these explode on heating. Their formation can be minimized by storage in the dark and addition of reducing agents such as hydroquinone or catechol or by storage over 20 percent sodium hydroxide solution.

The formation of unstable peroxides on exposure to light and air is a property of most of the lower ethers.

Glycol ethers and ether-esters

These derivatives of ethylene glycol have been found to be more toxic than was previously thought and their use in coatings has been discouraged. Propylene glycol derivatives, which show considerably lower toxicity, are being used as replacements. These are excellent solvents 'for a wide range of resins, are compatible with aliphatic and aromatic hydrocarbons and the majority are miscible with water. In addition to their use in solvent type paints they are used as coalescing solvents in emulsion paints and as co-solvents in water-soluble paints.

Table 8.1

Solvent	Specific gravity	Boiling point °C at 760 mm	Flash point °C*	Evaporation rate (Butyl acetate = 100)
Methoxy propanol	0·920	120	35	70
Ethoxy propanol	0·896	132	42	46
Methoxy propyl acetate	0·970	146	50	31
Ethoxy propyl acetate	0·946	158	54	19
isoButoxy propanol	0·873	161	60	14
isoButoxypropoxy propanol	0·906	220	110	3
Methoxypropoxy propanol	0·951	187	79	3
Dipropylene glycol monomethyl ether	0·945	176	73	—

*Pensky Martens closed cup

The physical characteristics of the most widely used members are set out below

Ketones

Ketones are a class of compound characterized by the presence of the carbonyl group, C = O. The carbon can be attached to two alkyl groups which are the same, as in acetone, $CH_3CO.CH_3$, or different as in methyl ethyl ketone, $CH_3COC_2H_5$. Alternatively the carbonyl group can form part of a ring, such as cyclohexanone (see below). Other reactive groups, such as hydroxyl may be present in the molecule as in diacetone alcohol,

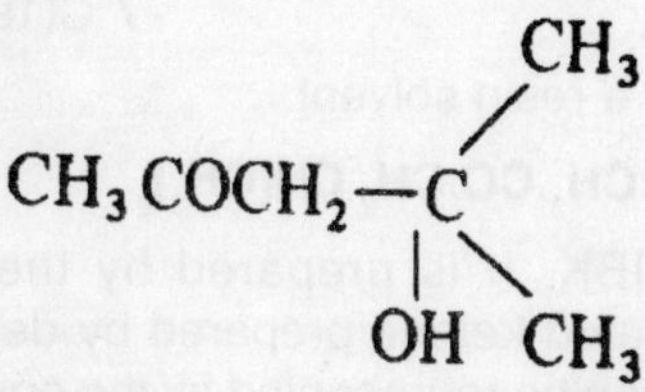

The lower members of the class are very volatile and highly flammable liquids and are soluble in water. With increasing size of substituent groups the members lose the water-solubility and become less volatile and less flammable. The highest members are solids.

The following ketones are among the most important paint and lacquer solvents.

Acetone (dimethyl ketone), CH_3COCH_3

This is prepared from isopropyl alcohol by passage over a copper catalyst at 500°C(932°F) and at three atmospheres pressure:

$$(CH_3)_2.CHOH \rightarrow CH_3COCH_3 + H_2$$

Acetone is an extremely volatile liquid with a flash point below 0°C. It therefore flashes at normal temperatures and very strict precautions are necessary in its use.

'It is one of the most powerful organic solvents and is used as a low-boiling solvent in some cellulose acetate and nitrate lacquers. The great solvent power renders it an attractive ingredient for paint strippers.

Acetone possesses the following characteristics:

Specific gravity (20°C)	0.790
Refractive index (D2O°C)	1.3599
Boiling point	56.2°C (133°F)
Flash point	- 16.5°C (2° F)

Methyl ethyl ketone, $CH_3COC_2H_5$

Known commercially as MEK, this is prepared by the high-temperature dehydrogenation of secondary butyl alcohol:

$$CH_3.CHOH.C_2H_5 \quad CH_3CO.C_2H_5 + H_2$$

This solvent is similar to acetone in basic reactions but differs in the higher flash point and lower rate of evaporation. The physical characteristics are:

Specific gravity (20°C)	0.805
Refractive index($D_{20°C}$)	1.379
Boiling point	79.6°C

Flash point	- 7°C(19°F)

MEK is used widely as a resin solvent.

Methyl iso-butyl ketone, $CH_3.CO.CH_2.CH(CH_3)_2$

Also known as MIBK. It is prepared by the hydrogenation of mesityloxide, an unsaturated ketone prepared by dehydrating diacetone alcohol. The two stages can be represented by the equations:

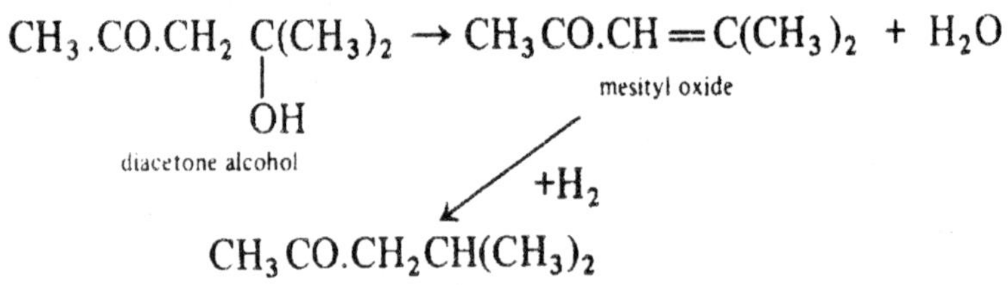

MIBK possesses the following characteristics:

Specific gravity (20°C)	0.802
Refractive index($D_{20°C}$)	1.396
Boiling range	95% between 114° and 117°C (237° and 243°F)
Flash point (Abel)	10°C (50°F)

It is a solvent for a very wide range of resins and is extensively used both in stoving enamels and lacquers where it functions as a medium boiling point solvent.

Cyclohexanone

This is a ring compound with the structure and can be produced by the dehydrogenation of cyclohexanol.

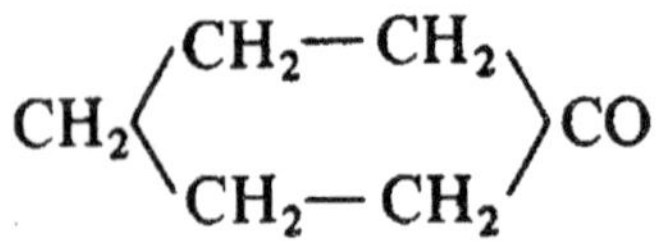

It has the following physical characteristics:

Specific gravity (20°C)	0.950
Refractive index-	1.443 - 1.451
Boiling range	95% between 150° and 158°C (302° and 316°F)
Flash point	47°C (117°F)

It is an excellent solvent for a number of resins and is used in cellulose nitrate lacquers, in which it tolerates considerable additions of diluents such as toluene.

Chlorinated hydrocarbons

The hydrogen atoms in both the saturated and unsaturated hydrocarbons can be replaced by chlorine, and many of these substitution products are useful solvents.

As a class they possess the following characteristics.

1 High specific gravity.

2 A low degree of flammability. The highly chlorinated members are completely nonflammable and whilst the lower chlorinated members can_be ignited, the heat of combustion is so low that the flame is extinguished.

3 Characteristic odours.

4 Anaesthetic and often pronounced toxic properties.

5 A low heat of vaporization, indicating high volatility in relation to the boiling point.

6 High solvent power for a wide range of organic resins and coatings.

It is unfortunate that the desirable properties of non- or low-flammability and high solvent power are accompanied by toxic properties. The range of application is therefore severely limited, and whenever they are used special precautions must be taken to protect operators from the toxic effects.

The following members of the class are encountered in the surface coatings industry.

Methylene chloride, CH_2Cl_2

A highly volatile liquid with boiling point 41°C (106°F) and specific gravity 1.336. It is a very powerful solvent and is the major component of many nonflammable paint strippers.

Ethylene dichloride, $ClCH_2.CH_2Cl$(1:2-dichloroethane)

Boils at 84°C (183°F) and has a specific gravity of 1.44. Like methylene chloride it is a powerful solvent and is used in paint strippers.

Trichloroethylene, $Cl_2C = CHCl$

Boils at 87°C (189°F) and has a specific gravity of 1.48. It is a powerful solvent and evaporates very rapidly. Among its many uses are extraction of oils from crushed seeds, dry-cleaning of fabrics, and recently it has been used successfully as the sole solvent in a dipping paint.

Perchlorethylene, $Cl_2C = C.Cl_2$

This is very similar to trichlorethylene in properties except for the evaporation rate which is lower.

PLASTICIZERS

Plasticizers are used in lacquers or non-convertible coatings which dry by solvent evaporation only, and in some types of stoving finish. Their function is to improve flexibility and extensibility of the film without impairing other properties. They should, ideally, be non-volatile, completely compatible with other film components, and chemically stable. The important classes of plasticizers are the following.

Esters

These comprise the largest class. The boiling points of esters increase

Table 8.2

Plasticizer	Boiling point (at 760 mm) (101·325 kN/m²)	Plasticizer for:
Triacetin	280°C(536°F)	cellulose acetate cellulose nitrate
Dimethyl phthalate	284°C(543°F)	cellulose acetate
Dibutyl phthalate	340°C(644°F)	cellulose nitrate ethyl cellulose vinyls
Dioctyl phthalate	230°C(445°F) at 5 mmHg (666·61 Nm²)	cellulose nitrate, vinyls
Tributyl phosphate	290°C(554°F)	cellulose nitrate
Tritolyl(tricresyl) phosphate	420°C(788°F)	vinyls, cellulose nitrate
Butyl stearate	365°C(689°F)	cellulose nitrate
Dibutyl sebacate	345°C(653°F)	cellulose nitrate
Tributyl citrate	225°C(437°F) at 5 mmHg (666.61 Nm²)	cellulose nitrate
Butyl oleate	203°C(397°F) at 10 mmHg (1333·22 Nm²)	chlorinated rubber ethyl cellulose

with increasing molecular weight until the volatility of the material decreases to the point where it can be used as a plasticizer. Esters with boiling points above 250°C (482°F) have, generally, a very low vapour pressure at normal temperatures.

Table 8.2 shows a few of the many ester plasticizers in common use, with their boiling points and the materials for ' which they are satisfactory plasticizers.

The properties of a range of interesting trialkyl phosphate plasticizers have been described by Quinn

Camphor

Camphor was the first plasticizer to be incorporated into cellulose nitrate, the product being known as 'celluloid'. Chemically it is a ring ketone of the terpene family and is available in both natural and synthesised forms. It is a solid with specific gravity 0.992, melting point 178°C and an appreciable vapour pressure. As a result of the latter there is a steady loss from the plasticized film resulting in progressive embrittlement. For this reason camphor is now used to a limited extent.

Castor oil

First pressings castor oil.

This is used in cellulose nitrate lacquers where permanent flexibility is required, as in leather finishes. It is a non-drying oil, completely non-volatile, and remains permanently in the film.

Blown castor oil

This is a higher-viscosity material produced by blowing air through the raw oil, and is used as a plasticizer in cellulose undercoats and primers.

Chlorinated waxes

A range of liquid plasticizers derived from hydrocarbon waxes is marketed under the trade name 'Cereclor' (ICI Ltd). They are completely non-volatile and are used as plasticizers for chlorinated rubber, vinyls, and cellulose nitrate.

Chapter - 5

SYNTHETIC RESINS

The very wide range of synthetic resins available to both the paint and plastic industries is the result of systematic investigation into the formation of resinous materials, which at one time were regarded as embarrassments in chemical laboratories. Such materials showed no tendency to crystallize and had no sharp melting point. It was realized gradually that these resinous bodies were materials of very high molecular weight and that their formation was associated with the presence of certain groups in the reacting molecules. Furthermore, resin formation depended on the relative quantities of reactants.

POLYMERIZATION

Modern synthetic resins are essentially polymers, i.e. they contain large molecules which have been built up from the normal molecules or monomers. The number of monomer molecules which go to a given polymer molecule is not constant, so that in a resin there is a range of polymer sizes or molecular weights. These are found to be distributed round a mean value, in much the same way as the particles in a pigment.

There are two general methods for the production of polymers. These are known as addition and condensation polymerization. The method employed depends on the type of monomer.

Addition polymerization

Certain types of monomer can be reacted - usually with the aid of a catalyst - to give polymers by simple addition. The reaction usually involves addition at double bonds, and an example is afforded by the polymerization of vinyl acetate. Long chain polymers are built up by rupture of the double bonds:

Long-chain polymers of this nature are thermoplastic.

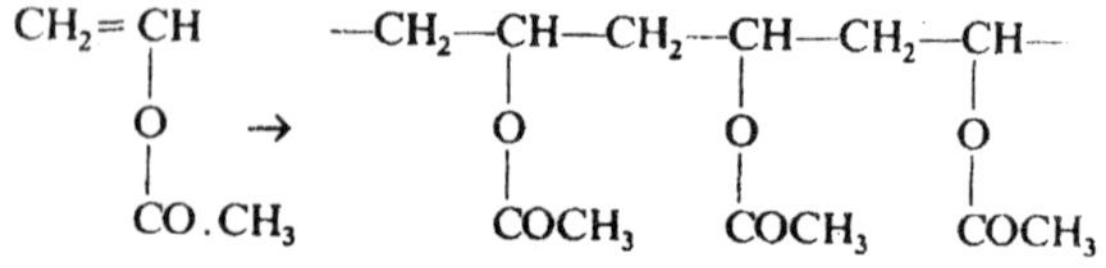

More than one monomer can take part in addition polymerization, and vinyl acetate can be co-polymerized with, for example, butyl maleate to give a copolymer:

The addition polymerization reaction involving the ethylene group

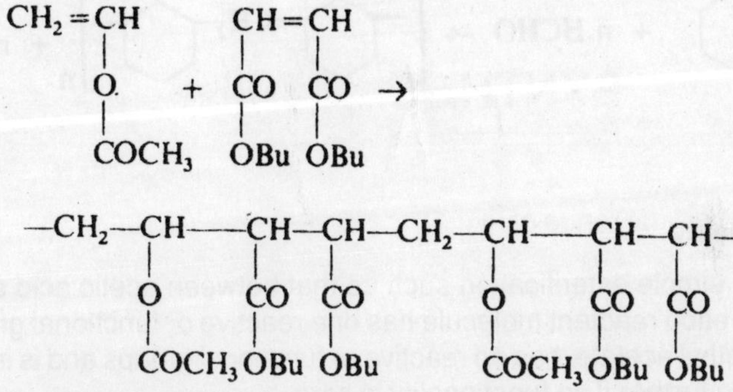

>C=C< is the basic reaction in the production of vinyl, acrylic and polystyrene resins. However, the ease with which the ethylene linkage is broken to produce polymers varies with the nature of the attached groups: Ethylene and propylene are much more difficult to polymerize than vinyl acetate.

Condensation polymerization

In a very simple reaction such as that between a monobasic acid and a monohydric alcohol, water is eliminated and a simple ester is produced:

$$CH_3COOH + C_2H_5OH \quad CH_3COOC_2H_5 + H_2O$$

No further reaction takes place. If, however, a dibasic acid is used with a dihydric alcohol a more complicated series of reactions can take place:

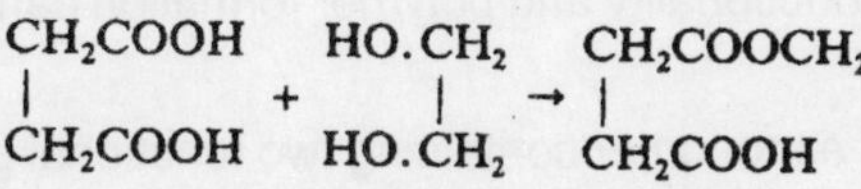

Half ester

This half ester can then lose water to give the cyclic ester:

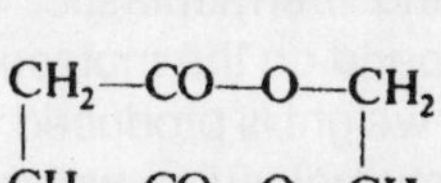

or it can react with further molecules of either acid or alcohol. In this way quite large molecules can be built up by a series of esterification reactions involving loss of water. This type of reaction is the basis of alkyd formation.

Esterification is but one type of condensation polymerization reaction involving the elimination of water. Another important type is that by which phenolformaldehyde resins are formed. Here the formaldehyde reacts to form a methylene bridge between adjacent phenol molecules. In its simplest form the reaction can be represented as follows:

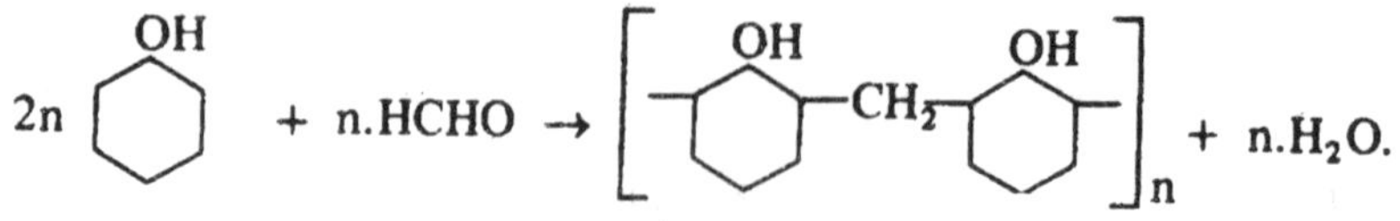

Functionality

In a simple esterification such as that between acetic acid and ethyl alcohols, each reactant molecule has one reactive or functional group. The product, ethyl acetate, has no reactive or functional groups and is incapable of reacting further. The functionality is zero.

A dibasic acid such as succinic has two reactive or functional groups and so a functionality of two. Similarly, ethylene glycol has a functionality of two. The half ester produced as the first reaction stage (above) also has two reactive or functional groups and therefore a functionality of two.

Maleic acid contains two functional carboxyl groups and also. an ethylene linkage. This linkage is capable of, addition at each carbon atom, i.e., it has two reactive points, and. is bifunctional. The total functionality of maleic acid is therefore four. Table 11.1 shows the functionality of a number of common reactants.,

The idea of functionality was first advanced by Kienle as a result of his work in alkyds, and was later developed further by Carothers The general principles relating functionality and polymer formation can be summarized as follows.

A molecule of a monomer containing two functional groups can react with 'a suitable.second bifunctional molecule to give a polymer. Such a polymer will be linear, and thermoplastic. The type of polymer, i.e. the molecular weight, will depend,on the molecular ratio of the reactants. At a 1:1 ratio a high molecular weight is produced, but an excess of one will stop the reaction and lead to low molecular.-weight polymers..

When a bifunctional molecule reacts with one which is trifunctional it is possible for cross-linking to occur, leading to a three-dimensional structure. Such polymers are further cross-linked on heating and yield insoluble and infusible films when stoved.

The basic reaction in alkyd preparation is the. reaction between bifunctional phthalic acid and trifunctional glycerine or tetrafunctional

Table 11.1 Functional groups

Material	Formula	Functional groups	Functionality
Glycerol	CH_2OH $CH.OH$ CH_2OH	—OH (3)	3
Pentaerythritol	$C(CH_2OH)_4$	—OH (4)	4
Phthalic acids	$C_6H_4(COOH)_2$	—COOH (2)	2
Adipic acid	$COOH(CH_2)_4COOH$	—COOH (2)	2
Sebacic acid	$COOH(CH_2)_8COOH$	—COOH (2)	2
Maleic acid	CH—COOH ‖ CH—COOH	—COOH (2) >C=C< (2 points)	4*
Fumaric acid	CH—COOH ‖ COOH—CH	—COOH (2) >C=C< (2 points)	4*
Formaldehyde	CH_2O or CH_2OH OH (hydrate)	—OH (2)	2
Phenol	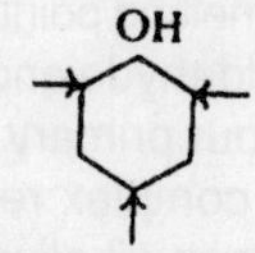	2 ortho reactive 1 para positions	3
Styrene	 $CH=CH_2$	>C=C< (2 points)	2

*This means a functionality of 2 for esterification and 2 for addition reactions.

pentaerythritol. A condensation polymerization of this type can lead rapidly to insoluble polymers and is discussed under Alkyd resins (below).

ALKYD RESINS

The alkyd resins form the largest group of synthetic resins available to the paint industry and the consumption is greater than that of any other resin. They form part of the larger group of polyesters which includes all products of the esterification of polybasic acids with polyhydric alcohols.

Alkyds differ from other polyesters in containing a monobasic fatty acid in the molecule and are often referred to as oil-modified alkyds, though the adjective 'oil modified' is redundant. The nature and often the amount of the monobasic fatty acid determines the drying characteristics of the resin.

Saturated fatty acids yield non-drying or plasticizing resins, while drying properties are conferred by unsaturated acids.

Raw materials for alkyds

The following are among the most important in common use.

Dibasic acids

Orthophthalic acid, used in the form of the anhydride, is the most extensively used of these acids.

Polyhydric alcohols (polyols) The two most widely used are glycerol and pentaerythritol, but small amounts of sorbitol and trimethylolpropane are sometimes employed.

Glycerol The general properties of glycerol have been discussed. It contains two primary and one secondary alcohol group and these react at the same rate with fatty acids to form glycerides. With dibasic acids the primary groups react more readily than the secondary; and it is likely that -the former react with phthalic anhydride to give the first stage syrup, and the secondary alcohol groups are available for reaction with fatty acids.

Glycerol can be used in alkyds of ail fatty acid contents or oil lengths.

Pentaerythritol, $C(CH_2OH)_4$ is a solid with melting point 253°C (487°F), and is manufactured by reaction between acetaldehyde and formaldehyde in the presence of water and alkali. It contains four primary alcohol groups which are all equally reactive and forms more complex resins than does glycerol. It can be used for medium/long and long oil alkyds only, as the short and medium/short oil types gel rapidly. Compared with the glycerol types, long oil alkyds produced from pentaerythritol dry harder to give more durable films with better -moisture resistance. They have a greater tendency to form crystalline bloom in urban atmospheres.

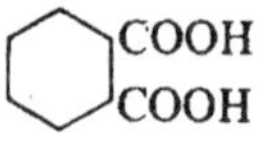

ortho-phthalic
(used as anhydride
m.p. 130 C, 266 F)

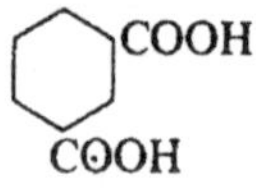

iso-phthalic
(m.p. >300 C, 572 F)

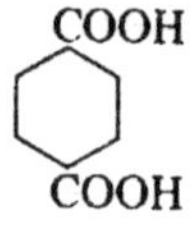

terephthalic
(sublimes on
heating)

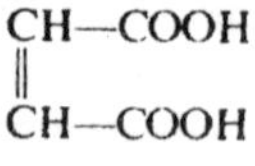

Maleic
(m.p. 130 C,
266 F)
(anhydride
m.p. 56 C,
132·8 F)

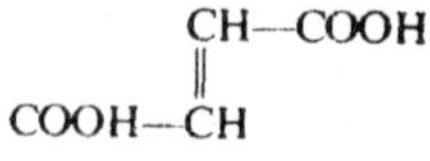

Fumaric
(sublimes at
200 C, 392 F)

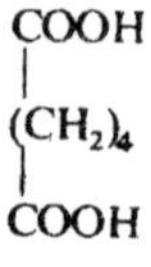

Adipic
(m.p. 151 C
303·8 F)

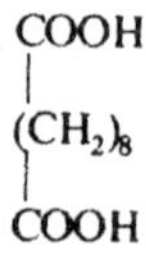

Sebacic
(m.p. 133 C,
271·4 F)

Fatty acids

It has been mentioned earlier that the drying characteristics of an alkyd are determined by the quantity and nature of the fatty acids, and they can be divided into two general groups, drying and non-drying.

The acids employed consist of mixtures derived from the parent oil by hydrolysis of the glycerides. In this way the acids can be separated and, if necessary, purified. An alternative method in which the acids are not isolated consists in heating together the oil and glycerol to produce monoglycerides as in the process of this name (below).

Alkyd formation

When two moles of glycerol and three moles of phthalic anhydride are heated together, a syrup is first formed which, on heating further, is converted to a gel. Continued heating causes the formation of a resin which ultimately becomes an insoluble and infusible mass. It is thought that a linear polymer is first formed, and this gradually cross-links to give a very complex structure. This is the type of resin usually formed from a bifunctional acid and a trifunctional polyol and is of no value as a surface-coating resin.

The polymerization to the very large polymers can be checked by the introduction of a monofunctional component into the system. This can be as an alcohol such as cyclohexanol or n-butanol, or as a monobasic fatty acid. In practice the latter is used and the fatty acid can be reacted with the first stage or syrup formed from phthalic anhydride and glycerol. On further heating the resin is much less reactive and does not reach the infusible state. This is the basis of the fatty acid method of alkyd manufacture.

Fatty acid process

There are two variants of this process.

1 The phthalic anhydride and glycerol are heated to 180°C (356°F) to the 'first stage' syrup, and molten fatty acids are added to esterify the free hydroxyl groups. Heating is continued at 180° to 220°C (356° to 428°F) until the desired acid value and solubility characteristics are reached. Foaming can be troublesome in this method.

2 The three raw materials, phthalic anhydride, glycerol and fatty acid, are placed in the reaction vessel together with a small quantity of xylol. The vessel is fitted with a condenser to which is attached a water separator of the Dean and Stark type. On heating, the water produced is carried off with the xylol and is separated. The condensing xylol serves to flush the sublimed phthalic anhydride back into the reaction vessel. The amount of water collected is an indication of the progress of esterification, but samples of the resin are removed from time to time for acid value and viscosity checks.

The reaction vessels are generally of stainless steel fitted with stirrer, charge hole, condensing system, and pipes for passing inert gas over the charge. The latter serves to reduce discoloration. Heating can be by immersion heaters or by passing hot oil or other liquid through a jacket surrounding the vessel.

The fatty acid process is being superseded by the alcoholysis process (below).

Alcoholysis or monoglyceride process

The formation of an alkyd resin involves esterification of glycerol or pentaerythritol with phthalic anhydride and a fatty acid. In glycerol-type alkyds (but not those from pentaerythritol-see below) the necessity for isolating the fatty acids can be avoided by the use of monoglycerides which are then further esterified with phthalic anhydride. The monoglycerides are formed by heating the drying oil with the necessary amount of glycerol to 250° to 280°C (482° to 536°F), when alcoholysis takes place according to the scheme:

$$\begin{array}{l} CH_2OCOR \\ | \\ CHOCOR \\ | \\ CH_2OCOR \end{array} + 2 \begin{array}{l} CH_2OH \\ | \\ CHOH \\ | \\ CH_2OH \end{array} \rightarrow 3 \begin{array}{l} CH_2OH \\ | \\ CHOH \\ | \\ CH_2OCOR \end{array}$$

The phthalic anhydride is added and the reaction completed at 180° to 250°C (356° to 482°F). The plant employed is similar to that used for the fatty acid process and the reaction is assisted by the use of xylol to remove the water.

This process is cheaper than that using the fatty acids, but it is not as versatile. A greater variety in the nature and purity of acids is possible with the fatty acid method.

Alkyds required to contain pentaerythritol as the sole polyol cannot be produced by the alcoholysis or monoglyceride process since the product will contain the glycerol introduced with the monoglyceride.

Dehydrated castor oil alkyds

These differ from other alkyds in their rather unique method of manufacture. The raw materials - raw castor oil, phthalic anhydride and glycerol - are heated together, slowly at first and then rapidly to 260° to 270°C (500° to 518°F). Under these conditions the raw castor oil is dehydrated by the phthalic anhydride, leading to the formation of dehydrated castor oil resins. It is of interest that during the dehydration reaction the viscosity of the mix falls, but rises again when polymerization of the resin commences.

Drying alkyds

These contain unsaturated fatty acids which control, to a large degree, the drying and performance characteristics of the resin. The amount of fatty acid present in the glycerol type can vary from 25 to 80 percent and is generally expressed as a percentage, although the varnish convention of long, medium and short-oil is sometimes used. The figures covered by these terms are not precise, but they refer roughly to fatty acid contents of 60 percent upwards, 45 to 60 percent, and 25 to 45 percent respectively.

Pentaerythritol is used only in alkyds with a fatty acid content of about 60 percent and upwards. It tends to gel rapidly when used with lower proportions of fatty acids.

Drying alkyds with fatty acid contents of 60 percent and above are soluble in aliphatic hydrocarbons such as white spirit, and are compatible with drying oils and varnishes. In the range of 45 to 60 percent fatty 'acid a proportion of stronger aromatic solvent is often necessary, but below 45 percent fatty acids the resins are soluble only in strong solvents such as xylol and naphtha. They are not compatible with drying oils or varnishes.

Driers

The drying times decrease progressively with decrease in fatty acid content, the actual figures depending on the type of acid used. The long and medium types are catalysed satisfactorily by mixtures of lead and cobalt in the form of naphthenates and octoates. The use of lead, however, is being discontinued and the metal has been eliminated from decorative paints; these dry satisfactorily with zirconium/cobalt mixtures. In decorative finishes a proportion of calcium (usually as octoate) is included to check the tendency to 'crystalline bloom' formation on exterior films. The short types of alkyd can be catalysed by cobalt alone, and this type is frequently cured by stoving without driers.

Types of fatty acid employed

Linseed fatty acids produce alkyds with good drying properties and durability but which yellow to a marked degree on exposure. This yellowing appears to be associated with the linolenic acid present. Linseed alkyds based on pentaerythritol dry harder and are more durable than those based on glycerol.

Soya bean fatty acids are widely used and, by reason of their very low linolenic acid content, the tendency to yellow on exposure is much less than with linseed. Alkyds made with these fatty acids and pentaerythritol as the polyol are in general use in the pale shades of decorative enamels.

Safflower, Sunflower and Tobacco seeds yield fatty acids free from linolenic acid and containing a high proportion of linoleic acid (like soya bean oil, they are described as 'linoleic rich'), and are used as alternatives to soya acids.

Dehydrated castor oil fatty acids (a mixture of 9:11-octadecadienoic and 9:12 octadecadienoic acids) yield non-yellowing alkyds. These are made in medium- and short-oil lengths and are used in air-drying and stoving (with amino resins) finishes respectively. These fatty acids are also used in some epoxy esters.

Tall-oil fatty acids (essentially linoleic) are derived from the wood-pulp industry. They can now be produced virtually free from rosin acids and yield non-yellowing alkyds exhibiting excellent gloss.

Tung-oil fatty acids are not used alone but often mixed with linseed in alkyds which can be further modified with phenolic resin. Such alkyds dry faster than the linseed type and the film has much greater water resistance. The durability is very good but the film yellows on exposure.

Applications of drying alkyds

Alkyd finishes, in general, show good gloss and gloss retention but are sensitive to moisture both during drying and afterwards. Exterior painting with alkyds during conditions of condensation, which often occur in early summer and autumn, can lead to loss of gloss on account of microrivelling.

When immersed in water for prolonged periods, alkyd films absorb appreciable quantities of water, and the resulting swelling frequently results in blistering. They are therefore not used under conditions of water immersion.

The long and medium types are used in air-drying finishes and undercoats for decorative and maintenance work and in marine topside and weatherwork paints. The medium types are used also in paints for machinery and implements.

Long-oil alkyds are versatile materials,-and some are compatible with other types of resin to give films with special properties. Blends with chlorinated rubber, for example, show greater adhesion to clean metal than does chlorinated rubber alone, and are sometimes used in primers for steelwork under chlorinated rubber systems.

'Mixtures of some long-oil alkyds and certain vinyl co-polymers show rapid through drying and are used in undercoats when short overcoating times are required. Care must be taken in the choice of resins and solvents since these mixtures can present stability problems.

Short-oil types find use in quick-drying primers and sometimes in 'half-hour' enamels. They are used also in stoving coatings often with amino resins.

Blends of emulsions of long-oil alkyds and acrylics form the basis of some decorative/preservative treatments for wooden window frames and doors.

Non-drying alkyds

These are produced either by the use of saturated fatty acids in the normal process, or by the polymerization of a bifunctional acid such as adipic with a bifunctional polyol such as ethylene glycol. The former types are the more common, and resins based on castor oil are very widely used. These are made by heating raw castor oil, glycerol and phthalic anhydride at a relatively low temperature (190° to 200°C, 374° to 392°F).

Non-drying alkyds are made from other oils by the fatty acid or alcoholysis process and are usually of short oil length.

They are used as plasticizers for cellulose nitrate lacquers and as film-formers in conjunction with amino resins. In the latter case the films are stoved to effect the necessary cross-linking between the resins.

The non-drying alkyds used in high quality white stoving enamels are frequently based on lauric acid or coconut oil fatty acids.

Vinyl toluenated (VT) alkyds

Vinyl toluene, $CH_3C_6H_4CH = CH_2$ (as well as styrene, $C_6H_5CH = CH_2$) will react with alkyds containing unsaturated linkages when heated in xylol solution in presence of a catalyst (e.g. a peroxide). Addition of vinyl toluene takes place at the double bonds in the fatty acid chain and has the effect of reducing the oil length. The products dry more rapidly and give harder and more chemically resistant films. They can take some time to develop their solvent resistance, and recoating can sometimes be a problem.

Vinyl toluenated alkyds are used for rapid air-dry and stoving finishes in industrial work. The longer oil types (with the lower vinyl toluene content) are less affected by adverse drying conditons than are the straight alkyds, but their durability is not as good.

Silicone alkyds

These are produced by co-polymerizing alkyds with certain silicone intermediates, e.g. low molecular weight siloxanes, so that the product contains up to 30 percent silicone. They are characterized by good drying properties, high gloss, and outstanding weather resistance. Some 'long life' coating systems are based on these resins.

Thixotropic alkyds

Certain modified polyamide resins will combine with conventional alkyds to produce resins with pronounced thixotropic properties.

If is possible, by the use of suitable types and quantities of reactants, to produce resins which can be pigmented to give finishes ranging from full-gloss to flat. These are the so called jelly or dripless paints which form firm gels at rest but lose their structure and exhibit flow when stirred or applied by brush.

Water-soluble alkyds

One of the most interesting developments of recent years has been the production of a!kyd (and other) resins capable of being solubilized in water, but which can be stoved to a waterresistant film. Water-qalubility is achieved by the introduction of a number of free carboxyl and hydroxyl groups which are well distributed in the polymer. These groups are neutralized by organic bases, the type of which depends on the type of polymer, but, in general, the tertiary bases are preferred. The products are soluble in water and can be pigmented and applied by spraying or dipping. The film is cured by stoving, when the organic base is volatilized and cross-linking occurs.

POLYESTER RESINS

Whilst alkyd resins are considered to be members of the polyester group, the resins considered here differ from alkyds in several respects but, in common, they can be unsaturated or saturated.

Unsaturated polyester resins

The product obtained from the condensation polymerisation of a glycol such as 1:2propylene glycol or 1:3-butylene glycol with an unsaturated acid such as maleic (or a mixture of maleic and saturated acid e.g. phthalic) in the form of anhydrides is a linear polymer containing unsaturation in the chain. This is dissolved in a suitable monomer, generally styrene, to produce the final resin. The film is produced by co-polymerization of the linear polymer and monomer by means of a free radical mechanism. The free radicals can be generated by heat, or more usually by addition of a peroxide. In order that curing can take place at room temperature the decomposition of peroxides into free radicals is catalysed by certain metal ions, usually colt. Caution: the solutions of peroxide and cobalt compound must not be mixed under any circumstances but should be added separately to the resin mix and well stirred in. A simple mixture of the two additives is highly explosive.

Films produced by curing in the air can show a residual surface tack for some hours. This is the result of inhibition of curing by the oxygen of the air and is difficult to overcome. One method consists in dissolving wax in the paint, so that the wax forms a skin on the surface of the film. When the latter is dry the wax is removed by polishing. The amount of wax used is of the order 0.01 to 1.0 percent. Wax-free types which are not inhibited by oxygen to the same degree incorporate an allyl group, such as the allyl ether of trimethylolpropane or glycerol, as part of the polyol ingredient.

Properties and uses of unsaturated polyester resins

Unsaturated polyesters give hard, mar-resistant films with good chemical and solvent resistance. The films are characterized by depth of gloss. These resins are used in considerable quantities for wood finishing.

The fact that these polysters cure by a free radical mechanism renders them suited to irradiation curing. This form of cure, in which no heat is produced, is particularly suited to films on wood or board.

Electron-beam curing is used on flat surfaces and it effects cure in less than one second. The more widespread use of electron-beam curing has been hindered by difficulties in the design of plant.

Ultraviolet irradiation curing is used on an increasing scale, particularly for clear coatings on wood or board. Difficulties have been experienced with pigmented coatings.

Saturated polyester resins

The main use of these resins is production of polyurethanes by reaction with isocyanates. The reaction involves hydroxyl groups and the components are selected to produce resins with high hydroxyl contents. Saturated dibasic acids such as adipic or phthalic are reacted with polyols such as glycerol, trimethylol propane or 1:3-butylene glycol.

Saturated polyester resins react also with some amino resins on stoving (see below).

AMINO RESINS

These are derived by reaction between formaldehyde and either urea or melamine to give urea-formaldehyde or melamine- formaldehyde resins respectively.

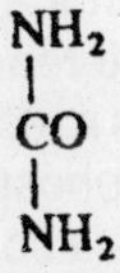

Urea
(m.p. 133 C, 271·4 F)

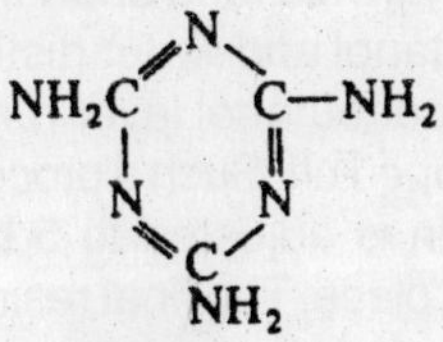

Melamine
(m.p. 350 C, 662 F)

Urea-formaldehyde resins

When urea is heated with formaldehyde solution (formalin) under slightly alkaline conditions, addition takes place to form methylol urea. Either mono-' or dimethylol urea is formed according to the ratio of urea to formaldehyde:

$$\begin{array}{c} NH_2 \\ | \\ CO \\ | \\ NH_2 \end{array} + H.CHO \rightarrow \begin{array}{c} NH.CH_2OH \\ | \\ CO \\ | \\ NH_2 \end{array} \quad \text{Monomethylol urea}$$

$$\begin{array}{c} NH_2 \\ | \\ CO \\ | \\ NH_2 \end{array} + 2H.CHO \rightarrow \begin{array}{c} NH.CH_2OH \\ | \\ CO \\ | \\ NH.CH_2OH \end{array} \quad \text{Dimethylol urea}$$

A water-soluble syrup is first formed, and on continued heating to 200° to 240°C (392° to 464°F) hardens rapidly to a colourless hard infusible resin. This resin is valueless as a coating material, but if the condensation is carried out in the presence of a high-boiling primary alcohol such as n-butanol, the hydroxyl groups in the methylol ureas are etherified:

$$\begin{array}{l} NH.CH_2OH \\ | \\ CO \\ | \\ NH_2 \end{array} + HO.C_4H_9 \rightarrow \begin{array}{l} NH.CH_2OC_4H_9 \\ | \\ CO \\ | \\ NH_2 \end{array} + H_2O$$

The butylated urea resin produced by polymerization of this ether possesses entirely different solubility properties from the original hard resin. It is soluble, in aromatic and some aliphatic hydrocarbons but insoluble in water. It is miscible with some alkyds and some varnishes. The solubility and compatibility with other resins increases with increasing chain length of the alcohol. When the films are cured by stoving, much of the alcohol breaks off and is lost, but some is retained as an integral part of the cured film.

Manufacture of urea resins

Urea and formalin are charged into -a stainless steel vessel fitted with stirrer, condensing system, and water collector. The pH of the mixture is adjusted to 8. It is warmed for a short time and then an excess of butanol is introduced. The butanol and water distil into the collector and separate into two layers. The upper butanol layer runs back into the reaction vessel and the water can be tapped off. Such a process is known as azeotropic distillation. The pH of the resin is adjusted to 5 by addition of phosphoric acid, and etherification takes place. The final resin is obtained as a colourless solution in n-butanol.

Properties and uses of urea resins

Alkylated urea resins are water white and are compatible with a number of alkyds, both drying and non-drying. The combination of urea resin with nondrying alkyd is used very widely for stoving finishes of almost all types. It appears that combination between the two resins takes place during stoving, probably by etherification of the hydroxyl groups of the alkyd with the butoxy or methylol groups of the urea.

For general purposes a urea:alkyd (solids) ratio of about 1:1 is used and stoved at 120°C (248°F) for 20 to 30 minutes.

Curing of the films at lower or ambient temperatures can be effected by addition of small quantities of mineral or phosphoric acid.

Melamine-formaldehyde resins

A molecule of melamine can react with up to six molecules of formaldehyde to give a series of methylol melamines:

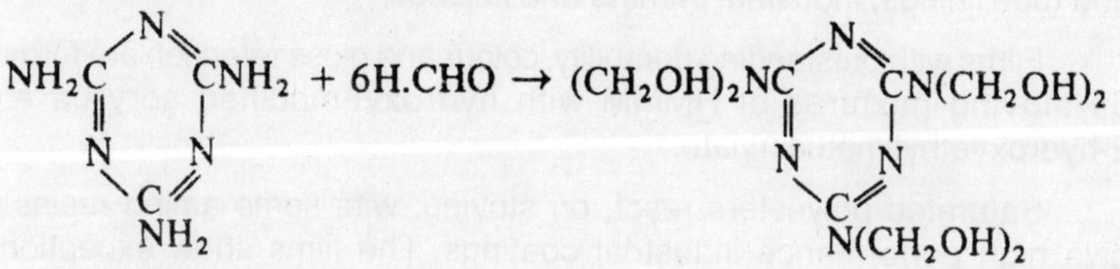

These methylol melamines are very reactive and the mono-, di-, and tricompounds tend to react, forming methylene bridges between melamine units. They form ethers with n-butanol, and this reaction is generally employed to limit the reactivity and to confer solubility in solvents and other media.

Manufacture of melamine resins

The process employed is similar to that used for urea resins, but conditions are modified in view of the greater reactivity of the melamine.

Properties and uses of melamine resins

Melamine resins are supplied in either n-butanol or n-butanol/xylol solutions and have limited compatibility with white spirit. They are miscible with drying and non-drying alkyds as well as with some epoxy resins and thermosetting acrylics.

Combinations of melamine resins and non-drying alkyds are widely used in white stoving finishes of domestic equipment and in car finishes. Melamines will tolerate larger quantities of alkyd than will ureas and the films show greater gloss retention, and heat and chemical resistance. The weather resistance and durability are excellent and they are used with thermosetting acrylics in car finishes.

Melamine/alkyd finishes can be cured at slightly lower temperatures than ureas. Like the latter they can be cured at ambient temperatures by addition of small amounts of mineral or phosphoric acid.

The mechanism of cure of alkyd/melamine systems by acid has attracted much attention.

Cross-linking reactions occur when amino resins are stoved with one of a number of hydroxyl-containing polymers e.g. alkyds, saturated polyesters, epoxies and acrylics. The resulting films show many outstanding properties.

The methylated melamines were a great improvement on the earlier butylated types in respect of compatibility and cost. One of the most widely used resins of ,this type is the highly versatile hexamethoxymethyl-melamine (HMMM). With epoxy resin this forms the well known Beetle BE 647 which, on stoving, yields films of outstanding gloss retention and resistance to heat, detergents, salt solutions and humidity. Typical applications are can and tube linings, industrial primers and finishes.

Films with outstanding durability, colour and gloss retention are formed on stoving mixtures of HMMM with hydroxyl-modified acrylics e.g. 2-hydroxyethyl methacrylate.

Saturated polyesters react, on stoving, with some amino resins to give high performance industrial coatings. The films show exceptional durability, colour retention and mechanical properties. They are used in coil and strip coatings, appliance finishes and metal decoration.

EPOXY RESINS

Epoxy resins are the products of condensation of epichlorhydrin and diphenylolpropane derivatives. The best known of the latter is bisphenol 2.2-bis (4-hydroxyphenyl) propane, also known as Bisphenol A. The product possesses the following structure:

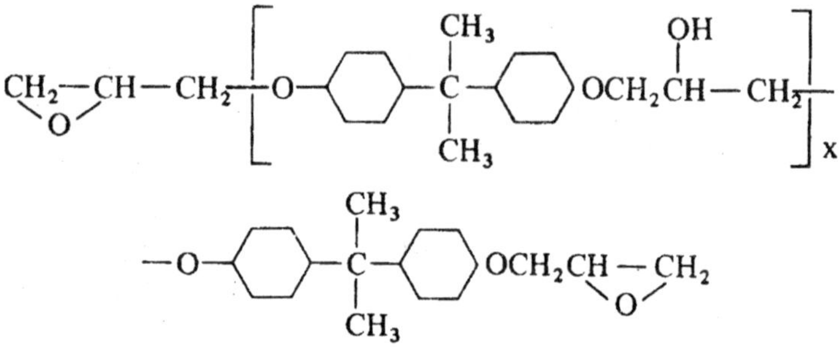

where x indicates the repeating unit. They are formed by condensing the reactants in the presence of alkali at about 100°C (212°C). A range of resins is produced, differing in molecular weight, and they are marketed under the trade names 'Epikote' (Shell Chemical Company) and 'Araldite' (CIBA/Geigy Ltd).

Epoxy resins contain hydroxyl and epoxy groups and the epoxy content is important in the evaluation of these resins. This may be quoted either as epoxy equivalent, i.e. the number of grams of resin containing one gram-equivalent of epoxy group, or as epoxy value, i. e. the number of epoxy groups in 100 grams of resin. The hydroxyl groups can be esterified with carboxylic acids to give epoxy esters (below).

Uncured epoxy resins are either viscous liquids (at lower molecular masses) or thermoplastic solids soluble in esters and ketones and in mixtures of these with aromatic hydrocarbons and some alcohols and propylene glycol derivatives. The following mixtures will illustrate some of the solvent blends used for epoxy resins but it will be realised that many different mixtures are possible. The composition of these will depend on the other ingredients present and the method of application of the paint. Figures represent percentages by weight.

(a)	Diacetone alcohol	25	(b)	Xylol	60
	Toluene	25		Methoxy propanol	10
	Ethanol 95%	25		Aromatic hydrocarbon	20
	Methylethyl ketone	25		Isobutanol	10
(a)	Methoxy propanol	25	(d)	Xylol	20
	Xylol 50			Methylethyl ketone	35
	Aromatic hydrocarbon	25		Toluol	35
				Isobutanol	10

Epoxy resins can be cross-linked by cold-curing or stoving with a range of materials which includes amino and phenolic resins, amines, polyamide resins and isocyanates. The resulting films are very abrasion resistant, resistant to chemical attack and show a high degree of adhesion to metal and other surfaces.

Curing by amino or phenolic resins

These materials cross-link with epoxy resins on stoving to give films of excellent adhesion, chemical resistance and flexibility. Films obtained from the amino resins possess slightly inferior resistance to the phenolic types but are more widely used on account of their better colour. Combinations with melamine resins, particularly hexamethoxymethyl melamine (HMMM) give very pale and resistant films and are used in white finishes for articles such as washing machines. The phenolic types are used where colour is of lesser importance, as in drum linings.

Curing by amines

Primary amines will react with epoxy resins at ambient temperatures to give long chain polymers according to the general scheme

The use of primary, di-, or triamines such as ethylene diamine or diethylene triamine leads to cross-linking and the formation of extremely resistant films. When the two components are mixed, set and cure of the film takes place at normal temperatures but can be accelerated further by the use of heat. Generally the amount of amine used is about 6 percent on the weight of the resin, and the two are mixed shortly before use. These systems are therefore supplied as two components and the mixture has a limited 'pot-life'. This depends on the type of solvent used, but it is unwise to mix more than is required for one day's working. The pot-life is extended slightly when the resins are pigmented.

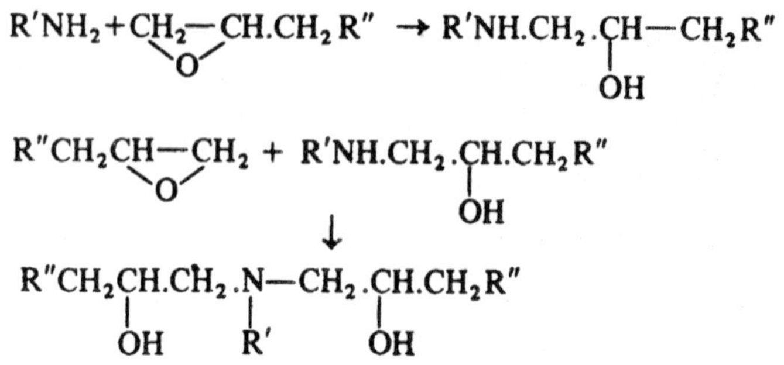

The amines used in these reactions are generally toxic and require careful handling. For this reason amine 'adducts' were introduced. In these materials the amino groups are rendered inactive by reaction with a proportion of the epoxy resin to give an adduct which can be handled safely. The amino groups are, however, available for reaction when mixed with additional epoxy resin. Adducts are available based on aliphatic and aromatic amines.

Solvent-free systems By the use of liquid (low molecular weight) epoxy resin and a liquid (amine) hardener it is possible to apply very thick coats and to avoid the faults which can arise from solvent retention in thick films. Drawbacks are high application viscosity and relatively short pot life. This type of coating is used where the absence of solvent is desirable as in painting tank interiors and underwater surfaces.

High solids systems incorporate a small quantity of solvent. This renders application a little easier and tends to lengthen the pot life. The use of this type of coating is increasing since it is environmentally more acceptable and application of fewer coats reduces labour costs.

Curing by polyamides

These resins contain the reactive group -CO.NH- and react with epoxy resins in a similar way to amines, but the reaction is slower and more amenable to control. The films produced are identical in many properties, but whereas polyamides yield the more flexible and water-resistant films, amines and amine adducts give films with higher chemical resistance. These differences are, on the whole, relatively small, and the lower toxicity of polyamides together with the more controllable reaction has resulted in these materials being more.widely used.

Curing by isocyanates

The higher molecular-weight epoxy resins are used in order to furnish the maximum number of hydroxyl groups for reaction with the isocyanate. The resulting film shows very high chemical resistance, adhesion, and general mechanical properties.

Epoxylpitch systems

Epoxy resins can be blended with certain grades of pitch and then cured by amines, amine adducts, polyamides or isocyanate to give products which are considerably cheaper than the straight cured resins and which can be applied in thick coatings to steel and other metals as protection against corrosion. Building materials such .as concrete, brick and stone also can be protected.

They are two-pack systems and are used on permanently or intermittently immersed structures such as piles, pier supports and ships' bottoms. They are unsuited to decorative work as the pitch 'bleeds' into the majority of superimposed coatings.

General properties and applications of epoxy resins

The mechanical properties of the films -high adhesion to the majority of clean surfaces combined with high impact and abrasion resistance - render epoxy coatings very suitable for use as floor paints which have to withstand heavy traffic. The solvent-free type is used in building mastics and in resinbonded screeds for seamless floors.

The high resistance to chemicals and many solvents makes the coatings suitable for use on alkaline surfaces such as concrete, cement render or cement screeds. They are used also in tank lining paints to resist lubricating oils and other petroleum products.

The heat resistance of epoxy films is moderate. They will withstand dry heat to about 150°C but under immersed conditions the maximum temperature is of the order of 80°C.

On exterior exposure epoxy films tend to chalk and so are generally used in primers for the more weather resistant polyurethanes

Large quantities of epoxy resins are used in powder coatings.

Blast primers based on epoxy resins are used in considerable quantities in the constructional and ship building industries. Pigmentation is by zinc powder ('zinc rich' primers), zinc phosphate, iron oxide or iron oxide/zinc chrome.

Epoxy esters

The hydroxyl groups in epoxy resins can be esterified with fatty acids. Acids derived from- linseed and dehydrated castor oils are commonly used. The linseed type containing 50-55 percent fatty acid is soluble in white spirit. With driers this type yields durable paint films and the paints are used on storage tanks and other exposed steelwork. They are used also on implements and machinery.

A problem sometimes arises in overcoating undercoats or primers based on epoxy esters. During the drying/curing period the film exhibits, over a period of several hours, a sensitivity to solvent with the result that brush application of a further coat during this period tends to lift the film. Outside this 'sensitive' period, which lasts from about 4 to 16 hours after application, overcoating can proceed normally in some cases the difficulty can be overcome by a change in the proportions of drier metals.

The dehydrated castor oil type usually contains about 40 percent fatty acids, is soluble in xylol but not in white spirit. It will cure either .by air drying (with driers) or by stoving and is used in chemical and abrasion resisting primers, undercoats and finishes for plant and machinery.

POLYAMIDE RESINS

These resins are formed by condensation of polyamines with dimer (or other polybasic) acids, the nature of the product being determined by the functionality rules enunciated by Carothers.

Dimer acids are long-chain aliphatic dicarboxylic acids containing two or more alkyl side chains. They are obtained by polymerization of refined unsaturated C_{18} fatty acids, and the long chains present confer a high degree of flexibility.

Apart from their use in polyamide resins they are used as part-replacements for dibasic or fatty acids in alkyds and epoxy esters.

Polyamide resins have two important applications.

1 They are used as curing agents for epoxy resins For this purpose they are more convenient to handle than the amines, but there are slight differences in the properties of the products.

2 When reacted with alkyd resins they produce the 'thixotropic' alkyds which are used in 'non-drip' decorative paints. The polyamide is added during the final stage of alkyd production, and the structure is thought to result from hydrogen bonding between carboxyl and amine groups.

POLYURETHANE RESINS

The basis of formation of these polymers is reaction of an isocyanate group (-NCO) with compounds containing an active hydrogen atom. The latter attaches itself to the nitrogen atom of the -NCO group. A number of materials contain active hydrogen atoms, and the reactions of an isocyanate group with some of these can be represented as follows.

$$-N=C=O + -OH \rightarrow \underset{\text{urethane 'unit'}}{-\overset{\displaystyle H}{\overset{|}{N}}-\overset{\displaystyle O}{\overset{\|}{C}}-}$$

1 Reaction with hydroxyl group

This reaction is used in the formation of surface films. A di-isocyanate is reacted with hydroxyl-containing polymers such as polyesters, alkyds, epoxies or acrylics.

2 ***Reaction with carboxyl group***

$$-N=C=O + HOOC- \rightarrow -NH-CO- + CO_2$$

3 ***Reaction with amine***

$$-N=C=O + H_2N- \rightarrow -NH.CO.NH-$$

(substituted urea)

4 ***Reaction with water***

$$-N=C=O + H_2O \rightarrow -NH_2 + CO_2$$

This reaction is used in foam production. The amine produced reacts immediately with further isocyanate to give a substituted urea, as in 3. The substituted urea can react further with free -NCO groups to give a highly cross-linked structure.

Film formation by moisture-cured polyurethanes results from a train of reactions of this nature.

In reaction 1, the hydroxyl groups may be phenolic or aliphatic, and the latter may be primary, secondary or tertiary. Saturated or unsaturated compounds may be involved.

The isocyanates may be long- or short-chain, aliphatic, or aromatic. Similar comments apply to reactions 2 and 3. It is therefore apparent that a very great number of technical combinations are theoretically possible.

Materials for polyurethanes

Polyurethanes are two-pack materials, i.e. the material containing the active hydrogen (polyester, alkyd or epoxy) and the isocyanate are packed in separate containers and mixed together immediately before use. The chemical reaction commences at once and consequently such mixed materials have a limited 'pot life'.

Isocyanates

Toluene di-isocyanate (TDI) is widely used in the form of polyisocyanate produced by treatment of the monomer. This, and other polyisocyanates, has a low vapour pressure and usually contains less than 0.7 percent of the highly toxic monomer. Inhalation of the latter can result in serious respiratory effects and can lead to impairment of lung function The dangers associated with the use of polyisocyanates prompted the Paintmakers' Association to issue a document entitled 'The Hazards arising from the Manufacture of Polyurethane Paints and Varnishes'. The toxic effects are confined to the isocyanate raw materials. The resulting polyurethanes are not hazardous (apart from solvent),

provided no unreacted isocyanate is present. Films produced from aromatic polyisocyanates yellow on exposure; the aliphatic compounds do not show this defect.

Resins

The resins most widely used for reaction with di-isocyanates are saturated polyesters, the general requirements being a high hydroxyl value and an acid value as low as possible to avoid liberation of carbon dioxide.

The nature of the film produced will depend on the chemical structures of both polyester and isocyanate. Soft films are formed from polyesters based on aliphatic acids, but harder and sometimes brittle films result from the use of alkyds based on phthalic and terephthalic acids. The type of polyol used in the resin also affects the film properties. Glycerol and pentaerythritol give hard films by cross-linking, but diols such as 1,4-butanediol or ethylene glycol give much softer films.

In view of the very wide range of properties, especially flexibility and hardness, required for different types of application and surface, manufacturers find it convenient to produce a limited range of polyesters of widely differing characteristics. The desired properties are then obtained by mixing the polyesters in the appropriate ratios.

Solvents

The polyesters used are soluble in esters and ketones, and a balanced mixture of low-, medium-, and high-boiling types is generally used. In some cases toluene or xylene is used as a diluent to reduce costs. Alcohols must be avoided. The di-isocyanates are generally dissolved in esters. All solvents should be dry to avoid reaction between water and the isocyanate group, leading to formation of carbon dioxide.

Film formation

Two pack type

This comprises the largest class and is used for both clear and pigmented coatings. The ratio of isocyanate to polyester is important in that low ratios of isocyanates give softer films.

Calculations of reacting ratios can be difficult with polyesters which may contain more than one polyol. The di-isocyanates are fairly pure and their equivalent weight is known. The polyester is calculated on the basis of an experimental value known as isocyanate equivalent. This is the weight of polyester (in grams) which reacts with one gram equivalent of isocyanate. The blend of polyesters is chosen to give the desired properties, and the isocyanate required is calculated from their isocyanate equivalents.

Polyester and isocyanate are made up in separate containers and mixed in the appropriate ratio shortly before use.

In pigmented finishes the pigment is dispersed in the polyester, and most pigments can be used safely. However, basic pigments such as red lead, zinc oxide and zinc chrome as well as Prussian Blue cause premature gelling of the system.

Additions of cellulose acetobutyrate or ethyl cellulose are often made to improve the flow properties and to avoid cissing.

Properties and uses

The curing of polyurethane films will take place at temperatures down to 0°C, a property which gives them an advantage over the epoxies. Depending on the type of polyester or polyol and hardener, films can be produced in a wide range of hardness and flexibility. It is usual for manufacturers to stock a limited range of polyesters and polyols and to blend these according to requirements. The films are characterised by good adhesion..to most clean surfaces but for exterior exposure, where they exhibit excellent weather resistance, they are generally applied over an epoxy primer. The films tend to yellow if aromatic isocyanates are used but retain their colour with aliphatic isocyanates. Other film properties are good resistance to moisture, chemical attack and many solvents.

Moisture-cured type

The polyether triols (prepared by reaction of glycerol with polypropylene glycol) contain secondary hydroxyl groups and react more slowly with isocyanates than do the normal polyesters. If these are mixed with an excess of di-isocyanate a reaction occurs giving virtually a solution of a prepolymer. Films of this material when exposed to the atmosphere react with the moisture present and cross-linking takes place.

These materials are marketed as solvent-free liquids which can be applied directly, with thinning if necessary, to a variety of surfaces. The films are very hard, adherent, glossy and show high abrasion resistance. They are used on wooden floors and also on concrete and similar floors where their alkali resistance is an advantage.

Pigmentation inevitably introduces traces of moisture which have to be removed. This can be affected by addition of an isocyanate 'moisture scavenger' which is added to the paint immediately after manufacture. Reaction with the moisture (with evolution of CO_2) takes place before the cans are closed.

Blocked urethanes

These are prepolymers in which an isocyanate has been reacted with a 'blocking agent' to produce a product from which the blocking agent is driven off on stoving. The regenerated isocyanate can then react with hydroxylcontaining materials Among the blocking agents used are phenol, methylethyl ketoxime, caprolactam and diethyl malonate.

One pack urethane alkyds

These are prepared by forming a mixture of mono- and di-glycerides from a drying oil and reacting the free hydroxyl groups with a di-isocyanate. The product is soluble in white spirit and cures by the normal drying process, usually with the addition of cobalt drier. One-pack urethane alkyds dry to hard and tough films, but the overall resistance is not as high as that of the two-pack type of polyurethane. The film hardness and resistance to solvents and chemicals is superior to normal alkyds, and they can be used to upgrade these materials.

The tough, hard wearing properties of the film has resulted in their wide use as clear varnishes for marine work. In pigmented form they are used where impact and abrasion resistance is necessary as, for example, in paints for kitchen or office furniture.

VINYL RESINS

Vinyl resins are straight-chain thermoplastic polymers produced by addition polymerization of compounds containing the vinyl group $CH_2 = CH$-. The polymers can be made from straight monomers to give homopolymers or from two or more monomers to give co polymers. In this way a very large number of co-polymers is possible, for example by polymerizing vinyl acetate with other unsaturated monomers. The polystyrene and acrylic resins are also members of this class.

Methods of polymerization

Two methods are employed: (a) solution polymerization in which the monomer is dissolved in a suitable solvent, and (b) emulsion polymerization in which the monomer is emulsified in a non-miscible solvent, usually water. In each case, a catalyst, e.g. benzoyl peroxide, is present. Polymerization is catalysed also by heat, irradiation or light.

' Emulsion polymerization is cheaper than the solution method and is also amenable to a greater degree of control. The process can be stopped at any stage of the polymerization and, in addition, emulsions can be produced in any desired particle-size range.

Polymers which are to be used in solution form can be separated by filtration after acidification of the emulsion. The product is dried and dissolved in a suitable solvent. Considerable quantities of the polymer emulsions are used directly in the manufacture of latex emulsion paints.

The following are the principal types of vinyl resin.

Polyvinyl acetate (PVA) is a colourless resin with a low softening point (about 38°C, 100°F), non-toxic and thermoplastic. It is supplied in a number of grades differing in degree of polymerization and, to some extent, solubility characteristics. The lower grades are soluble in ethyl alcohol, esters, ketones, and aromatic solvents. They are insoluble in white spirit. Films produced from solutions of the resin tend to be brittle and lack adhesion on smooth surfaces. They are usually plasticized with up to 20 percent ester-type plasticizer such as dibutylphthalate, but gradual loss of plasticizer by volatilization or absorption into a porous substrate will lead ultimately to embrittlement. The plasticized forms possess improved adhesion,'but all films of polyvinyl acetate tend to absorb appreciable quantities of moisture.

The polyvinyl acetate chain has the following structure:

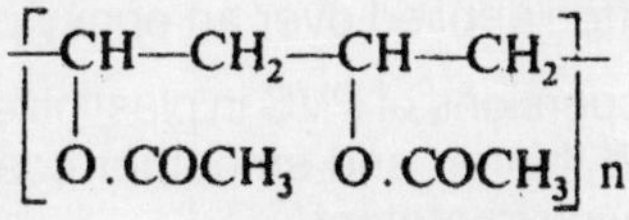

Polyvinyl alcohol This is produced by the incomplete hydrolysis (88-89 percent) of polyvinyl acetate. It is used in paper coatings, strippable coatings and in release agents for cast resin moulds.

Polyvinyl formal Reaction of polyvinyl alcohol with formaldehyde yields polyvinyl formal:

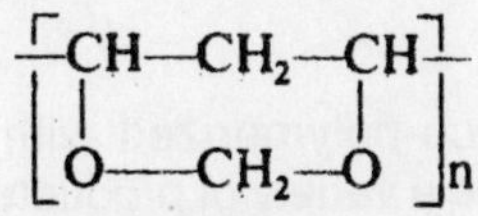

In combination with phenol-formaldehyde resins, polyvinyl formal is used in wire enamels.

Polyvinyl butyl This is produced in a similar way to polyvinyl formal, using butyraldehyde in place of formaldehyde:

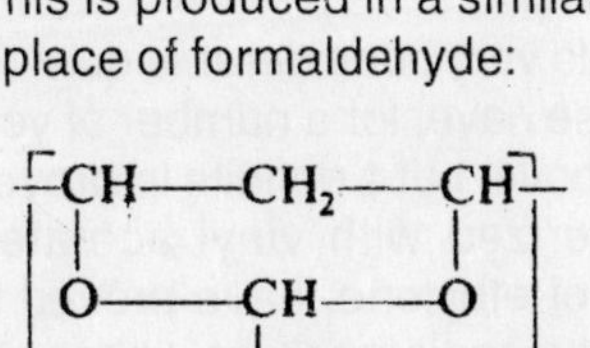

Polyvinyl butyral is used in etch and some types of blast primer. Both butyral and formal resins show very good adhesion to most surfaces.

Polyvinyl chloride (PVC) is produced from vinyl chloride (CH_2 = CH.Cl) by one of the recognized methods of polymerization, i.e. bulk, emulsion, or suspension. The operation must be carried out under very close control in view of the recognized carcinogenic properties of vinyl chloride.

It is a colourless polymer with a high Glass Transition Temperature (Tg) of approximately 80°C (176°F). (Tg is the temperature at which a polymer changes from a hard rigid state to a soft plastic condition.)

PVC has very limited solubility in common solvents, and in surface coatings it is used either as a suspension (plastisol or organosol) or as a co-polymer (below).

Plastisols consist of PVC dispersed in a suitable plasticizer. They are usually pigmented and yield thick coats which are stoved at 170°-193°C (338°-374°F). At this temperature the PVC absorbs the plasticizer and becomes sufficiently soft to form a continuous film. Such films are extremely hard and resistant to most reagents. On bare metal the adhesion is sometimes suspect, and they are often applied over an epoxy primer.

Organosols are dispersions of PVC in plasticizer and thinner. They are pigmented and can give thinner and smoother coats than the plastisols. They require similar stoving treatment.

The solids content of organosols is higher than that of vinyl solutions, and they are replacing these solutions in the internal coating of metal containers.

Both organosols and plastisols are used in the coil coating of metal strip.

Vinyl co-polyrners

Vinyl acetate can be co-polymerized with a wide range of other unsaturated monomers to give a variety of products with any desired degree of hardness or flexibility. The need for added plasticizer, so essential with the homopolymer, polyvinyl acetate, is eliminated. Among monomers commonly used are acrylates, maleates, and caprates. Emulsion polymerization is the common method of production.

In the decorative field very considerable quantities of vinyl co-polymer emulsions are used. These have, for a number of years, been based on the copolymers mentioned above, but a definite improvement -was made when ethylene was co-polymerized with vinyl acetate. These co-polymers, containing 8-25 percent of ethylene, have proved to be superior to other co-polymers in durability, resistance to reagents, and non-yellowing properties. An additional advantage, particularly in cold countries, is in film formation, i.e. coalescence of the dispersed polymer. This will take place down to 0°C (32°F).

A range of co-polymers of vinyl chloride and vinyl acetate containing 86-90 percent vinyl chloride is available These polymers are thermoplastic, nonreactive, very resistant to moisture penetration and to chemical attack. Some members have been partially hydrolysed in order to introduce polar groups to enhance the adhesion to smooth metal and other surfaces. The non-hydrolysed material is generally suspect in this respect.

Vinyl chloride/vinyl acetaie co-polymers are soluble, to varying degrees, in aromatic hydrocarbons, esters, ketones and chlorinated hydrocarbons. The solutions generally contain 15-30 percent solids so that multicoat systems are required to give a reasonable film thickness.

They are used in paints for the protection of chemical and process plants, particularly if these are in exposed situations. Some members are compatible with certain long oil alkyds to which they are added to upgrade chemical resistance and to shorten the drying time and overcoating interval.

POLYSTYRENE RESINS

Styrene or vinyl benzene, $C_6H_5CH = CH_2$, is the basic monomer for this type of resin. It is manufactured by reacting benzene and ethylene at high temperature and pressure in presence of a catalyst. Ethyl-benzene is produced which is then

dehydrogenated to yield styrene:

$$C_6H_6 + CH_2 = CH_2 \rightarrow C_6H_5CH_2CH_3$$

$$C_6H_5CH_2CH_3 - C_6H_5CH = CH_2 + H_2$$

The product is then fractionally distilled in vacuum, sulphur being present to prevent polymerization of the styrene. This and other methods of synthesis, as well as the properties and polymerization of styrene,,

Vinyl toluene, $CH_3C_6H_4CH = CH_2$, which consists of a mixture of the meta and para isomers, is manufactured in a similar manner. During the preparation a proportion of the ortho isomer is produced. This is separated by fractional distillation under vacuum.

Properties of styrene

It is a mobile liquid with a characteristic odour and polymerizes readily. Premature polymerization is inhibited by addition of a very small quantity of p-tertiary butyl catechnol or hydroquinone.

Polymerization of styrene

Polymers of styrene itself are of little interest to the paint industry, but styrene forms a number of interesting and useful co-polymers. The co polymerization reaction generally requires free-radical initiation and can be carried out either in solution (in aromatic hydrocarbon or carbon tetrachloride) or in emulsion. The exclusion of air is advisable, since oxygen retards the reaction.

Emulsion polymerization is the most widely used method, the free radical initiation being effected by either a redox system or a persulphate.

Copolymers of styrene

Co-polymers of styrene and acrylic acid derivatives form the basis of many thermosetting acrylic systems

The co-polymers of vinyl toluene and acrylic esters, in solution form, are used as binders in exterior masonry finishes. They show good durability. Styrene becomes an integral part of polyester finishes

One of the most interesting co-polymerization reactions of styrene and, more particularly, vinyl toluene, is with alkyd resins.

ACRYLIC RESINS

These are closely related to the vinyl resins. The acids acrylic, CH_2 = CH. COOH and methacrylic $CH_2 = C(CH_3)COOH$ as well as their esters can be polymerized to form long-chain thermoplastic resins:

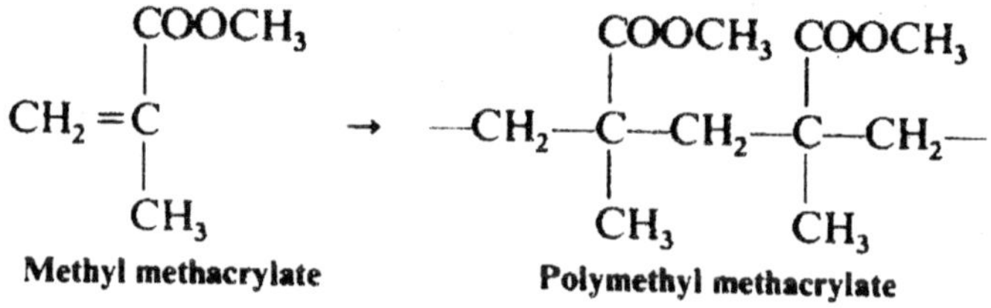

Polymers of methyl methacrylate and other esters containing alkyl side chains. are hard brittle solids but those from the 'straight' esters are soft and flexible. By copolymerising mixtures of the two types it is possible to produce polymers with any desired degree of hardness and flexibility. These are the so-called '100% acrylics'.

Acrylic acid, as well as the straight and branched esters, can be co polymerised with other unsaturated compounds such as styrene, vinyl toluene, vinyl acetate or vinyl chloride to give a variety of interesting and useful products.

Polymerisation of the acrylic monomers takes place readily by a free radical mechanism and is catalysed by heat and oxidising agents such peroxides. The reaction can be carried out by either solution or emulsion methods.

Properties of acrylic polymers and co-polymers

Generally these are colourless, thermoplastic solids soluble in esters, ketones and aromatic solvents. They are insoluble in aliphatic hydrocarbons and are resistant to water, alkali, mineral oils and greases. They also possess good lightfastness, adhesion and electrical properties. The exterior durability is very good, especially the co-polymers with styrene and vinyl toluene which are used as binders for masonry finishes. The co-polymers with vinyl acetate are used in emulsion paints.

Co-polymers of methyl methacrylate with butyl acrylate or ethyl hexyl acrylate have proved successful in acrylic gloss paints

Some of the softer members can be blended with chlorinated rubber and a small proportion of chlorinated paraffin to give tougher films than are obtained with chlorinated paraffin as the sole plasticiser. The films show better colour retention, durability and overcoating properties Good adhesion to galvanized and etched zinc surfaces is also claimed.

Thermosetting acrylic resins

The acrylic resins described above are long-chain thermoplastic materials and so not suited to stoving procedures. It is, however, possible to introduce reactive groups, spaced along the polymer chain, which can be cross-linked with other groups to give complex three dimensional structures. Groups introduced include carboxyl, hydroxyl, amino, and epoxy.

Thermosetting acrylic resins are, in general, based on the monomers methacrylic ester, acrylic ester, and styrene. Other monomers are incorporated to provide the reactive groups. The nature and relative amounts of monomers control the flexibility and other properties. For example, methacrylates and acrylates are used for maximum durability. The incorporation of styrene or vinyl toluene yields finishes resistant to detergents and household chemicals, particularly when cross-linked with epoxy resin (see below).

Carboxyl groups can be introduced by the use of a proportion of methacrylic acid. Cross-linking of the product with epoxy resins gives a film of outstanding chemical resistance, hardness, and adhesion.

Hydroxyl groups are introduced by using hydroxyalkyl methacrylates or acrylates. The resulting resin can be cross-linked with hexamethoxymethyl melamine to give films of outstanding weather-resistance and gloss retention.

They are used as stoving finishes on cars, or can be used as acid catalysed lacquers.

Acrylic resins incorporating acrylamide can be reacted with formaldehyde and butanol giving a butoxymethyl acrylamide monomer, containing the group.

$$CH_2\text{-}CH\text{-}CO\text{-}NH.CH_20C_4H_9$$

This group is similar to that in a butylated amino resin and will cross-link with other materials containing free -OH groups such as alkyds and epoxies. When cross linked with the latter, the resulting films have outstanding resistance to fats, oils and household chemicals. They are, therefore, used on domestic appliances.

Acrylic systems used for the finishing of furniture are suited to curing by ultra violet radiation. Whilst this form of cure has always proved successful with clear coatings, in the earlier years difficulties were encountered with pigmented coatings, particularly the high build types. Developments in photoinitiators have now largely overcome this problem

SILICONE RESINS

These are semi-inorganic high polymers containing both silicon and carbon, and from these elements it is possible to prepare a large number of silicone polymers according to the number and types of groupings. They can be 'tailored' for a great many specific purposes and are marketed as resins (solutions), oils, and rubbers.

Formation of silicones

The chemical reactions involved in the formation of silicone resins are many and complex. The following scheme indicates the general reactions involved:

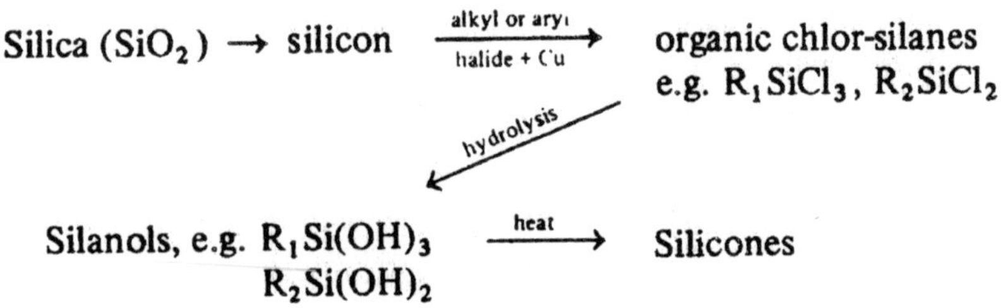

Properties of silicones

The nature of the alkyl and/or aryl groups determines, to a large degree, the properties of the resin. Methyl silicones are useful as waterproofing agents but find no application as paint materials. The introduction of a phenyl group confers heat resistance, but pure phenyl silicones are too brittle and fuse readily. All-round properties of a high standard are exhibited by co-polymers of methyl and phenylsilicone. These are far superior to the methyl or phenyl resins in respect of heat resistance, flexibility, electric properties, and durability.

Silicone resins are supplied in solutions in aromatic solvents, and can be thinned with similar solvents as well as esters and ketones. They are not soluble in white spirit.

Silicone resins will not cure at ambient temperatures and require heating to 200° to 250°C (392° to 482°F) for about two hours for complete cure. The process can be accelerated by the use of the naphthenates or octoates of zinc, cobalt or iron.

The films produced can vary froth rubbery to glass-like hardness. The softer types are the more resistant to heat and weathering, but to obtain the necessary mechanical properties the two types can be blended.

Uses of silicones

Silicone resins are used as the sole binder in paints to withstand high temperatures, particularly when pigmented with aluminium. Such paints require a curing period of 2 hours at 200°-220°C (392-428°F) after which they will withstand prolonged exposure to temperatures up to 430°C (806°F). With other heat-resisting pigments the service temperature is lower, about 280°-300°C

(536°-572°F).

Binders consisting of co-polymers of alkyds and silicones, containing up to' 30 percent silicone, are now being used for gloss paints with outstanding weather-resistance

Chapter - 6

CELLULOSE ESTER AND ETHER PRODUCTS

Cellulose comprises the bulk of the fibrous tissue of all plants, and the purest form is obtained from cotton in which it forms a protective fibre round the 'seeds. It is a member of the carbohydrate class and the composition of the repeating unit can be represented by the formula

$C_6H_7O_2(OH)_3$ or 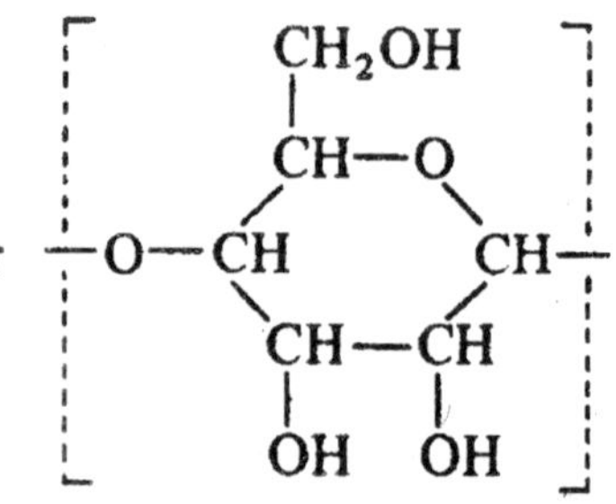

but the actual molecular weight is very high. The unit depicted above contains three alcohol groups, one of which is primary and the remaining two are secondary. The range of esters and ethers derived from cellulose is produced by reactions of these hydroxyl groups, and it is theoretically possible to produce mono-, di- and triderivatives. In practice, mixtures are usually obtained.

Esters of cellulose have been known for a considerable time and in 1855 A patent was taken out by Parkes in which he suggested the use of nitrocellulose solutions as protective coatings. He later suggested the use of camphor as a plasticizer

At first the use of cellulose esters as paint media was severely restricted by lack of solvents of suitable evaporation rate. The introduction of amyl acetate in 1882 provided a solvent of reasonably slow evaporation, but the high viscosity of the solutions necessitated considerable dilution before application, resulting in very thin films. In addition the plasticizer, camphor, slowly volatilized from the film, leading to embrittlement and breakdown. The production of low-viscosity cellulose nitrate and the introduction of a wider range of solvents and plasticizers led to the mass-production of cellulose nitrate lacquers, and over the last fifty years very large quantities have been produced.

CELLULOSE ESTERS

Cellulose nitrate

This is very often - but erroneously - called 'nitrocellulose'. It was first produced by Schoenbein in 1845, who treated cellulose with a mixture of nitric and sulphuric acids.

The modern method of manufacture employs the same reaction, the sulphuric acid acting both as a dehydrating agent to absorb the water produced and as a catalyst. The cellulose used is either cotton linters, which are short fibres attached to the seed and remaining after the longer fibres have been removed for spinning, or purified wood-pulp. The linters are subjected to preliminary treatments to remove fragments of seed and other impurities and are often given a mechanical treatment to open out the fibres before nitrating.

The cellulose is then treated in stainless steel vessels with a mixture of nitric and sulphuric acids, and the temperature controlled carefully until the desired degree of nitration is attained. The mixture is then run into a stainless steel centrifuge where -the bulk of the acid liquor is separated. The crude cellulose nitrate is drowned in water and then subjected to several washings with fresh water. Removal of acid impurities is essential for stability of the material in use, and after washing with water it is heated in slightly acidified water to about 140°C (284°F). This serves to release any sulphuric acid entrapped in the fibres and also reduces the viscosity of the product. The cellulose nitrate is then washed with hot water and centrifuged.

The material still contains about 30 percent water but cannot be dried owing to the dangerous nature of the dry compound. It is therefore 'dehydrated' by replacing the water by methylated spirit, butanol or isopropanol. The replacement of water by alcohol is carried out either by forcing the alcohol through the wet cellulose nitrate cake in a press or by spraying the material with the alcohol while it is being spun in a centrifuge.

The use of the higher alcohols has the advantage of more complete dehydration as they are less hygroscopic than the lower members. Nevertheless the material is never completely anhydrous. Cellulose nitrate then reaches the user 'damped' with one of the above alcohols; it should not be allowed to dry out after the drums are opened.

Properties of cellulose nitrate

The degree of nitration depends on conditions, and cellulose nitrates are divided into three classes according to the nitrogen content:

10.5 - 11.2% Low nitrogen (L)

11.2 - 11.8% Medium nitrogen (M)

11.8 - 12.2% High Nitrogen (H)

The nitrogen content has an important bearing on the choice of a cellulose nitrate for a given purpose. The most widely used are those with a high nitrogen content, whilst the low-nitrogen grades tolerate large amounts of alcohol and are used in paper lacquers.

The viscosity of a cellulose nitrate solution is of great importance and is influenced by the type of material and the nature of the solvent blend. It is generally measured in the form of a standard solution in aqueous acetone, the solvent consisting of 95 percent acetone and 5 percent water by volume. The concentfation of the solution varies with the grade of cellulose nitrate being tested, and viscosity ranges are designated by letters H (high), M (medium), L (low) and X (extra low). The accepted method of designating a cellulose nitrate gives information on type, nitrogen content and viscosity. For example, a material designated DHX 30/50 is a dense (D) type with high nitrogen content (H) and extra low viscosity (X) lying between 30 and 50 poise.

Testing

The quality of cellulose nitrate must be carefully controlled to ensure successful results. The following tests are among the most important.

Nitrogen content The older method consisted of measurement of the volume of nitrogen evolved when a known weight of the material is decomposed with concentrated sulphuric acid in a Lunge nitrometer. In the modern method the cellulose nitrate is hydrolysed by sulphuric acid in glacial acetic acid solution. The liberated nitric acid is estimated by titration electrometrically with standard ferrous ammonium sulphate solution in sulphuric acid.

Viscosity The solution of standard concentration in aqueous acetone is placed in a wide vertical tube in a thermostatically controlled bath at 20°C (68°F). The viscosity is then determined by the falling sphere method

Stability At normal temperatures a properly prepared cellulose nitrate is stable, or at least decomposes at a rate that can be ignored. However, any slight tendency to instability, i.e. decomposition, is accelerated by heat, and resistance to heat is therefore used to assess stability. It is usually carried out by the Bergmann and Junk test in which the cellulose nitrate is heated for 2 hours at 132°C (270°F) and the acid decomposition products are absorbed in water. These are estimated by titration.

Volatile content When lacquers are prepared from 'damped' cellulose nitrate the alcohol content must be taken into consideration. It is usually about 30 percent but is likely to vary. The figure is determined by heating a known weight of the damp material in an aluminium dish in an oven at 60° to 65°C (140° to 149°F). Heating is continued until the weight is constant, and high temperatures must be avoided. The dry material should be redamped as soon as the estimation is completed.

CELLULOSE LACQUERS

Cellulose lacquers are not simply solutions of cellulose derivatives, but also contain plasticizers to give the necessary film flexibility, and resins to increase the gloss and adhesion. They may also contain non-solvents or diluents to control the cost. A large proportion of the lacquers used is pigmented.

The performance is controlled by the type of cellulose derivative used and by the cellulose - plasticizer - resin ratio. The large number of materials available renders it possible to design cellulose lacquers for a very wide range of uses. Some of the general principles involved in lacquer formulation are discussed below.

Cellulose nitrate lacquers

Cellulose nitrate is the principal component of the film in most cases and there is a wide variety of types available. A low-viscosity type permits the formulation of high-solids lacquers leading to high-build films. Higher viscosity cellulose nitrate gives lacquers of lower solids at spraying viscosity, but the solids can be increased by the use of suitable resins. These lead to greater gloss and hardness of the film, and the types used are discussed below.

Ethyl cellulose is compatible with cellulose nitrate in all proportions and can be incorporated to reduce flammability and increase flexibility.

Resins These are used to improve the gloss and adhesion of the film. The film produced from cellulose nitrate alone is a semi-gloss and has poor adhesion. The resin must have good compatibility with cellulose nitrate and plasticizer in all proportions, and the amount used varies considerably.

Damars These are extensively used on account of good solubility, the dewaxed type being the most suitable. They have a pale colour and confer good gloss and adhesion. Damars are insoluble in alcohol and so cannot be used in the low-nitrogen type spirit lacquers.

Sandarac and mastic can be regarded as resins of the same type as damar but have the advantage of ready solubility in alcohol.

Dewaxed shellac is used in the spirit type of lacquer where it confers good adhesion, toughness and flexibility. Such lacquers are not suitable for exterior exposure.

Ester gums The glycerol types are completely compatible with cellulose nitrate and soluble in the solvents used. The pentaerythritol types are much less compatible. Low acid value in the ester gum is essential, and the plasticizer content is very important. Generally the proportion of ester gum is high for interior finishes and low in finishes for exterior exposure.

Maleic resins show good compatibility and produce very hard films. These must be well plasticized to avoid brittleness. They are not recommended in lacquers for exterior exposure.

Cyclohexanone resins possess no acidity and are useful in clear lacquers for metals. They have good compatibility and confer good gloss and adhesion on the film.

Alkyds have replaced a number of the natural resins such as kauri, Congo copal, and rosin. Both drying and non-drying types are used, but the latter find widest use. The addition of a non-drying alkyd plasticizes the film and confers good gloss and durability. The films are also resistant to alcohol and to heat.

The castor-oil modified types are used in greatest quantity, but other nondrying types are used for special purposes. The general requirements of such an alkyd are stated [1] to be: fatty acid content 30 to 40 percent; phthalic anhydride 40 to 50 percent; acid value 5 to 25.

Plasticizers

A characteristic "of cellulose esters is considerable swelling on addition of solvent before actual dispersion or solution. When a film of the ester solution dries, the process is reversed, resulting in a contraction of the film and a tendency to pull away from the surface. The function of a plasticizer is to correct this tendency and to confer elasticity on the film without destroying the hardness. The ratio of plasticizer to cellulose ester is important and generally is higher for the low-viscosity grades. If a proportion of ethyl cellulose is used in the lacquer, the amount of plasticizer can be reduced.

The ideal plasticizer for high-quality lacquers would be freely soluble in the solvents:used, completely compatible with the ester and resin, non-volatile, and chemically inert. With such a material the film would retain its elasticity indefinitely. In practice it is difficult to obtain the desired properties with one plasticizer, and blends are generally used. Even so, the ideal requirements are never completely met.

A great many plasticizers are available and the following are in common use.

Dibutyl phthalate	Tricresyl phosphate
Dioctyl phthalate	Triphenyl phosphate
Dimethylglycol phthalate	Trichlorethyl phosphate
Tributyl citrate	Castor oil

Solvents

The volatile portion of a lacquer usually consists of a blend of liquids, and these are conveniently divided into three groups, based on solvent power.

True solvents form the major portion of the volatile constituents.

Latent solvents are not solvents for the.principal film-formers, but increase the solvent power of the other volatile ingredients.

Diluents are not solvents for the principal film-formers but are added to reduce cost. They may also improve the solvent power of the mixture for the resin and plasticizer.

The range of true solvents is not extensive, and typical solvents for cellulose nitrate are ester, ketones and glycol ethers. Examples of the first two classes are:

Esters	**Ketones**
ethyl acetate	acetone
isopropyl acetate	methyl ethyl ketone -
n-butyl acetate	methyl isobutyl ketone
ethyl lactate	methyl cyclohexanone

Evaporation rate

The rate of evaporation of a solvent is one of its most important properties and is usually evaluated against ether. A solvent which evaporates too rapidly can cause severe chilling of the film to a temperature below the dew point; and moisture deposition on the soft film can lead to blushing. Also, if the true solvent leaves the film before the latent solvent or diluent, precipitation of the film-former can take place.

Viscosity

The viscosity of a solution of cellulose nitrate depends on the concentration and grade of ester used, the composition of the solvent mixture, and the temperature. The viscosity falls with increasing temperature as is usual. The effect of solvents is not as simple. With simple solvents, viscosity of the solution is lower with low molecular weight solvents than with those of high molecular weight. A mixture of solvents generally gives a lower viscosity than the same proportion of a single solvent. Thus a mixture of alcohol and butyl acetate gives a solution of much lower viscosity than butyl acetate alone. The alcohol here is acting as a latent solvent. Alcohols alone are not solvents for cellulose nitrate but they, possess a latent solvent power when mixed with other solvents. In practice an alcohol is usually present as the damping agent for cellulose nitrate and its presence is therefore an advantage.

Diluents

In order to keep the cost of a lacquer as low as possible, only sufficient solvent is used to dissolve the cellulose nitrate, the final consistency being. attained by dilution with an aromatic or petroleum hydrocarbon. These, are not actual solvents but are compatible with the mixture. The proportion of diluent used will depend on its compatibility with the active solvent and this is determined by the dilution ratio. This is given by the expression

$$\text{Dilution ratio} = \frac{\text{Volume of diluent which will just precipitate the dissolved cellulose nitrate}}{\text{Volume of solvent used}}$$

The determination is carried out by adding the diluent to a solution of cellulose nitrate in the specified solvent until the cellulose nitrate commences to precipitate and will not redissolve in the mixture. The value depends on the type of cellulose nitrate and the concentration. This is generally 10 percent. The dilution ratios in Table 12.1 are quoted by Durrans

Table 12.1

Solvent	Toluene	Xylene	Petroleum	Butanol
Acetone	4·5	3·9	0·6	7·0
Amyl acetate (*n*)	2·2	2·2	1·4	7·3
Butyl acetate (*n*)	2·7	2·4	1·4	7·3
Butyl phthalate	2·8	2·7	1·7	8·0
Butyl tartrate	10·6	7·7	1·4	15·0
Di-acetone alcohol	3·1	2·9	0·5	7·8
Ethyl lactate	5·6	4·8	0·7	10·2
Glycol mono-ethyl ether	5·0	4·7	1·0	6·9
Methyl ethyl ketone	4·5	3·3		
Tricresyl phosphate	3·3	4·2	0·7	4·9

Pigmented lacquers

The dispersion of pigments in cellulose nitrate lacquers follows broadly the same lines as for gloss paints. The pigment content is generally lower, and the lower viscosities of the media can result in troublesome settlement of heavy pigments. The desired properties of the pigment are maximum opacity, freedom from any tendency to bleed in lacquer solvents, resistance to ultraviolet light and freedom from toxicity (this applies to spray paints and any finishes for children's playthings).

The majority of pigments used in gloss paints can also be used in cellulose nitrate lacquers, but care should be exercised with the following-, which are either unsuitable or show the defects mentioned.

Zinc oxide	Reactive. Poor opacity but gives good gloss and colour.
	Can be used for interior work.
Ultramarine Blue	Poor strength and opacity.

Phthalocyanine Blue	Used mainly for tinting. When used alone shows tendency to give bronzy films of poor gloss.
Hansa Yellows	Tendency to bleed.
Ferrite Yellows	Poor gloss. Used for tinting.
Helio Red	Tendency to bleed.
Maroons	Many show poor exterior durability.
Lead Chromes Chrome Greens	Toxic.

Dispersion of the pigment can be effected in a ball or pebble mill, or the "pigment can be dispersed in plasticizer alone on a triple roll mill after premixing. A slow evaporating solvent can be used to ease the material over the rolls, but the process is slow.

Chip method This method is now widely used and consists in dispersing the pigment in a plastic cellulose dough in a heavy mixer. Dispersion of the pigment is effected by high shear forces resulting from high power input and high consistency. The dispersion process is carried out in a Bridge-Banbury mixer which incorporates a pair of bladed rotors turning in a closed chamber. The latter is jacketed for heating or cooling. The material to be processed is forced between the blades by hydraulic ram, and dispersion is effected in a short time.

In the chip process, the damp cellulose nitrate, pigment, and solvent (often a solvent plasticizer) are charged into the mill. When dispersion is complete the mass is passed through sheeting rolls and reduced to a thickness of about 2 mm ($\frac{1}{16}$ inch). The sheets are then broken up into chips.

Several companies now specialize in the supply of chips to the industry, and their use makes the manufacture of pigmented lacquers a relatively simple operation.

Cellulose acetate

Cellulose acetate was first introduced in 1865 by Schiitzenberger who prepared it by treating cellulose with acetic aciu and acetic anhydride. The formation of cellulose triacetate can be represented by the equation

$$C_6H_70_2(OH)_3 + 3CH_3COOH \rightarrow C_6H_7O_2(OCOCH_3)_3 + 3H_20$$

The triacetate is of little interest on account of limited solubility, but by controlled hydrolysis part of the acetate groups can be split off, yielding a product soluble in a number of solvents and useful for lacquer manufacture. It is usual to assess cellulose acetate by the acetyl value, which is the weight (grams) of acetic acid liberated on hydrolysis of 100 grams of ester.

Manufacture of cellulose acetate

Two methods are in use at the present time.

Dreyfus method This process involves a pretreatment of purified cotton linters or wood pulp with acetic acid containing a small amount of sulphuric acid. This serves to break down the cellulose structure and to increase the reactivity, The product is then added to a mixture of glacial acetic acid and acetic anhydride, the temperature being kept at 4° to 5°C (39-2° to 41 -0°F). When the reaction is complete, a clear viscous solution of triacetate is obtained which is then subjected to hydrolysis or 'ripening'. Water is added gradually and the whole then heated to 60° to 70°C (140° to 158°F) to effect the hydrolysis. For lacquer manufacture an acetyl value of 54 to 55 is considered suitable.

Methylene chloride process Dry cellulose is treated first with acetic anhydride and then with a mixture of acetic anhydride, methylene chloride and sulphuric acid. Rigid control of conditions, especially temperature, is essential. When the reaction is complete, some water is added and the mixture hydrolysed to the desired degree. The sulphuric acid is then neutralized by sodium acetate, and the methylene chloride recovered by distillation. The cellulose acetate is precipitated from the acetic acid solution by addition of water, washed well, and dried.

Properties of cellulose acetate

The cellulose acetates are white granular materials with specific gravities of about 1.36. They are thermoplastic and possess high but indefinite melting points. In the molten condition they decompose rapidly.

The general properties are determined largely by the degree of acetylation and the viscosity. They are soluble in a limited range of solvents, the most important of which are methyl acetate, ethyl acetate, acetone, methylethyl ketone, methylcellosolve acetate, carbitol acetate and diacetone alcohol. In addition they dissolve in mixtures of ethyl alcohol (10 parts) with methylene chloride or ethylene chloride (90 parts).

Films of cellulose acetate are very much less flammable than those of cellulose nitrate but have inferior water resistance. They are very resistant to degradation by sunlight and are very resistant to petrol, oils and greases. They are not resistant to alkali. For best results, plasticizers such as triacetin or phthalates are incorporated in quantities up to about 30 percent.

Cellulose acetates are used in lacquers for wood, metal, paper and leather; in strippable coatings, and in paint strippers.

Cellulose acetobutyrate

This material is in some ways very similar to cellulose acetate but possesses several advantages. It is more resistant to water, is soluble in a wider range of solvents, and is compatible with a greater number of plasticizers and resins.

Cellulose acetobutyrate can be prepared in methylene chloride solution using either a mixture of acetic and butyric anhydrides, or a mixture of acetobutyric anhydride, acetic anhydride and a small quantity of sulphuric acid.

The ratio of butyric: to acetic anhydride can be varied to give a range of products in which flexibility, solubility and. compatibility increase with increasing butyric content. They are used in lacquers for wood, wire, paper and plastics.

Safety Regulations

The highly flammable nature of cellulose nitrate and of the solvents used in cellulose lacquers has resulted in the issue of statutory regulations governing the manufacture, storage and use of these lacquers.

Cellulose nitrate is classed as explosive if the nitrogen content is greater than 12.3 percent. The type used in lacquers contains between 10.5 and 12.3 percent nitrogen and is supplied damped with at least 25 percent of butanol, isopropanol or ethanol.

CELLULOSE ETHERS

Ethyl cellulose

If purified cellulose is treated with concentrated sodium hydroxide solution an alkali cellulose is produced by reaction with the hydroxyl groups:

$$C_6H_70_2(OH)_3 + 3NaOH \rightarrow C_6H_70_2(ONa)_3 + 3H_20$$

The sodium compound can be reacted with an alkyl chloride such as ethyl chloride under appropriate conditions to give a tri-ether:

$$C_6H_70_2(ONa)_3 + 3C_2H_5Cl \rightarrow C_6H_70_2(OC_2H_5)_3 + 3NaCl$$

The method of manufacture is based on these reactions, the conditions being rigidly controlled to ensure the correct degree of ethylation. The tri-ether is of no interest as it has poor solubility and compatibility and is not thermoplastic. The type found most suitable contains between 2 and 2.5 ethoxyl groups per cellulose 'unit' which is equivalent to 42 to 48 percent ethoxyl content.

When the desired degree of ethylation has been reached, the excess of ethyl chloride is removed and the ethyl cellulose precipitated by addition of water. The material is washed free from chloride and dried.

Properties of ethyl cellulose

Ethyl cellulose is a white granular powder with specific gravity 1.14. It softens at about 140°C (284°F) and melts at between 200°C and 220°C

(392° and 428°F). The degree of flammability is very low. It is resistant to dilute acids and to alkalis.

Films of ethyl cellulose are tough and flexible, retaining the latter property over a wide range of temperature. The films are transparent and transmit ultraviolet light without discoloration. The water permeability is superior to that of cellulose acetate but inferior to that of cellulose nitrate.

Ethyl cellulose has the widest range of solubility of all the cellulose derivatives. It is soluble in alcohols, ketones, esters, aromatic and chlorinated hydrocarbons. The range of solubility is controlled by the degree of ethylation, reaching a maximum when about 2 - 5 of the three available hydroxyl groups are combined. It is also compatible with many drying oils, varnishes, and synthetic resins.

Uses of ethyl cellulose

Ethyl cellulose is incorporated into oleoresinous varnishes to improve drying characteristics, hardness and water resistance. It is also used in flowback lacquers, cable lacquers and coatings for foil and paper.

Water-soluble cellulose derivatives

These materials absorb water and slowly form gels or 'solutions' of high viscosity at low concentrations. With the exception of sodium carboxymethyl cellulose (SCMC) they are ethers which are tasteless and non-toxic. In addition to their extensive use as thickeners and protective colloids in latex emulsion paints they are used in foodstuffs. The most widely used are the following.

Methyl cellulose A methyl ether of cellulose which is obtained by methylating alkali cellulose with dimethyl sulphate or methyl chloride. The degree of etherification can vary and this controls the properties. When the number of methoxy groups per anhydroglucose unit lies between 1.3 and 2.4 the product is soluble in water, but with increasing methoxy groups it becomes soluble in organic solvents

Aqueous solutions of methyl cellulose are non-ionic and have surface tensions lower than that of water; consequently they form foams on vigorous agitation. The solutions form firm gels which coagulate reversibly on heating and require protection against bacterial attack.

When used as a thickener and protective colloid in emulsion paints the films show good moisture resistance and sizing properties, but in brushability and storage stability they are inferior to hydroxyethyl cellulose and SCMC.

Hydroxyethyl cellulose An ether in which the degree of etherification is approximately 8.5 hydroxyethyl groups per 10 anhydroglucose units. It produces firm gels and is soluble in both hot and cold water. The solutions are non-foaming and show excellent tolerance to electrolytes.

In latex emulsion paints it gives good scrub resistance, brushability, flow out and sizing properties on porous surfaces. In common with other cellulose ethers it requires protection against bacteria.

Sodium carboxymethyl cellulose (SCMC) This is prepared by reacting alkali cellulose with sodium monochloracetate. The degree of substitution-is of the order of 7 carboxymethyl groups per 10 anhydroglucose units. -The solutions in water are soft gels and exhibit pseudoplastic flow. They are anionic with a pH of 7.0 and are stable between pH 4 and pH 10.

SCMC gives precipitates with trivalent and some divalent metals, and when used as a protective colloid in emulsion paints it is usual to add a sequestering agent such as Calgon The emulsion paints show excellent brushing and storage properties but are inferior in other respects to those based on methyl and hydroxyethyl cellulose. Like the latter, SCMC solutions require protection against bacterial attack.

The choice of cellulose thickener for a specific purpose will be influenced by the relative importance of the desired properties. Each product has strong features as well as weaknesses, and a relative assessment is necessary before deciding on the type to be used.

Chapter - 7

VARNISHES

The term varnish is applied to a class of clear liquids of 2 to 3 poise viscosity which, when exposed to the air in thin coatings, dry to tough, glossy films. Whilst traditional varnishes are referred to as 'oil' and 'spirit' types, modern varnishes are frequently solutions of alkyds, polyurethanes, polyesters, and so on. In this section the traditional types are considered.

Oil varnishes.

Oil varnishes are combinations of drying oils and resins which are thinned to application viscosity with volatile solvent. Driers are incorporated to catalyse the drying process, and this will be controlled largely by the amount of oil present or the ratio of oil to resin. This ratio, by weight, is known as the oil length and can be varied considerably. Varnishes are described as long, medium, or short oil length, and these have roughly the following oil/resin ratios:

Long oil	3/1 to 4½/1
Medium oil	2/ 1 to 3/ 1
Short oil	1/3 to 2/1

In the USA oil lengths are expressed in gallons (US) of oil per 100 lb resin, so that a '10 gallon' oil length varnish would consist of 10 US gallons of oil to 100 lb resin. (Note: 1 US gallon = 0.833 Imperial gallon = 3.78 litres.)

Some of the short-oil varnishes retain a surface tack for some time and have been used as adhesives for gold leaf. Such varnishes are, in consequence, known as goldsizes.

The main use of oil varnishes has been the finishing of wood. The wood was either satained or grained before varnishing, although in some cases, where the wood presented a naturally attractive appearance, the varnish was applied without the preliminary staining. As a result of changing fashions in the use of wood and the growth of mass-produced furniture and wooden articles generally, oil varnishes for interior work have been largely replaced by lacquer, type finishes, notably cellulose nitrate, polyurethanes and polyesters.

The term 'mixing varnish' has long been applied to oil varnishes with are used' as paint media. Before the widespread use of alkyds, these mixing varnishes were the standard media for most gloss paints and undercoats, but today their uses are limited to certain metallic and maintenance paints.

Although oil varnishes are now manufactured on a reduced scale and the use of fossil resins is practically obsolete, a short account of these materials will, it is hoped, be of interest.

Oil varnishes contain the following four major ingredients.

Resins, which provide the hardness and gloss of the film. Both these properties increase with increasing ,resin content, but the durability decreases. Natural resins, especially the fossil copals, were formerly used extensively but these resins are no longer economically viable. Tung oil varnishes for special purposes were often made with ester gum or limed-rosin. Resins used in modern varnishes include pure and modified phenolics, maleics, coumarone, and hydrocarbon types.

Drying oils contribute the elasticity, toughness, and general durability. These properties improve with increasing oil content, but the effect is controlled by the type of oil. The commonly used oils are linseed (as VLO, stand oil, or enamel oil) and tung oil. Varnishes often contain both oils.

Driers catalyse the conversion (by oxidation and polymerisation) of the oil to the solid state. They are added as solutions of the naphthenates or octoates of zirconium, cobalt and, sometimes, manganese. Lead drier is no longer used in varnishes.

Thinners are added for the sole purpose of reducing the oil/resin complex to a suitable consistency for application. They should evaporate completely from the applied film. White spirit is the usual thinner for long-oil varnishes, but the shorter types, and especially some tung oil varnishes, require a proportion of stronger solvent such as xylene, naphtha, or aromatic petroleum solvent

Varnishes from fossil resins

The industrial production of durable oil varnishes was originally based on the combination of linseed oil with African hard fossils such as Animi and Sierra Leone copals. In their natural condition these resins are not soluble in drying oils but can be made soluble by heating for some time at a temperature just above the fusion point. This results in a partial depolymerization during which -about 20 to 30 percent of the weight of the resin is lost in volatile decomposition products. This process is known as gum running.

Congo copal has been used on a large scale by varnish manufacturers but has also been run in bulk, allowed to cool, and marketed as fused copal, or esterified with glycerol and marketed as copal ester.

The varnish-making operation consists of the following successive steps: (a) running the resin, (b) incorporating the run resin with the linseed oil, (c) cooling, dilution with thinner and addition of driers, (d) clarification and maturing. Clarification is necessary since the natural resins always contain a certain amount of extraneous matter.

Properties and uses of copal varnishes

The drying times of these varnishes vary with the oil length, the long-oil types taking from 16 to 20 hours and the short-oils from 1 to 2 hours.

The term 'copal varnish' has been used in the decorating trade for the bestquality varnish. Long-oil types are used for exterior work and medium-oil types for interior deeoration. The long-oil types were formerly used as carriage varnishes, and for many years were the standard type of medium for hard-gloss paints. Other types of varnish made on copal resins are the short-oil types known as 'hard church oak', 'flatting varnish', and the goldsizes.

Varnishes from modified phenolic resins

Modified phenolic resins are soluble in drying oils at comparatively low temperatures, so the varnish-making process is relatively simple. Again, the wide range of rosin-modified phenolic resins available enables varnishes to be designed to meet a wide spectrum of requirements.

Some of the softer types of modified phenolic resin are soluble in white spirit in the cold and can be made into varnishes by solution in this solvent. followed by addition of bodied oil and driers. This process is known as cold-cutting.

With the harder types, the resin and part of the linseed oil are heated to 250° to 260°C (482° to 500°F) until a drop forms a clear bead on cooling on glass. A second portion of oil is added and the test repeated. The process is continued until all the oil has been added and the varnish gives a clear solution in white spirit. It is then cooled and thinned, and driers are added in the normal way.

The softer types of modified phenolic resin can be treated in a similar way, but the oil and resin can be blended in fewer steps.

These varnishes are very similar in their general properties to those made from Congo copal but they are more easily made.

Tung oil is often incorporated into these varnishes along with the linseed oil and is best used in the form of enamel oil. These oils contain 20 to 25 percent tung oil co polymerized with linseed oil. Processing is similar to that for linseed oil, but the varnishes have appreciably greater water resistance.

Tung oil varnishes

Tung (or wood) oil can be used in varnish-making, either in the form of a stand oil (these are available in a range of viscosities) or as the cheaper raw tung oil. The stand oil can be blended with the softer modified phenolic resins or with coumarone resins at 200° to 220°C (392° to 428°F), but harder resins require a higher temperature, with its attendant risk of gelation. To reduce this risk the resin is best cooked with linseed oil and oiled out with the tung-oil stand oil. It is then cooled rapidly and thinned.

It is more economical to use raw tung oil and to effect the bodying during the processing, but this method requires close control and experience. The raw tung oil is mixed with half the resin and heated rapidly in an open pot to 280°C (536°F). This temperature is necessary to ensure that the tung oil is gas proof, i.e. that the film on drying will be unaffected by gases from combustion. It must be borne in mind that tung oil will gel in 12 to 20 minutes at 280° to 285°C (536° to 545 ° F), so all operations must be carried out smoothly and without delay.

When the temperature has reached 280°C the pot is moved away from the fire, and after about 2, minutes the remainder of the resin, in small pieces, is added rapidly, -with---stirring. The temperature of the mixture falls to 250° to 260°C (482° to 500°F) at which temperature bodying is completed. It is then cooled rapidly and thinned.

Many Lung-oil varnishes contain a proportion of linseed oil which is, often useful as a chill-back if the tung-oil bodying tends to get out of control.

Tung oil-pure (100 percent) phenolic varnishes

The two types of pure phenolic resin behave differently towards tung oil, the resole type being reactive and the novolac type being non-reactive but soluble in the oil.

Reactive resole resins The manufacture of varnishes from these resins is effected by hating the tung oil to 170° to 180°C (338° to 356°F), at which point the resin is added and the whole stirred until the resin is dissolved. The temperature is then raised to 230° C (446°f when reaction occurs accompanied by foaming. The intensity of foaming varies from one resin to another, and care must be taken to regulate the temperature so that the reaction proceeds slowly, otherwise there is a risk of the pot boiling over. The melt is held for about 25 to 30 minutes, the end-point being indicated by lessening or cessation of foaming. It is then cooled and thinned.

It is of interest that with reactive resins a gas proof varnish is obtained at the relatively low temperature of 230°C (446°F).

Non-reactive novolac resins These resins dissolve in tung oil but no reaction occurs between them, so bodying involves polymerization of the oil only. The varnishes are made in the normal way for tung-oil media, but the thinners must contain a high percentage of aromatic hydrocarbons as the resins have limited solubility in white spirit.

Properties and uses of tung oil-phenolic varnishes

These varnishes are all characterized by higher water resistance than linseed oil types, the highest water resistance and the quickest dry being shown by the 100 percent phenolic types. Of these, varnishes from the reactive types are the most popular. They are used as spar varnishes and as media for certain types of maintenance paints, for example, those pigmented with micaceous iron oxide and used on structural steelwork.

Tung oil-coumarone varnishes

These are usually made at about 2/ 1 oil length and are conveniently manufactured from bodied tung oil. The oil and resin are heated to 220°-230°C (430°-450°F) until a uniform melt is obtained, cooled rapidly, and thinned with white spirit. The alkali resistance of these varnishes is of a high order and they are used in primers for alkaline surfaces such as plasters, cement render, and asbestos board. The low acid value of these media renders them very suitable for use in metallic paints.

Physical properties of oil varnishes and films

Colour This is influenced by the colour of the oils and resins used and alsc by the care taken in manufacture. Excessive heating is a frequent cause of dark colour. The measurement of the colour of varnishes is carried out by methods similar to those used for oils

Viscosity Varnishes are generally applied by brush and the brushing properties are determined largely by the viscosity. If this is too high, brush-drag will be experienced and the varnish will be difficult to spread; if too low, the varnish will form runs on vertical surfaces and the film will be excessively thin. It is found that a viscosity of 2 to 3 poises at 25°C (77° F) is generally satisfactory for a brushing varnish. Viscosity measurements are carried out by the same methods as those used for oils

Drying time The drying time of a varnish is dependent on the composition but, in addition,it is influenced by film thickness, temperature and humidity of the air; nature of the substrate, and the amount of light reaching the surface. The methods for the determination of the drying times of varnishes are the same as those used for paints and are described in BS 3900, C_2 and C_3

Flexibility One of the functions of the oil in a varnish is to contribute flexibility, a property which enables a varnish film to accommodate the dimensional changes in the substrate without cracking. This is particularly important on exterior woodwork when expansion and contraction imposes great stresses on the varnish. The cold-check test is often applied to varnishes for woodwork. A wooden panel coated with the varnish in question is subjected to a number of cycles consisting of exposure to warm (60°C,140°F) and cold (-10°C, 23.3°F) conditions. Varnishes which lack flexibility will be found to crack after a few cycles.

The general methods for the determination of the flexibility of varnishes are identical with those used for paints

Hardness This property, like many others, cannot be assessed in isolation. The property which is important from a practical viewpoint is the resistance of the film to mechanical injury, and this depends on a combination of hardness and toughness. The methods for measuring these are identical, with those used for paint

Moisture absorption of films All oleoresinous varnishes absorb water to some extent and the amount present in the film will be in equilibrium with the moisture content of the air (or relative humidity). Moisture absorption is related, to a large degree, to the presence of water-attracting (hydrogen bonding) groups, such as hydroxyl and/or carboxyl, in the film as well as watersoluble oxidation products. It is also affected by the nature and amount of resin present. Tung oil/phenolic varnishes absorb considerably less moisture than, for example, a clear alkyd film whilst chlorinated rubber, which contains no water-attracting groups absorbs very little.

These facts are illustrated by the following figures:

Varnish	% water absorbed at 20 °C
Tung oil/phenolic	2.5
Alkyd	6.2
Chlorinated rubber	0.8

Measurement of water absorption can be carried out by casting films on weighed glass panels. When the varnish is dry the panels are re-weighed and immersed for the required time in distilled, tap or salt water:

Figures quoted for moisture absorption do not reflect exterior durability. The absorption of moisture is not a rapid process and is of importance only when films are allowed to remain wet for prolonged periods. This can occur under marine conditions but tung oil/phenolic varnish has.- nevertheless, been the standard marine varnish for many years. Alkyd resin films are little affected by showers of rain and the paints. show good exterior durability.

Ultimate breakdown of alkyd paint films is due to the combined effect of moisture and radiation Chlorinated rubber is usually employed in the form of pigmented coatings and these can show very good durability. Moisture permeability indicates the ease with which moisture will pass through a film and may or may not be accompanied by absorption. The least permeable films are those containing no water-attracting groups such as chlorinated rubber or vinyls. Measurement of film permeability can be carried out using a Payne cup. A detached varnish (or paint) film is secured firmly over the open end of a metal cup containing a desiccating agent. The cup is weighed and then exposed in a.humid atmosphere. It is re-weighed at invervals over a specified time. The increase in weight gives the amount of moisture which has passed through the film. The film permeability is expressed as grams (moisture)/ 100 cm^2/24 hours at 20°C.

Both moisture absorption and film permeability are affected to a marked degree by the amount and nature of any pigment present.

Non-volatile content This can be determined by weighing 1 to 2 grams of varnish into a circular flat-bottomed metal dish 75 mm in diameter and heating for 3 hours at 105° to 110°C (221 ° to 230° F). -It is then cooled and weighed. Difficulties are sometimes encountered with this method due either to skinning of the sample or to retention of solvents by certain types of resin. The method is useful for checking and correcting solvent losses which take place during the thinning of varnishes.

Flash points and specific gravities of varnishes are determined by the methods used for solvents and oils respectively.

Spirit varnishes

These consist of solutions of resins in volatile solvents, and dry entirely by evaporation. The resin film remains soluble in the parent solvent and is sometimes termed 'a non-convertible coating.

Shellac is the most widely used resin in this class and is dissolved in Industrial Methylated Spirit (IMS) by placing the resin and solvent in a wooden barrel churn. This is rotated until the resin is in solution. A number, of spirit varnishes and 'polishes'. are made from shellac alone or in admixture with other resins. The two members in current use are French polish and knotting.

French polish consists of a 25-30 percent solution of orange shellac in IMS. It is used for polishing good-quality furniture, especially antiques.

Knotting, a 35-40 percent solution of orange shellac in IMS, is used, as the name suggests, for sealing knots in new timber. The purpose is the prevention of exudation of resinous materials which would soften and discolour paint films.

Shellac solutions in ethanol are. highly acidic and can cause rapid corrosion leading to discoloration if packed in tinplate containers. The corrosion can be prevented by addition of a small quantity of ethylaniline phosphate.

Polyvinyl acetate is soluble in IMS to give water-white solutions of zero acid value. Such solutions require a plasticizer but yield films of limited weather resistance. They are used as coatings on polished metals and also as media for bronze and aluminium paints for interior use.

Chapter - 8

PIGMENTATION

The basic operation in the manufacture of a paint is the dispersion of the particles of pigment (often mixed with extender) in a paint medium to produce a uniform, stable system.

The techniques and associated theory applied to non-aqueous and watersoluble pants differ from those for aqueous emulsion paints, and the two will therefore be considered separately.

NON-AQUEOUS PAINTS

The process of pigment dispersion comprises three stages which are inter related and can take place simultaneously. -

1. Breakdown of aggregates to smaller units and individual particles.
2. Wetting of these units and particles by the paint medium.
3. Stabilization of the resulting dispersion.

Stage 1: Breakdown of aggregates

This is essentially a mechanical process involving pigment and medium. It is often referred to as 'grinding', although little breakdown of the individual particles takes place.

It is not always necessary to effect a complete breakdown of the aggregates to individual particles; for each type of paint there is an 'acceptable degree of dispersion' which, in production control, is assessed by the use of the 'fineness of-grind' gauge

The gauge consists of a steel plate on which are machined one or two wedgeshaped channels either 50 micrometres (0.002 in.) or 100 micrometres (0.004 in.) deep at one end and tapering to zero at the other. Calibration can be in micrometres, inches-3, or in Hegman units of 0-8 or 0-10, increasing from the deep end. On the 0-8 Hegman scale; acceptable figures for undercoats are about 6 and for finishes at least 7.5 and preferably 'off scale'. Readings are taken by placing a drop of the pigment dispersion in the deep end and then drawing it along the channel with a doctor blade held vertically. The film is viewed at grazing angle and the point noted where the surface shows the general appearance of aggregates or 'bittiness'.

Whilst the fineness-of-grind gauge is a useful instrument for use in production control of dispersion, the information provided is,insufficient for investigational work. Some knowledge is often required of the state of dispersion throughout the system, for example, particle size distribution, flocculation, etc. Among methods employed to obtain this information are determination of (a) tinting strength and (b) particle-size distribution by sedimentation rates, optical and electron microscope and centrifugal methods.

Stage 2: Wetting of pigment particles

The term 'wetting' is generally accepted as referring to the replacement of the pigment/air or pigment/moisture interface by a pigment/medium interface.

All solids adsorb a certain amount of moisture and in addition, air is held within the aggregates of pigment particles. The adsorbed film is often held very tenaciously and, with finely divided powders, can be of considerable area.

The process of wetting involves a number of factors, predominant among which are (a) the surface tension or, more correctly, the adhesion tension at the solid/liquid interface, and (b) the nature of the pigment surface.

Interfacial tension

The adhesion tension between pure liquids and solids can be studied by use of the classical contact angle.

Contact angle A drop of liquid in contact with a solid surface will assume a shape that is governed by the surface tension at the liquid-solid interface. Suppose a drop takes the shape illustrated in Fig. 14.2, which depicts a cross section through the drop and the surface.

The contact angle, θ, lies between the solid surface and the tangent to the liquid surface at C and is invariably measured in the liquid.

If y_1, y_2 and y_3 are the surface tensions at the liquid/air, liquid/solid and solid/air interfaces respectively, then the horizontal forces acting at C will be in equilibrium, or

$$W = \gamma_3 + \gamma_1 - \gamma_2$$

$$\therefore W = \gamma_2 + \gamma_1 \cos\theta + \gamma_1 - \gamma_2$$

$$= \gamma_1 (1 + \cos\theta)$$

In other words, the work of adhesion, which is a measure of the 'wettability' of a powder by a given liquid, can be obtained from a knowledge of the surface tension of the liquid and the contact angle between the liquid and the solid surface.

$$\gamma_3 = \gamma_2 + \gamma_1 \cos \theta$$

The work of adhesion, *W*, is given by

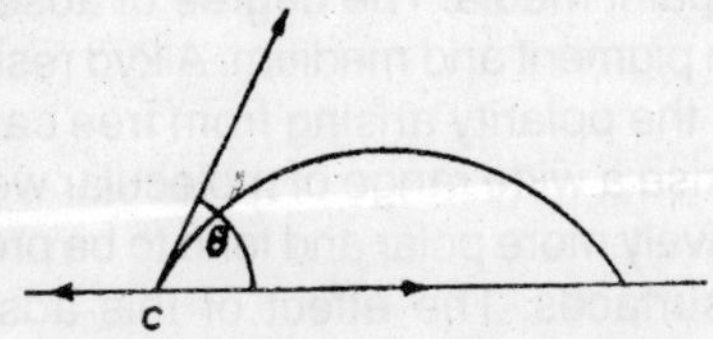

Fig 14.2 Section through a drop of liquid

Measurement of the contact angle between a pigment surface and a liquid presents difficulty. This technique is really applicable only to pure liquids, but, according to Crowl, it can be applied to dilute paint media and shows some correlation with rates of dispersion in the early stages of ball milling.

Generally, however, more practical methods for assessing wettability are desirable and these inevitably must involve a consideration of the characteristics of the pigment surface.

Nature of the pigment surface

It is generally accepted that pigments can be designated hydrophilic or hydrophobic according to their tendency to attract or repel moisture, respectively. These terms are, however, relative and there is no sharp line of demarcation between the two classes. For example, rutile titanium dioxide is more hydrophobic than anatase, but they are both hydrophilic in comparison with the arylamide yellows. The majority of inorganic pigments are hydrophilic and disperse more readily in water than in organic media. Most organic pigment dyestuffs are hydrophobic and are not readily dispersed in water. In fact, if a dispersion in water is mixed with oil, flushing takes place, i.e. the pigment migrates to the oil phase.

This hydrophilic or hydrophobic nature of pigments can be changed by surface treatment. Some inorganic pigments are coated to render them hydrophobic and so more readily wetted by organic media, whilst the hydrophobic organic pigment dyestuffs are made hydrophilic for use in aqueous emulsion paints.

Pigment powders possess large surface areas per unit of weight. This is related to the particle size distribution and varies from one type of pigment to another. Surface areas are usually measured by the well-known nitrogen adsorption method ' but for many practical applications involving comparisons of pigments, oil absorption determinations are a sufficient guide.

Also related to particle size is the surface energy which increases with decreasing particle size. Much of the energy is concentrated at the edges of the pigment crystals.

Most pigments, by virtue of their surface energies, tend to adsorb certain molecular species from paint media. The degree of adsorption can vary widely and depends on both pigment and medium. Alkyd resins contain a proportion of polar molecules, the polarity arising from free carboxyl and hydroxyl groups, and they comprise a wide range of molecular weights. The lower molecular weights are relatively more polar and tend to be preferentially adsorbed on certain pigment surfaces. The effect of this adsorption of medium by the pigment can be threefold.

1 At the dispersion stage, it assists in displacing the air and/or moisture at the pigment surface and so promotes the Wetting process.

2 It coats the particles with an envelope of resin. This reduces the interparticle attraction which can lead to -flocculation and it also prevents dense settlement of the pigment on standing.

3 If this dispersion is stored for any considerable time or, often, when pigments of very fine particle size are involved, the adsorption can result in a progressive increase in viscosity and, in some cases, gelling can be the final result. For example, if carbon black or phthalocyanine blue are milled into alkyd at high concentration, rapid gelling can take place. The viscosity increase and ultimate gelling result from the withdrawal of the lower molecular weight species from the alkyd solution. These normally act as solvents for the higher molecular weight fractions, the solubility of which becomes progressively lower until gelation occurs.

In addition to adsorption of molecules of the medium, some pigments adsorb drier metals, resulting in a progressive increase in the drying time of the paint. Carbon black is notorious in this respect, as well as in causing progressive increase in viscosity of paints in which it is the major pigment. Titanium dioxide also has been known to adsorb driers, but to a lesser degree than carbon black.

In cases of drier adsorption, re-milling of the paint will restore much, but not all, of the original drying property.

Instances occur when the wetting and dispersion of a pigment in a medium is extremely slow, as indicated by an extended milling time. This is often attributed to 'poor wetting by the medium' or a difficultly wettable pigment'. In such cases the use of an appropriate surface-active agent can be of assistance. Cationic or non-ionic types are employed in non-aqueous media. Both types are polar and tend to be adsorbed on pigment surfaces, so inducing wetting.

According to Stephen, the pigment/solvent relationship is important in the dispersion process and to ensure subsequent dispersion stability. The correct solvent balance also is required to prevent unnecessary flocculation. He considers that hydrogen bonding, HLB values of surfactants as well as solvent and resin characteristics are involved.

Surface-active agents (surfactants)

A very large number of surfactants is available for assisting pigment dispersion and for stabilising the resulting dispersions: They can be classified into a relatively small number of general types but within these types there are innumerable modifications and many surfactants being marketed are mixtures of two or more types. In the following the basic characteristics of the main types are considered and no attempt is made to include the very many modifications.

Anionic surfactants

These are water-soluble and used only in aqueous media.

Cationic surfactants

These are generally salts of primary, secondary or tertiary amines and the activity resides in the cation. They can be subdivided into (a) ammonia types and (b) quaternary ammonium salts.

Ammonia type Fatty acid amines or diamines form salts with free fatty acids to give products of the general type

$$\left[H_3\overset{+}{N}.R\overset{+}{N}H_3\right]\left[R'COO^-\right]_2$$

The cation is reactive and is adsorbed strongly on negatively charged surfaces such as oxidized metals, glass and paper. It will displace previously adsorbed moisture, and cationics of this type are used to assist the dispersion of pigments in organic media. The polar groups of the cation are attracted to the pigment surface, displacing the moisture, and the hydrocarbon chains are directed away from the surface. The latter becomes lyophilic and is' readily wetted by the organic medium.

Strongly hydrophilic pigments are difficult to flush but can be made to do so by addition of a cationic surfactant to the aqueous dispersion. Adsorption of the cation in the manner described above results in a hydrophobic surface, and flushing then takes place readily.

Quaternary ammonium salts These are of the following general type:

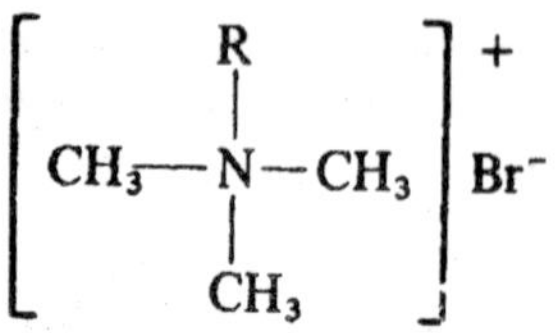

Alkyl trimethyl ammonium bromide

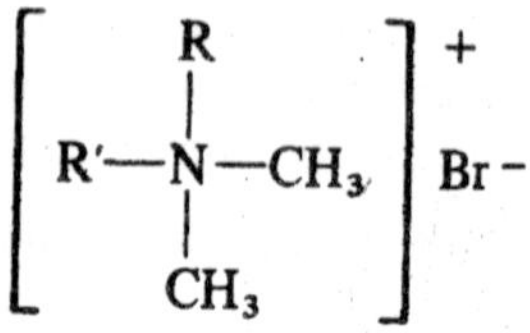

Dialkyl dimethyl ammonium bromide

The cations of these compounds are, like the ammonia type, strongly adsorbed on a number of surfaces, and their main use is in bituminous compositions and paints for application to wet surfaces.

Non-ionic surfactants

These do not dissociate in aqueous solution and their activity is due to polar groups such as hydroxyl or ether linkages within the molecule. Individually they are less hydrated than the ionized polar groups in anionics, but an equivalent total hydration can be achieved in the molecule if there is an adequate number of non-ionizing polar groups present. Non-ionic surfactants are made on this principle.

A number of types are available, the two most important being the polyglycerol esters of fatty acids and polyglycol ethers of polyethenoxy compounds. The latter are condensation products of compounds possessing an amido, hydroxyl or carboxyl group with a long-chain polyglycol ether radical, e.g.

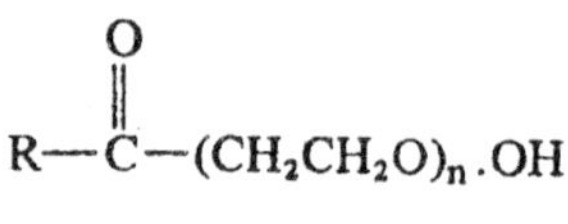

Ester linkage

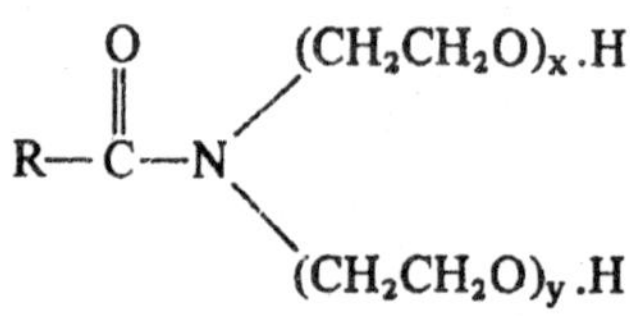

Amide linkage

These may be further esterified at the free hydroxyl groups to give polyoxyethyleneglycol diesters.

Properties of non-ionic surfactants

The water solubility of these non-ionics increases with increase in length of the polyoxyethylene chain. They can be subdivided on the basis of solubility into three types: (a) oil-soluble or slightly soluble in water, (b) self-dispersible in water, and (c) soluble in water. The water-soluble types can be used to replace anionics in most applications and possess the advantage of a lower tendency to promote foam formation. When used in aqueous paint systems they promote rapid wetting of the pigment when used at 0.5 to 1.0 percent (on the pigment). In emulsion paints they improve the brushability and levelling properties.

Non-ionics of the low ethylene oxide type are used to assist the dispersion of pigments in organic media. Small additions reduce the time required for dispersion and deflocculation. They show no preferential wetting in pigment mixtures. They are also used to assist the flushing of hydrophilic pigments.

Ampholytic surfactants

These are materials in which the polarity is internally neutralized. This type of structure occurs in the compound:

$$R{-}NH{-}\underset{\displaystyle CH_3}{\underset{|}{CH}}{-}CH_2COOH \quad \textbf{(Armeen Z) [8]}$$

and is also present in lecithin (below).

Lecithin This is a by-product obtained in the refining of natural drying oils such as linseed, soya, etc. The soya type is the more common and has been used as a surfactant on a wide scale for many years due to its versatility and relatively low cost. The material as marketed contains 35 to 45 percent of the parent oil together with a mixture of phosphatides. These contain a polyhydric alcohol such as glycerol or other alcohol, esterified partly with fatty acids and partly with phosphoric acid. The phosphoric acid is further esterified with a hydroxyamino compound such as choline, ethanolamine or serine.

Each molecule contains lyophilic fatty acid groups and hydrophilic phosphoric acid and amino groups. The latter confer ampholytic properties on the molecule. In non polar media and in aqueous dispersion the phosphatides assume the form of large micelles.

Uses Lecithin is used to assist pigment dispersion (0.5 to 1 percent on the pigment, but the amount may be critical for some systems) and generally as a modifier for pigment flocculation and dispersion.

Hyperdispersants

A range of specially designed dispersing agents which are claimed to raise dispersion efficiency as well as to improve the properties of the finished paint in respect of optical and flow properties They contain a synergist to enhance the attachment of the main surfactant chains to the pigment surface thereby promoting dispersion stability and the optimum effect is obtained by coating the pigment surface with a unimolecular layer of hyperdispersant. The amount required can therefore be calculated from a knowledge of the surface area of the pigment. Alternatively it can be determined practically by additions to a dispersed mill base. The type of hyperdispersant to be employed depends on the type of pigment as well as on the nature of the resin and solvent. Their use is claimed to effect appreciable savings in manufacturing costs as well as improvement in quality of product.

Stage 3: Stabilization of dispersions

A stable dispersion is one which, ideally, is free from any of the following defects.

1 Tendency of the pigment to settle to a dense mass.

2 Excessive flocculation of the pigment, a condition which can impair the rheological properties of the paint and influence the optical properties of the paint film.

3 Viscosity increase resulting from physical and/or chemical reaction between pigment and medium (as distinct from flocculation).

Pigment settlement

The familiar form of the Stokes equation applies to spherical particles falling through a large mass of liquid:

$$V=\frac{2r^2(p_1 - p_2)\,g}{9\eta}$$

where V = velocity of fall of particle,

r = radius of particle,

p_1 = density of particle,

p_2 = density of liquid,

η = coefficient of viscosity of liquid,

g = gravitational constant.

Although a pigment dispersion does not satisfy the requirements for the application of this equation there is a degree of compliance, and it serves as a useful basis for our discussion.

V can be kept as low as possible (preferably zero) by reducing the radius of the particles; by equating, as far as possible, the densities of pigment and medium (p_1 and p_2); and by increasing the viscosity of the medium, preferably by controlled thixotropy.

If we consider a pigment particle with adsorbed low-molecular-weight polymer or surfactant, the effective radius will be increased, tending to more rapid settlement, but this will be negated by a reduction in overall density or p_1. The effect of the increased particle radius, caused by adsorbed long-chain molecules, will be a steric hindrance to free settlement. This-will, nevertheless, take place slowly, but the settled layer of pigment will be more voluminous and will be more readily re-incorporated by agitation or stirring.

Prevention of dense pigment settlement is effected also by use of 'surface coated' precipitated calcium carbonate The coating consists of stearic acid (1.5-3.0 percent by mass on the calcium carbonate) which produces an enlarged hydrophobic particle. The presence of these particles introduces a steric hindrance to settlement of other pigment particles, but the quantity used should not exceed 10 percent of the total pigment. Above this figure, interference with flow properties can result.

The rate of pigment settlement is reduced by an increase in η, the coefficient of viscosity of the system. This can be achieved by introducing 'thixotropy' or structure into the paint. A thixotropic system is one which forms a gel when at rest but which becomes fluid and flows when a stress is applied and reverts to a gel as soon as the stress is removed. When a paint is in the gel condition, pigment settlement cannot take place. In practice, complete gelation is employed only in the 'non-drip' or thixotropic decorative paints. Generally a controlled degree of thixotropy or structure is built into the system and the following types of compounds are used.

1 Hydrogenated castor oils,' These require a temperature of 40°C to 60°C for gelling.

2 Organically reacted montmorillonite clays Types 6e available to suit solvents of different polarities. Some require to be pre-gelled but some newer types will gel spontaneously when mixed with paint.

3 Aluminium alcoholates

Pigment flocculation

A flocculated system is one in which the pigment particles have formed clusters of 'flocculates' after they have been dispersed. The flocculates contains liquid and may be closely-knit or loose associations according to the forces acting between the particles; prevention of flocculation requires some means of opposing or neutralizing these attractive forces. In aqueous systems the particles can be given an ionic charge to render them mutually repellent, but this method cannot be employed in organic media. In these it is thought that adsorption of long chain molecules of polymer or surfactant tends to prevent the particles from approaching each other sufficiently closely for the short-range Van der Waals forces to Operate.

In the more lightly pigmented pants such as gloss finishes, flocculates tend to settle rapidly, but their bulky nature results in a soft deposit of considerable volume which can readily be re-dispersed by stirring. The supernatant liquid is usually clear, whereas in nonflocculated or dispersed systems this layer is generally cloudy as a result of the very fine particles being kept in suspension by Brownian movement.

Flocculation in highly pigmented paints such as undercoats is usually accompanied by abnormal flow properties such as thixotropy and pseudoplastic flow.

Generally a controlled degree of flocculation can be of advantage in preventing pigment settlement on storage.

The Flocculation Monitor

An instrument developed by Tioxide UK Ltd, the uses of which are described by Gamon It is used to measure the degree of flocculation of pigment dispersions, especially titanium dioxide, in wet and dry paint films. In the latter it measures the amount of radiation of 2.5 µm wavelength which is reflected (back scattered) by dry paint films of differing thickness. A graph of reflectance plotted against film thickness gives a 'flocculation gradient'. High values indicate flocculation whilst low values indicate good dispersion. For liquid paints a sample is placed in a special cell but only one value is obtained.

Flocculation of stainers

In single pigment paints, flocculation generally presents no colour problems in the film. When, however, certain pale shades are produced by addition of dispersed stainer to a white base, for instance, difficulties can arise as a result of stainer flocculation. Pale blues, for example, made by addition of a dispersed phthalocyanine blue to a white base, have been known to flocculate on standing for a relatively short period. Many of the flocculates are redispersed on stirring but others can be more resistant. The latter are usually dispersed by shear, with the result that brushed films exhibit blue streaks whereas a mottled appearance results on spraying. The fault is reduced considerably by treatment of the phthalocyanine blue with surface-active agents to reduce the mutually attractive forces, and grades of 'flocculation-resisting' blues are available. The ideal situation is one in which co-flocculates are formed, involving both white pigment and stainer. This requires matching the relative free surface energies, a state difficult to achieve.

'Pigment shock' or 'dilution shock' is a severe form of flocculation which sometimes occurs during the 'letting down' of dispersed ball-mill bases. The latter consist of pigment dispersed in a dilute solution of resin solvent.

A state of equilibrium exists, the resin molecules being subjected to the. attractive forces of the pigment and the solubilizing characteristics of the solvent. This equilibrium can be disturbed very easily, . and the sudden introduction of a large quantity of resin solution of high concentration can lead to severe flocculation of the pigment; further milling is usually required to disperse the flocculates. The added resin solution should be as dilute as possible and should be added in small portions with mill rotation between additions.

Effect of solvent on flocculation

A high proportion of inorganic pigments are hydrophilic and when dispersed in certain non-polar solvents yield 'buttery' pastes. For this - reason these solvents have been described as 'poor wetters', but this may not be so. An example is afforded by the action of white spirit on anatase titanium dioxide, as quoted by Bowman and Hughes The 'buttery' dispersion, on treatment with a 2 percent resin solution, is converted to a free-flowing liquid. Actually the white spirit wets the anatase readily, but the dispersion is highly flocculated. The added resin is adsorbed on the anatase surface and probably inhibits the interparticle attraction. Deflocculation results and the dispersion flows freely.

Flotation (or 'floating')

Some paint films can exhibit a mottled appearance shortly after application. It occurs when mixtures of pigments are used, the individual members of which differ appreciably in colour, particle size, specific gravity, and wetting characteristics. The cause is also associated with the type of solvent evaporation and the influence of convection currents in the wet film. Flotation is accentuated when one of the pigments has a tendency to flocculate. Systems which can exhibit troublesome flotation are titanium dioxide/phthalocyanine blue, titanium dioxide/carbon black and lead chrome/ Prussian blue

Flotation can be converted to the less objectionable 'flooding' by addition of certain silicone oils (1 part to 40 000 parts of - paint) or proprietary materials.

Flocculation during drying

The loss of solvent from a freshly applied paint film results in film contraction and a reduction in distances between the pigment particles. As a result, flocculation can take place before the film has set, and the consequence is a loss of opacity and colour strength. Carr has presented evidence of the occurrence of flocculation during the drying of both decorative and industrial paints as well as printing inks It has also been observed during the cure of acid cured alkyd/amino finishes pigmented with rutile titanium dioxide. Here the flocculation appears to be associated with reaction between the basic surface coating of the rutile titanium dioxide and the added acid ,'

Increase in viscosity (on storage)

This can result from reaction between pigment and medium and may be physical and/or chemical in nature. The most common causes are the following.

1 Adsorption by the pigment of certain low molecular weight fractions of the polymer binder.

2 Chemical reaction between an acidic medium and basic pigments such as zinc oxide or certain grades of coated rutile titanium dioxide. The increase in viscosity is progressive and can result in gelling. In the early stages the thickening can be checked by addition of small quanitities of benzoic, salicylic or citric acids which act as peptizing agents.

3 Reaction between metallic aluminium pigment and an acidic medium can result in gassing accompanied by an increase in viscosity of the paint. This can lead to gelling.

WATER SOLUBLE PAINTS

Paints in which the polymer binder has been rendered soluble in water are used mainly for application by electrodeposition although they are also applied by conventional spray and dipping. In each case the films are cured by stoving.

Nature of the binders

These are of two types . Briefly they are (a) alkali silicates, which are now used only in certain types of zinc-rich paints and in fire-resisting compositions for interior use, and (b) the water-soluble resins. Water-solubility has been conferred by the introduction of either acidic or basic groupings followed by neutralization by bases or acids respectively. The main use of the water-soluble resins is in primers for application by electrodeposition, but appreciable amounts are used in stoving primers and finishes.

Pigmentation of water soluble resin solutions for conventional application generally follows normal procedure, dispersion stability being achieved by the use of appropriate surfactants.

AQUEOUS EMULSION PAINTS

Polymer emyulsion paints

These are usually three-phase systems consisting of aqueous (or continous) phase, pigment and dispersed polymer. The manufacturing operation involves two operation;(a) dispersion of pigment in the aqueous phase, followed by (b) mixing of the pigmented aqueous phase with the polymer emulsion.

Pigment dispersion in the aqeous phase

A very high proportion of the emulsion paint used is white or tints prepared from white; the pigment employed is rutile titanium dioxide and the following discussion relates to the dispersion of this pigment.

The aqueous medium consists, basically, of a dilute solution of either a cellulose ether or sodium carboxymethyl cellulose or an ammonium salt of a polyacrylic acid.

Rutile titanium dioxide is a hydrophilic pigment and usually has an adsorbed film of moisture on the surface of the particles. No great difficulty is encountered in wetting such a pigment by an aqueous medium, and the breakdown of the pigment aggregates is not taken to the degree required, for example, in gloss finishes. The main problem is the stabilization of the titanium dioxide dispersion. The particles must be prevented from flocculating and from any tendency to 'flush' to the organic polymer on storage. (With hydrophilic pigments, however, this tendency is very slight.).

The particles in the polymer emulsion are usually 'protected' by an anionic surface-active agent which gives them a negative charge. These emulsions are known as anionic,

Stabilization of the pigment dispersion

The dispersion of titanium dioxide particles can be effected by the use of either anionic or long-chain non-ionic surfactants. Both these surfactants confer a negative charge on the particles as a result of adsorption. The negativity in anionics is due-to the - COO - group, while in non-ionics it arises from the multiplicity of ether linkages. Non-ionics are usually preferred since the anionics have a great tendency to produce foam. In the presence of watersoluble thickners, foams can be difficult to break.

Adsorption of the surface-active agent results in an 'electric double layer' round the particle, the negative charges being accompanied or surrounded by a second layer of positive ions, as in fig. 14.3. An electrical double layer to this type is also produced by the adsorption of electrolytes (e.g. sodium polyphosphates).or anionic polyelectrolytes (ammonium salts of polyacrylic acid) on the pigment surface. Whilst sodium hexametaphosphate is used in emulsion paints as a sequestering agent for calcium and other polyvalent metal ions, reservations on the use of this type of material have been expressed by Capella and Bieleman They consider that polyphosphates can be hydrolysed to orthophosphates which not only act as pigment flocculants but also cause a loss of gloss and provide a nutrient for bacteria.

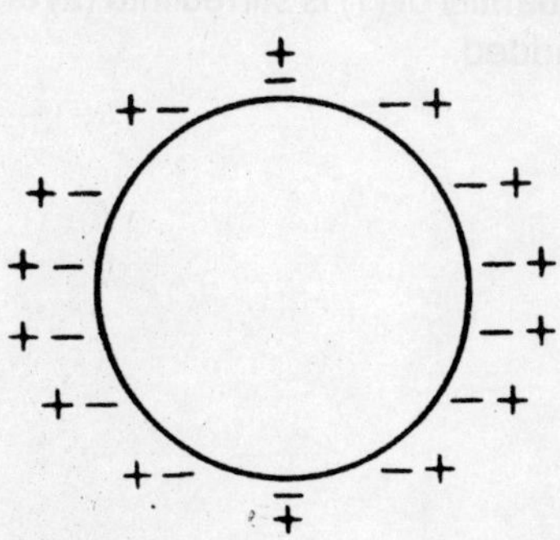

Fig 14.3

Further stabilization -of the titanium dioxide dispersion, and of the emulsion paint, is effected by the use of water-soluble colloids . or 'thickeners' which introduce structure in the system and so decrease the mobility of both pigment and polymer particles. Materials used For this purpose include methyl cellulose, hydroxyethyl- and hydroxypropyl-cellulose, ethylhydroxyethyl cellulose, and ammonium polyacrylates.

Dispersion of hydrophobic pigments

Pale shades of emulsion paints are produced by addition of dispersions of coloured pigments (stainers) to the white emulsion paint. The stainers must be efficiently stabilized to prevent flocculation and changes of colour. The majority of inorganic pigments and extenders are hydrophilic and, in general, are readily dispersed and stabilized in aqueous media. Many organic pigments, particularly the pigment dyestuffs such as the arylamide yellows and toluidine reds, are hydrophobic and require treatment with anionic surfactants for both wetting and dispersion. The level of surfactant is relatively high to ensure the stability of these dispersions when used as stainers. Unless they are protected in this way, hydrophobic pigments will flush readily to the organic (polymer) phase, with serious effects on the colour of the emulsion paint. Similar remarks on the necessity for adequate protection apply to hydrophobic pigments used as the principal pigments in full-colour emulsion paints.

These usually require organic pigments, which are generally hydrophobic, to give the necessary brightness. They can be made in the following manner.

1 A concentrated dispersion of the organic pigment is prepared in an aqueous solution of a cellulose ether and a non-ionic surfactant.

2 An emulsion 'base' is made by dispersing the extenders in an aqueous solution of a cellulose ether together with the surfactants and other additives. This is then mixed with part of the polymer emulsion.

3 The required quantity of (1) is stirred into (2) and the remainder of the polymer emulsion is added.

Chapter - 9

PAINTS (DECORATIVE & BUILDING)

For many years linseed oil in one or other of its various forms was the standard binder. for practically all paints. These oil paints were slow-drying, possessed poor initial gloss and gloss retention, and showed poor levelling. Nevertheless, they afforded reasonably good protection. The introduction of oleoresinous varnishes led to shorter drying times and harder films with, in the case of finishes, greater gloss and gloss retention. They gave rise to the so-called hard gloss paints. In gloss finishes and undercoats for decorative work oleoresinous varnishes have been replaced by alkyds but they continue to be used.. in some undercoats and primers for structural painting.

Paints for decorative and building work are generally applied by brush or hand-roller, but on new work, and especially on prefabricated sections, spraying is used. Generally, decorative paints are slow drying (4 to 16 hours according to type) and contain long media and slow-evaporating solvents. This combination allows large areas to be painted in sections without difficulties-in joining up.

The following discussion follows the sequence of application, namely sealers, primers, fillers and stoppers, undercoats and finishes. Special products receive separate treatment.

SEALERS

Wood often contains knots which slowly exude resinous matter which will soften and discolour paint. These knots can be sealed by the application of knotting which is a 25 to 30 percent solution of orange shellac in IMS.

Creosoted wood may also be sealed with knotting to prevent the creosote from bleeding into and discolouring, subsequent coats of paint, provided the creosote has been on for some years. Newly creosoted wood cannot be sealed in this way. PVA emulsion sealer is also effective on weathered creosoted wood and is appreciably cheaper than knotting.

Plasters, cement render, etc. These surfaces can be highly alkaline as well as porous and require an alkali-resistant sealer with low penetration properties, i.e. high molecular weight. Polyvinyl acetate emulsion is widely used, but dilute solutions of chlorinated rubber as well, as oleoresinous sealers based on tung oil/coumarone mixtures are also employed. PVA emulsions have an advantage for interior work as both aqueous and non-aqueous paints will adhere to the surfaces.

Plaster surfaces must be thoroughly dry and free from any tendency to efflorescence. Otherwise the coating of paint will be lifted by moisture or by crystallization of soluble salts beneath the film.

Hardboards and building boards can be sealed with PVA emulsion sealer. For hardboard the latttr can be made by addition of water to normal emulsion paint. Where surfaces are more porous, an effective sealer can be produced by mixing emulsion paint (2 volumes) with unpigmented emulsion (1 volume) and water (1 volume).

Preservatives for wood

Nature of wood A cross-section of a tree trunk shows a series of annular rings which comprise the sheaths of new wood formed each year. These completely cover the old wood and enclose any lateral branches. The heartwood, which occupies the central part of the trunk, has changed with age and is darker in colour, contains less water, and is less permeable to liquids than the more recent sapwood which surrounds it. Sapwood consists of alternate layers (grain) of spring wood, formed in the early part of the growing season, and summer wood which is formed later.

The grain consists of interconnected elongated cells with. rigid cellulose walls. Spring cells are thin-walled and large, but as the season advances the cells decrease in size and the walls thicken. There is a sudden change in cell structure from one year's summer wood to the following year's spring wood, and this is very evident in softwoods such as pine, spruce, larch and Douglas fir. A high proportion of the external joinery used in the United Kingdom is Scots pine or 'Baltic redwood' (Pinus sylvestris). The sapwood of this tree is very-porous and susceptible to attack by fungi and in the UK climate this presents a major problem Greater stability is shown by some of the South American hardwoods now widely used for window frames, etc., which usually are only varnished. Hardwoods are more irregular in structure, and the wood is frequently oily; common British hardwoods are oak, birch, chestnut, and walnut.

Types of preservative

Creosote is the time-honoured preservative for exterior joinery where preservation is more important than decoration as, for example, wooden fences or sheds. The preservative qualities are contributed by the phenolic compounds present. It is sometimes claimed that crecsoted timber which has been 'weathered' can be overpainted but the results with paints other than black are seldom satisfactory. 'Bleeding' takes place into the paint film resulting in patchy discolouration. Application of a sealer such as knotting can prevent bleeding on smooth timber but the treatment can be expensive and is not recommended on the rough-sawn timber of many fences.

A very large number of wood preservatives is available. These include the naphthenates and 8-hydroxyquinolinates of copper pentachlorophenol, zinc naphthenate and tributyl tin compounds. Busan 1009, is a mixture of methylene bis (thiocyanate) and 2-(thiocyanomethylthio) benzothiazole. Tests have indicated a high efficiency of this 'material against a wide range of fungi.

The Madison formula, a pigmented linseed oil/wax mixture, was designed for the restoration of --weathered cedarwood.

Application of wood preservatives

Water uptake along the grain is very much greater than across and so it is essential to seal the ends of timber effectively before units are assembled.

The efficiency of a preservative increases with the depth of penetration and whilst woodwork 'in situ' must necessarily be treated by-brush or spray, manufactured pieces can be dipped before assembly. Dipping is more effective than brush or spray for end grain but the deepest penetration of the entire members is achieved by immersion in .the preservative solution using a vacuum/pressure technique.

Preservative stains

In place of paint, exterior woodwork is now frequently treated with a preservative stain which can be either water-borne or solvent based.

The water-borne types are based on a mixture of alkyd and acrylic emulsions pigmented with transparent UV-absorbing oxides of iron or other light-fast pigments. The stains may be transparent, translucent or opaque and exhibit very good durability:

The exterior solvent-based stains are best suited to hardwoods. They are based on a specially designed flexible alkyd ; and pigmented with transparent UVabsorbing oxides of iron. Their performance is far superior to that of conventional alkyds.

The painting of wood

Behaviour of paint on wood

When paint is applied to wood it will fill the superficial cavities in the rough surface, and the medium will tend to enter the cell spaces, passing from one cell to another. The degree of penetration will depend on the molecular size and will be deeper for raw than for bodied oils. The paint medium does not enter the cell walls. Spring cells are larger than summer cells and so tend to absorb more medium, but pigment cannot pass into the cells. The result is a variation in pigment/binder ratio in the film over the spring and summer wood. This will be different for each type of wood.

The moisture in wood is in equilibrium with that in the atmosphere. It enters wood mainly along the grain, i.e. from one cell to another, and travels through the cell walls, which expand in the process. Lateral penetration also takes place but to a much lesser degree. Expansion is greater in 'the thicker summer-cell walls, and there will therefore be greatest movement of the wood at the junction of spring and summer cells. This movement, together with the difference in pigment/binder ratio, causes considerable strain along lines in the film and failure usually commences along these lines.

In order to maintain a,constant pigment/binder ratio in the dry primer film it is common practice to incorporate a proportion of polymerized oil or varnish which will show less tendency to penetrate the wood.

It was formerly thought that deep penetration into the wood was necessary for satisfactory adhesion, but from recent work it appears that unbodied oils penetrate only to a depth of 2 to 3 cells. The adhesion of paint films to wood depends, as with other substrates, on good wetting of the surface by the paint.

Hence the advisability of ensuring that the wood is dry when priming .is carried out. Rothwell, has pointed out that 'the method of drying timber, direction of grain, proportions of oil and resin in the timber (particularly in hardwoods) were all important in determining the degree of penetration and paint adhesion'.

The durability of a paint system on wood will be influenced by the ability of the system - particularly the primer - to accommodate the dimensional changes in the wood caused by absorption and loss of moisture. Two essential properties of the primer are adhesion and elasticity, but certain other properties, including a finite degree of moisture permeability, are also-important.

Preservatives for softwoods

Primers for softwoods

The traditional 'pink primer', based on a mixture of white and red leads in linseed oil,-gave excellent protection to exterior woodwork but has now been phased out for reasons of high toxicity.

Calcium plumbate primers also have given good results on softwoods and these have been marketed as 'universal' primers for use on wood, steel and galvanized iron. However, as lead compounds, calcium plumbate primers are also being phased out.

Leadless primers are manufactured on a number of media including oleoresinous varnishes, alkyds, and urethane oils. Non-toxic pigments and extenders are employed to give primers suitable for both interior and exterior joinery.

Most prefabricated timber units are primed at works and should of course be primed before assembly to ensure sealing of end-grain in joints. The primers employed are quick-drying types applied by spray or dip. The formulation below illustrates the general type:

	% by weight
Titanium dioxide	17.0
Paris white	11.8
Red oxide of iron	2.9
*Medium (50% solids)	67.7
Driers	0.6

*A variety of media can be employed, the type chosen being often influenced by the drying time required.

Prefabricated joinery units such as windows and frames can be exposed to weather on building sites for considerable periods; it is. essential, therefore, that good quality primers are used and that close attention is paid to application.

Primers for brush application can be made on the formulation set out above using a medium/long alkyd binder. Where highly porous sapwoods are encountered, the addition of 10-20 percent of light stand oil (with the appro priate driers) has been found advantageous.

Aluminium primer Lamellar pigments such as aluminium, are thought to even the strain at points where it is greatest in the film, i.e. at the junction of spring and summer woods. They also yield films resistant to moisture penetration. The following is a typical example:

	% by weight
Non-feafing aluminium paste	19 .0
Solvent naphtha	8 .0
Medium (60% solids)	72.8
Cobalt naphthenate (6%)	0.2

(Medium: 2/1 oil length tung oil/modified phenolic. 2 poise)

A leafing type of aluminium would give a superior moisture barrier, but the non-leafing type provides a more suitable surface for the adhesion of subsequent coats. This primer is suitable for use on both interior and exterior woodwork and dries in 4 to 6 hours.

Emulsion primers Suitably pigmented acrylic emulsions are used successfully on softwoods.

Acrylic emulsion primers are non-toxic, flexible and adhere well to wood surfaces. They tend to dry slowly at low temperatures and at high humidities. Difficulties have arisen in respect of the long-term adhesion of glazing putties over these primers

Painting of plywood

The use of plywood for exterior cladding has increased in recent years. It is more dimensionally stable than timber but is susceptible to surface cracking along the grain on weathering. Protective systems discussed by Gunn comprise textured coatings on oleoresinous media and heavily textured coatings based on vinyl and acrylic emulsions. The latter are stated to :be the more satisfactory.'~

Primers for hardwoods

Oil-type primers are unsatisfactory on hardwoods,, particularly if these are inclined to be oily. Adhesion is 'poor and flaking usually occurs in 12 to 18 months in the UK. More satisfactory results are obtained using the aluminium primer desribed. above. Other aluminium primers which have given very, promising results are based on epoxy esters and on urethane oils:

Finishing systems for wood

Interior The conventional alkyd-type primer, undercoat and finish gives satisfactory results and is the commonly used system " for interior decoraton.

Exterior .Several systems are in use.

1 The conventional alkyd-based primer, undercoat and finish can give satisfactory performance provided the wood has been effectively sealed against moisture penetration Unfortunately this - is often not -done , and the progressive embrittlement of the coating system leads, ultimately, to cracking and flaking.

2 The most interesting development in the painting of wood,has been the use of the acrylic emulsions. An acrylic primer and undercoat under an alkyd finish gives a fairly good life by reducing stress cracking and providing a degree of permeability

It is interesting to note the trend to water-borne systems either as all-acrylic paints or as acrylic/alkyd preservative stains.

Primers for plaster and other wall surfaces

Plasters used for the surfacing of internal walls are based on calcium sulphate and formed by the action of heat on gypsum. When the. latter is heated to 120°-130°C (248°-266 °F), partial dehydration occurs with formation of the hemihydrate plaster of Paris. When the latter is mixed with water, gypsum is formed. The two reactions can be represented in the following way:

$$\underset{\text{Gypsum}}{2CaSO_4.2H_2O} \underset{\text{Water}}{\overset{\text{Heat}}{\rightleftharpoons}} \underset{\text{Plaster of Paris}}{[CaSO_4]_2.H_2O} + 3H_2O$$

The reaction between plaster. of Paris and water takes place too rapidly for application to large areas and it is therefore, retarded by addition of alum or borax. The well-known 'Parian', 'Thistle' and 'Sirapite' plasters are retarded hemihydrates of this type.

These plasters are neutral and set to a porous mass. In practice a proportion of lime is added 'to facilitate spreading and the dry plaster- is therefore highly alkaline as well as porous. In the presence-of potassium sulphate (from alum), potassium hydroxide can be formed.

$$Ca(OH)_2 + K_2SO_4 \rightarrow CaS0_4 + 2KOH$$

and could cause saponification of certain types of media.

The type of treatment to be applied is determined largely by the degree of porosity. Highly porous surfaces require application of a sealer before priming, but on less porous surfaces the primer is used also as the sealer. Even so, it is usually necessary to apply two coats for satisfactory results.

Types of primer for internal walls

Oieoresinous type These are based on alkali-resisting highly polymerized media. Tung oil/phenolic and tung oil/coumarone have been found suitable. The following formulation illustrates the general type of oleoresinous primer:

	% by weight
Anatase titanium dioxide	9.3
Gypsum	18.0
Talc	5.5
Water-ground mica	3.7
Medium - (60% solids)	52.0
White spirit	11.5

(Medium: 2/ 1 oil length tung oil/Coumarone. 3 poise)

This primer dries in 6 to 8 hours. The alkali resistance can be upgraded by the incorporation of isomerized rubber. The finish is glossy and can be overpainted with non-aqueous systems.

Emulsion type This is a lightly pigmented vinyl emulsion applied at 25 to 30 percent solids. It has the necessary alkali-resistance and sealing properties and, in addition, shows the following advantages over the oleoresinous type.

1 The drying time is approximately one hour.

2 It is much cheaper.

3 It can be overpainted with emulsion, or solvent type paint or can be papered.

Primer for hardboard Hardboard is best primed with a vinyl emulsion paint which has been thinned with water. This acts also as a sealer and gives a finish suitable for application for either aqueous or non-aqueous paints.

Primer for chip-board Chip-board can be primed with vinyl or acrylic type emulsion paint which has been thinned a little with water.

Primers for exterior surfaces

The types of surface likely to be encountered are roughcast, stucco, concrete, asbestos sheeting, and brickwork. All these, when new, are highly alkaline (brickwork through the pointing) and porous, but the degree of alkalinity decreases on exposure to weather. Painting can be required on new surfaces or on old surfaces the condition of which may vary considerably. The latter is not difficult (provided the surface is properly prepared) but the former needs alkali resistance and sealing properties of a high order. The treatment will be determined by the nature of the following coats and the following primers are in use.

1 Vinyl co-polymer and acrylic emulsions. These are used under emulsion finishes and some of the proprietary masonry finishes.

2 Solution types based on styrene-acrylic type co-polymers. These are employed in some masonry paints and are alkali-resistant.

3 Chlorinated rubber is highly alkali-resistant and is used on very alkaline surfaces such as new asbestos sheeting and concrete. The application of chlorinated rubber paint is the usual treatment for concrete swimming pools where high resistance to water and alkali is required.

STOPPERS AND FILLERS

These are highly pigmented compositions used to fill deep or shallow. surface indentations. They are always applied over primers.

Stoppers .are paste materials used for deep indentations such as nail holes or cracks and are applied by knife. They are sometimes described as paste fillers. Pigmentation is kept very high to minimize shrinkage and to enable the dry material to be rubbed down to a smooth finish without clogging the paper. The resulting surface is porous and must be sealed before painting.

A white stopper for woodwork can be made on the following formulation:

	parts by weight
Titanium dioxide	20
Barytes	130
Whiting	120
Medium (60% solids)	60

(Medium: short-oil alkyd or oleoresinous varnish)

The hardness can be controlled by the extenders used, and this stopper could be made harder by replacing the whiting by ground natural silica or by slate powder., on a volume basis. The latter would give a grey stopper.

Glazing putty is a stopper based on iinseed oil, whiting and soft soap in the following approximate proportions: putty whiting 85.8 percent, raw linseed oil 13.8 percent, soft soap 0.4 percent. Putty is a flocculated system formulated at approximately the critical pigment volume concentration and for this reason does not stick to the hands. A slight. increase in oil content would deflocculate the system and it would become sticky.

This type of putty is used in glazing wooden frames and slowly forms a skin on the surface, the underlying mass remaining plastic for a considerable time.

Metal casement putty is generally similar to glazing putty but contains a small amount of fatty acid or sulphonated oil to improve the wetting characteristics and consequently the adhesion to the metal surface.

Fillers are highly pigmented liquid materials used to fill shallow indentations and irregularities in surfaces. They are applied by brush or spray, and dry to a hard surface which can be rubbed down. The stopper (formulation above) when thinned further with white spirit would make a suitable filler.

Coloured stoppers or fillers for wood These are used on natural coloured woods when the latter are to be polished or varnished. Semi-transparent pigments are used and the stainers can be varied to match the different types of wood. They are made on the following general lines:

	parts by weight
Burnt umber	20
Barytes	25
Whiting	25
Short oil alkyd	30

UNDERCOATS

Undercoats are highly pigmented paints which follow the primer and any filler or stopper and provide the necessary ground for the finishing coat.

An ideal undercoat would possess the following properties.

1 Good adhesion to the primer.

2 Satisfactory opacity

3 Good flow and levelling, i.e. the dry film should show no brushmarks.

4 Fairly rapid set to avoid sagging and pulling away from sharp edges, yet remain open long enough to be joined up to other areas.

5 An eggshell finish to the dry film so that the finishing coat can adhere satisfactorily.

6 A colour similar to, but preferably a little lighter than the finishing coat.

It is extremely difficult to embody all these desirable properties in any one undercoat and it is usually necessary, as with most paints, to produce the best compromise. The main difficulty is to produce the desired flow properties with the high pigmentation required to produce an eggshell finish. Pigmentation and flow properties are closely interrelated and merit brief discussion before considering undercoat formulation.

Pigmentation

For many years the relationship of pigment to binder was expressed as a simple ratio by weight, but this was of limited value in view of differing densities and therefore of differing volume of pigments. It is now usual to express the pigment content of a paint film in terms of the pigment percentage by volume. This is defined as the Pigment Volume Concentration (PVC) and has been discussed in Chapter 1. It is essential that paints be pigmented below the CPVC and thif is particularly important with undercoats. These are made just below the CPVC to ensure absence of porosity (which would lead to sinkage of the finish) and failure to produce the desired slight eggshell finish to the film.

The high pigment content of undercoats tends to reduce the overall mobility of the pigment particles, and as a result abnormal flow properties can be encountered.'

Flow properties of paints

When a liquid such as water or raw linseed oil is stirred, the rate at which it flows is directly proportional to the force applied.

Force applied (shear stress) = constant X rate of flow (rate of shear)

$$\text{or} \quad \frac{\text{Shear stress}}{\text{Rate of shear}} = \text{constant } (\eta)$$

η is defined as the coefficient of viscosity of the liquid and is expressed in poise

(P) -the unit of dynamic viscosity. If p is the density of the liquid, η/p = stokes

(u) - the unit of kinematic viscosity.

Liquids which behave in the manner of water or raw linseed oil are known as Newtonian liquids and are said to exhibit Newtonian flow (after Newton, whose Hypothesis of Viscous Flow forms the basis of viscosity measurements).

If the results are plotted on a graph, a straight line is obtained (Fig. 18.1) the slope of which gives the viscosity of the liquid.

Non-Newtonian flow

When a Newtonian .liquid is pigmented, the solid particles increase the viscosity, but at low concentrations the effect is small. When the volume of pigment present is large, interference with the flow properties can take place, and often a certain stress (force) has to be applied before the system will flow. This stress is known as the Bingham yield value (F) and is indicated graphically in Figs 18.2 and 18.3.

The yield value was postulated by Bingham to be the force expended in overcoming the internal stresses.

A paint which shows a yield value will, after this is exceeded, possibly give a straight line when shear stress is plotted against rate of shear. This line will not give the viscosity as this is not constant. Such behaviour is known as plastic flow.

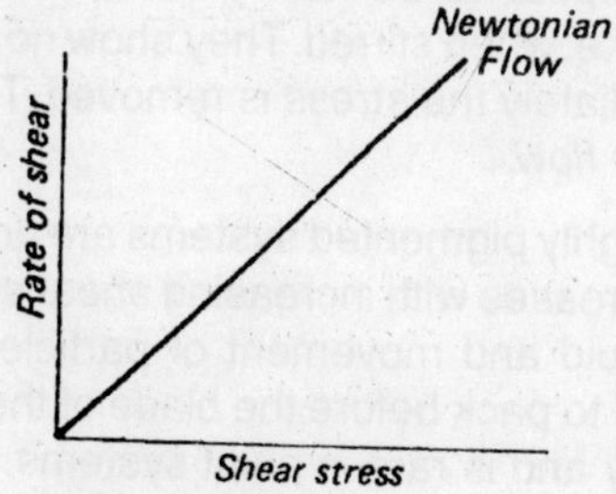

Fig 18.1 Newtonian flow

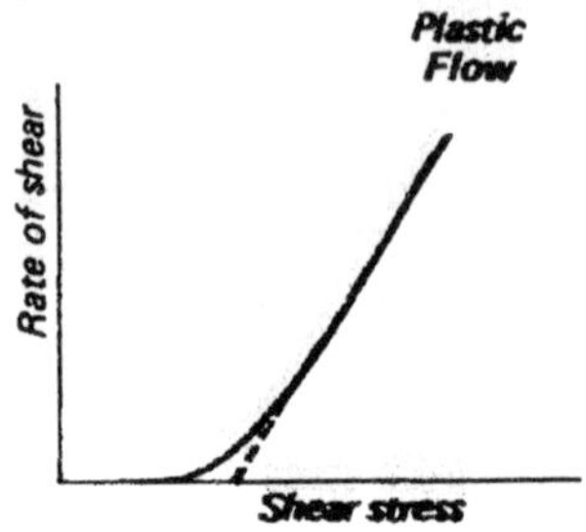

Fig 18.2 Yield value

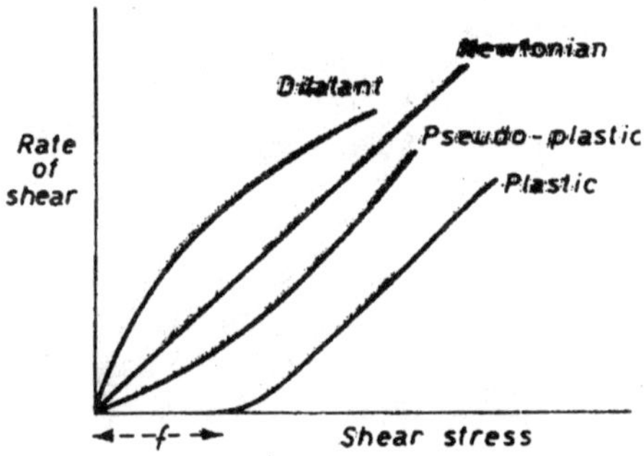

Fig 18.3 Flow curves

The presence of a yield value in a paint indicates the existence of structure, and when such a paint, which has become fluid on stirring, is allowed to remain at rest, the original structure is recovered. This behavious is known as *thixotropy* and the paint is said to be thixotropic (below). This has become a familiar phenomenon since the introduction of the thixotropic or jelly paints.

Some paints appear to be heavy but break down immediately on application of stress, i.e. when stirred. They show no yield value and recover their structure immediately the stress is removed. These paints are said to exhibit *pseudoplastic flow.*

Occasionally highly pigmented systems are encountered in which the resistance to flow increases with increasing shear stress. In these systems there is little free liquid and movement of particles is restricted. At high shear rates they tend to pack before the blade of the stirrer. This behaviour is known as dilatancy and is rare in paint systems.

The various types of flow are illustrated in Fig.18.3

Thixotropy

When the flow properties of a thixotropic paint are measured on a rotational viscometer two values are obtained for the shearing stress at the same rate of shear. One value is obtained when the rate of shear is increasing and the other when it is decreasing (Fig. 18.4). The area of the hysteresis loop is sometimes taken as. an indication of the degree of thixotropy in the paint.

A paint which exhibits thixotropy shows the following advantages: (i) it does not settle in the tin; (ii) provided the recovery rate is not too low, it does not sag on vertical surfaces nor pull away from sharp edges; (iii) heavier coats can be applied, so economizing in labour.

Application to flow properties of undercoats

Ideally, an undercoat should possess a degree of thixotropy, i.e. a yield value together with plastic flow. This ideal is extremely difficult to achieve since more than one type of flow is generally present. Pigment particles tend to flocculate (form clusters), and the degree of flocculation influences the type of flow property. Pseudo-plastic flow is often present, resulting in poor levelling properties. Brushmarks persist in the dry film and can mar the uniform gloss of the finishing coat.

Undercoat formulation consists largely of choosing pigments, and more particularly extenders, with the correct physical characteristics to give the desired flow and levelling. This calls for experience and a thorough knowledge of pigment properties in relation to the media being used. Further complications arise as a result of the little-understood inter-particle reactions, with the result that few undercoats approach the ideal type.

Undercoats generally are formulated at a PVC of 40 to 55 percent, depending on the type of pigment and medium used. The solid matter consists of true pigment (which is the more expensive solid and so used in minimum quantity to give the necessary colour and opacity) and extenders. The latter are used in sufficient volume to give the necessary degree of sheen, but care has to be exercised in their choice. There is little point, for example, in using large quantities of extenders of high specific gravity, such as barytes, which will give settlement troubles. Lower specific gravity pigments make a larger volume contribution for a given weight and are often cheaper.

Certain extenders, e.g. types of precipitated silica, possess very high oil absorptions and have a pronounced flatting effect on paint. These are generally used in small quantities. If too much is used they induce pseudo-plastic flow and :hence destroy the levelling properties of the paint.

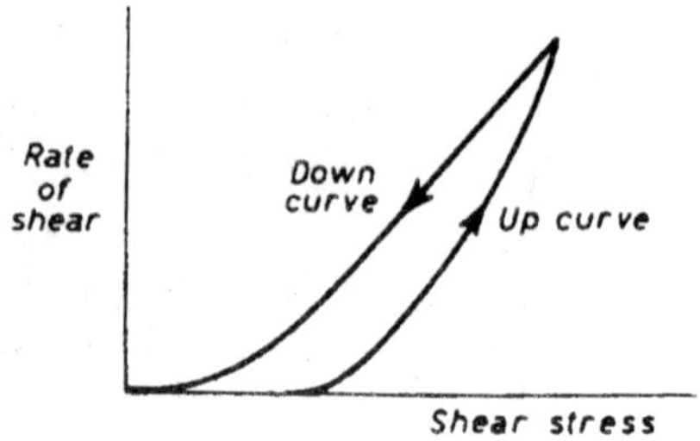

Fig 18.4 Thixotropy hysteresis loop

Formulation of undercoats

The properties required in the ideal undercoat have been listed on p. 324. Properties which are amenable to control are opacity, adhesion, degree of sheen, ease of. brushing, and drying characteristics. Flow properties present the most difficult problem. Ideally the paint should possess sufficient flow to eliminate brushmarks but, unfortunately, this degree of flow is accompanied by sagging on vertical surfaces and pulling away from corners and sharp edges. There is no ready solution to this problem and a compromise is necessary - as occurs so often in paint formulation. In order to minimize sagging on. vertical areas and pulling away from edges, a degree of brush-marking has to be tolerated.

In structural maintenance work, application is largely by airless spray, brushing being used only for small areas. Sagging is eliminated by the use of thixotropic or high-build paints whilst edges are given a 'stripe coat' to provide the necessary film build.

Media for undercoats

Experience has shown that the best performance of a paint system is achieved when undercoat and finish are based on the same general type of medium. Decorative finishes are usually formulated on long-oil alkyds, either straight or modified. The use of a long-oil alkyd in a highly pigmented undercoat usually results in a system showing poor flow and levelling properties. On the other hand, a highly polymerized alkyd provides excellent flow and levelling .properties, but the cost is high and the enamel 'hold-out' is sometimes suspect. A mixture of the two will provide a reasonable compromise which satisfies most requirements. Alternatively, the long-oil alkyd can be mixed with a thixotropic alkyd to provide a thixotropic undercoat. The degree of thixotropy can be controlled by the relative proportions of the two resins.

Pigments for undercoats

Whites and tints account for a very high proportion of decorative undercoats sold. Titanium dioxide is the white pigment used, the rutile type being preferred for the superior flow properties. A wide range of extenders is employed and the choice and quantity can be critical. Opinions differ on the best combination of extenders to provide the necessary film build with minimum interference with flow properties. Maximum 'flatting' is obtained with extenders of high oil absorption (fine particle size) but the amounts used are usually critical and flow can be impaired. Extenders of low oil-absorption (usually modular types) can be used in greater quantity to provide film build. A compromise is usually reached in which both types are employed.

For coloured undercoats the pigments must possess good opacity, but the brightness and lightfastness are not necessarily of the same standard as required in the finish. For this reason, inorganic pigments are used in undercoats whenever possible, but the more expensive organic. pigments have to be used on occasions with finishes which are very bright and/or lacking in opacity.

Replacement of one pigment by another in a formulation is sometimes required, without alteration of the essential characteristics such as gloss and consistency. Replacement must be on a volume basis, and this is satisfactory provided the two materials in question possess similar oil-absorptions. If these differ widely then they must be taken into account in the substitution. Often this means reformulation.

Examples of decorative undercoats

These formulations are intended to give the reader a general idea of the composition of undercoats. Appreciable latitude is possible in the choice of extenders and resins. The final formulation is often a matter of personal preference.

White: alkyd base	*% by weight*
Rutile titanium dioxide	21.8
White barytes(micronized)	17.4
Fine silica	5.5
Coated calcium carbonate	5.5
Long-oil alkyd (75% solids)	12.5
Polymerized alkyd (40% solids)	21.5
White spirit	12.4
Dipentene	2.5
Lecithin	0.3
Driers (Co/Zr octoates)	0.5
Methylethylketoxime	0.1
Specific gravity:	1.46
Solids by volume:	45.30%
PVC:	43.80%

(The figures for solvents may vary with the types of alkyd resin used and the solids content.)

Note on materials

Titanium dioxide the rutile type confers better flow properties than anatase.

Barytes and silica confer film build and strength. Silica provides 'tooth' and aids the adhesion of the finish.

Coated calcium carbonate prevents hard settlement. The effect is augmented by the lecithin.

Alkyds The flow properties of the undercoat are influenced by the relative proportions of the two alkyds. An increase in the polymerized alkyd content gives improved flow, whereas the long-oil alkyd confers a controllable degree of stickiness which assists film build by preventing the application of excessively thin coats. .

Dipentene is an excellent solvent for most alkyds and possesses some antiskinning properties. .

Methytethylketexime is a powerful anti-skinning agent and also extends the wetedge time. Both functions - are a consequence of complex formation between methylethylketoxime and cobalt which decomposes when the film is exposed to air. The freed cobalt then functions normally.

White Undercoat: sfkyd base, thixotropic

	% by weight
Rutile titanium dioxide	20.3
Micronized barytes	33.9
Talc	10.5
Thixotropic alkyd (50% solids)[10]	21.4
Pale boiled oil	2.5
ColZr drier	0.3
White spirit	11.0
Methylethylketoxime	0.1
Specific gravity:	1.68

Solids by volume: 53-4%
PVC: 53 - 8%

FINISHING COATS

Oil-based paints

The oldest types of gloss paint are those based on linseed oil in one or other of its forms. They are highly pigmented and contain only a small quantity of thinner. Consequently they give films of high build with a moderate degree of gloss.

Paint properties such as flow and levelling, as well as film properties such as elasticity, hardness and durability are dependent largely on the nature and degree of pigmentation. In this way oil finishes differ from the modern alkyd types in which the film properties are controlled to a large extent by the resin binder.

The demand for oil-based paints is now very small.

Modern gloss finishes

A considerable improvement was effected in gloss finishes by the replacement of oil by oleoresinous varnishes. These gave harder films with improved gloss and gloss retention. The earlier types were known as varnish paints and were heavily pigmented, but reduction in extender content, together with improved oleoresinous media, led to the superior hard gloss paints that were in general use until the Second World War. These paints were based on long-oil media produced from linseed oil with fused congo copal or copal ester, and gave finishes with high gloss, but the gloss retention was not as good as with modem alkyds. The durability was, by modem standards, reasonably good.

The first step in the introduction of alkyds was admixture with oleoresinous media, and such mixtures containing 50 percent and upwards of long-oil alkyd produced finishes with excellent gloss, gloss retention, and durability.

The earlier alkyds used were of the linseed/glycerol, and later linseed/pentaerythritol, types which stowed poor brushability on large areas. This brushability and the wet-edge time were improved considerably by admixture with oleoresinous media or enamel oils. These mixtures tended to yellow on exposure, a fault which was very apparent in white and pale shades.

The change to the modern all-alkyd type of finish became feasible with the introduction of the long oil pentaerythritol alkyds based on linoleic acid (or linoleic rich' acids) derived from soya bean and other semi-drying oils. These alkyds show excellent brushing properties and very little tendency to yellowing on exposure.

Formulation of alkyd gloss paints

The demand for whites and light colours is such that a high percentage of the alkyd gloss paints produced are pigmented with rutile titanium dioxide, with possibly a small quantity of anti-settling agent such as a coated calcium carbonate or a Bentone. These are pigmented at a PVC of 15-19 percent, the lower figures being used when stainers are to be added. A typical formulation for a white alkyd gloss is set out below at (A). Black finishes require only 2.5-3.0% of a good quality carbon black (Formulation B). In bright colours the pigment usually contains a high percentage of light-fast organic pigments, and examples of these are illustrated at (C) and (D) below.

(A) **White alkyd gloss**	**% by weight**
Rutile titanium dioxide	29.3
Coated calcium carbonate	1.4
Long-oil alkyd (70% solids)	52.2
White spirit	13.3
Dipentene	2.1
Methylethyiketoxime	0.1
Cobalt/zirconium octoate (6%Co, 9%Zr)	0.4
Calcium octoate (4%)	1.2

Specific gravity: 1.20
Solids by volume: 50.0%
PVC: 18.6%

(B) **Black alkyd gloss**	**% by weight**
Carbon black	2.7
Long-oil alkyd (70% solids)	71.2
Nuact [12]	0.1
White spirit	20.9
Dipentene	3.0
Methylethylketoxime	0.1
Cobalt/zirconium octoate (6%Co,,9%Zr)	0.5
Calcium octoate (4%) .	1.5

Specific gravity: 0.88
Solids by volume: 41.8%
PVC: 3.4%

(C) **Signal Red alkyd gloss**	**% by weight**
Toluidine Red	6.0
Permanent Red 2G	7.3
Rutile titanium dioxide	1.9
Long-oil alkyd (70% solids)	59.4
White spirit	20.4
Dipentene	3.0
Methylethylketoxime	0.1
Cobalt/zirconium octoate (6%Co, 9%Zr)	0.4
Calcium octoate (4%)	1.5

Specific gravity: 0.98
Solids by volume: 46.7%
PVC: 19.7%

(D) **Light Green alkyd gloss**	***% by weight***
Phthalocyanine Blue	1.0
Hansa Yellow G	10.0
Ferrite Yellow	3.5
Long-oil alkyd (70%solids)	59.9
White spirit	20.6
Dipentene	3.0
Methylethylketoxime	0.1
Cobalt/zirconium octoate (6%Co, 9%Zr)	0.4
Calcium octoate (4%)	1.5

Specific gravity: 0.97
§olids- by volume: 50.3 %
PVC: 25.5%

Note on materials

The ratio of thinners to alkyd resin will depend on both the nature of the alkyd and the viscosity. Alkyds based on the linoleic-rich oils, such as those derived from soya bean and safflower seeds, generally require less than the linseed type. The final paint viscosity is adjusted to 3 to 4 poise at 20°C (68°F).

Methylethylketoxime functions as an anti-skinning agent and also prolongs the wet-edge time. In warm weather, when wet-edge times are inclined to be short, the amount of methylethylketoxime can be increased without detrimental effects on other properties.

Decorative paints are now made on a leadless basis, and a mixture of cobalt and zirconium drier metals has been found to be the most satisfactory replacement for the, traditional-lead/cobalt mixture. Octoates (ethylhexoates) are preferred as the acid radicles to avoid the 'after odour' associated with the use of naphthenates.

In the black gloss a small quantity of Nuact is incorporated to prevent absorption of driers by carbon black on storage. Loss of driers leads to prolonged drying times.

The calcium naphthenate plays a dual role. It prevents. precipitation of the drier metals through reaction with phthalic-acid and also reduces the incidence of 'crystalline bloom' on the dry film.

Crystalline bloom consists of a -deposit -of fine crystals of ammonium sulphate and occurs under certain conditions in urban atmospheres containing ammonia and sulphur dioxide. It can be removed readily with water.

According to Holbrow, condensed water droplets on the film dissolve ammonia and sulphur dioxide which react slowly to produce ammonium sulphate. This remains as a bloom when the droplets evaporate. Calcium naphthenate induces condensation as a film rather than as droplets.

Evaporation is more rapid, and the time available for the formation of ammonium sulphate is reduced. It was shown, however, by Hill [that moisture is not essential for the formation of crystalline bloom. He produced the defect on painted panels by thermal precipitation of particles of ammonium sulphate.

General properties of alkyd enamels

The important attributes of alkyd enamels are good gloss retention and good durability. Application is usually by brush or roller and,. under normal conditions, they dry in 4 to 8 hours.

Alkyds are more sensitive than oleoresinous media to adverse conditions during drying, but there is an appreciable difference between types. Pentaerythritol alkyds are more sensitive than the glycerol types, but greater tolerance is claimed for the vinyl toluene types.

Low temperatures increase the drying time of alkyds considerably and they are very sensitive to moisture during the drying process. When alkyd enamels are applied on exterior surfaces during periods of heavy dew formation, application late in the day can result in moisture deposition during the drying process. Some moisture is absorbed by the surface layers of paint, resulting in swelling. Microrivelling occurs when the moisture dries out and the result is loss of gloss.

The sensitivity to moisture renders alkyds unsuitable for use on surfaces subject.to immersion in water. Poor alkali resistance renders them unsuitable for use on alkaline surfaces such as plaster or stucco.

Thixotropic paints

Decorative thixotropic paints are based on thixotropic alkyds and are also known as non-drip paints. They are made in the form of gloss, semi-gloss and eggshell finishes as well as undercoats.

The great advantage of thixotropic paints lies in the saving of time and labour. Thick coats can be applied which remain open long enough for levelling but set before sagging can set in. They can be made solely on thixotropic alkyds or on blends with conventional types. In the latter case the degree of thixotropy is reduced, i.e. the gels are less firm and the recovery time is greater

The behaviour of thixotropic paint films towards water and chemicals follows a similar pattern to that of conventional alkyds.

Fiat finishes, also known as flat wall paints, are used as interior wall finishes, but their use has declined considerably since the introduction of latex emulsion paints. The older types were based on stand oils or oleoresinous media heavily pigmented with lithopone and containing aluminium stearate as an anti-settling agent. They possessed poor levelling properties and were stippled to remove brush-marks.

Modern types are based on highly bodied alkyds of the non-yellowing linoleic rich type pigmented with titanium dioxide and extenders at a PVC of 55 to 60 percent. These modern types are more sensitive than the older oil finishes to variations in the porosity of the wall. It is important, therefore, that the wall should be adequately sealed, otherwise variations in sheen (flashing) will occur.

Eggshell and semi-gloss finishes are used to a limited extent as wall finishes and are made on conventional or thixotropic alkyds. Rigid control of PVC is essential for control of gloss.

Anti-condensation paints are used to provide a heat insulating barrier between the cold walls and the warm moist air of a room. Heat losses to the wall are reduced and condensation is minimised. They usually consist of an emulsion or flat oil paint to which is added a proportion of heat insulating material in the form of fine particles. Cork powder was formerly used but is no longer available. Very small polymer or glass spheres, such as 'Microsphere' are now commonly used.

Heat-resisting paints. The formulation of these paints will naturally be influenced by both the temperature to which the films are likely to be exposed and the exposure-time which is often for prolonged periods.

Considerable variations occur between the different types of organic binders and pigments (both inorganic and organic) in respect of resistance to heat. The number which will withstand prolonged exposure to temperatures above 120° to 130°C (248° to 266°F) is relatively small. The most usual effects of heat are darkening, which can be due to both pigment and binder, and embrittlement. The latter is a consequence of the acceleration of the normal ageing process brought about by the high temperature.

An investigation into the long-term heat stability of finishes was carried out by Berger who pointed out that temperatures of 90° to 120°C (194° to 248°F) were most frequently encountered in practice in central heating systems, chemical equipment, motors and so on. He found that at these temperatures the only finishes unaffected were silicones; polyurethanes cured by aliphatic isocyanate showed slight discoloration. With alkyds and with polyurethanes cured by aromatic isocyanates the protective value was retained in spite of discoloration.

Domestic radiators and heating panels are usually coated with a stoved finish at works. Repainting in light colours requires air-drying finishes in which colour stability of binde: (as well as the pigments) is as high as possible.

By basing the paints on a linoleic type alkyd, reinforced with a melamine/ formaldehyde resin, the discoloration can be minimized. Linseed type alkyd can be used for darker colours where darkening is not so apparent.

Krauss has shown that the greatest changes in film properties occur in the first 1000 hours of exposure and that little change takes place after 10000 hours.

In a number of industrial applications much higher temperatures are encountered. Oelsner [.studied the resistance of finishes at 150°C (302°F) and above and found that only silicones remained unchanged for 500 hours at these temperatures.

Temperatures of 600° to 700°C are reached in the lower sections of some steel chimney stacks, while many exhaust manifolds are only a little lower. These temperatures are above the limits of stability of most organic binders. For these surfaces aluminium paints based on silicone resins are usually employed. The silicone resins decompose at about 350°C (482°F), but the aluminium becomes sintered to the steel surface and provides protection.

Flame-retardant paints are designed to play a dual role. Firstly they must check or eliminate the spread of flame across the surface (flame will spread rapidly across most conventional paint films) and, secondly, they must in most cases be decorative. In this way they can reduce the fire hazard of combustible substrates and not detract from the flame-resisting properties of non combustible materials.

The earlier types of paint were based on alkali silicate solutions. Although they would not completely prevent damage or charring of combustible substrates such as wood as a result of excessive heat, they were very effective in preventing the spread of flame. Sodium silicate was the cheapest of the alkali silicates, but the paints developed an efflorescence which spoiled the colour. Potassium silicate paints were free from this defect and were used for stage scenery for many years. Very little silicate paint is used for flameretardant purposes today.

Modern flame-retardant paints are produced on both solvent and emulsion bases. They include the following types.

1 Oxygen-barrier coatings, often containing borates. On heating, these form a carbonaceous mass or a glassy barrier and evolve CO_2, and water rather than flammable products. Oxygen is excluded from the surface.

2 Media containing chlorinated compounds (such as chlorinated wax) and a pigment containing a high proportion of antimony oxide. Application of heat results in the formation of a blanket of volatile antimony chloride which prevents oxygen from reaching the surface. This type of paint, is protected by patents

3 Intumescent coatings which produce a substantial layer of foam when exposed to fire. These paints often contain starch, ammonium phosphate and a blowing agent to produce the foam.

The testing of flame-retardant paints is carried out on the desired substrate by the methods set out in BS 476; these include tests for ignitability, fire propagation, and surface spread of flame. For spread of flame the paint/ substrate combinations are assigned to one of four classes: (a) very low rate, (b) low rate, (c) medium rate, (d) rapid.

Aluminium paints for decorative and structural work are required to show maximum retention of brilliance over long periods. A high degree of leafing is essential and this requires a medium of low viscosity, low acid value and high solids. The most favoured media are tung oil/coumarone, tung oil/phenolic or urethane oil. Pigmentation is by aluminium paste to give about 130 to 150 grams of metal per litre. The final viscosity of the paint should be about 2 poise at 20°C (68°F).

Aluminium paints are used on metal lamp-standards, roof trusses and other structural work. They are not recommended in buildings where inflammable solvents are used since a spark can be generated if the, surface of the paint is struck with a steel object.

Bronze paints are made in a range of colours from Pale Gold to Antique Bronze. The metallic pigments used are copper alloys in flake form; pigmentation is usually at the rate of 400 to 500 grams per litre in a neutral medium such as a polymer, solution. Polyvinyl acetate, acrylics and polystyrene are used. Bronze paints are more sensitive than aluminium paints to acidic media and weathering; they are used only for interior decorative work.

Masonry finishes 'Masonry finish' is a general term applied to coatings used on exterior walls, excluding wood. Surfaces involved include stucco, cement render, brickwork, roughcast, and stonework.

Important reasons for painting exterior wall surfaces are (a) improvement in appearance, (b) prevention of water penetration, particularly, into stucco and brickwork, (c) prevention of spalling and disintegration resulting from frost, (d) reduction of dirt retention. Complete sealing of the surfaces is not desirable [23] and masonry paints are formulated with a microporous structure which provides a degree of permeability and so enables the wall to 'breathe'.

A number of binder types are in use but, in view of the alkaline nature of many of the materials, it is usual to employ alkali-resistant types. The following are among the types of binder most widely used. The finishes dry either to a smooth film or can be textured to exhibit an imitation stone effect.

1 100% acrylics or co-polymers of styrene/acrylate or vinyltoluene/ acrylate. These are generally in solution form and, when suitably pigmented, will produce films which adhere well and show very good durability.

2 Acrylic emulsions, in both flat and textured, finishes, also show very good durability.

3 Emulsions of vinyl co-polymers in which the second monomer can be either ethylene or an acrylic ester. Terpolymers produced from vinyl chloride, vinyl acetate and ethylene are also used and are claimed to possess very good weather resistance.

4 Chlorinated rubber, suitably plasticised. Lower-viscosity grades are recommended to assist penetration into the surface. Chlorinated rubber paints are highly resistant to alkali and to atmospheric contaminants.

5 Proprietary cement paints supplied in the form of dry powder and mixed with water immediately before use.

6 Long oil alkyd types which are usually applied as a two-coat system comprising sealer/undercoat and finish. They usually dry to a semi-gloss finish which can be smooth or textured.

Floor paints Floors are painted for the following reasons, (a) to improve appearance, (b) to protect the floor surface from abrasion, (c) to protect the surface from attack by spillages of various kinds and so present a surface from which they can be cleaned off without damage to the floor.

There is a wide selection of binder types which makes it possible to select the type best suited to the type of floor and the conditions of use. The following list sets out the most commonly used types and their main characteristics.

1 Medium-oil alkyd Used for general purpose floor paints where traffic is mainly pedestrian. Suitable for wood, quarry tiles, composites and mature concrete. Not resistant to alkali and so unsuitable for new concrete or cement screeds.

2 Epoxy ester Resembles alkyd insofar as usage is concerned but harder and more wear resistant.

3 Moisture-cured polyurethane Dries very hard and is very wear resistant. Used in clear form on parquet and other floors where appearance is to be retained. Used in pigmented form on other types of floor. Since this material cures by reaction with atmospheric moisture, ullage cans must be kept securely closed or the contents are likely to 'gel' and become useless.

Fungistatic paints are used in locations favourable to the growth of moulds and fungi. They are usually conventional paints to which has been added one to two percent of a fungistat. Among the latter are chlorinated phenols and dodecylamine salicylate but a number of proprietary .materials are available. Before application of fungistatic paint it is usual to neutralize any growths in the surface by application of a dilute solution of fungicide.

Multicolour paints produce films exhibiting two or more separate colours when applied as a single coat by spraying. They are polyphase systems containing one or more pigmented organic phases dispersed in a non-pigmented aqueous phase. The latter contains a thickener or stabilizer such as a cellulose ether and possibly an emulsifying agent.

The most widely used multicolour paints are based on cellulose nitrate as the medium for the dispersed organic phase. This is pigmented in the normal way and the lacquer stirred into an aqueous solution of stabilizer. More than one coloured lacquer can be used to produce the multicolour effect, but each is stirred into a separate portion of stabilizer solution and the individual dispersions are then mixed carefully.

The size of the coloured droplets varies from 1 to 8 mils in diameter, depending on the speed of stirring, and the shape depends on the viscosity of the lacquer. Low viscosity gives spherical and high viscosity elongated shapes.

Can stability of these paints depends on the densities of the aqueous and organic phases being as close as possible, and on the absence of water-miscible solvents in the organic phase.

Multicolour paints are used mainly for interior well decoration in public buildings, schools and offices.

Chapter - 10

COATINGS (WATER-BORNE)

The use of water as a paint solvent has always been attractive for reasons of low cost and absence of fire risk and toxicity. It was probably the first solvent used by man in his primitive paints and has,' of course, been used in artists' water colours for many centuries. A number of coating materials which are now virtually obsolete, among which were distemper and limewash, were water borne.

An impetus to the extended use of water as a paint solvent has been provided by the spiralling costs of solvents and considerations of environmental pollution.

The water-borne media in use today a can be divided into two main classes, (a) polymer emulsions, which are used chiefly in building paints and (b) watersoluble or water dispersible binders, used mainly for industrial paints especially metal primers applied by electrodeposition. An obviously attractive application of water-borne binders is in air drying decorative finishes and undercoats and considerable work has been done in attempts to produce suitable emulsions. It is now claimed that paint resins can be emulsified satisfactorily using a tailormade emulsifier possessing an appropriate HLB value (below).

POLYMER EMULSIONS

Nature of emulsions

An emulsion is a two-phase system consisting of a liquid, in the form of very fine droplets (the dispersed phase), suspended or dispersed in a second liquid (the continuous phase) in which it is insoluble. The commonest form of emulsion contains water as the continuous phase; polymer emulsions are of this type. When the dispersed phase is a solid the system is termed a 'dispersion', but although the polymer is usually more solid than liquid, the term 'emulsion' is always used for the polymer systems. (Emulsions exist in which water is dispersed in an organic continuous phase, but these are rarely encountered in surface coatings.)

Formation of emulsions

Suppose that it is desired to produce an emulsion of linseed oil in water. Rapid stirring of the two liquids together will produce a suspension of oil droplets, but when stirring ceases, the two liquids will separate into clearly defined layers (Fig. 19.1). If, however, the water contains a small quantity of a soap or a surface-active agent (or 'surfactant') the oil droplets remain dispersed in the water and an emulsion is formed. When this emulsion is allowed to stand for some time, the dispersed oil droplets will tend to rise (the specific gravity of linseed oil being lower than that of water). This is known as 'creaming' of emulsions, by analogy with the separation of cream from milk. The 'cream' is readily redispersed on stirring, but the formation of 'cream' can be prevented by increasing the viscosity of the water phase.

Among materials used for this purpose are cellulose ethers, alkali salts of polyacrylic acid, alginates and alkali caseinate. Such thickening agents are described also as 'emulsion stabilisers' or 'protective colloids'.

Surfactants

These are compounds which, when dissolved in a- liquid, reduce the surface tension of that liquid or the interfacial tension between two immiscible liquids or between the liquid and a solid. Their effectiveness is related to their chemical constitution and a very large number of these compounds are known. When a surfactant is used to produce an emulsion, as in the example given above, it is classed as an 'emulsifying agent', and the suitability of a surfactant for this purpose is related to the HLB value.

HLB value A surfactant molecule contains both hydrophilic and lipophilic (hydrophobic) groups and it is the relationship between these groups which controls the emulsifying properties of the surfactant. Empirical values were assigned to these groups by Davies and Rideal. Some of these values are quoted in Table 19.1.

Using these figures the HLB or Hydrophilic/Lipophilic Balance can be calculated using the expression:

$$HLB = \Sigma(\text{Hydrophilic groups}) - \Sigma(\text{Lipophilic groups}) + 7$$

Very good agreement was obtained between calculated and experimental values.

The correlation between HLB values and practical application of detergents is shown in Table 19.2

In practice the HLB value is useful in the choice of emulsifiers but is less important in detergents.

An interesting physico/chemical relationship between HLB value and emulsion stability was pointed out by Davies and Rideal

$$HLB = \log \frac{\text{coalescence rate W/O}}{\text{coalescence rate O/W}}$$

where W/O refers to the water in oil emulsion and O/W to the oil in water emulsion.

Surfactants are classified into four main groups designated anionic, nonionic, cationic, and ampholytic. The anionics are the more commonly used as emulsifying agents. The other classes are used in pigment wetting and dispersion and for special purposes.

Anionic surfactants

The most common types are the alkali metal salts of straight chain carboxylic or sulphonic acids of 11 to 17 carbon atoms. Sodium laurate is a typical example. When dissovled in water it ionizes:

$$CH_3(CH_2)_{10}COONa \rightleftarrows CH_3(CH_2)_{10}COO^- + Na^+$$

The surface activity is due to the polar nature of the anion which consists of the hydrophilic (water-attracting) COO- group and the hydrophobic or lipophilic (water-repelling or oil-attracting) hydrocarbon chain. Except at very low concentrations the anions form micelles (Fig. 19.2, where the anions are represented as-O) in which the hydrocarbon ends are directed inwards and the carboxyl groups outwards into the water.

When oil droplets are introduced (as in the introductory example) the hydrocarbon ends are attracted to the oil and the carboxyl groups project into the water (Fig. 19.3).

The oil droplets thereby acquire an overall negative charge and are mutually repellent. Coalescence of the droplets is prevented and an anionic emulsion results. The anions tend to concentrate at the surface of the solution and lower the surface tension by an amount proportional to the concentration. In a similar way they are adsorbed at the interface between the solution and a solid and so reduce the contact angle. Wetting of the surface is thereby facilitated.

Other types of compounds used as anionic surfactants are water-soluble salts of amines and fatty acids, e:g. triethanolamine oleate; sulphated higher alcohols, e.g. sodium lauryl sulphate; sulphonated compounds, e.g. sulphonated castor oil (Turkey Red Oil), and aromatic petroleum sulphonates.

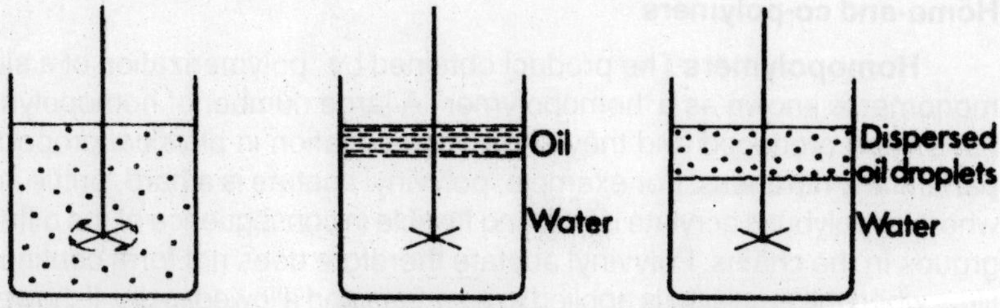

Oil droplets in suspension while stirring | Oil and water separate when stirring ceases | 'Creamed' emulsion

Fig 19.1

Table 19.1

Hydrophilic groups			Lipophilic groups	
$-SO_4^{2-}$	Na^+	38·7	$-CH_3$	0.475
$-COO^-$	Na^+	19·1	$-CH_2-$	
$-COOH$		2·1	$-\underset{\vert}{CH}-$	
$-OH$		1·9		
$-O-$		1·3		

Formation of polymer emulsions

When a liquid monomer, such as vinyl acetate, is added to an aqueous solution of an anionic surfactant under rapid stirring, droplets of various sizes are produced and these become coated with the anions. The smaller

Table 19.2

HLB range	Application
3·5– 6	W/O emulsifier
7 – 9	Wetting agent
8 –18	O/W emulsifier
13 –15	Detergent
15 –18	Solubilising agent

droplets become enclosed in micelles and are rapidly 'solubilized'. Addition of the polymerization catalyst results in rapid and vigorous reaction in which the solubilized monomer is converted to the polymer (polyvinyl acetate). The large droplets are solubilized more slowly, but ultimately the whole of the monomer is converted to polymer. The polymer particles are coated with anions, so acquiring a negative charge. The final system is an anionic emulsion. Emulsions produced in this way contain 45 to 55 percent of polymer by mass.

Homo-and co-polymers

Homopolymers The product obtained by . polymerization of a single monomer is known as a 'homopolymer'. A large number of homopolymers have been produced and they show wide variation in physical properties, particularly hardness. For example, polyvinyl acetate is a hard, brittle solid, whereas polybutyl acrylate is soft and flexible in consequence of the different groups in the chains. Polyvinyl acetate therefore does not form continuous films when the emulsion is applied to a surface and allowed to dry. If, however, a suitable plasticizer (up to 20 percent by mass on the polymer) is stirred into the emulsion, migration into the polymer takes place, resulting in softer particles which are capable of coalescing to form a film.

Ester-type plasticizers are the most suitable but, unfortunately, they possess drawbacks. On prolonged exposure of the plasticized film, loss of plasticizer takes place gradually, either by evaporation or by migration into the substrate. The result is progressive embrittlement, leading to failure.

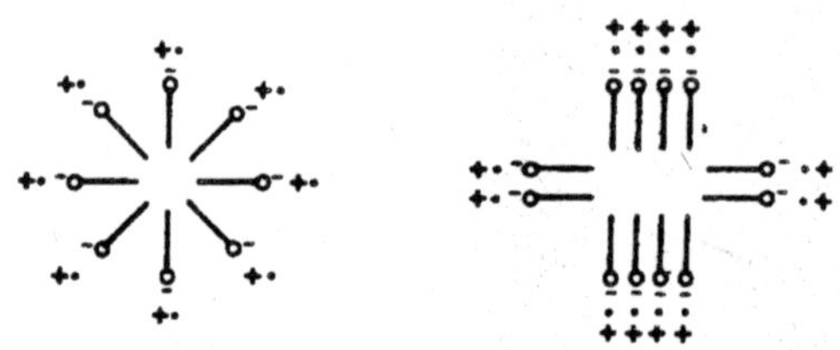

Fig 19.2

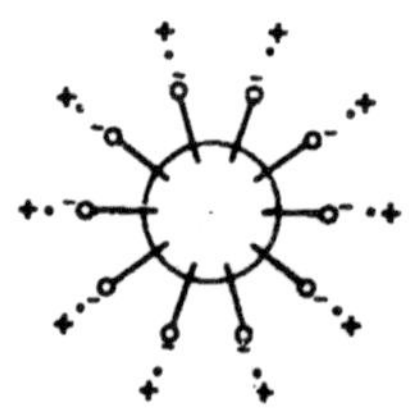

Fig 19.3

Co-polymers If vinyl acetate is co-polymerized with a second monomer, which itself gives a soft, flexible polymer, then by adjustment of the relative quantities, products can be produced with any desired degree of hardness and which are capable of yielding continuous films without addition of plasticizer. The proportion and type of second monomer can be varied, and the types used include ethylene and other olefines, vinyl chloride, VeoVa (a vinyl ester of a branched chain carboxylic acid), and acrylic esters. Other vinyl co-polymers with more specific applications include vinyl chloride/VeoVa, styrene/acrylic and vinyl toluene/acrylic.

A series of vinyl acetate/VeoVa 10 co-polymers has been designed to accept higher pigment loadings than normal without appreciable loss of scrub resistance. Matt finishes with a PVC of 70% are possible giving opacity by 'dry hiding'. Economies can be effected by replacement of a proportion of the titanium dioxide by extender. Co-polymers ,of this type are known as 'high binders'.

Vinyl co-polymers, particularly of the vinyl acetate/olefin type, are the standard media for the majority of emulsion paints for interior and, but to a lesser extent, exterior application.

A range of co-polymers of vinyl chloride and vinylidene chloride modified by inclusion of a proportion of acrylic ester has been produced by ICI and marketed under the trade name 'Haloflex' These anionic emulsions differ in several respects from the conventional types. A low level of stabiliser is used in manufacture and so it is necessary to add stabiliser to the paint formulation. A block co-polymer of ethylene oxide/propylene oxide (Synperonic PE 39/70-ICI) has been found very suitable.

'Haloflex' is marketed at a very low pH (1.0 - 2.0) since this type of polymer tends to undergo dehydrochlorination at higher pH levels. Emulsion paints based on 'Haloflex' are pigmented at a pH of 4 - 5 and this imposes some restrictions on the types of pigments which can be used. Zinc phosphate, modified aluminium triphosphate and 'Shieldex' have given satisfactory results when used in primers for steel.

Applications of the 'Haloflex' co-polymers include primers for blast cleaned steel (at 50 - 80 μm dry film thickness) and they show good adhesion to new galvanized steel, concrete, cement render, wood and many plastic surfaces.

The 'Haloflex' range includes co-polymers suited to finishes as well as to primers.

VINYL EMULSION PAINTS

Emulsion paints contain three distinct phases, (a) the aqueous or continuous phase in which the thickener, preservative and other additives are dissolved, (b) the dispersed polymer phase, and (c) the dispersed pigment phase. Table 19.3 illustrates typical compositions of flat and semi-gloss vinyl emulsion paints. They are followed by more detailed discussion of the components and of the finished paints.

Materials and manufacture of vinyl emulsion paints

Pigmentation

The pigments are dispersed in the aqueous phase, usually with the aid of a surfactant, preferably of the non-ionic type. This type is preferred to the anionic which has a great tendency to cause foaming. The greatest demand in emulsion paints is for whites and pale shades in which the major pigment is titanium dioxide. The rutile grade is preferred for chalk resistance and better flow properties.

Dispersion of the titanium dioxide is conveniently effected by a high-speed disperser of the Silverson type. The pigment (and extender, if used) is added to the aqueous solution of colloid, surfactant and other ingredients under the mixer. The degree of dispersion required is not as high as for gloss finishes. The pigment dispersion is then mixed with the emulsion, tinted if necessary, and pumped to the straining and filling area.

Where deep colours are required the strong pigments are generally used in the form of concentrated aqueous dispersions. Dry pigments can be used, provided care is taken to ensure that the dispersed pigment is in a completely hydrophilic condition (this applies particularly to many organic pigments which are hydrophobic) by using sufficient surfactant.,Extenders are used to make up the PVC to the required figure, the extenders being dispersed in the aqueous phase before addition of the concentrated pigment dispersion.

Protective colloids

These are used to,provide a degree of 'structure', so reducing the mobility of the dispersed pigment and polymer particles and improving stability. In addition they ar thought to be adsorbed on the dispersed pigment particles. Whilst the primary function of protective colloids is stabilization of the paint, they also exert a significant effect on flow properties (particularly levelling) and film formation.

In vinyl emulsion paints the types used are the non-ionic cellulose derivatives such as methyl-, hydroxyethyl- and ethylhydroxy ethyl-cellulose, the anionic sodium salt of carboxymethyl cellulose and the anionic ammonium polyacrylate. Mixtures are frequently required to meet formulation requirements.

Other types of thickening agents are the hydrophilic (montmorillonite) clays which absorb considerable amounts of water and disperse to form firm gels. They are more resistant to bacterial and fungal attack than are the cellulose ethers.

Preservatives

Protective colloids of the types enumerated above are prone to attack by bacteria in the can, the consequence being a drop in viscosity, often accompanied by gassing. Again, in damp situations the dried film can be attacked by moulds and fungi and it is necessary, therefore, to include a preservative in the formulation. Sufficient may be present to protect the liquid paint, but a higher concentration is necessary if the film is also to be protected. Paints of the latter type are marketed under the description 'Fungistatic Emulsion Paint'. (The adjective 'fungicidal' is often used but would be difficult to substantiate.) A fairly wide choice of preservatives is available and includes the chlorinated phenols, certain organotin compounds, chloroacetamide and a number of proprietary materials.

Table 19.3 Examples of vinyl emulsion paints

	Percentage composition	
	Flat finish	Semi-gloss finish
Rutile titanium dioxide	20·00	20·00
Whiting	13·50	–
Blanc fixe	9·40	–
Hydroxyethylcellulose	0·45	0·40
Water	29·45	13·70
Non-ionic surfactant	0·70	0·50
Sequestering agent	0·20	0·20
Water	1·30	1·30
Preservative	0·20	0·20
Anti-foam	0·15	0·15
Coalescing solvent	1·20	1·10
Co-polymer emulsion (50% solids vinylacetate/ethylene)	23·45	62·45
Specific gravity	1·48	1·22
Solids by volume	34·15%	40·70%
PVC	52·00%	15·0%
Water (by weight)	42·5%	46·2%

Sequestering agents

These are used in emulsion paints where hard waters or waters containing iron compounds are used. It is well known that polyvalent metal ions (cations) will precipitate anionic dispersions. The function of the sequestering agent is removal of these metal ions. Calgon which is commonly used, is a sodium hexametaphosphate and functions by ion exchange.

Anti-foam

Foam can be produced when dry pigment is added rapidly under vigorous stirring to an aqueous solution of cellulose ether or other colloid. The structure of the medium retards movement of the dispersed air-bubbles and the foams can be very persistent.

A diversity of 'anti-foams' or 'defoamers' is available but in some cases the mode of action is far from clear. It has been stated that the mechanism of one type consists in the rapid spread of a low tension insoluble oil over the surface of a system causing weaknesses in the bubble walls leading to their collapse. The oil used contains additives such as spreading agents and 'entering agents' to carry the defoamer into the inter-bubble spaces.

Film formation and coalescing solvent

When an emulsion paint is cast as a film, evaporation of water leaves a matrix of pigment and polymer particles interspersed with the minor components. If a continuous film is to be produced, the polymer particles must be sufficiently fluid to coalesce and to embody the particles of pigment. To reach this condition the temperature of the film must be at or above the 'minimum filmforming temperature' of the polymer. This is generally above the 'Glass Transition temperature' (Tg) which is the temperature at which a polymer or resin changes from a brittle solid to a plastic condition, or vice versa. The minimum film-forming temperature is a ,characteristic of a particular polymer or co polymer. The relationship between minimum film forming temperature and Tg has been examined by Nicholson It can be reduced to assist film formation at lower temperatures by addition of small quantities of certain solvents to the emulsion. These 'coalescing solvents' are absorbed by the polymer particles, resulting in softening and so facilitating coalescence. Among materials used as coalescing solvents are ethers of propylene glycol, Texanol and Dalpad A.

Whilst coalescing solvents are effective aids to film formation at lower temperatures they detract from the resistance of the paint to freezing. Soft polymer particles are more prone to coagulation as a result of freezing than the harder types.

In a study of factors affecting the optical properties of emulsion paint films. Williams and Fairless discuss film formation in some detail, particularly the part played by coalescing solvents.

Bondy and. Coleman have studied film formation and the factors which influence tensile strength and water permeability. They consider that coalescence of polymer particles is influenced by the presence of colloid stabilizers and the (usually uneven) distribution of pigment particles in the film.

The drying of an emulsion-paint, film is accompanied by the development of stresses before the film ultimately reaches a stable condition and this can result in detachment of the film from an unstable substrate: These stresses have been measured by Perera who has also shown how they are affected by the type and quantity of coalescing solvent.

Stainers for emulsion paints can be aqueous dispersions or the universal type. Inorganic pigments present little trouble, but hydrophobic organic pigment dyestuffs in aqueous dispersion must be treated with anionic or (prdferably) nonionic surfactant to avoid the risk of flushing to the polymer phase.

Properties and use of Vinyl Emulsion Paints

These paints have been very popular with both professional and amateur painters for a number of years. They are characterized by the following properties.

1 Absence of fire risk and toxic solvents.

2 Ease of application by either brush or roller.

3 Speed of drying, enabling a further coat to be applied within a few hours.

4 Tools and containers can be cleaned with water.

Their main application is on interior walls and ceilings where several coats can, if necessary, be applied in a working day. On absorbent surfaces such as new plaster it is advisable to thin the first coat with water (instructions are usually printed on the can), but no thinning is necessary for non-absorbent surfaces such as old paintwork. This should, of course, be thoroughly rubbed down. Vinyl emulsion paints (thinned if necessary) can be used also as primers for hardboard and many types of building board. They can be overpainted with conventional air-drying undercoat and finishing systems.

Some vinyl co-polymer emulsions are used on exterior surfaces. These usually contain mineral grit or mica, and the dry film resembles stonework.

ACRYLIC EMULSIONS AND PAINTS

The polymers employed, although frequently referred to as '100 percent acrylics' are, in effect, co-polymers of acrylic esters. Variations in properties can be obtained by varying the types and relative proportions of the esters. For example, polymerisation of ethyl acrylate yields an extremely soft polymer of little practical use; methyl methacrylate, on the other hand, yields a hard brittle product. By co polymerising the two esters in different proportions polymers differing in hardness and flexibility can be produced. Other esters co-polymerised with methyl methacrylate include butyl acrylate, and butyl methacrylate; styrene and acrylonitrile Also are used.

Acrylic emulsions being marketed today are characterised by fine particle size, good freeze-thaw stability and a high pH (9.5 -10.0).

Formulation is, in general, somewhat similar to that of the vinyls except for the appreciably higher pH (about 9.5) which requires fairly close control. Film formation takes place in a manner similar to that in vinyl emulsion paints, and the factors which influence the coalescence or fusion of the polymer droplets have been studied by van der Wiel and Zom The films are characterised by good adhesion to a wide range of surfaces, lasting flexibility and good durability. Among their applications are primers for wood and finishes for exterior surfaces such as cement render, stucco, roughcast and concrete.

The formulation below illustrates the general composition of an acrylic primer for softwoods.

	% by weight
Titanium dioxide	14.0
Calcium carbonate	11.4
Fine natural silica -	4.5
Ammonium polyacrylate 2% solution	8.6
Preservative	0.4
Non-ionic surfactant	0.6
Anti-foam	0.2
Propylene glycol	2.3
Acrylic emulsion (46% solids)	58.0
Ammonia solution	q.s.

Specific gravity, 1.26, solids by volume, 44%.

When dry this primer can be overcoated with conventional oxidising systems or with acrylic emulsion paint (below).

The following formulation for an exterior quality acrylic emulsion paint illustrates the general composition of this type.

Acrylic emulsion paint: exterior, white	**% by weight**
Water	5.2
Non-ionic surfactant	1.1
Anti-foam	0.2
Ammonium polyacrylate solution (2%)	9.6
Rutile titanium dioxide	20.5
Talc	8.4
Paris white	9.2
Proplene glycol	2.1
Pine oil	0.3
Preservative	0.2
Acrylic emulsion (46%)	43.0
Ammonia (0.880)	0.2

Specific gravity, 1.40; solids by volume, 41.0%; PVC, 38.7%; pH 9 5.9-9.6.

Properties and uses

Some of these have been mentioned above. In addition, the acrylic emulsion paints are more freeze-thaw resistant and less permeable to moisture than are the vinyls. Besides their use as wood primers and exterior finishes they are used on interior walls and ceilings; and, by incorporating the harder type of polymer, as floor paints. They have also been used successfully as primers for new galvanized iron.

Exterior joinery, such as window frames, is now frequently treated with a preservative stain instead of paint. A widely used stain is water-borne and consists of a mixture of alkyd and acrylic emulsions, together with light-fast pigments. Transparent, translucent and opaque stains are used. It is considered that the good durability of these stains is contributed by the acrylic component whilst the alkyd is responsible for penetration and adhesion. Low opacity red iron oxides, which are effective UV absorbers, are often used for pigmentation..

WATER-SOLUBLE BINDERS

Early types

Among the earliest binders for pigments used by man were the vegetable gums, some of which have been employed for special purposes down to the present day. Examples are gum tragacanth and gum arabic which are still used in limited quantities. Egg yolk is another material used by medieval painters and which continues to be used as a component of artists' 'tempera' medium.

Animal glues, obtained from hides and bones, were in general use until the middle of the present century as binders for 'soft' distempers (e.g. ceiling whites) and as protective colloids in oil-bound or washable distempers. These materials are now virtually obsolete.

Casein, a protein obtained from milk, is soluble in dilute alkali and was used as a binder per se in 'oil-free' distempers and as a protective colloid in the oilbound or washable types. Casein possessed one advantage over the animal glues. A solution in dilute ammonia gave a water-insoluble film by loss of the alkali. Alkali caseinate solutions continue to be used on a limited scale as a protective colloid in certain types of emulsion paint.

Alginates, obtained from certain species of seaweeds, form colloidal solutions of high viscosity. They have been used as binders for soft distempers.

Modern types

These can be divided into two classes: (a) alkali silicates, and (b) water-soluble resins. The latter are the more important.

Alkali silicates

Sodium silicate was used as the binder in fire-retarding paints (e.g. for fire curtains and stage scenery) for a number of years. However, the films tended to whiten due. to formation of sodium carbonate, and for this purpose sodium silicate was later replaced by potassium silicate. Sodium silicate was also used in paints required to resist moderately high temperatures, but the films were not sufficiently weather-resistant for outside work.

An interesting use of sodium silicate has been in the so-called 'inorganic zinc silicate' paints in which zinc dust is mixed with the sodium silicate solution shortly before use. The film consists of zinc silicate containing unreacted zinc and is an effective primer for steel. It is essential, however, that the SiO_2 / Na_2O ratio in the sodium silicate be kept within fairly narrow limits.

Lithium silicate was later used to replace sodium silicate in zinc silicate paints, but the use of alkali silicates for this purpose has dropped considerably since the introduction of the prehydrolysed ethyl silicates.

Water-soluble resins

A number of synthetic resins can be produced in water-soluble form by incorporating acidic groups, e.g. carboxyl, in the molecular structure. These groups are then neutralized by bases such as ammonia or amines to give products soluble in water.

Water-soluble resins have been used as binders in conventional type stoving enamels for a number of years, but surfaces to be coated must be very clean. The slightest traces of oil or grease can impair wetting of the surface and result in serious cissing or contraction.of the film

In 1963, metal primers based on water-soluble resins were introduced in the car industry and applied by electrodeposition. This has probably been the most important application of these resins to date.

Types of resin used

Alkyds

These are produced by selecting the appropriate polyol and acid to give the desired free acid groups in the molecule. A wide range of suitable acids is available among which are maleic and isophthalic and trimellitic anhydride. Caron et al. describe a method for introducing carboxyl groups during chain formation by using 2:2-bishydroxymethyl propanoic acid or by modification of the preformed chains using various aldehydes. The products are claimed to exhibit air drying times and application properties similar to those of conventional alkyd resins. A comparison of the performance of water-soluble alkyds with conventional solvent-based systems has been published by Engelhardt Burckhardt and Luthardt have examined water-soluble short-oil alkyds, particularly for use by conventional and electrostatic spray. They conclude that their behaviour is determined by the functional groups causing the solubility. Water-soluble methoxylated melamines are often added to crosslink with the alkyd in stoving finishes.

Solubilizing groups can be introduced by the use of appropriate fatty acids or by mkleinizatiom Certain solubilized epoxy esters can be cured by reaction with water soluble melamines or phenolics followed by stoving.

Other resins

Other water-solubilized resins of interest, particularly for electrodeposition, are polyesters, acrylics, aminos and phenol/formaldehyde. Appreciable amounts of water-soluble resins are used in paints for application by coil-coating. Polyesters and modified acrylics are widely used and are cross linked with water-soluble melamine during stoving.

Chapter - 11

METHODS OF APPLICATION

The transfer of a liquid paint from container to surface can be effected in a number of ways. Decorative paints are applied by brush or hand roller, but spraying is used on many large exterior surfaces. Both spray and brush application are employed in industrial maintenance painting as, for example, on bridges and other complex structures. A variety of methods are in use in industrial paint application. In the majority of cases these are followed by an accelerated curing operation.

The principal methods of paint application are listed below and later outlined in the text:

Brush	Spray - conventional (air-assisted),
Hand roller	hot, airless, electrostatic, and combinations
Dip coating	Tumbling or barrelling
Flow coating	Silk screen
Curtain coating	Electrodeposition
Roller coating	

Brush application

Brushes are made in many shapes and sizes, ranging from the small round 'pencils' to large flat types. The quality of the bristle is important, and hog bristle has long been regarded as the finest type. The bristles subdivide and so produce a number of fine ends which help to minimize brush-marking in the film. Nylon bristles also are used; these are more wear-resistant than the animal bristles.

New brushes are usually broken in by use with primers. Brush application is the most satisfactory method of applying primers to most surfaces as the paint can be 'scrubbed' in, giving good wetting and'adhesion. The scrubbing action, however, must be avoided in the application of undercoats and finishes. With these, the paint is applied more liberally and with longer strokes, cross-brushed, and finally laid off with light strokes across the surface.

After use, paint brushes should be cleaned in white spirit or other suitable solvent and stored suspended by the handle so that they do not rest on the bristles. Brushes used for decorative work can be kept in a 'soft' condition by immersing the suspended bristles in a mixture of white spirit (I volume) and raw linseed oil (I volume). They must, of course, be washed out in white spirit before further use.

Paints suited to brush application are the slow-drying types thinned with white spirit or other slow-evaporating solvent. By this means large areas can be painted in sections and the latter joined up smoothly before the film has dried. The period during which the paint film remains 'open' to enable joining up to be done is known as the wet-edge time.

Defects which can occur in brush painting include the following

Brush drag This can be due to excessively high viscosity, in which case the remedy is thinning, but this may be accompanied by loss of opacity and film build. Another cause is suction from an underbound priming coat or from a substrate which has been inadequately sealed.

Poor levelling or persistent brushmarks. This usually occurs in low-sheen paints and can result from excessive pigmentation,-flocculation, or incorrect choice and quantity of extenders. Addition of a surfactant may be effective in inducing flow but, if not, reformulation of the paint is necessary.

Sagging (or 'curtaining') on vertical surfaces, accompanied by pulling away from sharp edges, indicates, excessive flow or excessively heavy application. The former can be checked by introducing a limited degree of thixotropy by the use of a Bentone hydrogenated castor oil or a thixotropic alkyd.

Too short wet-edge time Wet-edge time has been defined above. It depends on the nature of the resin (linoleic-rich alkyds set up more slowly than the corresponding linseed types), the volatility of the solvents, and the temperature. Remedies include addition of an anti skinning agent such as methylethylketoxime to delay the initial oxidation of the film, or (if possible) an increase in the proportion of high-boiling solvent.

Hand rollers

The roller is made of lamb's-wool or soft plastic foam and is charged with paint by rolling to and fro in a shallow tray with a small quantity of paint. These rollers are very useful for painting large flat areas such as walls, and are popular with home decorators. The soft rollers can be removed easily for cleaning and must be washed out very thoroughly after use, or they will harden and become useless.

Pressure fed rollers

For large-scale work the use of the tray can be eliminated by conveying the paint to the roller through the hollow handle. The paint is pumped at low pressure and the flow can be controlled by a trigger mechanism, The use of an extension handle allows large areas to be painted with minimum use of scaffolding.

Dip coating

This is the simplest method of applying paint and provides a cheap and quick method of coating large numbers of articles.

The uniformity of the coating depends on the rate of withdrawal, and a rate of 2 to 4 inches (50 to 100 mm) per minute is usually satisfactory. It is necessary to adjust the viscosity of the paint and the rate of solvent evaporation, so that the film sets fast enough to ensure adequate thickness at the top of the article but slow enough for flow to ensure a uniform coating. Paint viscosities are low and many pigments tend to settle. Uniformity of the paint is maintained by pumping round an external circuit.

After removal from the tank, articles are allowed to drain and the excess paint is returned to the tank. Loss of solvent, and the fact that oxidizing types of paint are often employed, results in an increase in viscosity in the tank. The latter has to be checked daily for viscosity and solids content, and rectified as necessary.

A disadvantage of dipping is the quantity of paint required and, in large installations, the attendant fire risk. The risk is, of course, absent when the process is used for the application of water-soluble primers.

Hand-dipping allows rapid immersion and withdrawal, but bubbles and 'tears' can be troublesome. The article is then allowed to drain for about 15 minutes before stoving. Advantages of'hand-dipping are speed, low paint loss, and low cost.

Slow dipping involves withdrawal at about 1 inch per minute and gives superior results. The paints used can be of higher viscosity than in other forms of dipping and produce very uniform films. This method is used for brush and tool handles which are dipped in highviscosity cellulose nitrate lacquer. The articles are fixed in a suitable jig.

Automatic dipping The articles are suspended from a conveyor which dips over the tank and later rises. The excess paint drains on to a chute and is returned to the tank while the articles, after a 'flash off' period on the conveyor, pass through a camel-back or other type of oven. The viscosities of the paints used are of the order 0.7-1.0 poise at 25°C (77°F) so that bath contents must be kept in motion to avoid pigment settlement. This is achieved by pumping through an external circuit.

With articles which tend to retain drops of paint on the lower edges, the excess paint can be removed by the Ransburg electrostatic de-tearing process. The article is earthed (through the conveyor) and, after initial drainage, is suspended for a short time (20 to 100 seconds) over a negatively charged grid at 90 000 to 100 000 volts. Induced positive charges on the drops cause them to fly to the grid, leaving a uniform coating of paint on the article. With this process it is possible to use paints of slightly higher viscosity.

Rotational dipping, in which the article is rotated while immersed in the paint and while draining, is used for articles of complicated design or containing pockets from which the paint cannot otherwise drain.

Slipper-dip is used to 'apply an extra coat of paint to the lower half of car bodies. The latter are passed through the tank with only the lower half immersed.

Defects A number of defects can appear in dip coating; these have been summarized elsewhere The two most common are the following.

Fat edge and 'tears' These can be caused by poor flow properties, indicating an incorrect solvent balance. Alternatively, removal from the dipping tank may have been too rapid.

Excessive drainage from the top of the article due to excessive flow. A slight degree of thixotropy can be introduced by means of a Bentone or hydrogenated castor oil.

Types of paint employed Conventional stoving enamels of the medium/ short alkyd and alkyd/amino types are widely used. Paints thinned with trichlorethylene offer certain advantages in non-inflammability, excellent solvent power, and high evaporation rate. The latter allows higher rates of production with fewer fat edges and drips. Although trichlorethylene .is highly toxic, this hazard has been overcome by design of suitable plant.

Items coated by the dipping process include parts for agricultural and other implements, tools, and electrical components (with impregnating varnish). Dipping is also employed for the phosphate pretreatment of steel, particularly in the car industry.

Flow coating

This can be regarded as a variation of the dip process. The paint is either flowed over the objects and the excess returned for re-use, or the paint is directed at the objects from a number of strategically placed nozzles. In the latter case the objects are conveyed through a tunnel in which the paint application is carried out. Any drops which collect on the lower edges of the objects are removed by electrostatic de-tearing.

As a result of aeration the films may contain air-bubbles and other imperfections, and the objects are therefore passed through a chamber of solvent vapour, when the film flows out to a uniform coating. The articles are allowed to flash off, and are then passed into the stoving oven.

Flow coating is used for objects of intricate shape, or which are large in comparison with the area to be painted. For this reason it is used for agricultural machinery. The jets can be so positioned that every part of the object is coated.

Compared with the dip process relatively small amounts of paint are required, but solvent losses are much greater.

Curtain coating

This is, in effect, a refined form of flow coating. It is used for large flat panels, which may have raised mouldings, of wood, plywood, hardboard and similar materials. The panels are carried on a conveyor through a curtain of paint which is formed when the paint, from a pressure head, flows through a Vshaped slot which runs the width of the machine. The flow is controlled by the width of the slot, which can be varied from 0.1 to 5 mm and is adjusted to give the required film thickness.

Two-component systems can be applied by the use of two curtains about 3 inches apart. The film remains sufficiently fluid for the two components to mix.

Roller coating.

Application of paint is by transfer from rollers to one or both sides of flat materials such as strip metal, tin-plate sheets, and boards of various types. The paint is transferred through systems of rollers to the application rolls (Fig. 20.1). The thickness of the film is controlled by the gap between the feed and application rolls.

The basic requirements of the paint are high opacity, for one-coat coverage, good flow, and correct solvent balance. The solvent must not evaporate too slowly or the high production rates for which this process is well suited will not be achieved.

A wide variety of paints are used, including short-oil alkyds, alkyd/amino combinations, vinyl co-polymers, and modified epoxies. A high proportion of high boiling aromatic is included in the solvent mixture.

In 'reverse' roller coating the application roll rotates in the opposite direction to the movement of the sheets. The shearing action at the line contact results in a more uniform film. It is particularly useful in applying filler or primer to absorbent boards such as plywood and chipboard, where the filler is forced into the surface and a smooth finish is obtained.

Losses and wastage in roller coating are extremely low.

Coil coating

The coating of metals in the form of continuous strip is now well established. The strip, received in the form of a coil, is subjected to a sequence of operations, namely uncoiling, degreasing, pretreatment, roller coating with paint, cure by stoving, cooling and re-coiling. Aluminium and steel strip up to 5 ft (1.52 metres) wide are coated at speeds up to 600 ft (213 .4 metres) per minute The dry-film thicknesses of the paint are of the order of 25 to 35 micrometres.

Obviously a very high performance standard is required of the paints used. The major requirements are as follows.

1. Outstanding flexibility and adhesion to withstand forming operations.
2. High opacity, since one-coat systems are often employed.
3. Satisfactory inter-coat adhesion if more than one coat is applied.
4. A rapid stoving schedule (usually less than 60 seconds) without impairment of properties.

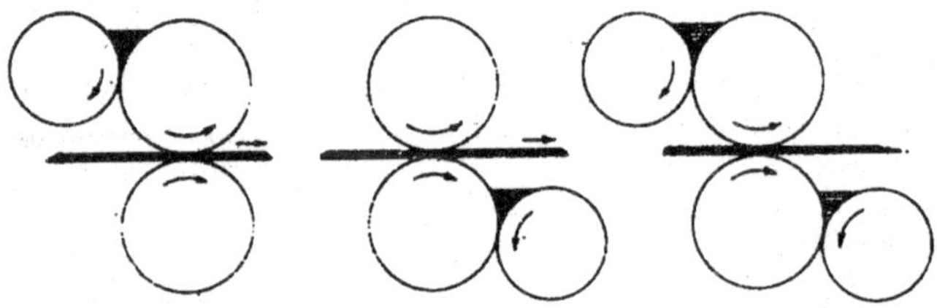

A *Top coater* B *Bottom coater* C *Double coater*

Fig 20.1 Roller coaters

Types of paint used include alkyd/amino combinations, modified alkyds, plastisols, organosols and polyvinyl fluorides. The use of aqueous coil coatings offers certain attractions, not the least being freedom from toxic and inflammable solvents.

Coated metal strip has a wide field of application, ranging from cladding for buildings to office filing cabinets and bottle tops.

Tumbling or barrel coating

This method is used to coat large numbers of small and irregular objects such as screws, nuts, clips, etc. These are placed in a barrel inclined at about 30 degrees to the vertical, and the precise amount of paint to coat the articles is added. The amount of paint required is determined accurately on a pilot run with a smaller number of objects.

After tumbling, the objects are tipped into a wire basket to flash off. If lacquered, they will dry rapidly, but oleoresinous or japanned finishes are stoved. The conventional alkyd/amino stoving enamels are unsuitable for this method of application.

Centrifuging is used for small objects such as artificial jewellery which would suffer damage in a barrel. They are placed in a wire basket, dipped, and finally centrifuged to remove surplus paint.

SPRAY METHODS

Conventional spray application

The general principle in spray application is atomization of the paint into a fine spray which is directed on to the object. A number of methods have been devised to perform this, and the earliest was the use of compressed air with a spray gun.

Spray guns

For small-scale work the paint is contained either in a cup fitted on top of the spray gun so that the paint feed is by gravity, or in a cup below the gun, from which the paint is drawn by suction. These guns are very useful if frequent colour changes are involved.

For large-scale and production work a continuous supply of paint to the gun is required. The paint is contained in a pressure vessel connected to comprrssedair and fed to the gun through pressure hose. A cut-away section of this type of gun is illustrated in Fig. 20.2. The paint leaves the needle valve and is mixed with the compressed air from jets surrounding the valve. Mixing of the paint and air can take place either outside or inside the tip of the gun, and this is determined by choice of gun fittings appropriate to the type of paint to be sprayed. A trigger mechanism controls both paint flow and compressed air and is arranged so that the air flow precedes the paint.

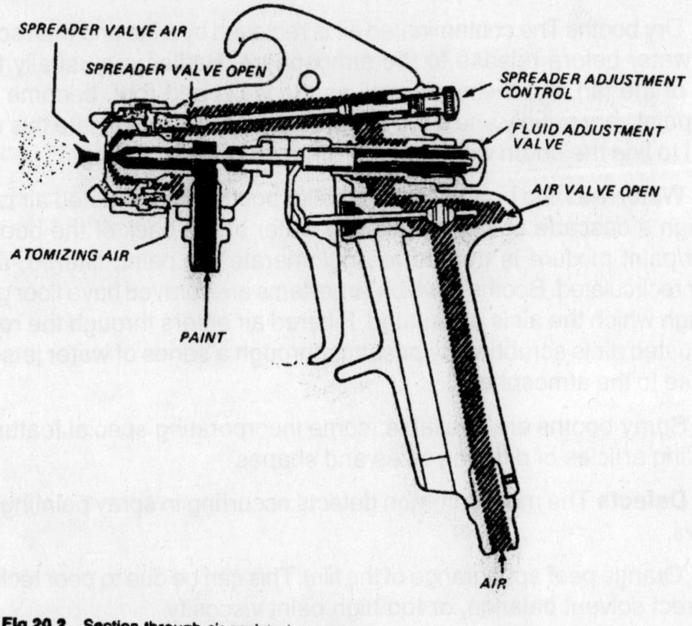

Fig 20.2 Section through air-assisted spray gun

Operation Apart from choice of the correct gun fittings, important factors are paint viscosity and air pressure. The viscosity of the paint influences the degree of atomization and the film properties. If too high, a coarse spray and orange peel film will result. If too low, it can give dry spray and a thin unsatisfactory film. The optimum spraying viscosity of a paint is characteristic of the type and can vary appreciably from one type to another.

The best air pressure is usually determined by preliminary tests, and it is essential to use the lowest pressure that will give adequate atomization. Pressures higher than this can lead to defects (below). The majority of paints can be sprayed at 40 to 601b/sq. in, but certain types require higher values.

The nature of the paint film is also determined by the distance of the gun from the surface. This should be about 9 to 12 inches and the gun should be held at right angles to the surface; movement should be in parallel lines, each overlapping the preceding one by 25 to 30 percent.

Spray booths A large volume of air passes through a conventional spray gun and there is, inevitably, a certain amount of overspray (the amount depending on the geometry of the article) together with rebound from the sprayed surface, which gives rise to 'spray fog'. To remove this paint-laden air the spraying operation may be carried out in a booth with open front and exhaust at the rear, so that the overspray is carried away as soon as it is produced. There are two general types of spray booth -'dry' and 'water washed'.

Dry booths The contaminated air is removed by a fan and then scrubbed with water before release to the atmosphere. Baffles are usually fitted in front of the fan, but these, as well as the walls and roof, become coated with-paint very rapidly and a fire hazard is created. To eliminate this risk it is usual to line the booth with paper or other strippable coating.

Water-washed booths In the smaller booths the extracted air is drawn through a cascade of slightly alkaline water at the back of the booth. The water/paint mixture is treated to agglomerate the paint, filtered, and the water recirculated. Booths in which large items are sprayed have floor gratings through which the air is exhausted. Filtered air enters through the roof. The exhausted air is scrubbed by passage through a series of water jets before release to the atmosphere.

Spray booths are available, some incorporating special features, for handling articles of differing sizes and shapes'

Defects The most common defects occurring in spray painting are as follows.

'Orange peel' appearance of the film. This can be due to poor technique, incorrect solvent balance, or too high paint viscosity.

Sagging indicating an excessively thick film. Causes are the gun being held too close to the work, or the use of excess high-boiling solvent, leading to slow set.

Dry spray The surface is rough and the paint droplets.have not coalesced to a smooth film. This can be due to excess of very volatile solvents, to too high pressure, or to holding the gun too far from the surface.

Hot spray application

When a paint is heated the viscosity is reduced, and in this state it can be sprayed at higher solids content, i.e. containing less solvent. It is not necessary to alter the basic composition of conventional spray types except to reduce the thinner content. The viscosity, measured at 25°C (77°F), will be influenced by a number of factors, but generally it is in the region of 2 to 3 poise.

The paint is heated in a special container and supplied to the gun at 60° to 71°C (140° to 160°F). Coatings of 2 to 4 mils dry-film thickness can be applied in one operation and this results in considerable savings in labour cost.

The Bede Airless Hot Spray is widely used and embodies the advantages of both systems. The pressures employed (400 to 6001b/sq.in) are considerably lower than those required by the cold airless method (below).

Airless, spray application

in this process no air passes through the spray gun but pressure is applied to the paint. The fluid pressure at the gun orifice is of the order of 1800 to 3000 1b/sq.in. (depending on the properties of the paint) and, on release, the sudden drop in pressure 'atomizes' the paint, the droplets of which are carried to the surface by their momentum. The orifice size is chosen to suit the consistency of the paint. Diameters range from 11 mils (for lower consistencies) to 21 or 23 for high consistency materials. Pressure is applied to the paint by a pump which may be operated by electricity or by compressed air. In the latter case the fluid (paint) pressure can be calculated from the expression

Fluid pressure = air pressure x pump ratio.

Heating the paint assists the atomization and produces a finer spray. It. also reduces the setting time of the film.

The use of high pressure enables high-build or thixotropic paints to be sprayed to give considerably thicker coats without sagging. The types of paint best suited to use as high-build coatings are the non-convertible (chlorinated rubber and vinyls) and chemically cured (two-pack, e.g. epoxy) types. It should be borne in mind that solvent release will be slower from the thicker films and overcoating intervals are, therefore, longer. This. does not apply, of course, to the solvent-free chemically cured (two-pack) coatings, and very thick coatings of these can be applied, the limiting factor being any tendency to sag.

A modified airless spray system is marketed under the name 'Airmix' By introducing a proportion of air the atomising pressure can be reduced from 1000-3000 psi to 200-500 psi. The slower speed of the particles results in reduced overspray and rebound and, it is claimed, produces a finer finish.

Oxidizing media, such as alkyds and oleoresinous binders, depend on absorption of oxygen for cure, and in consequence there is a limit to the thickness of film which will cure satisfactorily. With the high-build types, sufficient time must be allowed for solvent release and cure by oxidation before the film is overcoated.

The advantages of airless spray are summarized below.

1 Reduced overspray and rebound, making the process particularly suited to large areas.

2 High application rates.

3 Permits the use of high-build coatings with the result that fewer coats are required to achieve a specified film thickness, with consequent savings in labour costs.

Electrostatic spray

This process utilizes the fact that if atomized paint droplets are given a negative charge in the vicinity of a positively charged object, the droplets are attracted to, and form a uniform coating on, the exterior surfaces of the object.

This process was patented by Ransburg in the USA and named the 'Ransburg No. 1 Process'. The metal (or other conducting) articles to be painted are usually attached to a conveyor which is earthed. A system of electrodes or wires, well insulated and carrying a high negative potential of 150 000 to 200 000 volts, is fixed in a position to create an electrostatic field between the electrodes and the article. Paint droplets, produced by a conventional automatic gun, are injected into the field, whereupon they acquire a negative charge and are attracted to the earthed articles. Areas facing the electrodes are coated first with an insulating layer of paint. The charged droplets are then deposited on areas further away and, with many articles comprising cylindrical or rounded shapes, a 'wrap-round' effect results in the entire surface being coated from one side. Very few paint droplets are-lost and the operating costs are low. On the other hand, this process involves a high initial outlay and requires very careful control of paint viscosity and spray gun setting.

In the 'Ransburg No. 2 process an electrostatic field is created between the earthed articles and the gun. The paint is distributed from the edge of a disc or bell rotating at about 90 rpm and which is given a negative potential of about 90 000 volts. The paint, at a viscosity of 0.5 to 0.8 poise at 25°C (77°F) and with a resistivity within the range 400 to 500 kW, is fed to the centre of the disc by a pump and is thrown outwards and atomized as it leaves the edge. The charged droplets are attracted to the earthed objects on which a uniform wrapround coating is deposited. Many objects, except those which are large or flat, can be completely coated from one side.

In production units a horizontal disc is made to reciprocate vertically to cover large areas; large or difficult objects are taken round the disc and also rotate on their own axes to expose all surfaces to the gun.

A number of variations of this basic process have been produced. In some versions, low pressure air is used to assist the atomization, and under these conditions the voltage can be reduced. This air-assisted method has been found very suitable for electrostatic spraying of water-thinned paints.

Electrostatic spraying shows very considerable savings in paint compared with conventional spray processes, since there is virtually no overspray. The automatic nature of the process leads to very uniform results. Disadvantages are its inability to coat the insides of articles and a tendency, unless conditions are very rigidly controlled, to give hazy or orange-peel effects.

For smaller or special types of work an electrostatic hand gun can be used

Paints for electrostatic spray

A number of types can be applied by this method, but a correct solvent balance is highly important for the following reasons.

1 The evaporation rate must be slow enough for the charged droplets to reach the surface in a sufficiently fluid condition to flow out to a smooth film, but fast enough to avoid sagging. Furthermore, dry deposits must not form on the rotating discs or bells.

2 The resistivity of the paint must be sufficiently low to enable the paint droplets to acquire the maximum charge. A mixture of non-polar and polar solvents is usually employed to give a resistivity of the order of 400-500 KΩ at 20°C (68°F). Electrostatic spray is used also for the application of powder coatings

Silk screen coating

This technique is used for the application of lettering and decorative patterns to surfaces where sharp definition is required and repetitive work is involved.

The silk or other mesh is stretched tightly over a wooden frame and the stencil applied to the underside with water-soluble adhesive. The screen is placed on the surface to be treated and the ink or paint applied with a rubber or plastic squeegee.

The flow properties of the inks or paints must be controlled carefully and the types used include cellulose nitrate, drying-oil alkyds, and oleoresinous media. A thin coat is applied so pigmentation has to be high. In recent years thixotropic paints have been used. They work easily and give very sharp definition.

ELECTRODEPOSITION (also known as 'Electro-coating')

General principles

The majority of emulsions consist of a negatively charged dispersed phase, often stabilized by a water-soluble colloid. If two electrodes are immersed in an emulsion and potential difference applied, the negatively charged dispersed species will migrate to the anode (a process known as electrophoresis) where the charges are neutralized, and deposition or coagulation of the dispersed species takes place.

In the early part of this century this process was applied to the coagulation and deposition of crude rubber from the natural latices.

Later, in the 1930s, the deposition of can coatings from emulsified oleoresinous varnishes was investigated, but the process proved to be too slow for production lines.

The rapid development of electrodeposition as a viable commercial process followed the introduction of the water-soluble and the less soluble waterdispersible resins.

Until relatively recently electrodeposition was applied exclusively to the coating of metallic anodes, a process not without difficulties. Research on water-soluble resins has resulted in the production of types which can be deposited on the cathode and this process has proved to be so much more efficient than the anodic process that it has virtually replaced the latter. The anodic process is now largely of historic interest but still merits a brief description.

Anodic deposition

A range of resins, which includes modified alkyds, epoxy esters and maleinized oils, can be made water-soluble by introducing carboxyl groups followed by neutralization with ammonia or other base. In dilute aqueous solution these watersoluble resins ionize, giving a large anion embodying the resin complex (denoted by R) and the ammonium (or other) cation:

$$R.COONH_4 = R.COO^- + NH_4^+$$

When electrodes are immersed in the solution and a potential difference applied, electrophoresis takes place, the large anions migrating to the anode, where the following reactions are considered to take place.

1 Decomposition of water, yielding hydrogen ions and oxygen gas:

$$2H_2O - 2e^- \rightarrow 2OH^- + 2H^+$$
$$2OH^- \rightarrow H_2O + [O]$$
$$2[O] \rightarrow O_2\uparrow \text{ (gas evolved)}$$

2 Neutralization of the charged anion by hydrogen ion:

$$R.COO^- + H^+ \rightarrow R.COOH$$

The spongy deposit of resin is then consolidated by electro-osmosis (movement of water outwards from the mass).

Some anode metals tend to dissolve during the process, giving cations which react with the resinous anions. For example, a bare steel anode will yield ferrous ions and these react to give a coloured product:

$$2\,RCOO^- + Fe^2 \rightarrow (R.COO)_2Fe$$

This would discolour a white coating,. Phosphated steel and zinc-coated steel give no discoloration. The former yields no ions, whereas those of zinc (Zn^2+) are colourless.

Discolouration of product due to dissolution of steel anodes was one of the main drawbacks of the anodic process. Evolution of oxygen gas also caused problems. On the other hand, the water-soluble resins were cheaper to produce than those for the cathodic process.

Cathodic deposition

The article to be coated forms the cathode. The bath solution contains pigmented resinous cations or dispersed polymer. Types of binder containing amino/amide groups which are solubilised by acid.or dispersed non-ionic resins stabilised by cationic surfactants are described by Majia Precipitation or coagulation of the resin at the cathode results from the alkaline conditions at the surface.

Reactions at the cathode surface

1 Electrolysis of water, producing hydroxyl ions and hydrogen gas:

$$2H_2O \rightarrow 2H^+ + 2OH^-$$
$$2H^+ + 2e^- \rightarrow 2[H] \rightarrow H_2 \text{ (gas)}$$

2 Neutralization of charged cation (or cationic surfactant) by hydroxyl ions:

$$R-\overset{+}{\underset{\mid \atop H}{N}}-R_2 + OH^- \rightarrow R\text{-}NR_2 + H_2O$$

The range of resins employed in cationic depositions is more restricted than that used in the anionic process. Self-cross-linking properties can be built on to 'backbones' of epoxy/amine, epoxy/acrylic and epoxy/isocyanate resins, but cross linking agents may be included in the bath solution.

The advantages of cathodic electrodeposition are summarized below.

1 No dissolution of electrode. 2 No staining of pale shades. 3 Gives a hard dense coating with excellent corrosion resistance. Superior to anodically deposited films.

4 High utilisation of paint materials and no environmental contamination.

5 Excellent throwing power and hence ability to coat recessed areas difficult to treat by other methods.

POWDER COATINGS

Metal articles can be coated with certain resins by applying the powdered resin to the surface, followed by heating to melt the resin so that it flows and forms a uniform coating on the article. The method eliminates the fire and toxicity hazards associated with the use of solvent-based paints and also shows savings in cost.

There are three methods in use for application of the powders, namely (a) fluidized bed, (b) electrostatic spray, and (c) flame spraying.

Fluidized bed

The equipment is illustrated diagramatically in Fig. 20.5.

The rectangular container A is fitted with a porous plate B and inlet C for low-pressure air. The powdered resin rests on plate B. Compressed air is admitted at C, diffuses through porous plate B and then rises through the resin. The mass of powdered resin now behaves as a fluid and is said to be in a fluidized condition.

The metal article to be coated is heated to a temperature above the melting point of the resin and is then dipped in the fluidized bed. Resin particles in contact with the metal become attached by fusion, and the article is removed and passed through a stoving oven, when complete fusion of the resin takes place and a uniform coating is formed. The fluidized bed tends to give thicker coatings than the other methods.

The electrostatic fluidized bed eliminates the need to dip articles in the fluidized powder. The resin particles are given a high negative charge by means of electrodes in the container, whilst the articles are earthed. These pass over the bed of powder (or through a cloud of powder) when resin particles fly to the surface of the earthed article and are held by electrostatic attraction. The article then passes through a stoving oven to melt the resin into a uniform film. This method is suitable for continuous coating of small articles of simple shape.

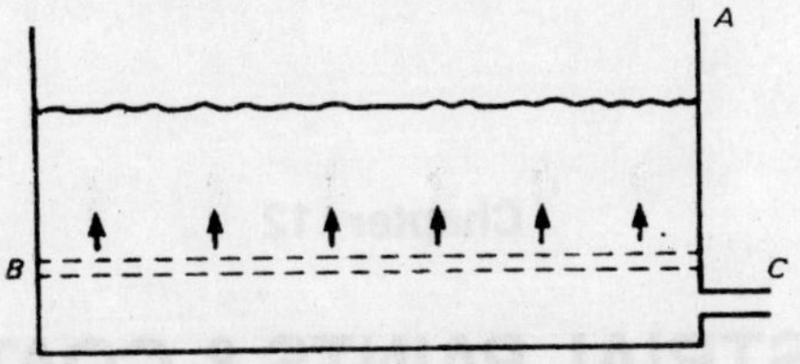

Fig 20.5 Fluidized bed for powder coating of metals

Electrostatic spray

The resin powder is blown through a special type of gun in which the particles receive a very high negative charge. The article to be coated is earthed, so that the resin particles are attracted to the surface and adhere by electrostatic attraction. The charges are lost only slowly and the article, with adherent resin, is then stoved to melt the resin into a continuous coating.

In electrostatic spraying, resin dust in the air at certain concentrations can create an explosion hazard, and precautions must be taken to ensure that no source of ignition is present.

The toxic hazard of resin dust is .matnly irritation.

Flame spraying

The resin powder is blown through the gun by compressed air. The particles are melted in a high-temperature flame and adhere well to the surface of the article. The process has been used widely with epoxy powders.

Chapter - 12

INDUSTRIAL PAINTS & COATINGS

Many industrial structures are difficult to paint, often as a consequence of difficult access or the fact that continuous processes are taking place. The paints employed, therefore, are designed to give maximum performance and durability, so that intervals between repaints are as long as possible.

UNDERCOATS FOR STRUCTURAL STEELWORK

The type of undercoat depends on the nature of the paint system chosen and this will be determined by the exposure environment and the life required. Often several coats are superimposed in one system to achieve the desired coating thickness.

Oleoresinous undercoats are employed to .a limited extent, pigmented mainly with micaceous iron oxide (MIO), in systems for the protection of bridges and other steel structures in moderate exposure conditions. They are generally applied over the PVB type of blast primer and can be self-overcoated or treated with decorative gloss finish. A typical oleoresinous/ MIO undercoat, based on a tung oil/phenolic or tung oil/modified phenolic varnish, is given below.

Oleoresinous/MI0 undercoat

	% by weight	
Micaceous iron oxide	48.0	
Wet ground mica	7.0	
Talc	5.0	
Bentone B34	1.4	pregelled
IPA 99%	0.5	pregelled
White spirit	2.0	pregelled
Tung oil/phenolic varnish (60% solids)	22.4	
White spirit .	13.0	
24% Lead naphthenate	0.3	
6% Cobalt naphthenate	0.2	
Methylethylketoxime	0.2	

Specific gravity, 1.65; solids by volume, 46%; PVC, 52%.

Undercoats of this type., containing a high percentage of lamellar micaceous iron oxide, are highly resistant to penetration by moisture and are sufficiently weather resistant to be self-overeoated and used as finishes. A brighter and more decorative finish is obtained by the addition of a small quantity (1 to 2 percent) of non-leafing aluminium pigment.

Greys and other light colours can be produced by the introduction of rutile titanium dioxide and other pigments. If a glossy decorative finish is required, the MIO undercoat can be overcoated with alkyd-type undercoat and finish or with alkyd finish only.

Other undercoats are designed for use with specific finishing systems and are described under the relevant headings.

FINISHING PAINTS: (1) NON-CONVERTIBLE

COATINGS

Chlorinated rubber

The use of chlorinated rubber paints for the protection of both structural steelwork and concrete structures has increased considerably in recent years, mainly on account of the following attractive properties.

1 Fast drying. The film is ready for overcoating as soon as the solvents have evaporated. This can be 2 to 6 hours according to the thickness of coating (high build types take appreciably longer), the volatility of the solvents, and the ambient temperature.

2 Good inter-coat adhesion. As a non-convertible coating, there is physical fusion between coats, and no difficulties are encountered in inter-coat adhesion. Furthermore there is no upper limit to overcoating intervals.

3 High resistance to moisture, alkalis, acids, a wide range of chemicals, and many solvents.

4 Good durability, resulting in maintenance intervals which are considerably longer than those with most conventional coatings.

5 One-pack systems with an indefinite storage life.

Chlorinated rubber films have the following weaknesses.

1 Difficulty with brush application. The application of chlorinated rubber primers to uneven or rough surfaces such as concrete is best carried out by brush, but brush application of further coats can result in 'pick up' due to softening of the primer. These further coats can be laid on with a full brush with no attempt to lay off, but this is wasteful and generally results in sagging on vertical surfaces. The difficulty can be mitigated to some degree by inclusion of a proportion of non-solvent, such as white spirit, which reduces the solvent power of the blend and increases the time required for softening of the primer coat.

2 Chlorinated rubber films are softened by animal fats and oils. In addition, they are dissolved by certain strong solvents, notably aromatic hydrocarbons and some esters and ketones.

Primers for chlorinated rubber systems

Alkaline surfaces The surfaces of new concrete, cement screeds and cement render are highly alkaline as well as absorbent. An effective primer/ sealer for such surfaces .can be prepared on the'following lines:

Chlorinated rubber primer/sealer (for alkaline surfaces)

	Parts by weight
Alloprene R 20 [3]	23
Cereclor 52 [3]	12
Cereclor 48 [3]	4
High aromatic solvent - (e.g. Aromasol H - ICI)	50
Methoxypropyl acetate	1
White spirit	10

Specific gravity, 1.02; volume solids, 28%,

Brushing is the preferred method of application so that 'bridging' of cavities is avoided.

Steel Whilst chlorinated rubber primers containing conventional plasticizers adhere to two-pack etch primer films, the adhesion to one-pack etch primer and to bare steel tends to be erratic. A range of chlorinated rubber primers containing rust-inhibitive pigments are available- for steelwork, but they are not used as widely as some other types.

The adhesion of chlorinated rubber primers to steel and non-ferrous metals is improved by the addition of resin, but the nature of the resin and the proportion used are of vital importance. A list of the resins which give good adhesion to steel when incorporated into chlorinated rubber primers has been compiled by Parker Certain long-oil alkyds have been found to give very satisfactory results; consequently primers for chlorinated rubber systems on steelwork are now frequently based on this mixture. The optimum ratio would appear to be two parts chlorinated rubber to one part long-oil alkyd (by weight). This type is illustrated by the following formulation:

White chlorinated rubber/alkyd primer (for airless spray application)

	% by weight
Zinc phosphate	20.3
Titanium dioxide	3.5
Barytes	4.0
Talc	5.3
Alloprene R5 chlorinated rubber [3]	11.8

Long-oil alkyd (65% solids)	9.1	
Cereclor 48 (plasticizer) [3]	2.8	
Solvesso 100 [4]	12.8	
Xylol	27.2	Pregelled with proportionof solvent
Bentone 38 [1]	2.3	
IPA 99%	0.6	
24% Lead naphthenate	0.2	
6% Cobalt naphthenate	0.1	

Specific gravity, 1.29; solids by volume, 34%; PVC, 37%.

Although formulated for airless spray application, this primer can be brushed on small areas and can be thinned for use as a blast primer. A brushing type can be prepared by increasing the proportion of high boiling aromatic solvent.

Other primers which can be used under chlorinated rubber systems are epoxy/zinc phosphate epoxy zinc-rich and inorganic zinc silicate

Chlorinated rubber/MI0 paints

Pigmentation of chlorinated rubber with lamellar micaceous iron oxide has been found to augment the already high moisture-resistance of the film and to improve the mechanical properties. The presence of the MIO also results in a reduced plasticizer demand. The following formulation for a high-build paint, which can be used both as undercoat and finish; has been suggested as a basis.

Chlorinated rubber/MI0, high build

	% by weight
Micaceous iron oxide	28.0
Barytes	6.3
Colloidal zinc oxide	0.7
Alloprene R1O [3]	14.5
Cereclor 52 [3]	5.7
Hydrogenated castor oil	1.2
Epoxidized oil	0.6
Xylol	34.0
Aromosol H [6]	9.0

Specific gravity, 1.38; solids by volume, 32%; PVC, 33%.

Paints of this type are widely used in the preservation of bridges and other steel structures which are exposed to severe environmental conditions.

Chlorinated rubber finishes

The formulation of finishes is, in the main, quite straightforward, but modifications can be made to meet special requirements. Table 21.1 illustrates two brushing-type gloss finishes and a high-build quality.

Table 21.1 Chlorinated rubber finishes: percentage composition

	White gloss	Black gloss	White high-build
Titanium dioxide, rutile	18·8	–	15·1
Carbon black	–	2·6	–
Micronized barytes	–	–	11·5
Alloprene R20 [3]	20·0	27·5	–
Alloprene R10	-	–	19·3
Cereclor 48 [3]	13·0	11·0	–
Cereclor 70	–	–	12·8
Cereclor 42	–	–	6·5
Hydrogenated castor oil	0·5	0·5	2·3
Xylol	–	3·0	27·2
High aromatic solvent [7]	39·6	47·5	5·3
White spirit	8·1	7·9	–
Specific gravity	1·19	1·04	1·36
Solids by volume	34%	29%	50%
PVC	16·6%	5·5%	17·6%

Formulations of this type allow appreciable latitude in the choice and amount of plasticizers (depending on the end use of the paint) and in the solvent blend.

Airless spray Application The white high-build formulation above yields a paint of which the consistency is too high for airless spray application. The addition of thinners to achieve spraying consistency will result in a porous film. For airless spray the solvent should contain a proportion of a higher boiling ingredient such as Methoxy propanol, and the PVC must be increased. The following formulation, quoted by Parker illustrates the type suited to airless spray.

	% by weight
Rutile titanium dioxide	12.5
Micronized barytes	12.5
Alloprene RIO [3]	12.5
Cerelor 70(3)	7.4
Cereclor 42	4.1
Hydrogenated castor oil (modified)	1.9
Methoxy propanol	9.7
Xylol	39.4

Specific gravity, 1.24; solids by volume, 31%; PVC, 24%.

The use of modified hydrogenated castor oil requires heat (42° to 45°C) (107° to 113 °F) for Gelation. It can be gelled separately in a portion of solvent, but if the paint is made in a high-speed disperser, the heat produced can be utilized. The rise in temperature occurring in ball mills is usually insufficient to gel a modified hydrogenated castor oil.

Other chlorinated rubber paints

Paints for concrete swimming pools These pools may be constructed with or without a waterproof membrane.

Pools with waterproof membrane on the outer surface of the concrete. This can take the form of bitumen, a layer of which is laid down before the bottom of the pool is cast and a thick coating is applied to the outer sides before the 'infilling' is done. Alternatively, the membrane may be thick plastic sheeting, care being taken to ensure that the joins of sheets are effectively sealed.

The purpose of this membrane is~prevention of seepage of water outwards from the pool in periods of drought or into the pool if the water table rises above the bottom of the pool. '

The concrete in these pools can be allowed to dry out thoroughly before painting. The surface of new concrete is highly alkaline (pH 11-12) and chlorinated rubber paints are used for their alkali resistance and impermeability to water. The concrete is given one or two coats (depending on the density) of chlorinated rubber primer/sealer, as described above, followed by one or two coats of chlorinated rubber finish. The following formulation is indicative of the type of finish employed.

	% by weight	
Rutile titanium dioxide	20.0	
Micronized barytes	9.8	
Alloprene R20 [3]	16.8	
Cereclor 48 [3]	11.2	
Bentone 34 [1]	0.5	Pregel with proportion of xylol
IPA 99%	0 2	
High aromatic solvent [7]	32.0	
White spirit	9.5	

Specific gravity, 1.32; solids by volume, 36%; PVC, 27%.

Pools without waterproof membrane When a membrane is not used, moisture is able to diffuse through the concrete from either side. An impermeable paint film, such as that above, could be forced off by hydrostatic pressure from the outside, particularly when the pool is empty. A permeable paint film, however, will allow the moisture to pass through without becoming detached. Such a paint can be based on the above formulation but the PVC is increased to a little above the critical point by the addition of extenders.

Chlorinated rubber is used also in the types of paint listed below:

- Flocr paints
- Road-marking paints
- Masonry finishes
- Fire-retardant paints
- Marine paints

Vinyl paints

Each primers both one- and two-pack, are generally based on polyvinyl butyral resin,

Vinyl coatings (primers, intermediate coats and finishes) are based on copolymers of vinyl chloride and vinyl acetate. Among the resins in common use are those manufactured by Union Carbide Ltd, and designated Vinylite VYHH, VYHD, VMCH, etc. The most widely used are the following.

VYHH The ratio of monomers, by weight, is approximately 87 parts vinyl chloride to 13 parts vinyl acetate. The solubility, even in strong solvent mixtures, is low; a mixture of equal weights of ketone and aromatic hydrocarbon dissolves only 15 to 20 percent (by weight) of the resin. Adhesion of the air-dried film to, metal is poor, but the film exhibits high resistance to chemical attack.

VMCH is similar in composition to VYHH but is modified with one percent dibasic acid. The presence of the carboxyl groups results in good adhesion to bare metal but can result in 'feeding' with basic pigments. This resin is recommended for air-drying maintenance paints, underwater coatings and finishes for light alloys.

VMCC is specially modified to give good adhesion to clean metal surfaces.

VAGH is partially hydrolysed and, compared with VYHH, shows wider compatibility and improved adhesion. Cross-linking properties result from the presence of hydroxyl groups. It is compatible with various types of long-oil; and short-oil drying alkyds, non-drying alkyds and certain urea- and melamineformaldehyde resins with which it will cross-link. VAGH is claimed to be the only vinyl resin which develops good adhesion on air-drying on WP 1 and other etch primers.

Formulation of vinyl paints

The vinyl co-polymers dissolve in ketones and certain esters such as propylene glycol derivatives to give solutions of low concentration. Aromatic hydrocarbons also can be incorporated. The paints usually contain a proportion of plasticizer such as tricresyl phosphate or Cereclor. The volume of solids is generally low (20 to 22 percent) so that a thixotropic agent or a thickener is required to produce a reasonable film build. Intercoat adhesion of vinyl paints is usually satisfactory, but care must be taken in the choice of resins for coatings to be applied to bare metal. For this purpose VMCH is used alone or in admixture with VYHH.

Typical formulations

Vinyl finish for metal

	% by weight
Vinylite VMCH	16.5
Tricresyl phosphate	3.3
Rutile titanium dioxide	13.2
Methylisobutyl ketone	33.0
Xylol _	33.0
'Anti-settle' [91	1.0

Specific gravity, 1.02; solids by volume, 19%; PVC, 17-4%.

This formulation yields a paint which dries to a gloss finish; the gloss can be reduced, if desired, by the incorporation of neutral extenders such as silica or talc. The low volume of solids results in a thin film; but a high-build paint, giving greater film build, can be produced by the use of Bentone or other thickening agent.

Intermediate coat (for use over etch primer)

	% by weight
Vinylite VAGH	17.4
Zinc tetroxychromate	9.0
Talc	2.7
Tricresyl phosphate	1.8
Methylisobutyl ketone	41.5
Toluene	27.6

Specific gravity, 1.0; solids by volume, 17%; PVC, 19.6%.

Properties and uses of vinyl coatings

They exhibit excellent resistance to chemicals, moisture and weather. Their solubility characteristics, however, result in paints of low solids content by volume and consequent lowfilm built. As mentioned earlier, greater film thickness can be obtained by the incorporation of gelling agents or thickeners.

The adhesion of the resins on different substrates varies considerably, and the following guide is taken from the Union Carbide literature.

Substrate	Most satisfactory resin
Clean smooth metal	VMCH, VMCC
Phosphated metal	VMCH, VMCC
Alkyd resin paint	VAGH
Vinyl butyral resin (etch primer)	VAGH
Concrete	VMCH, VMCC
Plaster	VMCH, VMCC

Vinyl coatings are used for the protection of steel, non-ferrous metals, concrete, and other surfaces exposed to very corrosive conditions. They are used also in certain types of marine paint- and anti-fouling compositions.

Bituminous paints

Bituminous paints made on straight bitumen solutions give water-resistant films and provide excellent protection for steelwork under certain conditions. Their principal use is protection of underground and submerged steelwork where highbuild types are often an advantage.

On exposure to weather, bitumen films undergo surface oxidation and hardening, while the underlying material remains soft. The surface then develops the familiar crazed pattern. The weather resistance of bitumen is improved by the introduction of drying. oil, and still further improvement is conferred by long-oil alkyds. The following formulations illustrate the three types:

Bituminous aluminium paint is used widely on roofs. The leafing of the aluminium provides a heat- and light-reflective surface and also improves the durability of the bitumen. The paint is used also as a barrier coat in the protection of ships bottoms.

(2) CONVERTIBLE COATINGS

Alkyd base

Paint systems based on medium- and long-oil alkyd resins are used extensively in general building and decorative work. Similar systems are used in industrial maintenance work where exposure conditions are relatively mild and decorative finish is required. Here the resins employed are usually of the medium-oil length to give shorter drying times and greater hardness. In many cases these medium oil length alkyds have shown better durability than the long-oil counterparts.

Formulation of alkyd undercoats and finishes for maintenance work follows lines similar to those for the decorative types,

Bituminous black

	% by weight
80/90 Bitumen	60·0
High aromatic solvent [7]	20·0
White spirit	20·0

Specific gravity, 0·97
Solids by volume, 53%

Bituminous black, oil modified

	% by weight
Gilsonite	30·7
Mexphalt	7·3
Boiled linseed oil	9·7
High aromatic solvent [7]	18·7
White spirit	33·3
24% Lead naphthenate	0·2
6% Cobalt naphthenate	0·1

Specific gravity, 0·92
Solids by volume, 41%

Bituminous black, alkyd modified

	% by weight
80/90 Bitumen	26·3
Long-oil alkyd solids	18·4
White spirit	36·6
High aromatic solvent [7]	18·0
24% Lead naphthenate	0·5
6% Cobalt naphthenate	0·2

Specific gravity, 0·9; solids by volume, 37%.

Silicone/alkyd co-polymers. These are used in place of unmodified alkyds in situations wnere a decorative system combined with long term durability is required. The co-polymer must contain 30 percent silicone to be effective. Formulation follows lines similar to those for the decorative types but they are more expensive.'

Alkyd/Chlorinated rubber The addition of a proportion of chlorinated rubber to certain long-oil alkyds results in an upgrading of both chemical and moisture resistance. The optimum effect is obtained from a mixture of three parts alkyd solids to one part chlorinated rubber.

This blend is used in quick-drying primers for alkyd systems and in marine fishes. A gloss finish is illustrated by the following formulation:

White alkyd/chlorinated rubber finish

	% by weight
Rutile titanium dioxide	18.4
Long-oil alkyd (70% solids)	36.4
Chlorinated rubber	8.5
High aromatic solvent	35.9
24% Lead naphthenate	0.5
6% Cobalt naphthenate	0.2
Methylethylketoxime	0.1

Specific gravity, 1.1; solids by volume, 36%; PVC, 14%.

Epoxy eaters

These are used as binders for primers, undercoats and finishes and can be blended with alkyds of the appropriate oil length to upgrade the chemical resistance and to shorten the drying time.

The air-dried epoxy ester films show good adhesion to most common substrates, good flexibility, and good resistance to chemicals and many solvents. Their resistance properties lie between those of alkyds and those of the two-pack epoxy systems. Complete epoxy ester systems have shown very good durability on storage tanks in both marine and industrial environments. The following formulations indicate the general composition of an epoxy ester undercoat and finish:

Epoxy ester undercoat (brushing)	**% by weight**	**Epoxy ester finish (brushing)**	**% by weight**
Rutile titanium dioxide	21.1	Rutile titanium dioxide	26.2
Micronized barytes	11.3	Micronized talc	1.2
China clay	6.2	Epoxy ester (60% solids)	47.9
Epoxy ester (60% solids)	37.7	Aromatic Solvent	3.4
Aromatic solvent	2.9	White spirit	21.1
White spirit	20.6	6% Cobalt drier	0.2
6% Cobalt drier	0.2		
Specific gravity,	1.22	Specific gravity,	1.10
Solids by volume, 37.5%		Solids by volume, 34%	
PVC, 33.1%		PVC, 22-6%	

Two-pack systems

Film formation in two-pack,systems results from chemical reaction between the two components' which are mixed immediately before use. The reaction commences in the container and the mixture, in consequence, possesses a limited pot-life. Reaction in the film takes place more rapidly as solvent evaporation results in an increasing concentration of reacting molecules.

Epoxies

An epoxy resin is produced by reaction between epichlorhydrin and diphenylol propane; the curing or cross-linking agent (sometimes referred to as 'hardener') can be a polyamine, amine adduct, polyamide or isocyanate. The pot-life of the mixed components depends on the type ,of resin modification and curing agent. The amount mixed should be capable of being used within the pot-life period; any material remaining unused at the end of the period should be discarded and not added to a new mix.

Since the curing of an epoxy resin film is a chemical reaction between resin and hardener, atmospheric oxygen is not involved, and there is, in theory, no upper limit to the thickness of coating which can be cured. The thickness is, however, controlled by other factors, the most important of which are the tendency to sag by thick films on a vertical surface and solvent retention by the film. Complete loss of solvent from a thick film can take a very considerable time. Nevertheless, the high build types of two-pack epoxy paints are used extensively. Solvent-free coatings are produced by the use of low molecularweight liquid resins and liquid hardeners.

When applied at 20°C (68°F) epoxies can be overcoated at not less than four hours and not more than 48 hours after application. If the overcoating is delayed beyond this time the film will have hardened to a degree when intercoat adhesion is likely to be poor, unless the first coat is abraded to provide a key.

A curing period of up to 7 days is usually required for the development of the maximum chemical and solvent resistance. The rate of cure is markedly influenced by temperature, and when amines or polyamides are used as curing agents, the material should not be applied when the ambient temperature is below 7°C (44°F). Actually curing becomes progressively slower as the temperature falls below 10°C (50°F). The use of isocyanate as curing agent allows epoxies to be applied and cured at temperatures down to 0°C.

Typical formulations

Primers for metal

Other epoxy-based primers include red lead (now being phased out on toxicity grounds), zinc phosphate and red oxide/zinc chrome. The following formulations illustrate the general composition:

Zinc phosphate/epoxy primer

Base	*% by weight*	
Zinc phosphate	38.4	
Titanium dioxide	8.5	
Talc	6.9	
Bentone B27	0.3	Pregelled with proportion of toluol
n-Butanol	1.7	
Epoxy resin 70% solution in xylol	16.7	
Methylethylketone	7.8	
Toluol	7.8	
Hardener		
Polyamide solution	8.4	
Methylethylketone	1.8	
Toluol	1.7	

Specific gravity (of mixed components), 1.53; solids by volume (of mixed components), 49%; PVC (of mixed components), 50%.

Red oxide/zinc chrome/epoxy primer

Base	% by weight	
Red oxide of iron	31.7	
Zinc chrome	9.0	
Talc	5.9	
Bentone B27	0.8	Pregelled with proportion of toluol
n-Butanol	1.8	
Epoxy resin,70% solution in xylol	16.6	
Methylethylketone	10.0	
Toluol	10.0	
Hardener		
Polyamide solution	8.4	
Methylethylketone	3.0	
Toluol	2.8	

Specific gravity (of mixed components), 1.44; solids by volume (of mixed components), 41%; PVC (of mixed components), 43%.

. Both these materials are used extensively as blast primers. They can be applied by airless spray, dry rapidly, and adhere tenaciously to blast-cleaned steel.

Epoxy finishes

These are produced in white, black, and a full range of colours, the pigments being dispersed in the resin phase. The curing agents can be polyamines, amine adducts, polyamides or isocyanates. Polyamines and amine adducts give the greatest chemical resistance; the amine adducts are the less toxic and the less unpleasant in use. Polyamides give greater film flexibility and water resistance. There is also more latitude in the ratio of curing agent to resin than exists With the polyamines. The following formulations illustrate the general composition of standard and high-build epoxy finishes.

Standard epoxy finish, white

Base	***% by weight***	
Rutile titanium' dioxide	27.0	
Epikote 1001	23.2	
Xylol	14.6	
Methoxy propanol	10.1	
isoButanol	1.7	Pregelled with proportion of xylol
Bentone B34	0.4	
Hardener		

Versamid 115X	16.4
Xylol	3.3
Methoxy propanol	3.3

Base and Hardener are mixed in the proportions shown.

Specific gravity (of mixed components), 1.22 solids by volume (of mixed components), 46%; PVC (of mixed components), 18%.

High build epoxy finish (for airless spray)

Base	*% by weight*	
Rutile titanium dioxide	23.0	
Micronized barytes	16.8	
Talc	4.9	
Epikote 1001 [14]75% solution in xylol	26.9	
Bentone B38 [i]	1.6	Pregelled with proportion of xylol
isoButanol	1.3	
Xylol	5.6	
Methoxy propanol	1.0	
Hardener		
Versamid 115X [12]	13.5	
Xylol	3.8	
isoButanol	1.6	

Specific gravity (of mixed components), 1.5; solids by volume (of mixed components), 57%; PVC (of mixed components), 29%.

Sotventless coatings By the use of low-viscosity liquid epoxy resins and lowviscosity hardeners, it is possible to dispense with the use of solvents. The fire hazard is virtually eliminated and the paints can be applied in thick films which do not shrink on drying; a high degree of protection is thereby achieved. Solventless coatings are used also for underwater application to steelwork and for the interiors of storage tanks and other vessels.

General properties of two-pack epoxy systems

Overcoating times Epoxy resins cure to extremely hard films, and overcoating times are restricted. They can be overcoated after minimum periods of 4 to 16 hours from time of application, the period depending on the resin and type of paint. Overcoating must not be delayed for more than 48 hours, since the film will then be very hard and abrasion will be necessary to promote adhesion.

Resistance The films show outstanding resistance to chemicals, solvents and abrasion. They tend to chalk on exterior exposure.

Adhesion to the majority of surfaces is outstanding, provided they are clean.

Uses Blast and holding primers for steelwork; finishes for structural steelwork and concrete where high resistance to chemicals and solvents is required: marine paints; flooring compositions; adhesives.

Epoxylpitch coatings

Epoxy resins can be diluted with certain grades of coal-tar pitch and the mixture can be cured by the normal curing agents. Extenders are usually incorporated to give high-solids products which are appreciably cheaper than the straight epoxies. They are applied by brash or airless spray to give thick films which are usually sag resistant up to 190°C (374°F). The films are tough and show excellent resistance to dilute acids, water and alkalis, but the resistance to solvents is lower than that of the undiluted resins. The following formulation is presented to show the general composition:

Epoxy/pitch coating

Base	*% by weight*	
Special pitch No. 4	33.6	
Epoxy resin solution	19.4	
Silica	1.9	
Talc	23.1	
Xylol	3.4	
Bentone B34	2.4	pregelled with xyloi
isoButanol	3.1	
Hardener		
Versamid 115X	10.0	
isoButanol	1.2	
Xylol	1.9	

Specific gravity (of mixed components), 1 - 27; solids by volume (of mixed components), 68%.

The relative proportions of pitch, resin/hardtner and extender can be varied, but any appreciable variation will be reflected in the properties.

Uses of epoxy/pitch coatings

They are used on steel and concrete surfaces which are exposed to severe conditions where protection rather than decoration is the prime consideration.

These include ships' bottoms, piers and pilings, lock gates, barrages, piping, dams and sewers.

Polyurethane coatings

These are two-pack materials consisting of a pigmented polyester or polyester/polyol mixture cured by reaction with an isocyanate. A wide choice of polyesters and polyols is available to produce films varying in elasticity and hardness from coatings suitable for soft rubber articles to tough, abrasion-resistant floor finishes. The use of aromatic di-isocyanates as second component produces films which yellow on exterior exposure. This defect can be avoided by the use of aliphatic di-isocyanates.

Polyurethane films show good weather-resistance and high resistance to abrasion. They show, also, outstanding resistance to chemicals and solvents.

The fact that any desired degree of flexibility can be built into the film, coupled with the intrinsically high durability,' has resulted in the widespread use of polyurethanes on exterior woodwork as well as metals. For use on wood they can incorporate the flexibility required to accommodate the dimensional changes which take place. Advantage is taken of their excellent durability in marine work where they are used as finishes on both steel and aluminium superstructures. The primer employed for aluminium is frequently a two-pack etch followed by zinc chrome primer, whilst for steel a two-pack epoxy primer is commonly used.

The following formulation illustrates the general composition of a polyurethane finish which exhibits good non-yellowing properties, gloss retention and weather resistance:

White polyurethane finish

Part A	***% by weight***
Rutile titanium dioxide	16.0
Desmophen 650	35.3
Cellulose acetobutyrate, 10% solution in Methoxypropyl acetate	8.3
Methoxypropyl acetate	8.2
Xylol	3.7
Part B	
Desmodur N75	28.5

Specific-gravity (of mixed components), 1.19, solids by volume (of mixed components), 49%; PVC (of mixed components), 10%.

PAINTING SPECIFICATIONS

It is generally agreed that the average life of a paint system on exposed iron and steel structures is considerably less than the potential life and this is frequently attributed, in the majority of cases quite erroneously, to deficiencies in the paint. An analysis of the causes of film breakdown has shown, however, that whilst the paint may occasionally be at fault, other factors also exert a major influence on the life of a paint system. Among these are the following.

1 Condition of the surface. Before painting, steel surfaces must be clean and free from scale, rust, grease and general dirt. Application of paint to a dirty or partly cleaned surface will result in poor adhesion and early failure.

2 The weather conditions under which application and drying take place. Painting at site is often dogged by adverse weather conditions such as low temperatures, mist, fog or high humidity. In consequence, items of new work are blast-cleaned and then painted, as far as possible, at the fabricator's works. 3 The paint film must be of uniform and adequate thickness. The protection afforded by a paint film is, within limits, proportional to the film thickness, and the maximum figure depends on the type of paint and exposure conditions. For exposed steelwork this can range from 150 to 300 micrometres (6 to 12 mils). 4 The location of the structure, i.e. industrial, marine or rural.

5 The design of the structure. It should be free from pockets or grooves which can retain dirt and moisture and-from sharp edges which are difficult to coat satisfactorily.

6 The paint may, for some reason, be unsuitable.

In order to achieve maximum protection of exposed steelwork it is essential to prepare a detailed painting specification and, in major works, to employ independent painting inspectors to supervise all stages of the work.

Chapter - 13

INDUSTRIAL FINISHES

The term 'industrial finish' covers a broad spectrum of coatings which are usually factory applied to a wide variety of articles.

Industrial finishes comprise both convertible and non-convertible coatings and differ from the decorative types in the following particulars.

1 The drying and curing times are very much shorter to satisfy mass production schedules. Methods used to attain this include the use of shorter oil media, more rapidly evaporating solvents, and the use of accelerated curing methods such as stoving and irradiation.

2 The resistance to impact, abrasion and general mechanical damage is greater.

3 The resistance to chemicals and solvents is of a higher order.

4 In many instances, the weather resistance is not of paramount importance. 5 They often have to withstand considerable temperature fluctuations or very high temperatures.

6 A high proportion of industrial finishes are applied to metal, either directly or over a primer.

For the purpose of the present discussion it is convenient to make a broad division into air-drying and stoving types, the former including lacquers, conventional air-drying, and chemically cured types; the last-mentioned can also be stoved.

AIR-DRYING TYPES

Lacquers and non-convertible coatings

Cellulose Nitrate Lacquers The principal use of pigmented cellulose nitrate lacquers is now in car refinishing and reproduction furniture. The resistance to heat and solvents of these lacquers can be improved by the use of modifiers and these improved lacquers are used on domestic furniture made from wood or wood-veneered chipboard."

Chlorinated rubber paints

Chlorinated rubber paints are used for the protection of steel and other vulnerable materials which are continuously exposed to water and/or chemicals. Examples are plant in plating shops, chemical plant, sewerage and water works.

Acrylic lacquers The acrylic resins used in solutions are polymers of methacrylic acid esters or co-polymers of, for example, methyl methacrylate and an acrylic ester such as methyl acrylate. A number of esters are available and, by judicious selection, it is possible to produce polymers with any desired degree of hardness and flexibility.

The resins are usually colourless and are soluble in esters, ketones, etheralcohols and aromatic hydrocarbons.

Drying of the films is by solvent evaporation only. The films show good gloss retention, good durability (in this respect they are superior to cellulose nitrate) and good resistance to lubricating oils and greases. Resistance to water is only fair. The films are resistant to heat (with only slight discoloration) up to 180°C (356°F).

A white acrylic gloss finish can be made on the following formulation:

	% by weight
Rutile titanium dioxide	16.5
Acrylic solution (55 %) [2]	43.3
Xylol	40.2

Specific gravity, 1.05, solids by volume, 28%; PVC, 15%.

Uses of acrylic lacquers These lacquers have a wide field of application which includes media-for metallic and fluorescent paints, clear lacquers for metal and sealers for sprayed metal, aircraft components, protective lacquer for vacuum-deposited metals, and pigmented finishes for kitchen cabinets and washing machines. Acrylic resins also form the basis of finishes for certain types of plastic articles.

Vinyl lacquers. They are based on co-polymers of vinyl chloride and vinyl acetate and are used where a high degree of resistance to chemical attack is required.

Cellulose acetate is used in strippable coatings which may be clear or pigmented. The following formulation gives a clear coating of this type:

	% by weight
Cellulose acetate	16.6
Diacetin	12.0
Acetone	66.0
IMS 64 O.P.	5.4

Shellac solutions in methylated spirit are pigmented, usually with bright non toxic pigments, and used on wooden playthings such as children's bricks. pigmentation follows normal procedure and for articles of uniform shape application is often by tumbling.

Shellac varnish provides a rapid drying film with high build and gloss. It is often used on timber to improve appearance and to reduce water penetration for limited periods.

The following is a typical formula:

	% by weight
Orange lac	42.5
Raw castor oil	2.5
Ethyl cellulose	2.1
IMS 64 O.P.	53.1

Convertible coatings,

Oxidizing types

Alkyd resins are probably the most widely used binders for industrial airdrying paints, especially in the medium- and short-oil. types. They are used alone, in modified form (VT or acrylic modifications), or in admixture with other resins such as chlorinated rubber, acrylic or expoxy ester. Tung oil and phenolic modified types possess excellent resistance to lubricating and cutting oils and are therefore suited to machinery finishes. Rapid air-drying primers and finishes can be based on short VT modified alkyds. For example, a grey oilresisting machinery enamel can be based on the following general lines:

	% by weight
Rutile titanium dioxide	19.2
Carbon black	0.7
Coated calcium carbonate	1.9
VT Alkyd solution (50% solids)	56.7
Xylol	11.2
Solvesso 100	10.0
6% Cobalt naphthenate	0.5

Specific gravity, 1.4, solids by volume, 35%; PVC, 19%; drying time, 1-2 hours: this can be reduced by replacement of Solvesso 100 by xylol.

Epoxy esters are used to upgrade the chemical and moisture resistance of long oil alkyds. They are also used alone, when they show very good adhesion to many surfaces and moderate to good resistance to chemicals. The linseed types exhibit good durability and have given satisfactory service as media for paints for steel storage tanks and gas holders. The DCO types give very hard and abrasion resistant films and are used in floor paints.

Straight epoxy esters are compatible with white spirit and dipentene and so can be applied by brush. This may be the most convenient method of application on some types of plant.

The following is a typical formulation for a brushing type of white base machinery enamel:

	% by weight
Rutile titanium dioxide	26.0
Coated calcium carbonate	1.9
Epoxy ester solution	47.6
Dipentene	8.1
White spirit	16.2
Cobalt naphthenate (6%)	0.2

Chemically cured coatings

The acid-cured alkyd/amino and the hydroxylated acrylic/isocyanate systems are described below. The other important members of this class are the polyesters, polyurethanes and epoxies.

Acid-cured alkyd amino systems

The use of certain acids or acidic materials as catalysts enables cure of alkyd/amino systems to be effected at normal temperatures.

The ratio of non-drying alkyd to amino resin is usually between 1.5:1 and 1:1 (by weight). Cure is effected by addition of controlled amounts of hydrochloric acid or acid butyl phosphate. Other acids, chiefly sulphuric and p-toluenesulphonic, are sometimes used.

Hydrochloric acid is very efficient and is added, in solution in ethanol or butanol, at the rate of 2%-5% (calculated as concentrated acid) on the weight of solid amino resin. At the higher concentration the pot-life of the mixture is very short. A drawback to the use of hydrochloric acid is the corrosion which can take place on metallic substrates.

Corrosion of metallic substrates can be avoided by the use of acid butyl phosphate as catalyst. It has a longer pot-life than systems using hydrochloric acid and is used at about 10 percent on the amino resin solids.

The acid-cured alkyd/amino systems yield films which are very tough, adherent and resistant to many solvents and other liquids. They are used, inter alia, for bar and counter tops.

Acrylic-isocyanate systems

Reaction between an hydroxylated acrylic resin and an isocyanate produces a binder possessing good durability and gloss retention. It is used in fast drying furniture finishes and in coatings for motor car refinishing.

STOVING TYPES

The application of heat to wet films of certain types of resin or resin mixtures accelerates the cross-linking reactions, and cure of the film takes place rapidly, often in a matter of minutes. This enables mass-produced articles, from small components to motor car bodies, to be painted and cured on a production line basis.

Stoving cannot be applied to the long-oil types of resin used in air-drying decorative and maintenance paints.

Primers Industrial stoving primers are, to a large degree, based on short/medium oil-length straight or modified alkyds. As an example, the widely used Red Oxide/zinc chrome primer can be produced on a formulation of the following type:

	% by weight
Red iron oxide	29.0
Zinc chrome, Type~2 BS 282, 389 [5]	8.2
Zinc oxide	1.9
Micronized talc	2.4
Whiting	1.9
VT Alkyd (50% solids)	31.5
Aromosol H [6]	16.6
Xylol	8.5

Specific gravity, 1.39, solids by volume, 35%; PVC, 42.7%.

This primer is used on steel articles and gives a tough, adherent film when stoved (convention oven) at 120°C (248°F) for ½ to ¾ hour.

Since zinc chrome is being phased out on toxicity grounds the coloured pigments in the above formula can be replaced by zinc phosphate. In many painting systems the use of a pale shade primer is an advantage. If corrosion is not likely to be a major problem, titanium dioxide can be used as the opacifying pigment. Modified alkyd binders are likely to give some discolouration but this can be avoided by the use of an alkyd/amino combination.

Alternatively, if stringent conditions such as hot detergents are likely to be met, a melamine/epoxy combination is preferable. The following primer is based on this type of medium and produces a tough, adherent and resistant film when stoved at 140°C (284°F) for about 10 minutes.

	% by weight
Titanium dioxide	14.8
Blanc fixe	13.6
Micronized talc	13.6
Beetle BE 649 [7]	29.2
Xylol	25.3
n-Butanol	3.5

Specific gravity, 1.33, solids by volume, 36.7%; PVC, 42.4%.

Primers of this type are used on certain types of domestic equipment such as washing machines and dish washers where detergent resistance is of paramount importance.

Finishes

Stoving finishes can be produced in a large number of possible resin combinations according to the degree of gloss, flexibility, adhesion, chemical resistance, etc. required.

Alkyd/amino resins Combinations of non-drying alkyds and ureaformaldehyde resins are the most widely used. Pigmentation is on conventional lines, the pigment usually being ball-milled into the alkyd solution. In whites where titanium dioxide is the standard pigment, the pigment/binder ratio is 0.6 to 0.8/1. Other pigments are used at concentrations similar to those used in decorative enamels.

The gloss and mar resistance of these finishes can be improved, if necessary, by replacement of part of the mixed resins by a medium/short drying alkyd based on dehydrated castor oil.

The following formulation illustrates a typical alkyd-U/F medium suitable for stoving at 120°C (248°F) for, 30 minutes or at 240°C (464°F) for 3½ minutes:

	% by weight
Rutile titanium dioxide	23.1
U/F resin solution (53%)	25.7
Non-drying alkyd solution (50%)	28.2
Aromosol H [6]	4.7
Xylol	16.3
n-Butanol	1.2
Ethyl lactate	0.8

Specific gravity, 1.14; solids by volume, 35%; PVC, 19.0%.

Ethyl lactate is added to promote secondary flow in the stoving oven and so eliminates surface imperfections.

Mixtures of non-drying alkyds and melamine-formaldehyde resins give finishes with high gloss and a high degree of resistance to heat and chemicals. The ratio of alkyd to amino resin is higher than in the alkyd/urea combinations. The following formulation illustrates an alkyd/melamine finish:

	% by weight
Rutile titanium dioxide	22.5
Beetle BE 615 [7]	15.0
Synolac 9063X [8]	45.0
Xylol	17.5

Specific gravity, 1.16, solids by volume, 38.3%; PVC, 17.0%.

The alkyd/amino stoving types formed the basis of finishes for refrigerators, washing machines and other kitchen equipment for some time, but in recent years an appreciable amount of epoxy resin has been incorporated. This has the effect of upgrading the adhesion and general resistance of the finishes. Additions of melamine/epoxy resins can be made to the alkyd/amino combinations, but for high chemical and solvent resistance the former can be used alone.

The following formulation illustrates an epoxy-reinforced type, though the proportion of epoxy to melamine resin can be varied to suit circumstances:

	% by weight
Titanium dioxide	22.9
Uramex P138 [9]	12.9
Uralac 1308X [91	38.2
Beetle 649 [7]	7.7
Xylene	18.3

Specific gravity, 1 - 16, solids by volume, 38-4%; PVC, 17-4%.

High solids coatings based on blends of melamine (HMMM) and polyesters are stated to possess outstanding durability and chemical resistance. They are claimed to be superior to conventional alkyd systems and are suggested for use as automobile finishing coats.

Epoxy resins can be reacted- with amino (chiefly melamine/formaldehyde) and with phenolic resins to give products which cure on stoving. With melamine/formaldehyde, the product is a very pale resin suitable for white finishes which possess very high resistance to wear and chemicals. An example is Beetle BE 649 mentioned above. The reaction with phenolic resins yields films with high resistance and adhesion but possessing poor colour. These are used as coatings for the interior of cans and drums.

The cure of epoxy resins by polyamines or polyamides, a reaction which is relatively slow at ambient temperature, is accelerated considerably by the application of heat.

Vinyl resins

Probably the most versatile of these are the copolymers of vinyl acetate and vinyl chloride which produce films with excellent toughness and flexibility but which are not resistant to temperatures above 150°C (302°F). The films are resistant to oils and greases, water, many chemicals and many solvents. They are used for container linings, chemicalresistant finishes, coatings for collapsible tubes, and in ships' bottom compositions.

The protective value is a function of the coating thickness, and hot spray application has been used to produce thicker coats. Considerably greater thickness of coating has been achieved by the use of plasticized polyvinyl chloride.

Plastisols are dispersions of polyvinyl chloride in plasticizer. They are of high consistency and are frequently referred to as 'PVC pastes'. These materials can be pigmented, but the pigments used must be resistant to the stoving temperature of 171° to 193°C (340° to 380°F).

Organosols are dispersions of polyvinyl chloride in plasticizer and solvent. The polyvinyl chloride is not soluble in the plasticizer at normal temperatures, but on stoving, the plasticizer is absorbed by and softens the PVC so that the particles sinter or fuse, forming a very hard and highly resistant coating. The stoving temperatures are in the region of 171 ° to 193°C (340° to 380°F). Under these conditions relatively thipk coatings can be applied in a textured or smooth finish according to the type of plasticizer and the stoving temperature.

Unfortunately these films have shown very poor adhesion to metal and have to be applied over a primer which is usually based on two-pack epoxy resin. Plastisols and organosols are used where hard wear is encountered, such as heavy test equipment and office furniture. They are frequently applied by the coil coating process.

Water-borne coatings Most polymer emulsions are air-drying but stoving is the normal method of cure for the majority of water-soluble and waterdispersible systems which are applied by either conventional methods or electrodeposition.

Silicone resins require temperatures in the region of 200° to 230°C (392° to 446°F) for satisfactory cure: They are used when resistance to high temperatures is required, and when pigmented with aluminium will give protection up to 600°C (1112°F). It is probable that before this temperature is reached the silicone resin has decomposed and the aluminium has been sintered to the surface. These paints are used on exhaust manifolds and steel chimney stacks. Their general composition it illustrated by the following formulation:

	% by weight
Silicone resin (50% in xylol)	17.6
Ethyl cellulose	1.8
Aromosol H -	55.9
Polished aluminium paste (78%)	24.6
Manganese naphthenate solution	0.1

Specific gravity, I.07, solids by volume, 17%.

The production of high temperature resisting blacks using polyalkoxysilane binders and a range of metal oxide pigments has been investigated by Bhatia et al. They found that cobalt oxide, manganese dioxide or a 1:1 mixture showed the best heat resistance (330°-500°C) and film properties.

Flamboyant finishes are two-coat systems in which a coloured transparent lacquer is applied over an aluminium base coat. The base coat contains nonleafing aluminium in a conventional alkyd/amino medium and the latter is also used for the coloured lacquer. The colour in the lacquer is provided by a soluble dyestuff which is fast to light and stoving. The general effect is that of a brilliant coloured metal with a deep gloss and it is popular on cycles. Formulations can be based on the following:

Aluminium base for flamboyant finish

	% by weight
Synolac 9063X ,	43.0
Uramex P 138	29.8
Xylene	21.1
n-Butanol	2.6
Fine non-leafing aluminium paste	3.5
Specific gravity, 0.98.	

Flamboyant finish	*% by weight*
Synolac 9063X	38.9
Uramex P 138	34.7
Xylene	14.4
Ethoxy propanol	5.0
n-Butanol	3.3
Dyestuff	3.7
Specific gravity,	0.98

Polychromatic finishes are pigmented or dyed stoving finishes to which is added a small quantity of non-leafing aluminium paste. The dyes or pigments must be fast to light and stoving. The general effect is a coloured metallic sheen; it is used for cars as well as cycles.

Wrinkle finishes, Early types were made on tung oil oleoresinous varnishes to which a proportion of raw tung oil was sometimes added, and the pattern was dependent on the gas-checking of the tung oil medium in a foul oven in the presence of cobalt and manganese driers. The texture of the wrinkle depended on the thickness of the coat.

Modern types are based on short-oil alkyds of the linseed/tung oil or linseed/DCO types. With these media the size and pattern of the wrinkle can be controlled to a greater degree than with oleoresinous media. The nature of the wrinkle is influenced by the pigmentation and the type of extenders used.Surface coated calcium carbonate enables great control to be exercised over the pattern. The texture of the wrinkle is also influenced by temperature, becoming finer as the temperature'rises.

These finishes are applied by spraying and can be stoved in any of the conventional type ovens. The following formulation is typical of a wrinkle finish:

	% by weight
Short linseed/tung alkyd (60% solids)	46.9
Carbon black	1.9
Diatomaceous silica	4.7
Xylol	46.5

Cobalt and manganese naphthenates are added to give 0.3 percent cobalt metal and 0.1 percent manganese metal on the resin solids.

Wrinkle finishes of this type are stoved for about 1 hour at 120°C (248°F). They are used mainly on instruments of various types and on typewriters, but have been displaced to a- considerable degree by hammer finishes. A serious drawback of wrinkle finishes is the tendency of the pattern to collect dust which cannot readily be removed.

Flock finishes are produced by application of a fairly heavy coat of oleoresinous varnish designed to remain very tacky for some time after'loss of solvent. The nylon or silk flock is then sprayed through a special type of spray gun.

Polyurethanes

They can be cold-cured, though the curing process can be accelerated by stoving. This also increases the hardness and general resistance of the film but also causes some yellowing. Generally, polyurethanes are stable only up to 150°C (302°F).

The stoved films show a high degree of adhesion, and resistance to chemicals and a number of solvents. Among their uses are corrosion-inhibiting primers for steel, interior coatings for tanks and drums, and finishes for chemical plant.

Stoving phenolic resins These are heat-reactive, alkali-catalysed resins in which the polymerization reaction has been terminated before the resin becomes insoluble in solvents. The resins are supplied as solutions in an alcohol, a solvent of the Cellosolve type, or a mixture. They are usually applied in non-pigmented form, and the article then being stoved when the polymerization reaction is completed. The films show excellent solvent- and corrosion-resistance and are employed as linings for cans and drums..

Hammer finishes These are so-called because they give the surface the general appearance of hammered metal. In this way they mask minor irregularities in the surface'and at the same time produce a pleasing appearance.

The hammer pattern can be produced either by using a carefully selected blend of solvents with a rapid drying medium such as a short-oil alkyd or by addition of certain silicone oils to a conventional type of stoving medium. The latter gives the more satisfactory' and consistent result and is generally employed. Pigmentation is by non-leafing aluminium at low concentration.

The following formulation illustrates the base paint for hammer finishes:

	% by weight
Butylated urea-formaldehyde resin (50% solids)	22.7
Short-oil DCO alkyd (60% solids)	68.1
Non-leafing aluminium paste	1.9
Xylol	4.9
n-Butanol	2.4

Silicone oils designed specifically to give the hammer effect are added in small quantity. The amount is critical, the size of the pattern varying inversely with the amount of silicone added. Too much silicone leads to cissing.

Application of hammer finishes is by spray at higher viscosities than used with conventional paints so as to minimize sagging on vertical surfaces. The viscosity range is 1-2 poise at 20°C (68°F). The articles are then stoved at 220°F (104°C) for about half an hour.

Coloured hammer finishes are produced by addition of conventional stainers to the above base paint. The quantity of stainers required is very small.

Uses Hammer finishes are used extensively on instruments, typewriters, office furniture such as filing cabinets, and sheet-metal work generally. They wear well and do not collect dirt to the same degree as wrinkle finishes.

Thermosetting acrylic systems

The film properties of these systems are controlled by the nature of the comonomers, the molecular weight, and the type of cross-linking mechanism.

One of the most widely used systems consists of reaction between an hydroxylated acrylic and a butylated melamine/formaldehyde resin. The. combination cures in 30 minutes at 120°C and is used as a motor car finish. The film shows excellent durability and gloss retention.

Hydroxylated acrylics react also with epoxy and with polyester resins to give coatings with a very wide field of application.

Coatings for wood, suitable for UV curing, are produced from hydroxylated acrylics modified with epoxy, isocyanate, polyester or silicone.

Carboxylated acrylics cah be reacted with the co-polymers mentioned above to give hard glossy films with outstanding resistance to chemicals, soaps and detergents. They are used on hospital equipment and laundry machines.

Powder coatings

The basic principles and methods of application of powder coatings have been described in previous pages.

Materials employed

The resins employed are drawn from both thermoplastic and thermosetting types.

Thermoplastic resins include the following.

Polyethylene (polythene) is of low density, with a softening point of 105°-114°C. It is used for wirework and articles such as supermarket baskets and trollies.

Polypropylene has a melting point of about 168°C and is tougher and more abrasion resistant than polyethylene.

Nylon (a polyamide) shows outstanding resistance to abrasion and is self lubricating. It is used far moving surfaces in contact such as sliding racks, ball joints and so on.

PVC (polyvinyl chloride) is resistant to water and impact and has a wide range of uses such as out-door furniture, playground equipment and fencing.

Generally these thermoplastic resins require a primer, for the following reasons.

1 Their adhesion to metal is of a low order. Adhesion to primers is usually satisfactory but the primer must withstand the temperature of fusion of the resin.

2 They form a protective 'envelope' round the article. If this envelope is pierced or broken in any way, moisture and air will enter allowing corrosion to take place unless an efficient primer has been used.

Thermosetting resins The main thermosetting resins used are epoxies, saturated polyesters and acrylics. Other resins are used but in smaller quantities.

Epoxies are usually polyamide cured. They show outstanding adhesion, electrical insulation and resistance to chemicals and solvents. Their usage covers a wide field.

Polyesters are often blended with 'blocked' isocyanates (isocyanate reacted with a material such as caprolactone. The compound decomposes on stoving to release the isocyanate). Polyester films, in general, exhibit excellent durability, electrical properties and gloss. They are often used without primer.

Acrylics can be reacted with epoxies, isocyanates and polyesters to yield films of outstanding durability and mechanical properties.

Liquid powders are aqueous dispersions of powder coatings in which stainers, flow promoters, etc., can also be dispersed in the water. The advantages and drawbacks compared with dry powders have been summarized by Ramsay.

Advantages include : (1) conventional equipment, with minor modifications, can be used for application; (2) stainers can be added to the dispersion, so facilitating colour-matching; (3) no explosion hazard; (4) finer particle-size means smoother and thinner films.

Disadvantages are instability to shear (care must be exercised in the choice of pumps) and to temperatures above 80°C (194°F).

Liquid powders are being applied to a variety of steel articles, including tractors, scaffolding and car wheels.

Chapter - 14

MISCELLANEOUS COATINGS AND ANCILLARY MATERIALS

Paints for special floors

Asphalt floors are encountered in factories, warehouses, car parks, playgrounds and so on. They can be subjected to considerable pedestrian and vehicular traffic. Paints applied must not soften or dissolve the bitumen (or tar if tarmacadam has been used), a restriction which precludes the use of materials thinned with aliphatic or aromatic hydrocarbons. The traditional type of paint for these floors has been based on resins soluble in alcoholic solvents (industrial methylated spirit or isopropanol), particular attention being paid to pigmentation to give maximum hardness and wear resistance. Even so, areas exposed to constant traffic require repainting at frequent intervals.

Films of greater hardness and abrasion-resistance are produced by the use of water-borne expoxies. These are solvent-free materials in which the resin/pigment and hardener components are dispersed in water and supplied in two packs which are mixed immediately before use.

'Self-levelling' and 'seamless' floors are based on two-pack epoxies, twopack polyurethanes or catalysed (benzoyl peroxide), polymethacrylates. The resin is mixed with sand or other aggregate before laying. Finishing paints can be based on the same general type of resin. With the very hard-drying epoxy systems the paint should be applied within 48 hours from setting of the floor. After this time the hardness of the floor surfaces affords poor adhesion for the paint coating, unless it is abraded.

Road marking paints are used on asphalt and concrete roabs, surfaces of car parks, aerodrome runways and factories. As mentioned, paints for asphalt surfaces must be based on resins soluble in alcoholic solvents. Manila resin dissolved in industrial methylated spirit is commonly used, suitably pigmented to give maximum abrasion resistance. The following formulations illustrate two possible pigmentations for white line paints. Yellow line paints can be pigmented with lead chrome or, if required for use on concrete, with an alkali resistant pigment of the arylamide type.

White line paint

	% by weight			% by weight
Lithopone	36.5		Rutile titanium dioxide	20.5
Fine silica	12.7		Barytes	16.0
Manila resin	25.4	or	Fine silica	12.7
IMS 64 O.P.	25.4		Manila resin	25.4
IMS	64		O.P.	25.4

This type of paint dries rapidly and, depending on conditions, takes traffic in ½-¾ hour. It can be used also on concrete, but here other paints with a higher degree of alkali resistance are preferable. These are based on chlorinated rubber, vinyl toluene/acrylic co-polymer and thermoplastic acrylics.

Paints for aircraft

Subsonic types of aircraft have a basic structure of aluminium alloy with hightensile steel and magnesium alloys for certain specialized parts.

For structural aluminium alloys, epoxy systems are favoured. Anodizing is followed by a primer based on epoxy/polyamide and pigmented with strontium chromate. Epoxy/polyamide finish is then applied. Painting is carried out before assembly. Steel parts are phosphated and the absorbent phosphate coating is impregnated with low-viscosity high-bake epoxy lacquer. This is followed by epoxy primer and finish

The outside skin of the aircraft presents -a smooth aluminium alloy surface and the finish must be decorative as well as protective. Protection is required against wide fluctuations of temperature, intense ultraviolet radiation at high altitudes; and impact with raindrops at high velocity. Paints must be resistant also to fuels and to hydraulic, brake and de-icing fluids. Temperature fluctuations can result in condensation of appreciable amounts of water inside the outer skin. This can boil at the temperature reached by the skin of some aircraft and is a potent source of corrosion.

The surface of the aircraft becomes increasingly hot as the speed increases; for subsonic civilian and transport aircraft this can be of the order of 100°C.

Priming and any pretreatment is carried out before assembly, and this usually follows the pattern outlined above for structural aluminium alloys. The metal is anodized and primed with an epoxy/polyamide resin paint. After assembly a second coat of primer is applied, followed by the finish and all decorative work. The finish which has been increasing in popularity in recent years is polyurethane based on aliphatic isocyanate. This provides good glossretention, colour and chemical resistance.

With high-speed aircraft, temperatures are higher. According to Hoey a Mach 2.2 aircraft flying at 60 000 ft is likely to develop a surface temperature of about 120°C (248°F) but this figure is likely to be modified to some degree by the reflectivity and emissivity of the paint coating.

The exterior finishing system employed is somewhat similar to that described above, namely pretreatment of the aluminium alloy followed by epoxy/polyamide/strontium chromate primer and polyurethane finish based on aliphatic isocyanate. Acrylics are sometimes used: they show good colour stability at the temperatures reached, but their resistance to the hydraulic fluids is not as good as that of the polyurethanes. Two-pack epoxies are not favoured for the exterior of modern aircraft. They chalk rapidly at high altitudes where the ultraviolet radiation is more intense than at lower levels.

The interior alloy surfaces are given the same pretreatment and primer as the exterior surfaces, but they are often finished in two-pack epoxy enamel.

Clear wood finishes

Interior The factors of prime importance are preservation of the appearance, resistance to heat and fluids of various types, and resistance to mechanical damage. Resistance to weather is not of importance. The finishes in use include the following.

Copal varnish This is now seldom made on copal resin which has become too expensive. Usually it is a linseed/tung/modified phenolic varnish which dries to a hard film that retains its gloss for a considerable period. It does, however, tend to 'yellow' on ageing.

One pack polyurethane varnish gives very hard and abrasion-resistant films.

It is resistant to heat, alcohol (beverages), water and detergents. Applications include table tops, bar counters, floors and interior woodwork generally.

Acid-cured alkyd/amino clear finishes are used for similar purposes.

Exterior Clear finishes on exterior woodwork suffer rapid breakdown as a result of ultraviolet penetration. This can, of course, be reduced by the incorporation of UV absorbers

Protection of the wood is largely dependent on film thickness of the varnish so that 4 or 5 coats are applied to give protection for 2 to 3 years. Woods vary in their absorption characteristics and the multicoat application ensures a uniform finish.

The use of 'water-repellent' finishes has become more general in recent years. These are clear or lightly pigmented materials which impregnate the surface layers of the wood with a water-repelling material. It is claimed that this allows the wood to 'breathe' more than paint does, but it does not bring out the grain as well as conventional varnishes. A fungicide is also incorporated.

The original formula contained boiled linseed oil, wax, zinc stearate, a fungicide (pentachlorophenol) and white spirit. It can be tinted to match the colour of woods. Application is by brush, the excess being wiped off after about two hours. In the UK it dries slowly and the film tends to hold dirt. Breakdown is by gradual erosion, the life being about three years. It can then be cleaned down and a further coat(s) applied.

A water-based clear finish based on a vinylidene co-polymer is claimed to accommodate the movement of wood without cracking, to possess high moisture-resistance, and to provide excellent grain enhancement It gives excellent results when used over a clear varnish (where it acts as an oxygen barrier) or as a four-coat system. The life is claimed to be at least two years.

Stains for wood consist usually of a solution of a dye in water, spirit or oil, but semi transparent pigments dispersed in oil or varnish are sometimes employed.

Water stains are the least popular as they tend to raise the grain of the wood. They frequently contain natural colouring-matter such as logwodd. A dilute solution of potassium permanganate confers a brown stain on softwood.

Spirit stains consist of dyes dissolved in a solution of shellac or other resin in industrial methylated spirit. They penetrate well and dry rapidly. Generally the stained wood is varnished.

Oil stains are either solutions of dye in linseed oil and white spirit or dispersions, in the same medium, of semi-transparent pigments. After staining, the wood is varnished. Staining and varnishing can be carried out in one operation, but the result is influenced to a marked degree by the nature of the wood.

Scumble stain (or 'graining' colour). Scumbling is a process which was formerly used extensively but is now used to a very limited extent. It was designed to enable a decorator to imitate the grain of wood or to produce special grain effects. The surface is first given a flat ground coat or undercoat in a white or pale colour. Over this is applied a coat of scumble stain which consists of semi-transparent pigment dispersed in a varnish medium containing a gelling agent (usually a metallic stearate). A graining comb or other suitable tool is used to produce the desired pattern which dries without flowing out. Finally the surface is varnished or glazed Scumbling was used mainly on outside doors.

Exterior woodwork can be treated with oil or varnish stains or with one of the many water-repellent preservative stains on the market. The latter are often based on oil or varnish media containing fungicide and are lightly pigmented with semi-transparent pigment. Over-varnishing is generally required.

Motor-car finishes

The basic requirements of paint systems for cars are protection of the metal, maximum durability, good polishing properties, and resistance to chipping.

The application of primers to the phosphated steelwork by electrodeposition has resulted in a very considerable improvement in protection, particularly in box sections and other parts which were not adequately coated by the conventional dipping methods.

Underbody protection, in addition to the electrodeposited primer, is generally provided by bituminous type coatings which exhibit good waterresistance. It is difficult to understand why this very necessary additional underbody protection or 'underseal' has for so long been an 'extra' for the purchaser and not a standard feature applied by the manufacturer. In recent years, however, PVC plastisols have been applied by some manufacturers to certain underbody areas. They are more resistant to petrol and oils than are the bituminous types and exhibit better durability.

For bodywork on new cars, the alkyd/amino type of stoving finish has been replaced very largely by hydroxy functional (thermosetting) acrylics, cross linked with melamine. These show very good durability, particularly in metallic finishes and can be cured at 120°C (248°F) for 30 minutes. Thermosetting acrylics, in the form of polymer dispersions in aliphatic solvents ('non-aqueous dispersions' or NAD) (ICI), give high-build finishes with good solvent release.

In 're-finishing' operations, stoving is not possible and so finishes must dry or cure at ambient temperatures. Finishes in use include modified alkyds, cellulose nitrate, and thermoplastic acrylics. Two-pack systems in which hydroxylated acrylic resins are cross-linked with isocyanate have shown excellent performance.

Paint removers

Alkaline type the oldest and cheapest type of paint remover is based on sodium hydroxide and relies on saponification to destroy the paint film. For this reason it is ineffective against many modern coatings and furthermore is not recommended for use on woodwork, zinc, aluminium, or porous surfaces. It is, in fact, suitable for use only on ironwork where other methods are too costly. Alkaline paint removers can be based on the following general type of formulation, but the figures quoted can be varied widely.

	% by weight
Sodium hydroxide	5.7
Water	28.3
Non-ionic surfactant	0.3
Glycerin	0.7
Whiting	58.0
China clay	7.0

Operatives using this material should wear face shields, gloves and protective clothing. The cleaned surfaces should be washed thoroughly with water and dried before repainting.

Solvent type This employs strong solvents to penetrate and swell the paint coating,, so destroying the adhesion to the surface. The solvents are kept .in contact with the film by the use of cellulose acetate and wax, which delay evaporation. An emulsifying agent is often added to permit the surface to be cleaned with water. These are described as 'water-rinsible'.

It is often stated that several applications are necessary to remove several coats in a system, but according to Hurst and Goodier ' this is unnecessarily expensive. They suggest that a thin coating of the paint remover be applied and allowed to remain for 20-30 minutes. A second coating is then applied as thickly as possible and left undisturbed until the paint film has softened throughout. This may take several hours but the coating would then be removed completely to the substrate. The surface is then cleaned thoroughly with white spirit or water.

Solvent type paint removers may be either flammable or non-flammable, the latter being the more common. -In each case gloves and protective clothing should be worn, and care taken to avoid inhaling the solvent vapours.

The following formulation illustrates the general type of composition of a non-flammable water-rinsible paint remover:

	% by weight
Methylene chloride	88.8
Cellulose acetate	1.2
IMS 64 O.P.	4.9
Paraffin wax	0.8
Acetone	0.4
Toluene	2.8
Triethanolamine	1.1

Grease paints (also known as 'non-oxiding' paints)

The traditional type was based on green petroleum jelly, drying oil and pigment. Manufacture consisted in melting the petroleum jelly, adding the pigment ground in oil, and stirring until the mass had set sufficiently to avoid pigment settlement.

Thick films are applied by brush, but although the films remain soft and flexible, they are sufficiently rigid to resist the movement of water and rain.

This type of grease paint has been applied to some types of structural steelwork and steelwork difficult of access, such as bilge and ballast tanks on ships. Recent applications have included use as an anti-vandal or anti-thief treatment for walls and down pipes.

A more modern type is based on the calcium soaps of acids produced by the oxidation of higher petroleum hydrocarbons and waxes. These dry sufficiently hard to withstand occasional foot traffic. They are used for coating the interiors of box sections of bridges and for areas of steel structures which are difficult or impossible to clean sufficiently for conventional paint systems.

Trichlorethylene paints

These paints derive their name from the solvent employed which confers several advantages on the paints. Among these are (a) rapid evaporation - the articles dry in 60 to 120 seconds and so allow fast operation of production lines; (b) rapid set-up of the film eliminates sagging in dipping operations; (c) good cover of edges; (d) no flash point and therefore no fire risk. In view of the toxicity of trichlorethylene, special attention is paid to plant design.

Bacteriostatic and tungistatic paints

Liquid paints Bacterial attack is generally confined to aqueous systems containing suitable nutrients such as cellulose ethers, starches, animal and vegetable glues and casein. Of these, the cellulose ethers are the most widely used, generally as thickeners for emulsion paints. The bacteria secrete enzymes which act as catalysts and break down the cellulose molecules into simple substances which are then assimilated by the bacteria. Biocides are effective against bacteria but not against enzymes which can be present in the paint raw materials.

A number of materials have been proposed and evaluated for 'in-can' preservation of emulsion paints. The earlier types included phenolic derivatives such as orthophenylphenol, p-chloro-m-cresol (PCMC) and sodium pentachlorphenate. Organic mercurials and organotin compounds have both proved very effective, but the former type is no longer used in view of its toxic nature. A range of effective organic bacteriostats is available : including fluorinated sulphonamides, organic amides and fatty-acid modified amides. 1:2 -benzisothiazolin-3-one is widely used and is highly effective at a concentration of 0.01 to 0.05 percent on the paint.

Fungistatic paints

Fungi and moulds of many types will grow on most surfaces under the appropriate conditions; fungistats should, therefore, be effective against a wide spectrum of growths.

In interior conditions of high humidity or damp walls, both emulsion and solvent-type coatings can be affected. Emulsion paint films, by virtue of the presence of water-soluble cellulose derivatives and other ingredients, offer a favourable nutrient and are most affected. In an investigation into the preservation of emulsion paint systems, Carter has stated that, in addition to the necessary fungicidal activity, biocides must show low solubility in water, low vapour pressure, and stability both to ultraviolet radiation and to sulphur staining. Fungicidal activity must also be sustained in the dry film. 2-(4: thiazolyl) benzimidazole is claimed to give protection against a wide variety of fungi, but it has no 'in-can' preservative properties.

The protection of paint films against fungi and moulds under exterior conditions has been discussed by Pauli who emphasizes the importance of evaluating fungistats in the specific coating and under specific conditions. He lists a number of materials possessing the necessary sustained activity in addition to the other essential properties. These include modified barium metaborate (which, however, has to be used at 15 to 20 percent by weight on the solids content),, dithiocarbamates (used mainly in interior emulsion paints), phthalimide derivatives, substituted sulphonamides and sulphones.

Fungistatic paints generally contain sufficient biocide to prevent fungus growth on the film, but they are not fungicidal. When it is desired to paint surfaces which are infected with mould, steps must be taken to remove the growth and to sterilize the surface. The time honoured method has consisted in scraping and/or hard brushing followed by treatment with a fungicidal wash.

Fungicidal wash

A variety of fungicides are employed, some in solution in water, others in solvent such as white spirit or aromatic solvent. The aqueous type is preferred for interior use where solvent vapour can be objectionable, whilst the waterinsoluble solvent type is used on exterior work. The surface is thoroughly soaked with fungicide solution and is then allowed to dry out before being painted.

Methods for cleaning infected walls have recently been investigated by Whiteley and Bravery' I who consider that fungicidal washes are less effective in preventing further growth than very thorough cleaning by water jet, preferably containing abrasive.

The preservation of stonework

The exterior architecture of many of our older cathedrals, churches and other buildings is a valuable heritage of which we are temporary custodians with a responsibility to future generations. Unfortunately neglect over many years has allowed progressive decay to take place, in consequence of which structures have become unsound and the intricate architectural features severely eroded. The problems and dangers are now recognized and remedial measures are being undertaken as rapidly as finances permit, cost being the rate controlling factor.

Causes of decay Much of the stonework consists of either limestone (calcium carbonate) or magnesium limestone (calcium and magnesium carbonates), both of which are highly susceptible to attack by the following.

Frost Damage from frost occurs only on parts of structures which are frequently frozen while very wet. In this country this seldom occurs between the eaves and the damp-course

Crystallization of salts resulting from the action of atmospheric sulphur dioxide producing calcium sulphate in the pores of limestone and calcium sulphate with magnesium sulphate in the magnesium limestone. Repeated crystallization of these salts results in disintegration of the surface of the stone and can produce deep cavities.

Dissolution of carbonates is caused by carbon dioxide in rainwater, forming water soluble bicarbonates of calcium and magnesium.

Protective treatment The earlier treatments for preservation of the stone consisted in application of water-repellents such as emulsions of resins, waxes and other materials. These were not successful since the applied films were not sufficiently thick. Water penetration was not prevented and differential expansion effects accelerated the breakdown.

More modern approaches entail deep impregnation by resins or precipitation of other insoluble inorganic salts in the pores of the stone.

Resin impregnation is achieved by application of suitable monomers to give deep penetration followed by in situ polymerization. Monomers of interest include acrylics, epoxies and alkoxysilanes.

The second process involves precipitation of barium salts within the pores of limestones. Evaluation of the effectiveness of any process of stone preservation is slow and requires a number of years before conclusions can be drawn.

Paints for plastics

The extensive use of plastics has created a demand for coatings which are both decorative and protective. Many different types of plastic resin are in use with differing surface characteristics and, in some cases, properties vary between members of the same group.

It is generally accepted that the main problem in painting plastics is that of adhesion. Good adhesion requires a thoroughly cleaned surface but, other factors in the surface such as traces of mould release agent or migrated additive can play an important part.

It was formerly thought that a strong solvent which would 'bite' into the plastic surface was necessary for good adhesion. However, in many cases this led to swelling and subsequent crazing of the surface. It is now accepted that good adhesion is associated with the presence of polar groups at the paint/plastic interface but with non-polar plastics, such as the polyolefins, special surface treatments are required. In order that the polar groups can function, not only must the surface be clean but the paint must 'wet' the surface effectively. The topic of wetting is discussed by Arnoldous in relation to the use of aqueous dispersions of acrylic and polyurethane resins on plastics. A knowledge of the critical surface tension of the plastic is useful in formulating a suitable coating. The surface tension of an aqueous paint can be adjusted to the same order by means of water-miscible solvents. The acrylic and urethane dispersions are now being used widely.

A number of solvent-borne coatings are in use among which are the two-pack polyurethanes, thermoplastic acrylics, PVA/PVC and modified alkyds. As mentioned above, the coating is usually matched to the plastic and many coatings are in use reflecting the ingenuity of the paint technologist.

Coating of pipelines.

The principal materials of construction are mild steel, concrete, uPVC and polyethylene. Problems of protection are most difficult with mild steel and to a lesser extent with concrete. The majority of concrete pipelines are buried and are treated' with bitumen or tar compositions before being in-filled.

Steel pipelines are used both below and above ground. A number of protective systems is in use generally preceded by blast cleaning. The following schemes are in common use.

Buried lines (a) Wrapping at works with glass fibre impregnated with bitumen or tar. A special adhesive primer is used. The joints then require protection at site. (b) Electrostatic spray application of a heavy coating of epoxy powder. The pipes are preheated to fuse and cure the resin.

Exposed (above ground) The pipes are primed and are commonly wrapped with adhesive PVC or polyethylene tapes which often, are coloured as an aid to pipe identification. When black is used the polyethylene tape is stated to be more durable than the PVC material Glass fibre tapes impregnated with bitumen followed by a bituminous paint are also in use.

Chapter - 15

TESTING AND EVALUATION

TESTS ON LIQUID PAINTS

Production control

Tests applied in production control are designed to ensure that the product conforms to a predetermined standard or set of values. Where quantitative measurements are involved, the maximum deviation from mean values will also have been established. Generally, samples are drawn at various stages of manufacture, and the factory mixing sheets are usually designed to show the results on intermediate and final tests on a batch of paint.

The following tests are carried out in normal production, but specialized products may require other tests.

Degree of dispersion

Often known as 'fineness of grind' degree of dispersion is determined on samples drawn from bead mill, ball mill, etc., before the final thinning down. The material is applied to a 'Hegman' or fineness-of-grind gauge.

Using the 0 to 8 scale, an acceptable limit for undercoats is 6 and for the finishes 7½ or preferably 'off scale'.

Viscosity

Viscosity measurement is not only a useful check on make-up, but uniformity of viscosity is essential for modern production lines and other applications involving continuity of supply.

A number of instruments are in use for its determination. The most widely used are the following.

The -ICI cone and plate viscometer The instrument is illustrated in Fig. 25.1. The thermostatically controlled plate can be set at the desired temperature (usually 20° or 25°C) (68° or 77°F), while the rotating cone, which has an apical angle of 178°, gives a fixed rate ,of shear of 10 000 sec^{-1}.

A drop of the paint is placed in the centre of the plate and the cone lowered into position. The scale reading, in poise, is noted when it reaches a steady value.

A high proportion of modern paints, particularly the high-build types designed for airless spray, exhibit thixotropy to a greater or lesser degree, and the viscosity of such paints cannot be measured in the efflux type of viscometer. In the cone and plate, thixotropy is eliminated by shear before the viscosity reading is obtained. Other advantages are speed of measurement, small quantity of material required, and ease of cleaning.

The Ferranti-Shirley viscometer is a more elaborate and sophisticated cone and plate instrument which can be used to study flow properties over a range of shear rates and temperatures. A recording instrument can be attached to furnish results in the form of flow curves. This viscometer is more suited to research or project work than to routine quality control.

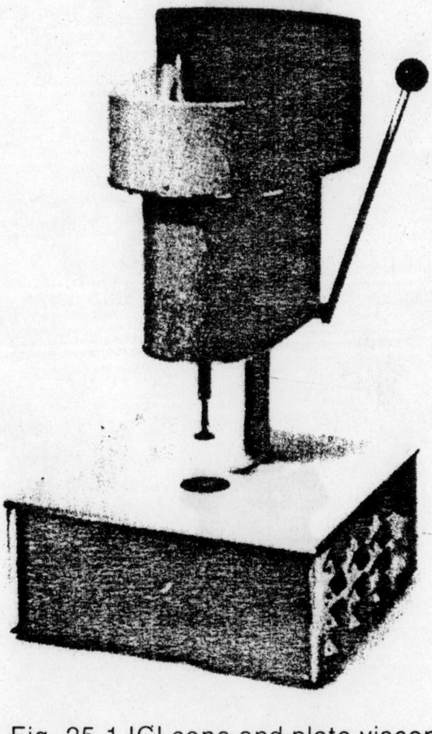

Fig. 25.1 ICI cone and plate viscometer

The Ferranti portable viscometer is a co-axial cylinder instrument, the outer cylinder being rotated. The inner cylinder is connected through a spring to a dial, and this shows the torque transmitted through the liquid by the rotation of the outer cylinder. Three speeds are used and sets of cylinders of different sizes are supplied to cover a range of viscosities.

This instrument is very useful not only for assessing. the degree of thixotropy in a paint, but, what is more important in practice, the rate of recovery of gel structure.

The Rotothinner is a dual-purpose instrument used both as a thinning mixer and as a viscometer. It is illustrated in Fig. 25.2.

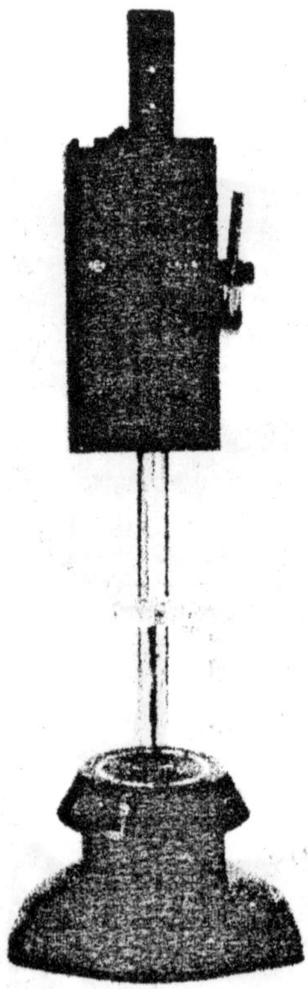

Fig. 25.2 Rotothinner

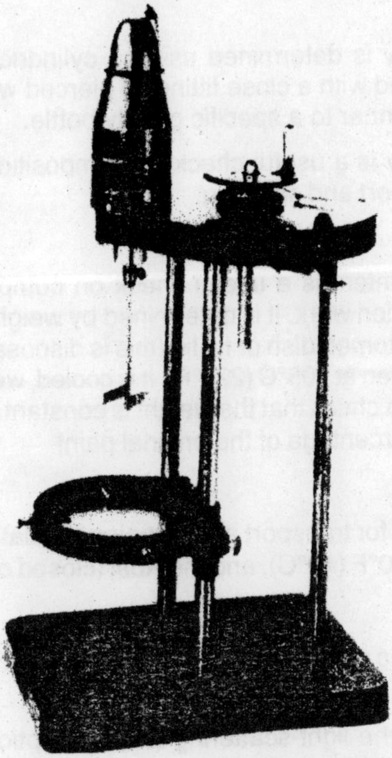

Fig. 25.3 Stormer Viscometer

A frequent task in the control laboratory is the determination of the amount of thinner to be added to a batch to attain a specified viscosity, and with the conventional efflux cups this can be a time-consuming operation.

Using the Rotothinner, a given amount of paint is placed in a 250 cm^3 tin on the turntable and the stirrer lowered. The torque transmitted through the liquid exerts a twist on the turntable, the base of which is marked off in poises, and a fixed pointer indicates the viscosity. Thinners can be added from a graduated cylinder until the desired viscosity is reached.

The Brookfield viscometer is a portable instrument which indicates viscosity directly in centipoises by the torque on a rotating spindle immersed in the paint. A number of spindle sizes are available to cover a wide viscosity range.

The Stormer viscometer (Fig. 25.3) can be fitted either with a paddle or with a temperature-controlled rotating cylinder. In the former type the paddle is immersed in a sample of the paint and rotated by string and falling weights. The weights are adjusted to give a uniform speed of rotation as indicated by a stroboscope, and by means of tables the weights are converted to Krebs units.

Specific gravity

Specific gravity is determined using a cylindrical cup of 100 cubic centimeters furnished with a close fitting lid pierced with a small hole. It is used in a similar manner to a specific gravity bottle.

Specific gravity is a useful check on composition and is, of course, necessary for transport and shipping.

Volatile content

The volatile content is a useful check on composition and is often required in specification work. It is determined by weighing out 2 to 3 grams of paint into a flat bottomed dish or tin lid (this is disposable) and heating for about 3 hours in an oven at 105°C (221°F). It is cooled, weighed, and reheated for a further ½ hour to check that the weight is constant. The volatile content is expressed as a percentage of the original paint.

Flash point

This is required for transport and shipping regulations. The majority of paints flash below 120°F (49°C), and the Abel (closed cup) method is used.

Opacity

Opacity or hiding power is the ability of a paint to hide or obliterate the surface.

It depends on the light-scattering and absorption properties of the dispersed pigments and on the thickness of the film. Opacity measurements are usually made on dry films of known thickness, but occasionally the need arises for the measurement on the liquid paint. This is best carried out by the use of the Pfund Cryptometer

APPLICATION AND WET FILMS

Brushability

Although the viscosity figure can afford a guide to the ease of brushing or suitability for spraying, other factors are involved which appear only during the application process. Brushability tests of decorative paints are made by application to areas of about 2 feet (0.6 metre) square to one side of which a piece of moulding is attached. The latter will show the behaviour of the paint on sharp edges and in hollows. On the panel, properties such as brush drag and ease of spreading, tendency to sag, levelling and wet-edge time can be assessed. For the latter, one half of the panel is coated, left for a short time, then the second half coated so that the two halves can be joined at the specified time. It should be possible to join up without leaving any visible sign.

Sag resistance

This test is used for high-build paints to be applied by airless spray or brush. The paint is applied at a predetermined thickness to a steel or glass panel. A sag

comb (Fig. 25.4) is drawn across the film so that the substrate is based in strips of graded width (Fig. 25.5).

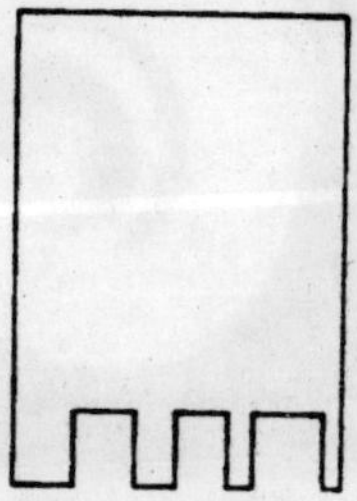

Fig. 25.4 Sag comb

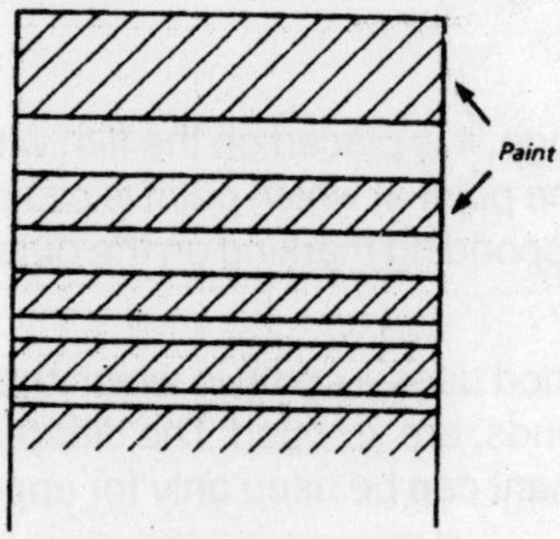

Fig. 25.5 Sag test

The panel is immediately placed in a vertical position. Any sagging becomes apparent by flow across the bared strips.

Measurement of wet-film thickness

A knowledge of the wet-film thickness is required in the sag resistance test.

It is an invaluable aid in on-site painting. From a knowledge of the wet-film thickness and the solids content of the paint by volume, the dry-film thick, ness can be calculated.

The most successful instrument for this purpose is the Wet-Film Thickness. Gauge and is illustrated in Fig. 25.6. It consists of two solid metal disks and between them is mounted a slightly smaller third disk which is eccentric to the other two, and at one point the three circumferences are in the same plane. This point is marked O and the point opposite is marked - the difference in diameter (in mils) between the centre and outside disks.

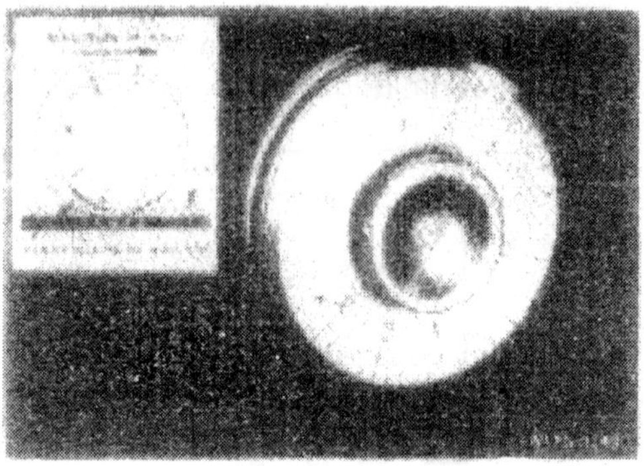

Fig. 25.6 Wet film thickness gauge

To use the gauge, it is placed on the film with point 4 downwards and then rolled along. The point at which paint is picked up on the centre disk is noted and the corresponding marking on the outer disk gives the thickness of the film.

A second method uses a comb in which the teeth, with the exception of those at the two ends, are stepped. The differences in length are usually 1 mil, so the instrument can be used only for approximate measurements.

In use the comb is held vertically on the paint film and a note made of the tooth which just touches the film.

Spraying properties

A high proportion of industrial air-drying and stoving paints are applied by one or other of the spraying methods. Application of paint by the appropriate method will reveal any tendency to poor atomization, spray, orange peel, etc.

Covering power

Covering. power, often referred to as spreading rate, is expressed in square metres per litre or per 5 litres and represents the area which can be covered when the paint is applied at a given thickness by the specified method.

A theoretical figure for covering power can be calculated from the wet (or dry) film thickness . and the volume solids, but 'practical' figures can be appreciably lower and depend on the nature-of the substrate, the application technique, prevailing conditions and sundry losses. In fact, practical figures can vary from 60 to 90, percent of the theoretical values.

An approximate figure for brushing paints can be obtained by application of sufficient paint to cover a known Area and then weighing the amount used.

Covering power or spreading rate should not be confused with opacity or hiding power.

Drying time

The drying time of a paint is the time required for the film to change from the liquid condition, as applied, to a solid film. Three types of drying or hardening are encountered.

1 Loss of volatile thinner, leaving a hard film. Drying times are short and of the order of 10 to 30 minutes. This type of drying occurs with lacquers and other non-convertible coatings generally.

2 Loss of volatile thinner followed by oxidation and polymerization of unsaturated fatty chains, as in oleoresinous varnishes and drying-oil alkyds. Drying times vary from 1 to 20 hours.

3 Chemical reaction between film components, where solvent may or may not be present. Examples ale amine- and polyamide-cured epoxies, polyurethanes, and acid-cured amino/alkyd coatings. In each case the rate of change is increased by a rise in temperature.

Type 2 materials will be considered in the present discussion, but many of the methods can be applied to type 3 and, with limitations, to type 1 . The drying times of type 2 are influenced by humidity, air circulation, light intensity, and film thickness, in addition to temperature.

The drying process is characterized by two periods known as surface dry and hard dry. A film is surface dry when it is free from tackiness; it is also known as tack free.

Assessment of drying time

Preparation of films Measurements of drying time require films of uniform and known thickness, particularly if used for comparison purposes. Both hand and automatic applications are in use.

Hand application includes brush and spray methods, as well as 'spreaders'. Among the latter are bar applicators (usually embodying an adjustable gap), steel shims with doctor blade, and spiral rod applicators. An interesting 'block spreader', which eliminates the personal factors associated with hand instruments, has been described by Monk. The ICI Spinner is an automatic spreader in which the paint is applied to the centre of a panel which is then spun at a uniform speed in its own plane. The thickness of the resulting film depends on the speed, duration of rotation, and the film properties of the paint.

Surface dry This condition, also known as 'touch dry', requires no definition, following are the salient points.

The coated panel, at the end of the specified period, is laid horizontally. 0.5 gram ballotini is then sprinkled on to the surface from a height of 15 cm (6 inches) and allowed to remain on the surface for one minute. If the paint is surface dry, the ballotini -should be capable of removal by means of a soft camel-hair brush without damage to the film. Automatic instruments are available,- to determine surface drying time when the yes/no method is not applicable.

Hard dry For many years decorators have used thumb pressure and rotation as a test for hardness of dry of a paint film. The principle has been embodied in an instrument known as the Hard Dry Apparatus, or 'mechanical thumb', The following is a very brief summary of the method.

A vertical steel plunger is tipped with rubder at the lower end. This rubber tip is capped with white drill which is renewed for each test. The plunger assembly is loaded to a total weight of 4 lb. By an automatic devico, the plunger is lowered gently on to the paint surface, rotated through 270° and then raised. A film is hard dry if the substrate or previous coat is nowhere exposed.

The BK drying recorder provides information on the whole of the drying process (Fig. 25.7). Films of known thickness are cast on long glass strips and, by means of a moving carriage, a vertical round-ended needle is drawn slowly through the paint film. The speed can be chosen so that the glass strip is traversed in 6, 12 or 24 hours. In the early period of drying, the paint flows found the needle and no record remains. As the paint sets, the needle cuts a groove and the appearance of this groove gives information on the relative speeds of surface- and through-drying. Rapid surface drying is shown by tearing of the skin. Too-slow surface dry is accompanied by an extended groove. When the paint film is hard dry, the needle rides on the surface and leaves little or no record.

Machines are available to hold six or ten samples and are used to provide an overnight record of the drying of production samples as well as for investigational work.

Fig. 25.7 BK drying recorder

Overcoating time

With brushing paints, this corresponds to the British Standard definition of 'hard dry' With spray paints, however, overcoating times do not necessarily require the film to be hard dry; they depend on both the nature of the film and of the paint to be used for overcoating.

Non-convertible films, such as cellulose nitrate, chlorinated, rubber, vinyl and acrylic lacquers can be overcoated by spray with similar materials at any time, provided the bulk of solvent has evaporated. Fusion of coats takes place and no difficulties are encountered in respect of intercoat adhesion. Attempts to apply a second coat of these materials by brush normally leads to softening and working up of the first coat.

Oxidizable films such as alkyds and epoxy esters require atmospheric oxygen for curing and should be hard dry for recoating. For gloss on gloss the interval should not exceed 48 hours. After this time the film will be hard enough to resist penetration or 'bite' by solvents from the next coat, and adhesion is likely to be poor. The first coat, in this case, should be rubbed down. Alkyd undercoats and primers can, if necessary, be overcoated up to one week after application, but this time should not be exceeded.

Overcoating times of two-pack epoxy and epoxy/coal-tar pitch systems are restricted. Generally the solvents have largely evaporated and the film has set sufficiently at 16 hours to be overcoated. This can be carried out up to 48 hours, after which the first coat will be very hard, and if glossy, will require abrasion to promote adhesion.

Metal primers based on two-pack epoxy resins dry rapidly to a matt or semimatt film. They can be overcoated at much shorter intervals than finishes. One pack materials can be spray applied after 1 to 2 hours and two-.pack materials after 3 to 4 hours. If the overcoating materials are brushed, double these times should be allowed. Since they dry to matt finishes, the maximum overcoating times are not as critical as for the gloss finishes, and when used as 'holding primers' two-pack epoxy types have been overcoated with undercoat after some months.

TESTS ON DRY FILMS

Measurement of film thickness

For most of the tests involving mechanical properties described below, a knowledge of the thickness of the dry film is essential for the correct interpretation of results. Dry film thickness can be calculated from wet film thickness and volume of solids but often it has to be checked as, for example, in specification work on structures.

According to circumstances, either destructive or, non-destructive methods are employed.

Destructive methods are of three types. (a), Micrometer: used for plates or panels where a small area of paint can be removed'; if necessary, to obtain the panel thickness. (b) Microscope method: a small area of the paint film is removed and mounted vertically on the microscope stage. (c) Dial thickness gauge: this has two legs which are planted on the paint film, and the probe, which is between them and attached to a dial, is set to rest firmly on the film. The dial reading is noted. The instrument is moved, the area of paint on which the probe had rested is removed, and the instrument replaced in the same position as before. The probe is now brought into contact with the substrate and the new reading noted.

Non-destructive methods A number of instruments are available using magnetic or electrical effects for ferrous and non-ferrous metals respectively.

With ferrous metals it is possible to use a permanent magnet and to measure the pull-off force required when it is placed on the surface. The presence of a paint film between magnet and steel reduces the force by an amount proportional to the thickness. This principle is employed in a widely used portable instrument in which the pull-off force is applied to the magnet by turning a calibrated circular dial until the magnet detaches from the painted surface. Other instruments, for use on non-magnetic metals, employ an eddy-current principle.

Optical properties

Gloss Paint films can exhibit any degree of gloss from high gloss (98 to 100 percent reflectance) to dead matt (no reflectance) but the following five categories are often used: high gloss, semi-gloss, eggshell gloss, eggshell flat, and matt. There is no universally agreed standard of gloss or sheen for any of these, and manufacturers, painters and public bodies all differ in their interpretation of the terms. It is not feasible, therefore, to quote gloss values for any except the high gloss.

The measurement of gloss values is usually carried out by the method set out in BS 3900, Part D5. The following is a brief summary.

A film of uniform thickness is cast on a plane glass surface-by means of 2-mil steel shims and a doctor blade. The film is allowed to harden for 24 hours. The gloss determination is carried out using a gloss head connected to a galvanometer.

Three gloss heads are available in which the angle of reflectance (relative to the normal to the surface) is 20°, 60° or 80°. The 60° instrument is used for high gloss finishes, the 20° for low sheen finishes, and the 80° for special effects. (For many years a 45° gloss head has been in use for gloss finishes, but the three instruments mentioned above provide a much wider range of measurements.) The equipment is standardized with a glossy black tile which is assumed to give a reflectance of 100 percent. The gloss head is placed on the sample and several readings taken at right angles to each other, the mean of the figures being taken as the gloss reading.

With high-gloss finishes the gloss retention is as important as the initial gloss, and the panel is therefore examined at weekly intervals over a period. The loss of gloss should not exceed 10 percent in the first 4 weeks.

Opacity of dry films

This is required for most specification work and is measured by the method described in BS 3900, Part D4. The following is a brief summary of the method.

Contrast ratio method A film of uniform thickness is cast on a thin sheet of cellulose acetate by fixing this on a plane surface under two steel shims of 2 mils thickness. The paint is spread over the surface with a doctor blade and allowed to dry.

The opacity or contrast ratio is obtained by measuring the total reflectance from the film when placed over a white and then over a black substrate. The difference is a measure of the amount of light which penetrates the film and is absorbed by the black.

The substrate consists of blocks of white and black glass fused together. The reflectance characteristics of these are first measured by reference to a magnesium carbonate standard. The paint film is placed on the white surface and the reflectance measured by means of the opacity reflectometer (Fig. 25.8) which comprises a lamp and photoelectric cell. It is connected to a galvanometer and the latter reading, with the opacity head and film on the white substrate, is set at 100. The film. and opacity head are then placed on the black and the galvanometer reading noted. After making the correction for surface reflectances the opacity or contrast ratio of the paint is expressed as a percentage.

Opacity can also be measured by means of Morest charts in the same manner as for pigments.

Colour comparison

In production work a great deal of colour assessment is done visually, using either dry or wet standards. Dry standards are panels or patterns which are compared with the sample after the latter has been applied to a suitable panel and allowed to dry. The comparison should be made in a north light. With a wet standard, this should be applied to a panel alongside the sample and the panel allowed to dry before comparison in a north light.

When a number of batches of the same colour are produced, colour comparisons should be made with the previous batch as well as with the standard. This ensures continuity of shade and prevents 'drift' from the standard colour.

Changes in the standards can be guarded against by recording the colour by means of a spectrophotometer or colorimeter.

Fig. 25.8 Opacity reflectometer

Mechanical properties

The mechanical properties of a paint film are so interdependent that it is difficult to measure a single property without involving at least one other to some degree. Many ingenious methods designed to minimize the involvement of other properties have been evolved, and the most widely used are described below.

Hardness

It is probable that the oldest method for assessing hardness was the use of the thumb-nail. This was very much a personal assessment.

Scratch test This method is widely used and is described in detail in BS 3900: Part E2. The following is a brief summary.

The paint is applied to clean abraded tin-plate, allowed to dry for the appropriate time, and fixed in a horizontal position in a slide in the apparatus (Fig. 25.9). Fixed over the slide is a pivoted counterbalanced arm to which

Fig. 25.9 Automatic scratch test unit

is attached a needle with a hemispherical hardened steel point, 1 mm in diameter. This arm can be lowered so that the needle, which can be weighted, is vertical when in contact with the paint film.

In use the weighted needle is lowered gently on to the paint surface and the slide pulled out, causing the needle to move along the paint film. This may produce a scratch through to the metal, cut a groove in the paint, or the paint may be unaffected. The result recorded is the maximum load which can be applied to the needle before bare metal is visible through the scratch. Good adhesion between paint and metal is essential for consistent results. Manual and automatic forms of the apparatus are available.

Pendulum methods These are 'rocking' methods which assess hardness by a damping effect. In the Persoz instrument the pendulum is attached to a horizontal bar to the underside of which two 8 mm diameter polished steel balls are attached. For standardization the pendulum is arranged with the steel balls in contact with plate glass, the pendulum displaced through 12° and the time noted for the amplitude to decrease to 4°. This is converted to.100. The test is then repeated on the paint film.

The Koenig pendulum works on a similar principle, but 5 mm polished steel balls are used. The opinion has been expressed that the Persoz pendulum is to be preferred for softer films and the Koenig instrument for the harder types.

Pencil hardness test This is a very simple and useful test for assessing hardness. Pencils of decreasing hardness (6H to 4B) are drawn across the surface until one is found which leaves a black line. The method involves a number of variables but is very useful when experience in its use has been acquired.

Indentation methods These are based on measurement of the depth of penetration of a film by a ball-ended needle under an applied constant load. The penetration is recorded as a function of time. Film recovery after removal of the load can also be recorded so that resilience as well as hardness can be assessed. Several forms of apparatus are available, the best known being the ICI Micro-indentation Recorder In this apparatus measurements can be carried out over a wide range of temperatures. It can be used also for assessing changes in film properties with age and exposure.

Flexibility and extensibility

To some degree these terms are synonymous. The flexibility of any material is usually assessed by some kind of bending or flexing operation (often repeated several times), but on a paint film, to be meaningful, it has to be assessed on the film attached to a substrate. By their nature, bending operations involve extending both the film and metal panel surface but to different degrees. In the film the internal cohesive forces are put under strain as is also the adhesion between paint film and metal. Both extensibility and adhesion are therefore involved. Methods used for assessing extensibility with adhesion include bending (Bend test) and forming a 'dome' in the coated metal by a force applied either slowly (Erichsen or 'cupping' test) or rapidly (Impact test). These tests are summarized below.

Bend test This is described in detail in BS 3900, Part E1. The paint is applied to a strip, 4 in. by 2 in. (10 cm x 5 cm) of 30 s.w.g. chromate-dipped soft aluminium and allowed to harden for the specified time. The panel is then placed, paint side outermost, under a mandrel of prescribed diameter embodied in a hinge. The panel is bent through 180° in one second, removed, and the bend examined for cracks and loss of adhesion. Mandrels are in use ranging from 1 in. (25 mm) to 1/8 in. (3.2 mm) in diameter. A conical mandrel is available which provides the information given by a series of hinge types. In this case a steel panel can be used with the appropriate bending aids.

Erichsen (cupping) test This measures the extensibility of a paint film when a portion of the substrate is extended into a 'dome' or 'cup'. The paint is applied to a prepared deepdrawing steel panel, and when ready for test is mounted against a rigid steel plate containing an orifice. A hemispherical hardened steel tool is placed against the back of the panel in line with the aperture. Pressure is applied to the tool so that a dome is gradually formed. It can be continued until the film ruptures or for a specified distance. The paint on the dome is then examined for cracking and loss of adhesion. This method is described in more detail in BS 3900, Part E4.

Impact test The following is a brief summary of the method described in BS 3900, Part E3. The paint is applied to an 18 B. G. steel panel, 10 cm by 5 cm and allowed to dry for the specified time. It is then fixed, painted side down, between two horizontal die-blocks which have holes in the centres. The steel indentor has a hemispherical end and forms part of a steel block, the total weight of which is 10½ lb (4.77 kg). The block slides smoothly on two vertical steel supports and is allowed to fall on the test panel by a release mechanism. The dome formed in the panel is then examined for cracking and loss of adhesion of the paint. The depth of penetration, i.e. the height of the dome, can be controlled by spacing washers between the die-blocks.

Adhesion

The adhesion of a paint to a surface is influenced by a number of factors, chief among which are the nature of the binder and of the surface.

Generally, adhesion to wood and plaster surfaces presents few problems, provided the surfaces are clean and dry. On metals the van der Waals forces of attraction are not augmented, as on wood and plaster, by absorbency of the surface.

Adhesion to a metal surface is improved by increasing the effective area by chemical pretreatment or abrasion but the nature of the binder and cleanliness of the surface are of paramount importance.

Nature of the binder It is generally agreed that binders possessing polar groups (e.g. - OH, -COOH) show better adhesion than do those containing no such groups. For this reason, epoxy resins, epoxy esters and alkyds show good adhesion, whereas certain vinyls and polyethylene (applied by the powder coating process) do not adhere well to metals and require an appropriate primer.

Cleanliness of the surface The adhesion of a paint to a surface depends on good wetting and therefore on the absence of contamination. In practice it is extremely difficult, and in some conditions impossible, to remove all impurities. Most paints must therefore be able to tolerate a degree of contamination, but difficulties often arise in determining an acceptable degree of cleanliness.

Both chemical and physical methods are employed in preparing metal surfaces for painting.

Some of the methods used in its assessment are here described briefly.

Direct pull-off methods The most simple of these is the 'snatch' method using adhesive tape. This is pressed on to the paint surface, often over a cross hatch and then pulled off sharply.

Cross-hatch test Using a sharp knife, a number of parallel cuts are made through the film to the substrate at 1 mm intervals. These are crossed by a second series, making a number of 1 mm sided squares, and it is convenient to make 100 squares. If the adhesion is poor, some of these squares will fall out and the number can be expressed as a percentage. More often, however, the severity of the test needs to be increased by pressing a strip of adhesive tape across the squares followed by a quick pull-off.

The Arco knife is a mechanical cutting instrument which uses a cutting tool tipped with a 60° conical diamond. Successive parallel cuts are made in the film at decreasing distances apart until the film is removed by the lateral force of the tool. The result is expressed as the greatest distance between the two cuts when the coating begins to be detached.

The Houndsfield tensometer is capable of measuring adhesion in more precise terms by a direct pull-off test. The paint is applied to the thoroughly cleaned ends of two cylinders of the appropriate substrate and these are then glued together, end to end. The composite specimen is placed in the tensometer and the two cylinders drawn part. The force required to pull the paint from the surface is noted. The precise significance of the results provides an interesting speculation.

Chapter - 16

MISCELLANEOUS FORMULAE

Hardening without losing its transparency. It is used to give a shining. Transparent,hard, and preservative covering to the finished surface of woodwork, capable of resisting in greater or less degree the influence of the air and moisture. This coating, when applied to metal or mineral surfaces, takes the name of lacquer, and must be prepared from rosins at once more adhesive and tenacious than those entering into varnish.

The rosins,commonly called gums, suitable for varnish are of two kinds- the hard and the soft. The hard varieties are copal, amber, and the lac rosins. The dry soft rosins are juniper gum (commonly called sandarac), mastic, and dammar. The elastic soft rosins are benzoin, elemi, anime, and turpentine. The science of preparing varnish consists in combining these classes of rosins in a suitable solvent, so that each conveys its good qualities and counteracts the bad ones of the others, and in giving the desired color to this solution without affecting the suspension of the rosins, or detracting from the drying and hardening properties of the varnish.

In spirit varnish (that made with alcohol) the hard and the elastic gums must be mixed to insure tenderness and solidity, as the alcohol evaporates at once after applying, leaving the varnish wholly dependent on the gums for the tenacious and adhesive properties; and if the soft rosins predominate, the varnish will remain "tacky" for a long time. Spirit varnish, however good and convenient work with, must always be inferior to oil varnish, as the latter is at the same time more tender and more solid, for the oil in oxidizing and evaporating thickens and forms rosin which continues its softening and binding presence, whereas in a spirit varnish the alcohol is promptly dissipated, and leaves the girms on the surface of the work in a more or less granular and brittle precepitate which chips readily and peels off.

Varnish must be tender and in a manner soft. It must yield to the movements of the wood in expanding or contracting with the heat or cold, and must not inclose the wood like a sheet of glass. This is why oil varnish is superior to spirit varnish. To obtain this suppleness the gums must be dissolved in some liquid not highly volatile like spirit,but one which mixes with them in substance permanently to counteract their extreme friability. Such solvents are the oils of lavender, spike, rosemary, and turpentine, combined with linseed oil. The vehicle in which the rosins are dissolved must be soft and remain so in order to keep the rosins soft which are of themselves naturally hard. Any varnish from which the solvent has completely dried out must of necessity become hard and glassy and chip off. But, on the other hand, if the varnish remains too soft and "tacky," it will "cake" in time and destroy the effect desired.

Aside from this, close observers if not chemists will agree that for this work it is much more desirable to dissolve these rosins in a liquid closely related to them in chemical composition, rather than in a liquid of no chemical relation and which no doubt changes certain properties of the rosins,and cuts them into solution more sharply than does turpentine or linseed oil. It is a well-known fact that each time glue is liquefied it loses some of its adhesive properties. On this same principle it is not desirable to dissolve varnish rosins in a liquid very unlike them, nor in one in which they are quickly and heghly soluble. Modern effort has been bent on inventing a cheap varnish, easily prepared, that will take the place of oil varnish, and the market is flooded with bezine, carbon bisulphide, and various ether products which are next to worthless where wearing and durable properties are desired.

Alcohol will hold in solution only about one-third of its weight in rosins, Turpentine must be added always last to spirit varnish. Turpentine in its clear recently distilled state will not mix with alcohol,but must first be oxidized by exposing it to the air in an uncorked bottle until a small quantity taken there from mixes perfectly with alcohol. This usually takes from a month to six weeks mastic must be added last of all to the ingredients of spirit varnish, as it is not wholly soluble in alcohol but entirely so in a solution of rosins in alcohol. Spirit varnishes that prove too hard and brittle may be improved by the addition of either of the oils of turpentine, castor seed, lavender, rosemary, or spike, in the proportion required to bring the varnish to the proper temper.

Colouring "Spirit" Varnishes.- In modern works the following colouring substances are used, separately and in blends: Saffron (brilliant golden yellow), dragon's blood (deep reddish brown), gamboge (bright yellow), Socotrine or Bombay aloes (liver brown), asphalt, ivory, and bone black(black), sandalwood, pterocarpus Santalinus, the heartwood(Dark Red), Indian Sandalwood, Pterocarpus-indica, the heart-wood (orange red), brazil wood (dark yellow), myrrh (yellowish to reddish brown; darkens on exposure), madder (reddish brown), logwood (brown), red Scammony rosin (light red), turmeric (orange yellow), and many others according to the various shades desired.

Manufacturing Hints.- Glass, coarsely powdered, is often added to varnish when mixed in large quantities for the propose of cutting the rosins and preventing them from adhering to the bottom and sides of the container. When possible, varnish should always be compounded without the use of heat, as this carbonizes and otherwise changes the constituents, and, besides, danger always ensues from the highly inflammable nature of the material employed. However, when heat is necessary, a water bath should always be used; the varnish should never fill the vessel over a half to three-fourths of its capacity.

The Gums Used in Making Varnish, Juniper gum or true sandarac comes in long, yellowish, dusty tears, and requires a high temperature for its manipulation in oil. The oil must be so hot as to scorch a feather dipped into it, before the gum is added; otherwise the gum is burned. Because of this, juniper gum is usually displaced in oil varnish by gum dammar. Both of these gums, by their dryness, counteract the elasticity of oil as well as of other gums. The usualsandarac of commerce is a brittle, yellow, transparent rosin from Africa, more soluble in turpentine than in alcohol. Its excess renders varnish hard and brittle. Commercial sandarac is also often a mixture of the African rosin with dammar or hard Indian copal, the place of the African rosin being sometimes taken by true juniper gum. This mixture is the pounce of the shops, and is almost insoluble in alcohol or turpentine. Dammar also largely takes the place of tender copal, gum anime, white amber, white incense, and white rosin. The latter three names are also often applied to a mixture of oil and Grecian wax, sometimes used in varnish. When gum dammar is used as the main rosin in a varnish, it should be first fused and brought to a boiling point, but not thawed. This eliminates the property that renders dammar varnish soft and "tacky" if not treated as above.

Venetian purpentine has a tendency to render varnish 'tacky" and must be skillfully counteracted if this effect is to be avoided. Benzoin in varnish exposed to any degree of dampness has a tendency to swell, and must in such cases be avoided. Elemi, a fragrant rosin from Egypt, in time grows hard and brittle, and is not so soluble in alcohol as anime, which is highly esteemed for its more tender qualities. Copal is a name given rather indiscreminately to various gums and rosins. The East Indian or African is the tender copal, and is softer and more transparent than the other varieties; when pure it is freely soluble in oil of turpentine or rosemary. Hard copal comes in its best form from Mexico, and is not readily soluble in oil unless first fused. The brilliant, deep-red color of old varnish is said to be based on dragon's blood, but not the kind that comes in sticks, cones, etc, (which is always adulterated), but the clear, pure tear, deeper in color than a carbuncle, and as crystal as a ruby. This is seldom seen in the market, as is also the tear of gamboge, which, mixed with the tear of dragon,s blood, is said to be the basis of the brilliant orange and gold varnish of the ancients.

Of all applications used to adorn and protect the surface of objects, oil varnishes or lacquers containing hard rosins are the best, as they furnish a hard, glossy coating which does not crack and is very durable even which exposed to wind and rain.

To obtain a varnish of these desirable qualities the best old linseed oil, or varnish made from it,must be combined with the residue left by the dry distillation of amber or very hard copal. This distillation removes a quantity of volatile oil amounting to one-fourth or One-fifth of the original weight. The residue is pulverized and dissolved in hot linseed-oil varnish, forming a thick, viscous, yellow-brown liquid, which, as a rule, must be thinned with oil of turpentine before being applied.

Hard rosin oil varnish of this sort may conveniently be mixed with the solution of asphalt in the oil of turpentine with the aid of the simple apparatus described below, as the stiffness of the two liquids makes hand stirring slow and laborious. A cask is mounted on an axle which projects through both heads, but is inclined to the axis of the cask, so that when the ends of the axle are set in bearings and the cask is revolved, each end of the cask will rise and fall alternately, and any liquid which only partly fills the cask will be thoroghly mixed and churned in a short time. The cask is two-thirds filled with the two thick varnishes(hard rosin in linseed oil and asphalt in the oil of turpentine) in the desired proportion, and after these have been intimately mixed by turning the cask, a sufficient quantity of rectified oil of turpentine to give proper consistence is added and the rotation is continued until the mixture is perfectly uniform.

To obtain the best and most durable result with this mixed oil, rosin, and asphalt varnish it is advisable to dilute it freely with oil of turpentin and to apply 2 or 3 coats. allowing each coat ot dry before the next is put on. In this way a deep black and very glossy surface is obtained which cannot be distinguished from genuine Japanese lacquer.

Many formulas for making these mixed asphalt varnishes contain rosin-usually American rosin. The result is the production of a cheaper but inferior varnish. The addition of such soft rosins as elemi and copaiba, however, is made for another reason, and it improves the quality of the varnish for certain purposes. Though these rosins soften the lacquer, they also make it more elastic, and therefore more suitable for coating leather and textile fabrics, as it does not crack in consequence of repeated bending, rolling, and folding.

In colouring spirit varnish the alcohol should always be coloured first to the desired shade before mixing with the rosin, except where ivory or bone black is used. If the color is taken from a gum, due allowance for the same must be made in the rosins of the varnish. For instance, in a varnish based on mastic, 10 parts, and tender copal, 5 parts, in 100 parts, if this is to be colored with, say, 8 parts of dragon's blood (or any other color gum), the rosins must be reduced to mastic, 8 parts, and tender copal, 4 parts. Eight parts of color gum are here equivalent to 3 parts of varnish rosin. This holds

ture with gamboge, aloes, myrrh, and the other gum rosins proportion is due to the inert matter and gum insoluble in alcohol, always present in these gum rosins.

Shellac Varnish.- This is made in the general proportion of 3 pounds of shellac to gallon of alcohol, the color, temper, etc.,to be determined by the requirements of the pruchaser, and the nature of the wood to which the varnishis to be applied. Shellac varnish is usually tempered with sandarac, elemi, dammar, and the oil of linseed, turpentine, spike, or rosemary.

Various impurities held in suspension in shellac varnish may be entirely precipitated by the gradual addition of some crystals of oxalic acid stirring the varnish to aid their solution,and then setting it aside overnight to permit the impurities to settle. No more acid should be used than is really necessary.

Rules for Varnishing - 1. Avoid as for as possible all manipulations with the varnishes; do not dilute them with oil of turpentine, and least of all with siccative, to expedite the drying. If the varnish has become too thick in consequences of faulty storing it should be heated and receive an addition of hot, well-boiled linseed-oil varnish and oil of turpentine. Linseed-oil varnish or oil of turpentine added to the varnish at a common temperature renders it streaky (flacculent) and dim and has an unfavorable influence on the drying; oil of turpentine takes away the gloss of varnish.

2. Varnishing must be done only on smooth, clean surfaces. if a fine, mirrorlike gloss is desired.

3. Varnish must be poured only into clean vessels, and from these never back into the stationary vessels, if it has been in contact with the brush. Use only dry brushes for varnishing which are not moist with oil of turpentine or linseed oil or varnish.

4. Apply varnishes of all kinds as uniformly as possible; spread them out evenly on the surfaces so that they form neither too thick nor too thin a layer. If the varnish is put on too thin the coating shows no gloss; if applied too thick it does not get even and does not form a smooth surface, but a wavy one.

5. Like all oil-paint coatings, every coat of varnish must be perfectly dry before a new one is put on; otherwise it is likely that the whole work will show cracks. The consumer of varnish is only too apt to blame the varnish for all defects which appear in his work or develop after some time , although this can only be proven in rare cases. As a rule, the ground was not propared right and the defferent layers of paint were not sufficiently dry, if the surfaces crack after a comparatively short time and have the appearance of maps. The cracking of paint must not be confounded with the cracking of the varnish, for the cracking of the paint will cause the varnish to crack prematurely. The

varnish has to stand more than the paint; it protects the latter, and as it is transparent, the defects of the paint are visible through the varnish, which frequently causes one to form the erroneous conclusion that the varnish has cracked.

6. All varnish coatings must dry slowly, and during the drying must be absolutely protected from dust, flies, etc., until they have reached that stage when we can pass the back of the hand or a finger over them without sticking to it.

The production of faultless varnishing in most cases depends on the accuracy of the varnisher, on the treatment of his brush, his varnish pot, and all the other accessories. A brush which still holds the split points of the bristles never varnishes clear; They are rubbed off easily and spoil the varnished work. A brush which has never been used does not produce clean work; it should be tried several times, and when it is found that the varnishing accomplished by its use is neat and satisfactory it should be kept very carefully.

The preservation of the brush is thus accomplished : First of all do not place it in oil or varnish, for this would form a skin, parts of which would adhere to it, rendering the varnished surface unclean and grainy; besides these skins there are other particles which accumulate in the corners and cannot be removed by dusting off; these will also injure the work. In order to preserve the brush properly, insert it in a glass of suitable size through a cork in the middle of which a hole has been bored exactly fitting the handle. Into the glass pour a mixture of equal parts of alcohol and oil of turpentine, and allow only the point of the brush to touch the mixture, if at all. If the cork is air-tight the brush cannot dry in the vapor of oil of turpentine and spirit. From time to time the liquids in the glass should be replenished.

If the varnish remains in the varnish receptacle, a little alcohol may be poured on, which can do the varnish no harm. At all events the varnish will be prevented from drying on the walls of the vessel and from becoming covered by a skin which is produced by the linseed oil, and which indicates that the varnish is both fat and permanent. No skin forms on a meager varnish, even when it drys thick.

After complete drying of the coat of varnish it sometimes happens that the varnish becomes white, blue, dim, or blind. If varnish turns white on exposure to the air the quality is at fault. The varnish is either not fat enough or it contains a rosin unsuitable for exterior work (copal). The whitening occurs a few days after the drying of the varnish and can be removed only by rubbing off the varnish.

Preventing Varnish from Crawling. - Rub down the surface to be varnished with sharp vinegar. Coating with strongly diluted ox gall is also of advantage.

Amber Varnish - This varnish is capable of giving a very superior polish or surface, and is especially valuable for coach and other high-class work. The amber is first bleached by placing a quantity- say about 7 pounds- of yellow amber in a suitable receptacle, such as an earthen ware crucible, of sufficient strength, adding 14 pounds of salgemmae (rock of fossil salt), and then pouring in as much spring water as will dissolve the sal gemmae. When the latter is dissolved more water is added, and the crucible is placed over a fire until the color of the amber is changed to a perfect white. The bleached amber is then placed in an iron pot and heated over a common fire until it is completely dissolved, after which the melting pot is removed from the fire, and when sufficiently cool the amber is taken from the pot and immersed in spring water to eliminate the sal gemmae, after which the amber is put back into the pot and is again heated over the fire till the amber is dissolved. When the operation is finished the amber is removed from the pot and spread out upon a clean marble slab to dry until all the water has evaporated, and is afterwards exposed to a gentle heat to entirely deprive it of humidity.

Asphalt varnishes. Natural asphalt is not entirely soluble in any liquid. Alcohol dissolves only a small percentage of it, ether a much larger proportion. The best solvents are benzol, benzine, rectified petroleum , the essential oils, and chloroform, which leave only a small residue undissolved. The employment of ether as a solvent is impracticable because of its low boiling point, 97° F., and great volatility. The varnish would dry almost under the brush. Chloroform is not open to this objection, but it is too expensive for ordinary use. Rectified petroleum is a good solvent of asphalt, but it is not desirable ingredient of varnish because, though the greater part of it soon evaporates, a small quantity of less volatile substances, which is usually present in even the ,most thoroughly rectified petroleum, causes the varnish to remain "tacky" for a considerable time and to retain a disagreeable odor much longer. Common coal-tar benzine is also a good solvent and has the merit of cheapness, but its great volatility makes the varnish dry too quickly for convenient use, especially in summer. The best solvent, probably, is oil of turpentine, which dissolves asphalt almost completely, producing a varnish which dries quickly and forms a perfect coating if the turpentine has been well rectified. The turpentine should be a "water white," or entirely colorless, liquid of strong optical refractive power and agreeable odor, without trace of smokiness A layer 1/5 of an inch in depth should evaporate in a short time so completely as to leave no stain on a glass dish.

But even solutions of the best Syrian asphalt in the purest oil of turpentine, if they are allowed to stand undisturbed for a long time in large vessels, deposit a thick, semi-fluid precipitate which a large addition of oil of turpentine fails to convert into a uniform thin liquid. It may be assumed that this deposit consists of an insoluble or nearly insoluble part of the asphalt which, perhaps, has been deprived of solubility by the action of light. Hence, in order to obtain a uniform solution, this thick part must be removed. This can be done, though imperfectly be carefully decanting the solution after it has stood for a long time in large vessels. This tedious and troublesome process may be avoided by filtering the solution as it is made, by the following simple and quite satisfactory method: The solution is made in a large cask, lying on its side, with a round hole about 8 inches in diameter in its upper bilge. This opening is provided with a well fitting cover, to the bottom of which a hook is attached. The asphalt is placed in a bag of closely woven canvas, which is inclosed in a second bag of the same material, The diameter of the double bag, when filled, should be such as to allow it to pass easily thtorgh the opening in the cask, and its length such that, when it is hung on the hook its lower end is apout 8 inches above the bottom of the cask. The cask is then filled with rectified oil of turpentine, closed, and left undisturbed for several days, The oil of turpentine penetrates into the bag and dissolves the asphalt, and the solution, which is heavier than pure oil of tupentine, exudes through the canvas, and sinks to the bottom of the cask. Those parts of the asphalt which are quite insoluble, or merely swell in the oil of turpentine, cannot pass through the canvas and are removed with the bag, leaving a perfect solution. When all soluble portions have been dissolved., the bag, with the cover, is raised and hung over the opening to drain. If pulverized asphalt has been used the bag is found to contain only a small quantity of semi fuild residue. This, thinned with oil of turpentine and applied with a stiff brush and considerable force, forms a thick, weather-resisting. and very durable coating for planks, etc.

The proportion of asphalt to oil of turpentine is so chosen as to produce, in the cask, a pretty thick varnish, which may be thinned to any desired degree by adding more turpentine. For use, it should be just thick enough to cover bright tin and entirely conceal the metal with a single coat. When dry, this coat is very thin, but it adheres very firmly, and continually increases in hardness, probably because of the effect of light, This supposition is supported by the difficulty of removing an old coat of asphalt varnish, which will not dissolve in turpentine even after long immersion, and usually must be removed by mechanical means.

For a perfect, quick-drying asphalt varnish the purest asphalt must be used, such as Syrian, or the best Trinidad. Trinidad seconds, though better than some other asphalts, yeild and inferior varnish, owing to the presence of impuritites.

Of artificial asphalt, the best for this purpose is the sort known as "mineral" caoutchouc," which is especially suitable for the manufacture of elastic dresssings for leather and other flexible substances. For wood and metal it is less desirable, as it never becomes as hard as natural asphalt.

FORMULAS:

I.- A solution of 1 part of caoutchouc in 16 parts of oil of turpentine or kerosene is mixed with a solution of 16 parts of copal in 8 parts of linseed-oil varnish. To the mixture is added a solution of 2 parts of asphalt in 3 or 4 parts of linseed-oil varnish diluted with 8 or 10 parts of oil of turpentine, and the whole is filtered. This is a fine elastic varnish.

II.- Coal-tar asphalt, American asphalt, rosin benzine, each 20 parts; linseed-oil, varnish, oil of turpentine, coaltar oil each 10 parts; binoxide of manganese, roasted lampblack, each 2 parts. The solid ingredients are melted to gether and mixed with the linseed-oil varnish, into which the lampblack has been stirred, and, finally, the other liquids are added. The varnish is strained through tow.

Bicycle Varnish.- This is a spirit varnish, preferably made by a cold process and requires less technical knowledge than the preparation of fatty varnishes. The chief dependence is upon the choice of the raw materials. These raw materials, copal, shellac, etc., are first broken up small and placed in a barrel adapted for turning upon an axis, with a hand crank, or with a belt and pulley from a power shaft, The barrel is of course simply mounted in frame of wood or iron, whichever is the most convenient. After the bareel has received its raw material, it may be started and kept revolving for 24 hours.Long interruptions in the turning must be carefully avoided, particularly in summer, for the material in the barrel, when at rest, will, at this season, soon form a large lump, to dissolve which will consume much time and labour. To prevent the formation of a semi-solid mass, as well as to facilitate the dissolving of the gum, it would be well to put some hard, smooth stones into the barrel with the varnish ingredients.

Bicycle Dipping Varnish (Baking Varnish).- Take 50 parts. by weight of Syrian asphalt; 50 parts, by weight of copal oil; 50 parts, by weight, of thick varnish oil, and 105 parts, by weight,turpentine oil, to which add 7 parts, by weight, of drier. When the asphalt is melted through and through, add the copal oil and heat it until the water is driven off, as copal oil is seldom free from water. Now take it off the fire and allow it to cool; add first the siccative, then the turpentine and linseed oil,which have been previously thoroughly mixed together. This bicycle varnish does not get completely black until it is baked.

Black Varnishes.- Black spirit lacquers are employed in the wood and metal industries. Different kinds are produced according to their use. They are called black Japanese varnishes, or black brilliant varnishes.

Black Japanese Varnish.- Sculpture varnish, 5 parts; red acaroid varnish, 2 parts; aniline black, ¼ part; Lyons blue, .0015 parts. If a sculpture varnish prepared with heated copal is employed, a black lacquer of especially good quality is obtained. Usually 1 per cent of oil of lavender is added.

II.-	Shellac	4 parts
Borax	2	parts
Glycerine	2	Parts
Aniline Black	5	Parts
Water	50	Parts

Dissolve the borax in the water, add the shellac, and heat until solution is effected; then add the other ingredients. This is a mat-black varnish.

For Blackboards.- For blackening these boards mix ½liter(1.05 pints) good alcohol, 70 grams (1,080 grains) shellac, 6 grams (92 grains) fine lampblack, 3 grams (46 grains) fine chalk free from sand. If red lines are to be drawn, mix the necessary quantity of red lead in alcohol and shellac.

Bookbinders' Varnishes -

	I Per Cent	II Per Cent	III Per Cent	IV Per Cent	V Per Cent
Shellac	14.5	6.5	13.5	6.3	8.3
Mastic	6.0	2.0	..	..	1.1
Sandarac	6.0	13.0	..	1.3	1.1
Camphor	1.0	..	0.5	1.5	..
Benzoin	..	..	..	..	13.7
Alcohol	72.5	78.5	86.0	79.2	75.8

Scent with oil of benzoin, of lavender, or of rosemary. Other authors give the following recipes.

	VI Per Cent	VII Per Cent	VIII Per Cent	IX Per Cent
Blond shellac	11.5	13.0	9.0	..
White Shellac	11.5	..	..	..
Camphor	..	0.7	..	..
Powdered Sugar	..	0.7	..	..
Sandarac	..	..	18.0	6.6
Mastic	..	..	..	13.0
Venice turpentine	..	..	2.0	6.6
Alcohol	77.0	85.6	71.0	73.8

All solutions may be prepared in the cold, but the fact that mastic does not dissolve entirely, must not be lost sight of.

Bottle Varnish.- Bottles may be made to exclude light pretty well by coating them with asphaltum lacquer or varnish. A formula recommended for this purpose is as follows: Dissolve asphaltum, I part in light coal-tar oil, 2 parts, and add to the solution anout 1 percent of castor oil. This lacquer dries somewhat slowly, but adheres very firmly to the glass,. Asphaltum lacquer may also be rendered less brittle by the addition of elemi. Melt together asphaltum, 10 parts, and elemi, 1 part, and dissolve the cold fused mass in light coal-tar oil, 12 parts.

Amber coloured bottles for substances acted upon by the actinic rays of light may be obtained from almost any manufacturer of bottles.

Can Varnish.- Dissolve shellac,15 parts, by weight; Venice turpentine,2 parts, by weight; and sandarac, 8 parts, by weight, in spirit, 75 parts, by weight.

Copal Varnish.- Very fine copal varinsh for those parts of carriages which require the highest polish., is prepared as follows;

I.- Melt 8 pounds best copal and mix with 20 pounds very clear matured oil. Then boil 4 to 5 hours at moderate heat until it draws threads; now mix with 35 pounds oil of turpentine, strain and keep for use. This varnish dries rather slowly, therefore varnishers generally mix it one half with another varnish; which is prepared by boiling for 4 hours, 20 pounds clear linseed oil and 8 pounds very pure, white anime rosin, to which is subsequently added 35 pounds oil of turpentine.

II.- Mix the following two varnishes:

(a) Eight pounds copal, 10 pounds linseed oil, ½ pound dried sugar of lead, 35 pounds oil of turpentine.

(b)Eight pounds good anime rosin, 10 pounds linseed oil,¼ pound zinc vitriol, 35 Pound oil of tupentine.Each of these two sets is boiled separately into varnish and strained, and then both are mixed. This varnish dries in 6 hours in winter, and in 4 hours in summer. For old articals which are to be re-varnished black, it is very suitable.

Elastic Limpid Gum Varnishes- I- In order to obtain a limpid rubber varnish, it is essential to have the rubber entirely free from water. This can be obtained by cutting the rubber into thin strips, or better, into shreds as fine as possible, and drying them, at a temperature of from 104^0 to 122^0 F., for several days or until they are water free, then proceed as follows:

II.- Dissolve 1 part of the desiccated rubber in 8 parts of petroleum ether (benzine) and add 2 parts of fat copal varnish and stir in, Or, cover 2 parts of dried rebber with 1 parts of ether; let stand for several days, or until the rubber has taken up as much of the ether as it will, then liquefy by standing in a vessel of moderately warm water. While still warm, stir in 2 parts of linseed oil, cut with 2 parts of turpintine oil.

ENAMEL VARNISHES:

Antiseptic Enamel. - This consists of a solution of spirituous gum lac, rosin, and copal, with addition of salicylic acid, etc, Its purpose is mainly the prevention or removal of mold or fungous formation. The salicylic acid contained in the mass acts as an antiseptic during the painting, and destroys all fungi present.

Bath -Tub Enamel Unaffected by Hot Water,-I- In order to make paint hold on the zinc or tinned copper lining of a bath tub, a wash must be used to produce a film to which oil paint will adhere. First remove all grease, etc., with a solution of soda or ammonia and dry the surface thoroughly; then apply with a wide, soft brush equal parts, by weight, of chloride of copper, nitrate of copper, and sal ammoniac, dissolved in 64 parts, by weight, of water. When dissolved add 1 part, by weight, of commercial muriatic acid. This solution must be kept in glass or earthen ware. It will dry in about 12 hours, giving a grayish-black coating to which paint will firmly adhere.

The priming coat should be white lead thinned with turpentine, with only just sufficient linseed oil to bind it. After this is thoroughly dry, apply one or more coats of special bath-tub enamel, or a gloss paint made by mixing coach colors ground in Japan with hard drying varnish of the best quality. Most first-calss manufacturers have special grades that will stand hot water.

II.- The following preparation produces a brilliant surfaces on metals and is very durable, resisting the effect of blows without scaling or chipping off, and being therefore highly suitable for cycles and any other articles exposed to shock:

For the manufacture of 44 gallons, 11 pounds of red copper, 8.8 pounds of yellow copper, 4.4 pounds of hard steel and 4.4 pounds of soft steel, all in a comminuted condition, are well washed in petroleum or mineral spirit, and are then treated with concentrated sulphuric acid in a lead- lined vessel, with continued stirring for 2 hours. After 12 hours rest the sulphuric acid is neutralized with Javel extract, and the fine powder left in the vessel is passed through a silk sieve to remove any fragments of metal, then ground along with linseed oil, ivory black, and petroleum, the finely divided mass being afterwards filtered through flannel and incorporated with a mixture of Bombay gum, 22 pounds; Damascus gum, 11 pounds; Judea bitumen, 22 pounds; Norwegian tar rosin, 11 pounds; and 11 pounds; of ivory black ground very fine in refined petroleum. When perfectly homogeneous the mass is again filtered, and is then ready for use. It is laid on with a brush, and then fixed by exposure to a temperature of between 400^0 and 800^0F. The ivory black may be replaced by other coloring matters, according to requirements.

A colour Enamel.-On the piece to be enameled apply oil varnish or white lead, and add a powder giving brilliant reflections, such as diamantine, brilliantine, or a gentine. Dry in a stove. Apply a new coat of varnish. Apply the powder again, and finally heat in the oven. Afterwards, apply several layers of varnish; dry each layer in the oven Apply pumice stone in powder or tripoli, and finally apply a layer of Swedish varnish, drying in the oven. This enamel does not crack. It adheres perfectly, and is advantageous for the pieces of cycles and other mobiles.

Cold Enamelling. - This style of enamelling is generally employed for repairing puposes. The various colors are either prepared with copal varnish and a little oil of turpentine, or else they are melted together with mastic and a trifle of oil of spike. In using the former, the surface usually settles down on drying, and ordinarily the latter is priferred, which is run on the cracked-off spot by warming the article. After the cooling, file the cold enamel off uniformly, and restore the gloss by quickly drawing it through the flame. For black cold enamel melt mastic together with lampblack, which is easily obtained by causing the flame of a wick dipped in to linseed oil to touch a piece of tin.

White.- White lead or flake white.

Red.-Carmine or cinnabar (vermilion).

Blue-Ultramarine or prussian blue.

Green- Scheele,s green or Schweinfurt green.

Brown.-Umber.

Yellow- Ocher or chrome yellow.

The different shades are produced by mixing the colours.

Enamel for Vats, etc.- Two different enamels are usually employed, viz., one for the ground and one for the top, the latter being somewhat harder than the former. Ground enamel is prepared by melting in an enamelled iron kettle 625 parts brown shellac,125 parts French oil of turpentine, with 80 parts colophony, and warming in another vessel 4500 parts of spirit (90 per cent) . As soon as the rosins are melted, remove the pot from the fire and add the spirit in portions of 250 parts at a time, seeing to it that the spirit added is completely combined with the rosins by stirring before adding any more. When all the spirit is added, warm the whole again for several minutes on the water bath (free fire should be avoided, on account of danger of fire), and allow to settle. If a yellow colour is desired, add yellow ocher, in which case the mixture may also be used as floor varnish.

The top enamel (hard) consists of 500 parts shellac, 125 parts French oil of turpentine, and 3500 parts spirit (90 percent). Boiling in the water bath until the solution appears clear can only be of advantage. According to the thickness desired, one may still dilute in the cold with high strength spirit.

Tinting may be done, as disired with earth colors, viz., coffee brown with umber. red with English red, yellow with ocher, silver gray with earthy cerussite, and some lampblack. Before painting, dry out the vats and putty up the joints with a strip of dough which is prepared from ground enamel and finely sifted charcoal or brown coal ashes, and apply the enamel after the putty is dry. The varnish dries quickly, is odorless and tasteless, and extraordinarily durable. If a little annealed soot black is added to this vat enamel, a fine iron varnish is obtained which adheres very firmly. Leather (spattering leather on carriages) can also be nicely varnished with it.

Finishing Enamel for White Furniture - Various methods are practiced in finishing furniture in white enamel, and while numerous preparations in tended for the purpose named are generally purchasable of local dealers in paint supplies, it is often really difficult, and frequently impossible, to obtain a first-class ready-made enamel. To prepare such an article take ½ pint of white lead and add to it ¼ pint of pure turpentine ¼ gill of pale coach Japan, and ½ gill of white dammar varnish Mix all the ingredients together thoroughly. Apply with a camel's hair brush, and for large surfaces use a 2 inch double thick brush. There should be at least three coats for good work, applied after an interval of 24 hours between coats; and for strictly high-class work four coats will be necessary. Each coat should be put on thin and entirely free from brush marks, sandpapering being carefully done upon each coat of pigment. Work that has been already painted or varnished needs to be cut down with, say, No. ½ sandpaper, and then smoothed fine with No. ½ paper. Then thin white lead to a free working consistency with turpentine, retaining only a weak binder of oil in the pigment,and apply two coats of it to the surface. Give each coat plenty of time to harden (36 hours should suffice), after which sandpapering with No, 1½ paper had best be done. Ordinarily, upon two coats of white lead, the enamel finish, as above detailed, may be successfully produced. For the fine, rich enamel finish , adapted to rare specimens of furniture and developed in the mansions of the multimillionaires, a more elaborate and complex process becomes necessary.

Quick-Drying Enamel Colours.- Enamel colours which dry quickly, but remain elastic so that applied on tin they will stand stamping without cracking off, can be produced as follows:

In a closed stirrer or rolling cask place 21.5 parts, by weight, of finely powdered pale French rosin, 24½ parts, by wieght, of Manila copal, as well as 35 parts, by weight , of denaturized spirit (95 percent), causing the cask or the stirrer to rotate until all the gum has completely dissolved, which, according to the temperature of the room in which the stirrer is and the hardness of the gums, requires 24 to 48 hours, When the gums, are entirely dissolved add to the mixture a solution of 21½ parts, by weight, of Venice oil turpentine in 0.025 parts, by weight, of denaturized spirit of 95 percent, allowing the stirrer to run another 2 to 3 hours. For the purpose of removing any impurities present or any undissolved rosin from the varnish, it is poured through a hair sieve or through a three fold layer of fine muslin (organdie) into suitable tin vessels or zinc-lined barrels for further clarification. After 10 to 14 days the varnish is ready for use. By grinding this varnish with the corresponding dry pigments the desired shades of color may be obtained; but it is well to remark that chemically pure zinc white cannot be used with advantage because it thickens and loses its covering power. The grinding is best carried out twice on an ordinary funnel mill. Following are some recipes:

1.- Enamel White.- Lithopone, 2 parts, by weight; white lead, purest, ½ part, by weight; varnish, 20 parts, by weight.

II.- Enamel Black.- Ivory black, 2 parts, by weight ; Paris blue, 0.01 part, by weight; varnish, 23 parts, by weight.

III.-Pale Gray.- Graphite, 2 parts, by weight;ultarmarine, 0.01 part,by weight; lithopone, 40 parts, by weight; varnish, 100 parts, by weight.

IV.-Dark Gray.- Graphite, 3 parts, by weight;ivory black,2 parts, by weight; lithopone, 40 parts, by weight; varnish, 110 parts, by weight.

V.-Chrome Yellow, Pale - Chrome yellow, 2 pars, by weight; lithopone, 2 parts, by weight : varnish, 40 parts, by weight ; benzine, 1½ parts, by weight.

VI. - Chrome Yellow, Dark. - Chrome yellow, dark, 2 parts, by weight; chrome orange, 1/8 part, by weight; lithopone, 1 part, by weight; varnish, 35 parts, by weight; benzine, 1 part, by weight.

VII. Pink, Pale- Carmine, ½ part, by weight; lithopone, 15 parts, by weight; varnish, 40 parts, by weight; benzine, 1½ parts, by; weight.

VIII. Pink, Dark- Carmine, ½ part, by weight; Turkey red, 1 part, by weight; lithopone, 15 parts, by weight; varnish, 40 parts, by weight.

IX. - Turkey Red, - Turkey red, pale 2 parts, by weight; lithopone, 1 part, by weight; Turkey red, dark, 1 part, by weight; white lead, pure, ½ part, by weight; varnish, 18 parts, by weight; benzine, ½ part, by weight.

X.- Flesh Tint. - Chrome yellow, pale 1½ parts, by weight; graphite, 1/8 part, by weight; lithopone, 15 parts, by weight; Turkey red, pale, 2 parts, by weight; varnish, 42 parts, by wieght; benzine, ½ part, by weight.

XI. - Carmine Red. - Lead sulphate, 5 parts, by weight; Turkey red, pale, 6 parts, by weight; carmine, 1½ parts, by weight; orange minium, 3 parts, by weight; vermilion, 2parts, by weight; varnish, 50 parts, by weight; benzine, 1½ parts, by weight.

XII.-Sky Blue- Ultramarine, 5 parts, by weight; lithopone, 5 parts, by weight; ultramarine green, 0.05 parts, by weight; varnish, 30 parts, by weight; benzine, 1 parts, by weight.

XIII.- Ultramarine.- Ultra blue, 5 parts, by weight; varnish, 12 parts, by weight; benzine, ½ part, by weight.

XIV. - Violet. - Ultramarine, with red tinge, 10 parts, by weight; carmine, 0.5 parts, by weight; varnish, 25 parts, by weight.

XV. - Azure.- Paris blue, 10 parts, by weight; lithopone, 100 parts, by weight; varnish, 300 parts, by weight.

XVI. - Leaf Green- Chrome green pale, 5 parts, by weight; varnish, 25 parts, by weight; benzine, ½ part, by weight.

XVII. - Silk Green. - Silk green, 10 parts, by weight; chrome yellow, pale, ½ part, by weight; lead sulphate, 5 parts, by weight; varnish, 30 parts, by weight; benzine. ½ part, by wieght,

XVIII.-Brown.- English red, 10 parts, by weight; ocher light, 3 parts, by weight; varnish, 30 parts, by weight; benzine, ½ part, by weight.

XIX. - Ocher, - French ocher, 10 parts, by weight; chrome yellow, dark, ½ part, by weight; varnish, 30 parts, by weight; benzine, ½ part , by weight.

XX. - Chocolate. - Umber, 10 parts, by weight; Florentine lake, 1/8 part, by weight; varnish, 25 parts, by weight; benzine, ½ part, by weight.

XXI. - Terra Cotta. - Chrome yellow, pale, 10 parts by weight; Turkey red, dark, 3 parts, by weight; varnish, 35 parts, by weight.

XXII. - Olive, Greenish. - French ocher, 5 parts, by weight; Paris blue, ½ part, by weight; graphite, ½ part, by weight; varnish, 25 parts, by weight; lithopone, 5 parts, by weight.

XXIII. - Olive, Brownish.- Chrome orange, 5 parts, by weight; Paris blue, 2 part, by weight; lead sulphate, 10 parts, by weight; english red, 1 part, by weight; varnish, 40 parts, by weight; benzine, 1½ parts, by weight.

XXIV. - Olive, Reddish. - Turkey red, dark, 75 parts, by weight; sap green, 75 parts, by weight; ocher, pale, 5 parts, by weight; varnish, 300 parts, by weight; benzine, 1½ parts, by weight.

Engravers' Varnishes.

In copper-plate engraving the plate must be covered with a dark-colored coating which, though entirely unaffected by the etching fluid, must be soft enough to allow the finest lines to be drawn with the needle and must also be susceptible of complete and easy removal when the etching is finished. Varnishes which possess these properties are called "etching grounds." They are made according to various formulas, but in all cases the principal ingredient is asphalt, of which only the best natural varieties are suitable for this pupose. Another common ingredient is beeswax, or tallow.

Etching ground are usually made in small quantities, at a single operation, by melting and stirring the solid ingredients together and allowing the mass to cool in thin sheets, which are then dissolved in oil of turpentine. The plate is coated uniformly with this varnish through which the engraver's tool readily penetrates, laying bare the metal beneath. After the lines thus drawn have been etched by immersing the plate in acid, the varnish is washed off with oil of turpentine.

The following formulas for etching grounds have been extensively used by engravers:

	I	II	III	IV
Yellow wax	50	30	110	40 parts
Syrian asphalt	20	20	25	40 parts
Rosin				20 parts
Amber			20	parts
Mastic	25	25	25	parts
Tallow				2 parts
Bergundy pitch				10 parts

FLOOR VARNISHES

I. Manila copal, spirit soluble	12 parts
Ruby shellac, powdered	62 parts
Venice, turpentine	12 parts
Spirit, 96 percent	250 parts

The materials are dissolved cold in a covered vat with constant stirring, or better still, in a stirring machine, and filtered. For the pale shades take light ocher; for dark ones, Amberg earth, which are well ground with the varnish in a paint mill.

II.- Shellac, A C leaf, 1.2 parts; sandarac, 8 parts; Manila copal, 2 parts; rosin, 5 parts; castor or linoleic acid or wood oil acid, 1.50 parts; spirit (96 percent), 65 parts.

French Varnish.- So called French varnish is made by dissolving 1 part of bleached or orange shellac in 5 parts of alcohol, the solution being allowed to stand and the clear portion then being decanted. The varnish may be colored by materials which are soluble in alcohol.

For red, use I part of eosin to 49 parts of the bleached shellac solution for blue, use 1 part of aniline blue to 24 parts of the bleached shellac solution, as the orange shellac solution would impart a greenish cast. For green, use 1 part of aniline green (brilliant green) to 49 parts of the orange shellac solution. For yellow, use either 2 parts of extract of turmeric or 1 part of gamboge to 24 parts of the solution, or 1 part of aniline yellow to 49 parts of the solution. For golden yellow, use 2 parts of gamboge and I part of dragon's blood to 47 parts of the orange shellac solution. The gamboge and dragon's blood should be dissolved first in little alcohol.

Golden Varnishes

I. Powdered benzoin. 1 part

Alcohol enough to make 10 parts. Pure saffron, roughly broken up, about 6 threads to the ounce.

Macerate 3 days and filter. Vary the quantity of saffron according to the shade desired. Mastic and juniper gum may be added to this varnish if a heavier body is desired.

II. Benzoin, juniper gum, gum mastic, equal parts.

Dissolve the gums in 9 times their weight of alcohol (varied more or less according to the consistency wanted), and color to the desired shade with threads of pure saffron. This varnish is very brilliant and dries at once.

India-Rubber Varnishes-I-Dissolve 10 pounds of India rubber in a mixture of 10 pounds of turpentine and 20 pounds of petroleum by treating same on a water bath. When the solution is completed add 45 pounds of drying oil and 5 pounds of lampblack and mix throughly.

II-Dissolve 7 pounds of India rubber in 25 pounds of oil of turpentine. By continued heating dissolve 14 pounds of rosin in the mixture. Color while hot with 3 pounds of lampblack.

Inlay Varnish -

Ozokerite	17	parts
Carnauba wax	3	parts
Turpentine oil	15	parts

Melt the ozokerite and Carnauba wax, then stir in the turpentine oil. This varnish is applied like a polish and imparts to the wood a dark natural colour and a dull luster.

Japanning Tin- The first thing to be done when a vessel is to be japanned, is to free it from all grease and oil, by rubbing it with turpentine. Should the oil, however, be linseed, it may be allowed to remain on the vessel, which must in that case be put in an oven and heated till the oil becomes quite hard.

After these preliminaries, a paint of the shade desired, ground in linseed oil, is applied. For brown, umber may be used.

When the paint has been satisfactorily applied it should be hardened by heating, and them smoothed down by rubbing with ground pumice stone applied gently by means of a piece of felt moistened with water. To be done well, this requires care and patience, and, it might be added, some experience.

The vessel is next coated with a varnish, made by the following formula :

Turpentine spirit	8	ounces
Oil of lavender	6	ounces
Camphor	1	drachm
Bruised copal	2	ounces

Perhaps some other good varnish would give equally satisfactory, results.

After this the vessel is put in an oven and heated to as high a temperature as it will bear without causing the varnish to blister or run. When the varnish has become hard, the vessel is taken out and another coat is put on, which is submitted to heat as before . This process may be repeated till the judgment of the operator tells him that it is no longer advisable.

Some operators mix the coloring matter directly with the varnish; when this is done, care should be taken that the pigment is first reduced to an impalpable powder, and then thoroughly mixed with the liquid.

Label Varnishes

1.-Sandarac	3	ounces av.
Mastic	3/4	ounce av.
Venice turpentine	150	grains
Alcohol	16	fluid ounces

Macerate with repeated stirring until solution is effected, and then filter.

The paper lables are first sized with diluted mucilage, then dried, and then coated with this varnish. If the lables have been written with water-soluble inks or color, they are first coated with 2 coats of collodion, and then varnished.

II.- The varnished lables of stock vessels often suffer damage from the spilling of the contents and the dripping after much pouring.

Formalin gelatin is capable of with standing the baneful influence of ether, benzine, water, spirit of wine, oil, and most substances. The following method of applying the preservative is recommended: having thoroughly cleaned the surface of the vessel, paste the label on and allow it to dry well. Give it acoat of thin collodion to protect the letters from being dissloved out or caused to run, then after a few minutes paint over it a coat of gelatin warmed to fluidity 5 to 25 being careful to cover in all the edges. Just before it solidifies go over it with a tuft of cotton dipped into a 40 percent formalin solution. It soom dries and becomes as glossy as varnish, and may be caoted again and again without danger of impairing the clear white of the label or decreasing its transparency.

Leather Varnishes.- 1. An excellent varnish for leather can be made from the following recipe: heat 400 pounds of boiled oil to 212^0 F., and add little by little 2 pounds of bichromate of potash, keeping the same temperature. The addition of the Bichromate should take about 15 minutes. Raise to 310^0 F., and add gradually during 1 hours at that temperature, 40 pounds prussian blue. Heat for 3 hours more, gradually raising to 482^{0}to 572^0 F., with constant stirring.In the meantime, heat together at 392^0 F., for ½ and hour, 25 pounds linseed oil, 35 pounds copal, 75 pounds turpentine, and 7 pounds cerasine. Mix the two varnishes, and dilute, if necessary, when cold with turpentine. The varnish should require to be warmed for easy application with the brush.

II.- Caoutchouce, I part: petroleum, 1 part; carbon bisulphide, 1 part; shellac, 4 parts; bone black, 2 parts; alcohol, 20 parts. First the caoutchouc is brought together with carbon bisulphide in a well closed bottle and stood aside for a few days. As soon as the caoutchoue is soaked add the petroleum and the alcohol, then the finely powdered shellac, and heat to about 125^{0}f. When the liquid appears pretty clear, which indicates the solution of all substances, the bone black is added by shaking thoroughly and the varnish is at once filled in bottels which are well closed. This pouch composition excels in drying quickly and produces upon the leather a smooth, deep black coating, which possesses a certain elasticity.

Metal Varnishes

The purpose of these varnishes is to protect the metals from oxidation and to render them glossy.

Aluminium Varnish - The following is a process giving a special varnish for aluminium, but it may also be employed for other metals, giving a coating unalterable and indestructible by water or atmospheric influences : dissolve, preferably in an enameled vessel, 10 parts, by weight, of gum lac in 30 parts of liquid ammonia. Heat on the water bath for about 1 hour and cool. The aluminium to be covered with this varnish is carefully cleaned in potash, and, having applied the varnish, the article is placed in a stove, where it is heated, during a certain time, at a suitable temperature (about 1062° F.).

Brass Varnishes Imitating Gold - I - An excellent gold varnish for brass objects, surgical or optical instruments, etc., is prepared as follows: Gum lac, in grains, pulverized, 30 parts; dragon's blood, 1 part; red sanders wood, 1 part: pounded glass, 10 parts; strong alcohol, 600 parts; after sufficient maceration, filter. The powdered glass simply serves for accelerating the dissolving, by interposing between the particles of gum lac and opal.

II - Reduce to powder, 160 parts, by weight, of turmeric of best quality, and pour over it 2 parts, by weight, of saffron, and 1,700 parts, by weight, of spirit; digest in a warm place 24 hours, and filter. next dissolve 80 parts, by weight, of dragon's blood; 80 parts, by weight, of sandarac; 80 parts, by weight, of elemi gum; 50 parts, by weight, of gamboge; 70 parts, by weight, of seedlac. Mix these substances with 250 parts, by weight, of crushed glass, place them in a flask, and pour over this mixture the alcohol colored as above described. Assist the solution by means of a sand or water bath, and filter at the close of the operation. This is a fine varnish for brass scientific instruments.

Bronze Varnishes - I - The following process yields a top varnish for bronze goods and other metallic ware in the most varying shades, the varnish excelling, besides, in high gloss and durability. Fill in a bottle, pale shellac, best quality, 40 parts, by weight; powdered Florentine lake, 12 parts, by weight; gamboge, 30 parts, by weight; dragon's blood, also powdered, 6 parts, by weight; and add 400 parts, by weight, of spirit of wine. This mixture is allowed to dissolve, the best way being to heat the bottle on the water bath until the boiling point of water is almost reached, shaking from time to time until all is dissolved. Upon cooling, decant the liquid, which constitutes a varnish of dark-red color, from any sediment that may be present. In a second bottle dissolve in the same manner 24 parts, by weight, of gamboge in 400 parts, by weight, of spirit of wine, from which will result a varnish of golden-yellow tint. According to the hue desired, mix the red varnish with the yellow variety, producing in this way any shade from the deepest red to the colour of gold. If required, dilute with spirit of wine. The application of the varnish should be conducted as usual, that is, the article should be slightly warm, it being necessary to adhere strictly to a certain temperature, which can be easily determined by trials and maintained by experience. In order to give this varnish a pale-yellow to greenish-yellow tone, mix 10 drops of picric acid with about 3 parts, by weight, of spirit of wine, and add to a small quantity of the varnish some of this mixture until the desired shade has been reached. Picric acid is poisonous, and the keeping of varnish mixed with this acid in a closed bottle is not advisable, because there is danger of an explosion. Therefore, it is best to prepare only so much varnish at one time as is necessary for the immediate purpose.

Brown Varnish - An excellent and quickly drying brown varnish for metals is made by dissolving 20 ounces of gum kino and 5 ounces of gum benjamin in 60 ounces of the best cold alcohol; 20 ounces of common shellac and 2 ounces of thick turpentine in 36 ounces of alcohol also give a very good varnish. if the brown is to have a reddish tint, dissolve 50 ounces of ruby shellac, 5 ounces balsam of copaiba, and 2 to 5 ounces of aniline brown, with or without 1/2 to 1 ounce of aniline violet, in 150 ounces of alcohol.

Copper Varnishes.-These two are for polished object :

I.-One hundred and ten parts of sandarac and 30 parts on rosin, dissolved in sufficient quantity of alcohol; 5 parts of glycerine are to be added.

II.-Sandarac	10 parts
Rosin	3 parts
Glycerine	½ part

Alocohol, a sufficient quantity. dissolve the two rosins in sufficient alcohol and add the glycerine.

Decorative Metal Varnishes.-

	I Per Cent	II Per Cent	III Per Cent	IV Per Cents
Seed lac	11.5	..	..	..
Amber	7.6	..	..	13.5
Gamboge	7.6	..	..	..
Dragon's blood	0.18	..	..	..
Saffron	0.16	..	..	..
Sandarac	..	11.2	15.9	16.6
Mastic	..	6.5	14.0	3.4
Elemi	..	3.3		
Venice turpentine	..	..	1.0	3.4
Camphor	..	1.5	..	..
Aloe	..	..	7.0	..
Alcohol	72.96	77.5	66.1	63.2

As will be seen, only natural colours are used. The so-called "gold lacquer" is composed as follows : Sandarac, 6.25 parts; mastic, 3 parts; shellac, 12.5 parts; Venice turpentine, 2.5 parts; aloe, 0.75 parts; gamboge, 3 parts; alcohol, 72 parts. The solution is filtered. Applied in a thin coating this varnish shows a handsome golden shade. Other metal varnishes have the following composition:

	V Per Cent	VI Per Cent	VII Per Cent
Shellac	17.5	..	18.0
Yellow acaroid gum	13.1	25.0	13.1
Manila	..	8.0	9.0
Alcohol	69.4	67.0	63.0

Gold Varnish. - I- A good gold varnish for coating moldings which produces great brilliancy is prepared as follows: dissolve 3 pounds of Shellac in 30 quarts of Alcohol, 5 pounds of mastic in 5 parts of alcohol, 3 pounds of sandarac in 5 quarts of alcohol 5 pounds of gamboge in 5 quarts of alcohol, 1 pound of dragon's blood in 1 quart of alcohol, 3 pounds of saunders in 5 quarts of alcohol, 3 pounds of tupentine in 3 quarts of alcohol. After all the ingredients have been dissolved separately in the given quantity of absolute alcohol and filtered, the solutions are mixed at a moderate heat.

II.- A varnish which will give a splendid luster, and any gold colour from deep red to golden yellow, is prepared by taking 50 ounces pale shellac, 15 pounds Florentine lake (precipitated from cochineal or redwood decoction by alum onto strach, kaolin, or gypsum), 25 ounces of sadalwood, and 8 ounces of dragon's blood. These in fine powder are disolved on the water bath, in 500 ounces rectified spirit. the spirit must boil and remain, with occasional shaking, for 2 to 3 hours on the bath. Then cool and decant. In the meantime heat in an other flask on the bath 30 ounces of gamboge in 500 ounces of the same spirit. The two liquids are mixed until the right colour needed for the particular purpose in hand is obtained. dilute with spirit if too thick. The addition of a little picric acid gives a greenish-yellow bronze but makes the varnish very liable to explode. These varnishes are applied to gently warmed surfaces with a soft bristle brush.

Gold Varnish for Tin. - This is obtained in the following manner; Spread out 5 parts, by weight, of finely powdered crystallized copper acetate in a warm spot, allowing it to lie for some time; then grind the powder, which will have acquired a light-brown shade, with oil of turpentine and add, with stirring, 15 parts, by weight, of fat copal varnish heated to 140^0 F. When the copper acetate has dissolved (in about ¼ hour), the mass is filled in a bottle and allowed to stand warm, for several days, shaking frequently. the gold varnish is then ready for use. coat the articles uniformly with it, and heat in a drying chamber, whereupon, according to the degree of temperature, varying colorations are obtained, changing from green to yellow, then golden yellow, and finally orange to brown. When good copal varnish is employed, the varnish will adhere very firmly, so that the article can be pressed without damage.

Iron Varnishes.-I.-A varnish obtained by dissolving wax in turpentine is useful. It gives a fairly hard coat, but has the drawback of filling up fine grooves. and so injuring the appearace of many metal ornaments.

II.- Shellac, 15 pounds; Siam benjamin, 13 pounds; alcohol, 80 pounds; formylchloride, 20 pounds.

III. - Sierra Leone copal, 6 pounds; dammar, 18 pounds; oleic acid, 3 pounds; alcohol, 40 pounds; oil of turpentine, 20 pounds; formylchloride, 15 pounds. The formylchloride not only effects the rapid drying necessary to prevent the varnish gravitating into hollows, but enables the alcohol to make a perfect solution of the rosin. The varnishes are excessively volatile, and must be stored accordingly.

Stove Varnishes-

Shellac	12 parts
Manila copal	14 parts
Rosin	12 parts
Gallipot	2 parts
Benzoin	1 part
Lampblack	5 parts
Nigrosin, spirit-soluble	1½ parts
Alcohol	250 parts

Tin Varnishes. - I.- For Tin Boxes. - In 75 parts of alcohol dissolve 15 parts of shellac, 2 parts of Venice turpentine, and 8 parts of sandarac.

II. - For Trays and Other Tinware.- The ground is prepared by adding to the white lead the tinting colours ground in good rubbing varnish and half oil of turpentine. For drier an admixture of "terebine" is recommended. With this lean and dull paint. coat the tins 2 or 3 times and blend. Next, grain with water or vinegar glaze, and varnish with pure Zanzibar copal varnish. or finest amber table-top varnish There are other tried methods for varnishing tin, which are applicable for new goods, manufactured in large quantities, while they are less advantageous for the restoration of old, repeatedly used articles.

Varnish substitutes.

A substitute for varnish is produces by adding to 100 parts of casein 10 to 25 parts of a 1 to 10 per cent soap solution and then 20 to 25 parts of slaked lime. The mixture is carefully kneaded until a perfectly homogeneous mass results. Then gradually add 25 to 40 parts of turpentine oil and sufficient water for the mass to assume the consistency of varnish. If it is desired to preserve it for some time a little ammonia is added so that the casein lime does not separate. The surrogate is considerably cheaper than varnish and dries so quickly that paint ground with it may be applied twice in quich succession..

Zapon Varnishes. - In the case of many articles which have been colored mechanically or by the battery. particularly with large pieces, an opaque varnish is used as a protection against atmospheric influences. The so-called brassoline, of a brown colour, negroline, black, and zapon which is colourless, are employed, according to the colour of the article. the last-named varnish is most commonly used, and gives a fine and durable coating, insoluble in almost all liquids which would come into consideration here, except that it will wash off in soap and water. Zapon varnish is a solution of collodion cotton and camphor in amyl acetate and amyl alcohol, and was formerly used to preserve old manuscripts and legal documents. In the process of zaponizing, the article is slightly warmed and immersed in the varnish, or the latter is applied with a brush. The solution is very durable, and has the advantage that after drying it will not show edges, ring, or spots. Zapon varnish which has become too thick must be diluted, and the brushes must be kept from becoming dry. If it is desired to give an especially warm tone, the article is treated with brushes which have been drawn over beeswax or mineral wax.

For the production of zapon or celluloid varnish, pour 20 parts of acetone over 2 parts of colourless celluloid waste, allowing it to stand for several days in a closed vessel, stirring frequently until the whole has dissolved into a clear, thick mass. Admix 78 parts of amyl acetate and clarify the zapon varnish by allowing it to settle for weeks.

PAINT BASES :

Dry Bases for Paints - The following colours and minerals, mixed in the proportions given and then ground to fine powder, make excellent dry paints, and may be thinned with turpentine oil, and a small percentage of cheap varnish to consistency required.

Buff.-

Yellow ocher	44	pounds
Whiting	6	pounds
Oxide of zinc	5	pounds
Plaster of Paris	1/2	pound

Brick Brown.-

Yellow ocher	26	pounds
Calcined copperas	4	pounds
Red hematite	1 1/4	pounds
Best silica	7	pounds
Whiting	18	pounds

Gray.-

Oxide of zinc	30	pounds
White lead	6	pounds
Whiting	12	pounds

Bone black	1/4	pound
Yellow ocher	2	pounds
Crimson.-		
Indian red	25	pounds
Crocus martis	7	pounds
Oxide of zinc	6	pounds
Whiting	6	pounds
Vandyke Brown.-		
Yellow ocher	25	pounds
Whiting	18	pounds
Umber	4	pounds
Oxide of zinc	7	pounds
Purple oxide of iron	1	pound
Blood Red.-		
Crocus martis	30	pounds
Whiting	20	pounds
Hematite	3	pounds
Silica	6	pounds
Venetian red	2	pounds
Drab.-		
Yellow ocher	40	pounds
Whiting	10	pounds
Oxide of zinc	8 1/2	pounds
Sulphate of barytes	1	pound
Paint for Blackboards.-		
Shellac	1	pound
Alcohol	1	gallon
Lampblack (fine quality)	4	ounces
Powdered emery	4	ounces
Ultramarine blue	4	ounces

Dissolve the shellac in the alcohol. Place the lampblack, emery, and ultramarine blue on a cheese-cloth strainer, pour on part of the shellac solution, stirring constantly and gradually adding the solution until all of the powders have passed through the strainer.

Dark-Green Paint for Blackboards.- Mix 1 part Prussian blue and 1 part chrome green with equal parts of gilders' size and alcohol to a thin cream consistency. Apply with a large, stiff brush and after an hour a second coat is given. After 24 to 48 hours smooth the surface with a felt cloth. This renders it rich and velvety. The shade must be a deep black green and the quantities of the colours have to be modified accordingly if necessary. Old blackboards should be previously thoroughly cleaned with soda.

BRONZING SOLUTIONS FOR PAINTS.

I.- The so-called "banana solution" (the name being derived from its odor) which is used in applying bronzes of various kinds, is usually a mixture of equal parts of amyl acetate, acetone, and benzine, with just enough pyroxyline dissolved therein to give it body. Powdered bronze is put into a bottle containing this mixture and the paint so formed applied with a brush. The thin covering of pyroxyline that is left after the evaporation of the liquid protects the bronze from the air and keeps it from being wiped off by the cleanly housemaid. Tarnished picture frames and tarnished chandeliers to which a gold bronze has been applied from such a solution will look fresh and new for a long time. Copper bronze as well as gold bronze and the various coloured bronze powders can be used in the "banana solution" for making very pretty advertising signs for use in the drug store. Lettering and bordering work upon the signs can be done with it. Several very small. stiff painters' brushes are needed for such work and they must be either kept in the solution when not in use, or, better still, washed in benzine or acetone immediately after use and put away for future service. As the "banana solution" is volatile, it must be kept well corked.

II.-A good bronzing solution for paint tins, applied by dipping, is made by dissolving Syrian asphaltum in spirits of turpentine, etc., and thinning it down with these solvents to the proper bronze colour and consistency. A little good boiled oil will increase the adherence.

Paint Brushes.-To soften a hard paint brush, stand the brush overnight in a pot of soft soap and clean in warm water. Afterwards clean in benzine. If the brush is wrapped with a string do not let the string touch the soap.

Paint brushes which have dried up as hard as stone can be cleaned in the following manner: Dissolve 1 part soda in 3 parts water; pour the solution in a cylinder glass, and suspend in it the brushes to be cleaned, so that they are about 2 inches from the bottom of the vessel. Let it remain undisturbed at a temperature of 140° to 158° F., 12 to 24 hours, after which the most indurated brushes will have become soft, so that they can be readily cleaned with soap. It is essential, however, to observe the temperature, as bristle brushes will be injured and spoiled if the heat is greater.

Black- A permanent Black of Rich Luster for Metal Boxes-Dissolve chlorate of potassium and blue vitriol, equal parts, in 36 times as much water, and allow the solution to cool. The parts to be blacked may be either dipped in the solution, or the solution may be flowed on and allowed to remain until the metal becomes black, after which the fixtures should be rinsed in clean water and allowed to dry. Those parts of the surface which show imperfections in the black should be recoated.

Dead White on Silver Work, etc.-Bruise charcoal very finely and mix it with calcined borax in the proportion of 4 parts of charcoal to 1 of borax. Of this make a paste with water; apply this paste on the parts to be deadened; next expose the piece to the fire of well-lit coal until it acquires a cherry-red shade; allow to cool and then place it in water slightly acidulated with sulphuric acid. The bath must not be more than 5^0 Be. Leave the piece in the bath about 2 hours, then rinse off several times.

White Coating for Signs, etc.-A white colour for signs and articles exposed to the air is prepared as follows for the last coat: Thin so-called Dutch "stand" oil with oil of turpentine to working consistency, and grind in it equal parts of zinc white and white lead, not adding much siccative, as the white lead assists the drying considerably. If the paint is smoothed well with a badger brush, a very durable white colour of great gloss is obtained. Linseed oil, or varnish which has thickened like "stand" oil by long open storing, will answer equally well.

To Prevent Crawling of Paints-Probably the best method to pursue will be to take an ordinary flannel rag and carefully rub it over the work previous to varnishing, striping, or painting. This simple operation will obviate the possibility of crawling.

In some instances, however, crawling may be traced to a defective varnish. The latter, after drying evenly on a well-prepared paint surface will at times crawl, leaving small pitmarks. For this, the simple remedy consists in purchasing varnish from a reputable manufacturer.

FIREPROOF PAINTS:

Fireproofing paints of effective quality are prepared in different ways. Naturally no oily or greasy substances enter into their composition, the blending agent being simply water.

I.-One of the standing paints consists of 40 pounds of powedered asbestos, 10 pounds of aluminate of soda, 10 pounds of lime, and 30 pounds of silicate of soda, with the addition of any non-rosinous coloring matter desired. The whole is thoroughly mixed with enough water to produce a perfect blend and render an easy application. Two or more coats of this is the rule in applying it to any wood surface, inside ro outside of building.

II.-Another formula involves the use of 40 pounds of finely ground glass, a like amount of ground porcelain, and similarly of China clay or the same quantity of powdered asbestos, and 20 pounds of quicklime. These materials are ground very fine and then mixed in 60 pounds of liquid silicate of soda with water, as in the preceding formula. Two or more coats, if necessary, are given.

Each of these paints is applied with a brush in the ordinary way, the drying being accomplished in a few hours, and, if coloring matter is desired, the above proportions are varied accordingly.

III.-A surface coated with 3 coats of water glass, these 3 coats being subsequently coated with water glass containing enough whiting or ground chalk to make it a trifle thicker than ordinary paint, is practically non-inflammable, only yielding to fierce consuming flames after a somewhat protracted exposure.

IV.-Zinc white, 70 pounds; air-slaked lime, 39 pounds white lead, 50 pounds; sulphate of zinc, 10 pounds; silicate of soda, 7 gallons. The zinc white and lime are mixed together, then ground in elastic oil, after which the silicate of soda is added, this addition being followed by the white lead and sulphate of zinc. This white paint can be coloured to meet any desired shade and it may be classed as a good working paint and probably fireproof to the same extent that most of the pretentiously sounded pigments on the markets are.

Fireproof and Waterproof Paints-

The following recipes are claimed to resist both fire and water: A preparation for protecting wood against the action of fire and of moisture, and also for producing on the surface of wood and metal a coat, insulating with reference to electricity and preservative from corrosion, has been introduced in france by Louis Bethisy and Myrthil Rose. The bases or fundamental raw materials quire distinct from those hitherto employed for the same purpose, are 100 parts, by weight, of nitro-cellulose and 30 parts, by weight, of chloride of lime, dissolved in 50 per cent alcohol.

Preparation of the Bases-The cellulose (of wood, paper, cotton, linen, ramie, or hemp) is put in contact with two-thirds part of sulphuric acid of 66° Be. and one-third part of nitirc acid of 42° Be. for some 20 or 30 minutes, washed with plenty of water, and kept for 24 hours in a tank of water supplied with an energetic current.

The nitro-cellulose thus obtained is bleached for this purpose; a double hypochlorite of aluminum and magnesium is employed. This is obtained by grinding together 100 parts of chloride of lime, 60 parts of aluminum sulphate, 23 parts of magnesium sulphate, with 200 parts of water.

When the nitro-cellulose is bleached and rewashed, it is reduced to powder and dried as thoroughly as possible. It is then placed in a vat hermetically closed and put in contact with the indicated proportion of calcium chloride dissolved in alcohol. This solution of calcium chloride should be prepared at least 24 hours in advance and filtered.

Composition of the Coating.-This has the following constituents; Bases (nitro-cellulose and solution of calcium chloride), 1 part; amyl acetate (solvent of the bases), 5 parts, by weight; sulphuric ether of 65°, 1.650 parts, by weight; alcohol, 0.850 parts, by weight; one of these powders, alum, talc, asbestos, or mica, 0.100 parts. Other solvents may be employed instead of amyl acetate; for example, acetone, acetic acid, ether alcohol, or methylic alcohol. The ether alcohol furnishes a product drying very quickly. If a very pliant coating is desired, the amyl acetate is employed preferably, with addition of vaseline oil, 0.20 parts, and lavender oil, 0.010 parts.

Method of Operating.-The sulphuric acid is mixed with the alcohol, and left for an hour in contact, shaking from time to time. Afterwards the amyl acetate is added, and left in contact for another hour under similar agitation. In case of the employment of vaseline oil and lavender oil, these two are mingled in ether alcohol. The base is introduced and left in contact for 24 hours, with frequent agitation. The fluidity of the product is augmented by increasing the quantity of the solvent.

Properties.-Wood covered with this coating is fireproof, non-hygrometric, and refractory to the electric current. It also resists the action of acids and alkalies. Metals covered with it are sheltered from oxidation, and effectually insulated on their surface from the electric current. The coating is liquid in form, and applied like colloidons, either by the brush or by immersion or other suitable method.

Paint Deadening.-In order to obtain an even dullness of large walls, proceed as follows: After all the dirt has been carefully swept off, oil with 2 parts linseed oil and 1 part turpentine and rub down the smooth places in the wet oil with pumice stone, When the oil coating is dry, mix the ground paint, consisting of whiting, 2 parts; and white lead, 1 part; both finely ground and diluted as above. Do not apply the grounding too thin, because the chalk in itself possesses little covering power. It is not the mission of the chalk, however, to adulterate the material, but to afford a hard foundation for the subsequent coats. For the third coating take white lead, 1 part; and zinc white, 1 part; thin as above and blend with a soft hair pencil. For the final application use only zinc white, ground stiff in oil with any desired mixing colour and thinned with turpentine and rain water. Mix the water and the turpentine with the colour at the same time, and this coat may be dabbed instead of blended. By the addition of water the paint becomes dull more slowly and is a little more difficult to lay on; but it does not show a trace of gloss after a few days and never turns yellow, even in places less exposed to the air, and besides excels by great permanency.

Another way is to add white wax instead of water to the last coating. This wax paint also gives a handsome dullness but is more difficult of treatment. A nice matt coating is also obtained by addition of Venetian soap, dissolved in water instead of the wax. This is very desirable for church decorations where exceptionally large surfaces are to be deadened.

PAINT DRYERS :

I.	Ordinary barytes	25	pounds
	Whitting	4	pounds
	Litharge	2	pounds
	Sulphate of zinc	2	pounds

	Sugar of lead	2	pounds
	Boiled linseed oil	5	pounds
	Plaster of Paris	1/2	pound
II.	Whiting	16	pounds
	Barytes	16	pounds
	White lead	3	pounds
	Boiled linseed oil	3/4	gallon

PAINTS FOR GOLD AND GILDING :

Gold Paints formulas of the various gold paints on the market are carefully guarded trade secrets. Essentially they consist of bronze powder mixed with a varnish. The best bronze powder for the purpose is what is known in the trade as "French flake," a deep gold bronze. This bronze, as seen under the microscope, consists of tiny flakes or spangles of the bronze metal. As each minute flake forms a facet for the reflection of colour, the paint made with it is much more brilliant than that prepared from finely powdered bronze.

For making gold paint like the so-called "washable gold enamel" that is sold by the manufacturers at the present time, it is necessary to mix a celluloid varnish with the French flake bronze powder. This varnish is made by dissolving transparent celluloid in amyl acetate in the proportion of about 5 percent of celluloid.

Trnasparent celluloid,		
finely shreded	1	ounce
Acetone, sufficient quantity.		
Amyl acetate to make	20	ounces.

Digest the celluloid in the acetone until dissolved and add the amyl acetate. From 1 to 4 ounces of flake bronze is to be mixed with this quantity of varnish. For silver paint or "aluminum enamel." flake aluminum bronze powder should be used in place of the gold. the celluloid varnish incloses the bronze particles in an impervious coating, air-tight and water-tight. As it contains nothing that will act upon the bronze, the latter retains its luster for a long period, until the varnished surface becomes worn or abraded and the bronze thus exposed to atmospheric action.

All of the 'god" or, more properly, gilt furniture that is sold so cheaply by the furniture and department stores is gilded with a paint of this kind, and for that reason such furniture can be offered at a moderate price. The finish is surprisingly durable, and in color and luster is a very close imitation of real gold-leaf work. This paint is also used on picture frames of cheap and medium grades, taking the place of gold leaf or the lacquered silver leaf formerly used on articles of the better grades; it is also subsituted for "Dutch metal," of imitation gold leaf, on the cheapest class of work.

A cheaper gold paint is made by using an inexpensive varnish composed of gutta percha, gum dammar, or some other varnish gum, dissolved in benzole, or in a mixture of benzole and benzine. The paints made with a celluloid-amyl-acetate varnish give off a strong banana like odor when applied, and may be readily recognized by this characteristic.

The impalpably powdered bronzes are called "lining" bronzes. They are chiefly used for striping or lining by carriage painters; in bronzing gas fixtures and metal work; in fresco and other interior decoration, and in printing; the use of a very fine powder in inks or paints admits of the drawing or printing of very delicate lines.

Lining bronze is also used on picture frames or other plastic ornamental work. Mixed with a thin weak glue sizing it is applied over "burnishing clay," and when dry is polished with agate burnishers. The object thus treated, after receiving a finishing coat of a thin transparent varnish, imitates very closely in appearance a piece of finely cast antique bronze. To add still more to this effect the burnishing clay is colored the greenish black that is seen in the deep parts of real antique bronzes, and the bronze powder, mixed with size, is applied only to the most prominent parts or "high lights" of the ornament.

Since the discovery of the celluloid amyl-acetate varnish, or bronze liquid, and its preservative properties on bronze powders, manufacturers have discontinued the use of liquids containing oils, turpentine, or gums, since their constitutents corrode the bronze metal, causing the paint finally to turn black.

Gilding in Size.-The old painters and gilders used to prepare the gold size themselves, but nowadays it is usually bought ready made, barring the white of egg additional. The best and most reliable, and especially suited for fine work, is undoubtedly the red French gold size. It is cleaned, as far as possible, of all impurities, and powdered. For 246 grains take 1 white of egg; put it into a glass, taking care to exclude the yolk entirely-otherwise the burnish will show black spots. Beat the white of egg to a froth with a long, well-cleaned bristle brush; add the froth to the size and grind finely together, which is soon done. When grinding, a little water and red size, if necessary, may be added (use only water for thinning). After being ground, the size is forced through a very fine hair sieve into a perfectly clean vessel, and covered up well, for immediate or subsequent use.

The raw stuff of the red size is bolus, which is dug in France and Armenia in excellent quality. Besides the red size there are yellow, white (pipe clay), blue, and gray (alumina), which are used for certain purposes, to enumerate which here would lead too far.

For burnish gold, always take yellow size for ground work. Dip a finely ground bristle brush in the gold size prepared for use; fill a well-cleaned glass (holding 1 pint) half full of water, and add the size contained in the brush, also about 4 to 5 spoonfuls of pure alcohol. It is advisable not to take too much size; the liquid, when applied, must hardly have a yellow tint. When this is dry soon after, commence applying the size, for which a hair pencil is used. The essentials are to paint evenly and not too thickly, so that the tone remains uniform. Apply three coats of size.

When the size is laid on correctly and has become dry, brush the whole with a special brush, or rub with a flannel rag, so as to obtain the highest possible luster. The size must not stand too long; otherwise no gloss can be developed. After brushing, coat the work with weak glue water and wrap it up in tissue paper if the gilding is not to be done at once.

The strictest cleanliness is essential, as the red gold size is very sensitive. The parts where the size has been applied must not be touched with the hand, else grease spots will ensue, which will make a flawless gloss in gilding impossible. The least relaxation of the necessary attention may spoil the whole job, so that everything has to be ground off again.

The necessary tools for the application of gold leaf are: Hair pencils of various sizes, tip, cushion, and gilding knife, as with oil-gilding. Take pure alcohol or grain brandy, and dilute with two-thirds water. When ready to apply the gold leaf, dip a hair pencil of suitable size into the fluid, but do not have it full enough that the alcohol will run on the size ground. Moisten a portion of the ground surface as large as the gold leaf, which is laid on immediately after. Proceed in the same manner, first moistening, then applying the ready-cut gold leaf. The latter must not be pressed on, but merely liad down lightly, one leaf a little over the edge of the previous one, without using up too much gold. Technical practice in gold-leaf gilding is presupposed; through this alone can any skill be acquired, reading being of no avail.

The leaf of gold being applied, all dust must be swept off by means of a light, fine hair pencil (but never against the overlapping edges), and the burnishing is commenced. For this purpose there are special agate tools of the shape of a horn. Flint stone, blood stone, and wolf's teeth are sometimes, but gradually more seldom, employed. Burnish till a full, fine luster appears; but very carefully avoid dents and lines, not to speak of scratches, which would be very hard to mend.

Gold Enamel Paints -

I.	Pure turps	6	pints
	Copal varnish	1	pint

Good gold bronze	6 1/2	pounds
Calcis hydrate (dry-		
slaked lime)	1/2	ounce

Mix the varnish and turps at a gentle heat, then slake well with the lime, and settle for a few days, then pour off the clean portion and mix with the powder.

II. White hard varnish	1	gallon
Methylated spirit	3/4	gallon
Gold bronze	12	pounds
Finely powdered mica	3	ounces

Mix the varnish and the spirit, reduce the mica to an impalpable powder, mix with the gold, then add to the liquid. Many bronze powders contain a goodly proportion of mica, as it imparts brilliancy. Powdered mother-of-pearl is used also.

GRAINING WITH PAINT :

Oak Graining-Prepare a paint of two-thirds of white lead and one-third of golden ocher with the requisite amount of boiled linseed oil and a little drier, and cover the floor twice with the mixture, which possesses great covering power. When the last coating is dry, paint the floor with a thinly liquid paint consisting of varnish and sienna, applying the same in the longitudinal direction of the boards. Trat a strip about 20 inches wide at a time, and draw at once a broad paint brush or, in the absence of such, an ordinary brush or goose feather along the planks through the wet paint, whereupon the floor will acquire a nicely grained appearance. The paint requires several days to dry. A subsequent coating of varnish will cause the graining to stand out still more prominently.

Birch-Imitations of birch are usefully employed for furniture. The ground should be a light, clean buff, made from white lead, stained with either yellow ocher or raw sienna in oil. In graining, brush over the surface with a thin wash of warm brown, making the panel of 2 or 3 broad color shades. Then take a large mottler and mottle the darker parts into the light, working slantwise, as for maple, but leaving a broad and stiff mark. While this is still wet soften the panel and then slightly mottle across the previous work to break it up. When thoroughly dry, carefully wet the work over with clean water and clean mottler, and put in darker over grain with a thin oak overgrainer of overgrainer in tubes.

Maple-Sixty pounds white lead; 1 ounce deep vermilion; 1 ounce lemon chrome.

Ash-Sixty pounds white lead; 1 pounce deep vermilion; 1 ounce lemon chrome.

Medium Oak-Sixty pounds white lead; 2 pounds French ocher; 1 ounce burnt umber.

Light Oak-Sixty pounds white lead; 1 ounce lemon chrome; 1/2 pound French ocher.

Dark Oak-Sixty pounds white lead; 10 pounds burnt umber; 1 1/2 pounds medium Venetian red.

Satin Wood-Sixty pounds white lead; 1 ounce deep vermilion; 1 1/2 pounds lemon chrome.

Pollard Oak-Seventy-five pounds white lead; 20 pounds French ocher; 3 pounds burnt umber; 2 1/2 pounds medium Venetian red.

Pitch Pine-Sixty pounds white lead; 1/2 pound French ocher; 1/2 pound medium Venetian red.

Knotted Oak-Sixty pounds white lead; 9 pounds French ocher; 3 1/2 pounds burnt umber.

Italian Walnut-Sixty pounds white lead; 6 pounds French ocher; 1 1/2 pounds burn umber; 1 1/4 pounds medium Venetian red.

Rosewood-Nine and one-half pounds burnt umber; 40 pounds medium Venetian red; 10 pounds orange chrome.

Dark Mahogany-Nine and one-half pounds burnt umber; 40 pounds medium Venetian red; 10 pounds orange chrome.

Light Mahogany-Sixty pounds white lead; 3 pounds burnt umber; 10 pounds medium Venetian red.

American Walnut-Thirty pounds white lead; 9 pounds French ocher; 4 pounds burnt umber; 1 pound medium Venetian red.

LUMINOUS PAINTS.

The illuminating power of the phosphorescent masses obtained by heating strontium thiosulphate or barium thiosulphate is considerably increased by the addition, before heating, of small quantities of the nitrates of uranium, bismuth, or thorium. Added to calcium thiosulphate, these nitrates do not heighten the luminosity or phosphorescene. The product from strontium thiosulphate is more luminous than that of the barium compound. Among the best luminous paints are the following:

I.-Lennord's-One hundred parts, by weight, of strontium carbonate; 100 parts, by weight, of sulphur; 0.5 parts, by weight, of potassium chloride; 0.5 parts, by weight, of sodium chloride; 0.4 parts, by weight of manganese chloride. The materials are heated for three-quarters of an hour to one hour, to about 2,372^{o} F. The product gives a violet light.

II.-Mourel's-One hundred parts, by weight, of strontium carbonate; 30 parts, by weight, of sulphur; 2 parts by weight of sodum carbonate:0.5 parts, by weight, of sodium chloride:0.2 parts, by weight, of manganese sulphate. The method of treatment is the same as in the first, the phosphorescence deep yellow.

III.-Vanino's.-Sixty parts by weight, of strontium thiosulphate; 12 parts, by weight, of a 0.5 per cent acidified alcoholic solution of bismuth nitrate; 6 parts, by weight, of a 0.5 per cent alcoholic solution of uranium nitrate. The materials are mixed, dried, brought gradually to a temperature of 2,372° F., and heated for about an hour. The phosphorescence is emerald green.

IV.-Balmain's.-Twenty parts, by weight, of calcium oxide (burnt lime), free from iron; 6 parts, by weight, of sulphur; 2 parts, by weight, of starch; 1 part, by weight, of a 0.5 per cent solution of bismuth nitrate; 0.15 parts, by weight, of potassium chloride; 0.15 parts, by weight, of sodium chloride. The materials are mixed, dried, and heated to 1,300° C. (2,372° F.). The product gives a violet light.

To make these phosphorescent substances effective, they are exposed for a time to direct sunlight; or a mercury lamp may be used. Powerful incandescent gas light also does well, but requires more time.

PAINTS FOR METAL SURFACES

Blackening Ornaments of Iron.-I.

To give iron ornaments a black-brown to black color, proceed in the following manner: The articles are treated with corrosives, cleaned of all adhering grease, and placed in a 10 per cent solution of potassium bichromate, dried in the air, and finally held over an open, well-glowing, non-sooting fire for 2 minutes. The first coloring is usually black brown, but if this process is repeated several times, a pure black shade is obtained. Special attention has to be paid to removing all grease, otherwise the greasy spots will not be touched by the liquid, and the coloring produced will become irregular. Benzine is employed for that purpose and the articles must not be touched with the fingers afterwards.

II.-This process protects the iron from rust for a long time. The -treatment consists in coating the objects very uniformly with a thin layer of linseed-oil varnish, and burning it off over a charcoal fire. During the deflagration the draught must be stopped. The varnish will first go up in smoke with a strong formation of soot, and finally burn up entirely. The process is repeated; i. e., after one coating is burned off a new one is applied. until the parts exhibit a uniformly handsome, deep- black colour. Next, wipe off the covering with a dry rag and heat again, but only moder ately. Finally, the articles are taken from the fire and rubbed with a rag well saturated with linseed-oil varnish. The black turns completely dull, and forms a real durable covering for the objects.

Black for Polished Iron Pieces.-Apply successive layers of a very concentrated solution of nitrate of manganese dissolved in alcohol over a gentle fire and the water bath. The surfaces to be blackened should be previously heated. By repeating the layers all the tints between brownish black and bluish black may be obtained.

Glossy Black for Bicycles, etc.

Amber	8	ounces
Linseed oil	4	ounces
Asphaltum	1 1/2	ounces
Rosin	1 1/2	ounces
Oil turpentine	8	ounces

Heat the linseed oil to boiling point, add the amber, asphaltum, and rosin, and when all melted remove from the fire and gradually add the turpentine.

Japan Black.-The following is a good japan black for metal surfaces: Take 12 ounces of amber and 2 ounces of asphaltum. Fuse by heat, and add 1/2 pint boiled oil and 2 ounces of rosin. When cooling add 16 ounces of oil of turpentine.

Brass and Bronze Protective Paint.

As a protective covering, especially for brass and bronze objects. a colorless celluloid solution is recommended, such as is found in trade under the name of "Zapon" (q. v.).

Paint for Copper.-Dissolve 1 ounce of alum in 1 quart of warm soft water. When cold add flour to make it about the consistency of cream, then add 1/2 thimble of rosin and 1/2 ounce of sugar of lead.

Priming Iron.-The following, if carefully carried out, gives the best satisfaction: The first step consists in thoroughly cleaning the surface of the iron, removing all adhesions in the way of dirt, rust, etc., before the question of priming is considered. As paint in this instance is applied more with a view of protecting the iron from atmospheric influences, rather than for a decorative effect, careful attention should be devoted for securing a base or surface which. is calculated to produce a thorough and permanent application. A great deal depends upon the nature of the metal to be painted. Common cast iron, for instance, possessing a rough exterior, with ordinary precautions can be more readily painted with the prospect of a permanent adhesion of the paint, than a planed steel or wrought-iron surface. With the latter it has been demonstrated that a hard and elastic paint is needed, while with regard to cast iron, other paints containing iron oxides are more suitable. For good drying and covering properties, as well as elasticity, a good boiled oil to which has been added an adequate proportion of red lead will be found to form an excellent paint for smooth metal surfaces. The primary object is to protect the surface of the iron from moisture for the purpose of avoiding - rust. The priming must therefore be carried out so that it will stick, after which subsequent coats may be added if desired.

It is advisable that articles made of iron should first be coated with linseed oil varnish. It dries slowly, hardens, and enables the operator afterwards to exercise an effective control over the condition of his material. Iron must be absolutely dry and free from rust when it is to be painted. It is best to apply next a coating of hot linseed oil; when dry this should be followed by a priming of pure red lead in good linseed oil, and the iron should then be painted as desired, using ground oil paints and leaving an interval of a week between each coating Cementing should be done after the red lead priming but the last coat must not be given until the whole is thoroughly dry. Bright oil paints and an upper coating with plenty of oil resist the effects of heat better than thin coatings; moreover, rust can be detected in its early stages with the former. Coatings of tar and asphalt (asphalt dissolved in turpentine) are practicable for underground pipes but are not adspted for pipes exposed to the air, as they are quickly spoiled. Asphalt varnish, used for coating coal scuttles, fire screens, etc., consists of asphalt dissolved in linseedoil varnish. Iron stoves and stovepipes are best coated with graphite.

Galvanized Iron.-For galvanized iron there has been recommended a wash consisting simply of dilute hydrochloric acid,. which produces chloride of zinc, that in combination with the oxygen of the air is said to produce a film upon which oil color takes as good a hold as it would upon ordinary sheet iron.

Another method which has been tested and found effective is to make a solution as follows: One ounce of chloride of copper; 1 ounce nitrate of copper;

1 ounce sal ammoniac, dissolved in 2 quarts of soft water, to which is added 1 ounce of crude or commercial hydrochloric acid. This solution should be made in an earthenware dish or pot, or in glass or stoneware, as tin will precipitate the copper salts and make the solution imperfect. To large surfaces this solution is applied with a broad brush, when the surface assumes a deep black colour, which in drying out in from 12 to 24 hours becomes a gray white, upon which the properly prepared primer will take a permanent grip On the fiim so produced a much thinner paint will cover very much better than a stouter paint would on the untreated galvanized or ordinary iron surface. A single trial will convince the craftsman that this treatment is a method that will give lasting results, provided he tries the same priming, paint on the treated and untreated surface.

To Paint Wrought Iron with Graphite.- In order to make wrought iron look like new mix fine graphite with equal parts of varnish and turpentine oil, adding a little siccative. Paint the iron parts with this twice, allowing to dry each time. Especially the second coating must be perfectly dry before further treatment. The latter consists in preparing graphite with spirit and applying it very thinly over the first coat. After the drying or evaporation of the , spirit the graphite last applied is brushed vigorously, whereby a handsome, durable gloss is produced.

Paint for Iron Bodies Exposed to Heat. Dilute 1 part soda water glass with 2 parts water and mix intimately with the following pigments:

White.-White lead or sulphate of barium.

Yellow.-Chromate of barium, ocher, or uranium yellow.

Green.-Chromic oxide or ultramarine green.

Blue.-Ultramarine.

Brown.-Oxide of cadmium, oxide of manganese or terra di sienna.

Red.-English red or chrome red.

Bronze powder in a suitable quantity may be added to the mixture, but not more paint should be prepared than can be used up in a few hours. The bronze powder may also be strewn on the fresh paint, or applied with a dry brush, to enhance the gloss. This paint is not affected by heat, and is inodorous.

Protective Coating for Bright Iron Articles.-Zinc white, 30 parts; lamp black, 2 parts; tallow, 7 parts; vaseline, 1 part; olive oil, 3 parts; varnish, 1 part. Boil together ¼ hour and add 1/2 part of benzine and 1 part of turpentine, stirring the mass carefully and boiling for some time. The finished paste-like substance can be readily removed with a rag without the use of solvents.

Rust Paints.-I.-A new rust paint is produced by the following process: Mix 100 parts dry iron sulphate and 87 parts sodium chlorate and heat to 1,500° to 1,800° F. The chlorine set free seems to have a very favorable action on the colour of the simultaneously forming iron oxide. In order to avoid, however, too far-reaching an effect of the chlorine gas about 18 pounds of a substance which absorbs the same mechanically, such as kaolin, ground pumice stone, ocher, etc., are added to the mixture.

II.-A material known under the names of lardite, steatite, agalmatolite, pagodite, is excellently adapted as a substitute for the ordinary metallic protective agent of the pigments and has the property of protecting iron from rust in an effective manner. In China, lardite is used for protecting edifices of sandstone, which crumbles under the action of the atmosphere. Likewise a thin layer of powdered steatite, applied in the form of paint, has been found valuable there as a protector against the decay of obelisks, statues, etc. Lardite, besides, possesses the quality of being exceedingly fine-grained, which renders this material valuable for use in ship painting. Ground steatite is one of the finest materials which can be produced, and no other so quickly and firmly adheres to the fibers of iron and steel. Furthermore, steatite is lighter than metallic covering agents, and covers, mixed in paint, a larger surface than zinc white, red lead, or iron oxide. Steatite as it occurs in Switzerland is used there and in the Tyrol for stoves, since it is fireproof.

Steel.-An excellent coating for steel, imitating the blue colour of natural steel, is composed of white shellac, 5 parts; borax, 1 part; alcohol, 5 parts; water, 4 Parts ; and a sufficient quantity of methylene blue. The borax is dissolved in water, the shellac in alcohol. The aqueous solution of the borax is heated to a boil and the alcoholic solution of the shellac is added with constant stirring. Next add the blue color, continuing to stir. Before this coating is applied to the steel, e. g., the spokes of a bicycle, the latter are first rubbed off with fine emery paper. The coat is put on with a soft rag. The quantity of pigment to be added is véry small. By varying the quantity a paler or darker coloring of the steel can be produced.

PAINTS FOR ROOFS AND ROOF PAPER:

Carbolineum.-This German preparation is made in three colours.

I.-Pale.-Melt together in an iron kettle, over a naked fire, 30 parts of American rosin F and 150 parts of pale paraffine oil and stir in 10 parts of single rectified rosin oil.

II.-Dark.-Melt 100 parts of anthracene oil and 20 parts of American rosin F on a slow fire. Next stir in 2 parts of Para rubber solution (or solution of caoutchouc waste) and keep on boiling until all is dissolved. When this is done there should be still added 5 parts of crude concentrated carbolic acid and 5 parts of zinc chloride lye, 50° Be., stir. ring until cool. The last-named admixture is not absolutely necessary, but highly advisable, owing to its extraordinary preservative and bactericidal properties.

III.-Colored.-For red, melt 100 parts of coal-tar oil, then stir in 50 parts of pale paraffine oil, and finally 75 parts of bole or iron minium, and pass through the paint mill. Although the addition of iron minium is very desirable, it is considerably more expensive. For gray, proceed as above, with the exception that metallic gray is used in place of the bole. For green, metallic green is employed. The colours are identical with those used in the manufacture of roof varnish. To increase the antiseptic properties of the colored carbolineum, any desired additions of phenol or zinc chloride solutions may be made, but the chief requirement in the case of colored carbolineum is good covering power of he coating.

Paints for Roofs Covered with Tar Paper, for Roofing Paper, etc.

I.-	Distilled coal tar	70	parts
	Heavy mineral oil		

	(lubricating oil)	10	parts
	American rosin	20	parts
II.-	Distilled coal tar	50	parts
	Trinidad asphalt	15	parts
	Mineral oil, contain ing paraffine	10	parts
	Dry clay, finely ground	25	parts

Imitation Oil Paint.-Sohulz's German patent paint is cheap, and claimed to be durable, weatherproof, and glossy, like oil paint. The application consists of a ground coat, upon which the surface coat proper is applied after the former is dry. For the preparation of the grounding dissolve 1,000 parts, by weight, of Marseilles soap in 10,000 parts of boiling water and stir. In a separate vessel dissolve 2,000 parts of glue in 10,000 parts of boiling water, adding 17,500 parts of spirit of sal ammoniac. These two solutions are poured together and well stirred. Then dissolve 400 parts of chrome alum in 5,000 parts of water, and pour into the above mixture. To this mixture add 10,000 parts of pipe clay, stirring the whole well and tinting with earth colours, ocher, Vandyke brown, etc. The solid ingredients must be dissolved in boiling hot water, and sifted so as to obtain a finely divided ground colour. This priming is applied in a warm state. The coating proper is put on the ground coat after it is dry, in about one-half to one hour. For this coat dissolve 2,000 parts of crystallized alum in 10,000 parts of boiling water and add to this liquid a solution of 2,000 parts of glue in 10,000 parts of water; in a special vessel prepare soapsuds of 1,000 parts of Marseilles soap in 12,000 parts of boiling water; dissolve 120 parts of chrome alum in 1 500 parts of boiling water, and mix the three solutions together with diligent stirring. This paint or liquid should also be put on hot, and assures a durable exterior paint.

PAINTS, STAINS, ETC., FOR SHIPS.

Anti-Fouling Composition.-Make an agglutinant by heating together

		By weight
White lead, ground in oil	2	parts
Red lead, dry	1	part
Raw linseed oil	14	parts

While hot stir in yellow ocher, kaolin, baked clay in powder, or any inert body, such as silica, barytes, gypsum etc., to form a stiff dough, and, without allowing this compound to become cold (the vessel should not be removed from the source of heat), dilute with more or less manganese linoleate to the required consistency.

Marine Paint to Resist Sea Water. First prepare the water-resisting agglutinant by heating together

Dry white lead, carbonate only	1	part
Litharge	1	part
Linseed oil (fluid measure)	14	parts

Heat these and stir until of the consistency of thick glue, and for every 36 parts, by weight of this compound add 3 parts, by weight, of turpentine, and 1 part, by weight, of mastic varnish (mastic rosin dissolved in turpentine); reheat the whole, and for every 32 parts, by weight, stir in and mix the following:

Baked and powdered clay	4	parts
Portland cement	16	parts
Zinc white	1	part
Red lead	1	part

After well mixing, dilute with more or less turpentine (not exceeding 25 per cent of the whole), or linoleate of manganese, the latter being preferable, as it has greater binding power. For colored paints use red oxide of iron or green oxide of chrome, but do not use chrome green or lead, as they will not stand the action of the sea water.

Compositions for Ships' Bottoms.

Green.

Pale rosin	25	pounds
Prepared mineral green	8	pounds
D. L. zinc	13	pounds
Boiled oil	2	pounds
Mineral naphtha	1	gallon
Petroleum spirit	1½	gallons

Prepared Mineral Green.

Dry levigated mineral green	28	pounds
Turpentine	7	pounds
Turpentine varnish	7	pounds
Refined linseed oil	7	pounds

Copper Color.

Pale rosin	25	pounds
Light Italian ocher	15	pounds
D. L. zinc	5	pounds
Turkey red paint	7½	pound
Petroleum spirit	1½	pounds
Mineral naphtha	1	pound

Pink.

Pale rosin	25	pounds
D. L. zinc	16	pounds
Deep vermilion	7	pounds
Mineral naphtha.	1	gallon
Petroleum spirit	1½	gallons

PAINTS FOR WALLS OF CEMENT, PLASTER, HARD FINISH, ETC.

Coating for Bathrooms.-As a rule cement plastering, as well as oil paint, suffices for the protection of walls and ceilings in bathrooms, but attention must be called to the destructive action of medicinal admixtures. For such rooms as well as for laboratories, an application of Swedish wood tar, made into a flowing consistency with a little oil of turpentine and put on hot, has been found very excellent. It is of advantage previously to warm the wall slightly. To the second coat add some wax. A very durable coating is obtained, which looks so pleasing that it is only necessary to draw some stripes with a darker paint so as to divide the surface into fields.

Cement to Paint Over Fresh.-The wall should be washed with dilute sulphuric acid several days before painting. This will change the surplus caustic lime to sulphate of lime or gypsum. The acid should be about one-half chamber acid and one-half water. This should be repeated before painting, and a coat of raw linseed oil flowed on freely should be given for the first coat. While this cannot be always guaranteed as effectual for making the paint hold, it is the best method our correspondent has heard of for the purpose, and is worth trying when it is absolutely necessary to paint over fresh cement.

Damp Walls, Coating for.-Thirty parts of tin are dissolved in 40 parts of hydrochloric acid, and 30 parts of sal ammoniac are added. A powder composed of freestone, 50 parts; zinc oxide, 20 parts; pounded glass, 15 parts; powdered marble, 10 parts; and calcined magnesia, 5 parts, is prepared, and made into a paste with the liquid above mentioned. Coloring matter may be added. The composition may be used as a damp proof coating for walls, or for repairing stonework, or for molding statues or ornaments.

Facade Paint.-For this zinc oxide is especially adapted, prepared with size or casein. Any desired earth colors may also be added. The surfaces are coated ,3 times with this mass. After the third application is dry, put on a single coating of zinc chloride solution of 30° Be. to which 3 per cent borax is added.

This coating is very solid, can be washed, and is not injured by hydrogen sulphide.

Hard-Finished Walls.-The treatment for hard-finished walls which are to be painted in flat colors is to prime with a thin coat of lead and oil well brushed into the wall. Next put on a thin coat of glue size; next a coat mixed with 1/3 oil and 2/3 turpentine; next a coat of flat paint mixed with turpentine. If you use any dry pigment mix it stiff in oil and thin with turps. If in either case the paint dries too fast, and is liable to show laps, put a little glycerine in, to retard the drying.

PAINTS, WATERPROOF AND WEATHERPROOF :

The following are claimed to be both waterproof and weatherproof :

I.-In 50 parts, by weight, of spirit of 96 per cent, dissolve 16 parts, by weight, of shellac, orange, finely powdered; 3 parts, by weight, of silver lake, finely powdered; and 0.6 parts, by weight, of gamboge, finely powdered.

This paint may be employed without admixture of any siccative, and is excellently adapted for painting objects which are exposed to the inclemencies of the weather, as it is perfectly weatherproof.

II.-Mix glue water with zinc oxide (zinc white) and paint the respective object with this mixture. When this is dry (after about 2 hours) it is followed up with a coating of glue water and zinc chloride in a highly diluted state. Zinc oxide enters into a chemical combination with zinc chloride, which acquires the hardness of glass and a mirror-like bright surface. Any desired colors can be prepared with the glue water (size) and are practically imperishable. This zinc coating is very durable, dries quickly, and is 50 per cent cheaper than oil paint.

Water- and Acid-Resisting Paint. Caoutchouc is melted with colophony at a low temperature, after the caoutchouc has been dried in a drying closet (stove) at 158° to 176° F., until no more considerable increase in weight is perceptible, while the colophony has completely lost its moisture by repeated melting The raw products thus prepared will readily melt upon slight heating. To the melted colophony and caoutchouc add in a hot liquid state zinc white or any similar pigment. Thin with a varnish consisting of 50 parts of perfectly anhydrous colophony, 40 parts of absolute alcohol, and 40 parts of benzine. The whole syrupy mass. is worked through in a paint mill to obtain a uniform product, at which operation more or less colophony varnish is added according to the desired consistency.

Water and Air-Proof Paint.-An airproof and waterproof paint, the subject of a recent French patent, is a compound of 30 parts, by weight, acetone; 100 parts acetic ether; 50 parts sulphuric ether; 100 parts camphor; 50 parts gum lac; 200 parts cotton; 100 parts paper (dissolved in sulphuric acid); 100 parts mastic in drops. These proportions may fluctuate according to need. The paper is reduced well and dissolved without heat with sufficient sulphuric ether; the cotton is dissolved in the acetone and the whole is mixed together with the other ingredients and stirred well. The application is performed as with any other varnish. The coating is said not to crack or shrink and to be particularly useful as a protection against moisture for all stuffs.

PAINTS FOR WOOD:

Floor Coating.-Anew paint for floors, especially those of soft wood: Mix together 2.2 pounds joiners' glue; a little over 1 ounce powdered bichromate of potash; 3 1/2 ounces aniline brown; and 10 1/2 quarts water in a tin vessel. After 6 hours have elapsed (when the glue is completely soaked), heat gradually to the boiling point. The coating becomes perfectly water-tight after 2 or 3 days; it is not opaque, as the earthy body is lacking. The glue causes the wood fibers to be firmly united. It becomes insoluble by the addition of bichromate of potash, under the influence of light. Without this admixture a simple glue coat has formerly not been found satisfactory, as it dissolves if cleaned with water.

Durable House Paint. - I. - New houses should be primed once with pure linseed oil, then painted with a thin paint from white lead and chalk, and thus gradually covered. The last coat is prepared of well-boiled varnish, white lead, and chalk. The chalk has the mission to moderate the saponification of the linseed oil by the white lead. Mixing colors such as ocher and black, which take up plenty of oil, materially assist in producing a durable covering.

II.-Prime with zinc white and let this be succeeded by a coating with zinc chloride in glue water (size). The zinc oxide forms with the zinc chloride an oxy-chloride of great hardness and glossy surface. By admixture of pigments any desired shade may be produced. The zinc coating is indestructible, dries quickly, does not peel, is free from the smell of fresh oil paint, and more than 5 per cent cheaper.

Ivory Coating for Smooth, Light Wood.

In order to cover the articles, which may be flat or round, with this coating, they must first be polished quite smooth and clean; then they are coated with thin, hot, white glue. When the coat is thoroughly dry, the glue is rubbed off again with fine glass paper. The mass is prepared as follows: Take 3 pounds (more or less according to the number of articles) of the purest and best collodion; grind upon a clean grinding stone twice the quantity that can be taken up with the point of a knife of Krems white, with enough good pale linseed oil as is necessary to grind the white smooth and fine. Take a clean bottle, into which one half of the collodion is poured; to this add the ground white, which can be removed clean from the stone by means of a good spatula and put in the bottle. Add about 100 drops of linseed oil, and shake the mass till it looks like milk.

Now painting with this milky substance may be commenced, using a fine hair pencil of excellent quality. The pencil is not dipped in the large bottle; but a glass is kept at hand with an opening of about 1 inch, so as to be able to immerse the pencil quickly. The substance is not flowing like the alcohol lacquers, for which reason it may be put on thick, for the ether, chiefly constituting the mass, evaporates at once and leaves but a very thin film which becomes noticeable only after about 10 such applications have been made. Shake the bottle well each time before filling the small glass, as the heavy Krems white is very apt to sink to the bottom of the bottle. If it is observed that the substance becomes too thick, which may easily occur on account of the evaporation, a part of the remaining ether is added, to which in turn 30 to 40 drops of oil are added, shaking it till the oil appears to be completely dissolved.

The operator must put on the mass in quick succession and rather thick. After about 10 coats have been applied the work is allowed to rest several hours; then 3 or 4 coats of pure collodion, to which likewise several drops of oil have been added, are given. Another pause of several hours having been allowed to intervene, application of the mass is once more begun.

When it is noticed that a layer of the thickness of paper has formed, the articles, after (drying thoroughly, should be softly rubbed off with very fine glass paper, after which they require to be wiped off well with a clean linen rag, so that no dust remains. Then coating is continued till the work seems serviceable.

A few applications of pure collodion should be made, and when this has become perfectly hard after a few hours, it can be rubbed down with a rag, tripoli, and oil, and polished by hand, like horn or ivory. This work can be done only in a room which is entirely free from dust. The greatest cleanliness must be observed.

MISCELLANEOUS RECIPES, PAINTS ETC.:

Bathtub Paint.-Take white keg lead, tint to any desired color and then add, say, 1/8 boiled oil (pure linseed) to 7/8 hard drying durable body varnish. Clean the surface of the tub thoroughly before applying the paint. Benzine or lime wash are good cleaning agents. Coat up until a satisfactorily strong, pure color is reached. This will give good gloss and will also wear durably.

Coating for Name Plates.-A durable coating for name plates in nurseries is produced as follows: Take a woolen rag, saturate it with joiners' polish, lay it into a linen one, and rub the wooden surface with this for sometime. Rub down with sandpaper and it can be written on almost like paper. When all is dry, coat with dammar lacquer for better protection. If the wood is to receive a colour it is placed in the woolen rag before rubbing down, in this case chrome yellow.

To Keep Flies from Fresh Paint.-For the purpose of keeping flies and other insects away from freshly painted surfaces mix a little bay oil (laurel oil) with the oil paint, or place a receptacle containing same in the vicinity of the painted objects. The pungent odor keeps off the flies.

Heat-Indicating Paint.-A heat-indicating paint composed of a double iodide of copper and mercury was first discovered years ago by a German physicist. At ordinary temperatures the paint is red, but when heated to 206° F. It turns black. Paper painted with this composition and warmed at a stove exhibits the change in a few seconds. A yellow double iodide of silver and mercury is even more sensitive to heat, changing from yellow to dark red.

To Keep Liquid Paint in Workable Condition. To prevent liquid paint which, for convenience sake, is kept in small quantities and flat receptacles, from evaporating and drying, give the vessels such a shape that they can be placed one on top of the other without danger of falling over, and provide the under side with a porous mass-felt or very porous clay, etc.which, if moistened, will retain the water for a long time. Thus, in placing the dishes one on top of the other, a moist atmosphere is created around them, which will inhibit evaporation and drying of the paint. A similar idea consists in producing covers with a tight outside and porous inside, for the purpose of covering up, during intermission in the work, clay models and like objects which it is desired to keep soft. In order to avoid the formation of fungous growth on the constantly wet bottom, it may be saturated with non-volatile disinfectants, or with volatile ones if their vapors are calculated to act upon the objects kept underneath the cover. If the cover is used to cover up oil paints, it is moistened on the inside with volatile oil, such as oil of turpentine, oil of lavender, or with alcohol.

Peeling of Paints.-For the prevention of peeling of new coatings on old oil paintings or lakes, the latter should be rubbed with roughly ground pumice stone, wet by means of felt rags, and to the first new coat there should be added fine spirit in the proportion of about 1/10 of the thinning necessary for stirring (turpentine, oil, etc.). This paint dries well and has given good results, even in the most difficult cases. The subsequent coatings are put on with the customary paint. Fat oil glazes for graining are likewise mixed with spirit, whereby the cracking of the varnish coating is usually entirely obviated.

Polychroming of Figures.-This paint consists of white wax, 1 part, and powdered mastic, 1 part, melted together upon the water bath and mixed with rectified turpentine. The colours to be used are first ground stiffly in turpentine on the grinding slab, and worked into consistency with the above solution.

Priming Coat for Water Spots-A good way to remove rain spots, or such caused by water soaking through ceilings, has been employed with good results. Take unslaked white lime, dilute with alcohol, and paint the spots with it. When the spots are dry-which ensues quickly, as the alcohol evaporates and the lime forms a sort of insulating layer-one can proceed painting with size colour, and the spots will not show through again.

TIRE PRESERVING PAINT:

Mix thoroughly: 2 pounds Linseed Oil; 2 pounds Petroleum; 1 pound Cottonseed Oil.

Then to this mixture add just enough dry white lead to give it a colour similar to a new tire.

Chapter - 17

ALUMINIUM PAINT

Aluminum paints are no longer limited to the simple pigmented gloss oil bronzing liquid of the early days of this century. A great variety of aluminium pigmented maintenance, industrial and trade sales coating are now available. These are applied by a brush, spray, dip, roller, knife and a number of other methods.

USES AND APPLICATIONS

Aluminium paints are use in painting exterior's exposed to acid fumes acid condition are common is paper mills nitration and pickling plants.

Aluminium paints formulated with phenolic resin varnish may be used under condition of milk alkaline exposure.

MANUFACTURING PROCESS

Aluminium paint is composed of pigments vehicle, solvent and additives spirit xylene, toluene, butanol as the common solvents. Additives like wetting and dispersing agents, antifloating agents anti skinning agents, plasticiser's and drier etc. are added in small amount to improve the specific property of a paint. The process of manufacture of Aluminium paint consist of two stages.

i. Aluminium paste making,

ii. Varnish making.

For Aluminium paste, the Aluminium powder are ground in a Ball Mill to get the desired degree of fineness. For general finish and maintenance a leafing pigment the aluminium powder is passed 325 mesh, (44 μ) screen to get a desired degree of fineness compatible for aluminium paint and mixed with linseed stand oil in quantity sufficient to get aluminium paste of desired consistency normally the Aluminium paste is purchased directly from the market. Secondly the varnish is prepared in a M.S. varnish kettle as per formulation.

Aluminium paint are supplied in a dual container one container consist of Aluminium paste and the other container consist of medium or varnish. Aluminium paints get black if mixed with the medium and packed. Hence they are mixed at the time of Application.

Two typical formulation of varnishes are given below.

			Parts by Wt.
1.	Coumarone resin	-	20 kgs
	Boiled linseed oil	-	50 litre
	Xylol	-	10 litre
	Mineral spirit	-	78 litre
	Cobalt naphthenate (6%)	-	0.32 kgs.
2.	Silicone resin (60%)	-	31 parts
	Acrylic ester resin	-	37 parts
	Zinc octate	-	1.2 parts
	White spirit	-	7.8 parts

The latter varnish gives a high heat resistant paint. The varnish should be such that the final paint gets hard dry, less then 8 hours. The aluminium paste paint and varnish are mixed before use in proportion so that the pigment concentration is not less than 15%

PLANT ECONOMICS

Rated Plant Capacity = 300000 KG/YEAR

LAND & BUILDING (Land reqd. 1000 sq.mts.) Rs. 14,30,000.00

PLANT & MACHINERY

1. M.S. ball mill
2. M.S. Varnish kettle
3. Planetary mixer
4. Triple roll mill
5. Paint storage tanks
6. Solvent storage tank
7. Laboratory testing equipment
8. Semi Automatic, can filling & sealing machine
9. Miscellaneous tools, pipes & pipe fitting, Zig fixture screens etc.

FIXED CAPITAL

1. Land & Building	Rs.	14,30,000.00
2. Plant & Machinery	Rs.	7,75,000.00
3. Other Fixed Assets	Rs.	85,000.00
TOTAL	Rs.	22,90,000.00

RAW MATERIALS

1. Aluminium paste
2. Coumarone resin
3. Linseed stand oil
4. White spirit
5. Solvent Naphtha
6. Cobalt Naphthenate
7. Tin containers for Aluminium paste
8. Tin container

TOTAL WORKING CAPITAL/MONTH

1. Raw Material	Rs.	18,15,928.00
2. Salary & Wages	Rs.	72,125.00
3. Utilities & Overheads	Rs.	25,400.00
TOTAL	Rs.	19,13,453.00

TOTAL CAPITAL INVESTMENT

Total Fixed Capital	Rs.	22,90,000.00
Total Working Capital for 3 Months	Rs.	57,40,359.00
TOTAL	Rs.	80,30,359.00

TURN OVER/ANNUM

Receipt by sale of Aluminium paint 3,00,000 kgs	Rs.	2,85,00,000.00

Profit Sales Ratio = Profit / Sales x 100 = 12.28 %
Rate of Return = Operating profit / T.C.I x 100 = 43.58 %
Break Even Point (B.E.P) = 41.74 %

Chapter - 18

ACRYLIC EMULSION PAINTS

Acrylic emulsion paints are considered to be outstanding in adhesion to glossy surfaces. They are also excellent with coloured pigments conventional additives such as antifoamers and preservatives against mildew, fingus, mould and bacteria may be required, depending on formulation and application conditions.

Coalecing agents (although rather less necessary than with vinyl copolymers) may be included. They are more likely to be desirable in systems with high pigment volume ratios or for application to exceptionally porous surfaces. These coalescing solvents should be first diluted with water before addition to the emulsion system, and rice acrylic emulsions normally contain polymerised acid, it is desirable to maintain a constant pH level, which should normally be between 8.5 and 9.5.

PROPERTIES

Acrylic emulsion paints contain polymers of acrylic esters and have shown a number of outstanding properties. They are very stable, resistant to freezing and less permeable to moisture than polyvinyl acetate. When made into paints they show very good chemical resistance, adhesion and flexibility and durability. An example of their adhesion and flexibility is afforded by the successful use of acrylic emulsion and exterior woodwork over lead-based primers. Acrylic emulsions are coming into extensive use of alkaline plasters and for external painting over new stucco and cement.

The particle size of acrylic latices is almost invariably much finer than that of vinyl acetate product, and is of the order of 0.1 - 0.2 μ. This implies that the individual particles require a much larger quantity of surfactant as "cover" in order to impart stability. This acrylic emulsion polymers often include a level of surfactant as high as 7 - 8 percent.

Correctly formulated acrylic paints are, however, of low viscosity and as a result of the time particle reactor in the series is itself in a steady - state condition, however, the concentration of reactants in a particular reactor remains constant. One might consider carrying out an emulsion polymerization continuously under steady state conditions in single reactor. Since the concentration of initiator, monomer, emulsifier, and modifier are constant. This would be expected to lead to a more homogenous polymer compared with a batch reaction where the concentrations are constantly diminishing. This is not necessarily found, however, since residence time in a single stage reactor under ideal stirring conditions is only an average.

Some latex particles will be in the reactor for much less than average residence time and others for a much longer period. Among the advantages of the continuous reactor type over the batch process are :

a. the uniformity of the reaction

b. the operational control, and

c. the fact that no time is lost in filling and emptying the reactors.

The techniques employed in emulsion polymerization of acrylic monomers usually follow conventional lines. Emulsion stabilizers may be non-ionic surfactants like the polyethylene glycol ethers of hydrocarbons, long chain alkyl sulphates fatty acid soaps and similar surface tension depressant with micelleforming ability. In addition, hydrophilic colloids are sometimes employed, especially synthetic materials such as the alkali metal or ammonium salts of polyacrylic and polymethacrylic acid. The most commonly employed polymerization invitiators are the alkali metal or ammonium salts of peroxide-sulfuric acid, after in conjunction with organic peroxides such as tertiary butyl hydroperoxide, and the redox activators such as sulphoxylates, hydrosulphites, bisulphites or ferrous salts. Acrylic emulsions normally have rather fine particles with diameter of the order of 0.05 to 0.3 microns. They dry to clear, glossy, colourless water-resistant films. The excellent light resistance combined with oil and tar resistance has contributed to the recent developments in U.S.A. Automobile finishes containing methacrylic acid ester polymers. Occasionally, the acid value of these products is deliberately raised buy copolymerizing the acrylic or methacrylic acid ester with a small proportion of acrylic methacrylic acid itself.

The case with which acrylic monomers can be copolymerized with each other and with vinyl or other unsaturated compounds makes these very versatile starting materials for surface coating media, and commercial acrylic ester resins are generally copolymers. Combined to produce the optimum drying and film properties. The composition of commercial resin is generally not available.

So far, only relatively few of the many possible acrylic copolymers have been studied in a commercial scale. The paints media which have undergone the most extensive field trials are emulsions of acrylate - methyl methacrylic copolymers containing ethyl acrylate as the major constituents. Any generalization of the behaviour of acrylic media would at this stage appear a little preventers. A great deal remains yet to be discovered and no doubt the recent substantial reduction in manufacturing costs of higher alkyl esters will stimulate extensive trials with acrylic media in the near future.

MANUFACTURING PROCESS

A polymerisable acid, usually acrylic or methacrylic, is almost invariably included in the polymerization formulation. The normal quantity is 1-2 percent which is included in the monomer mix. Apart from imparting greater stability to the emulsions the acid helps in wetting out the pigments and after assists in increasing the gloss of paint films. An acrylic copolymer including a higher quantity of acid is beneficial when it is desired to prepare paints of high pigment/volume loading.

Whilst polyvinyl acetate type emulsions are usually manufactured with the aid of colloid, acrylics in general have comparatively poor colloid acceptance, other than for certain polyartrolytes. Inclusion of a cellulosic thickener in an acrylic formulation generally produces a product of coarse particle size and impaired stability. Polyacrylates, e.g. sodium polymerthacrylate produces, as a rule, more stable products, but their inclusion does not normally enable any marked reduction to be made in the quantity of anionic or cationic surfactants present.

Most of the earlier technical emulsions have a composition which is about 62-64 percent ethyl acrylate, 1-2 percent acrylic or methacrylic acids, with a balance of methyl methacrylate. Products with solids content of 50 percent are available commercially, with a pH adjusted with alkali, most frequently ammonia, to about 6-8.5. Various blends of nonionic and ammoniac emulsifiers are employed, recommended formulation depending on the ultimate application of the final product.

Pigment binding power of acrylic latices tend to be markedly greater than that of vinyls, and thus a high PVC can be employed to give corresponding results, with some redress to the cost of the final paint. A wide variety of pigments can be employed, and equally the paints can be utilized in many different applications, whether exterior or interior, and on a wide variety of substances. They are exceptionally useful as clear sealers for porous surfaces, and as primer sealers, which may be followed by almost any form of top coat whether a further emulsion coating, or an oil paint, varnish or enamel.

Evidence has been accumulating in recent years that chalk resistance and tint retention of acrylic emulsion paints can be maintained by using less titanium dioxide than has been customary in the past a maximum of 2 to 2.5 lb. per gallon being suggested. Above this level, although brightness increases, hiding power does not increase quantities, of titanium dioxide, the binder demand of the system is reduced and the pigment volume can be increased. This produces tighter, stronger, more chalk-resistant paints, with reduced erosion, and improved grain crack resistance.

Formulation

Acrylic type Gloss Emulsion Paints :

Ingredients	Parts by weight
Pigment grind Rutile titanium dioxide	187.0
Sodium hexameta phosphate (10% aq.)	5.2
Hydroxy ethyl cellulose (2% aq.)	9.4
Defoamer	1.0
Hexylene glycol	12.3
Ethylene glycol	12.3
Water	22.0
Emulsion :	
Acrylic Emulsion	597.0
Water	91.8
Add to the mix of above two	
Hexylene glycol	28.5
Ethylene glycol	28.5
Silicon adolitine	5.0
	1000.0
Total solids content (%)	50.0
Pigment : binder ratio	0.6-1.0
Pigment - volume concentration (%)	150

Chapter - 19

BITUMINOUS ROAD EMULSIONS

Bitumen is the general them applied to any block, tarry substance occurring in nature or produced by heat from petroleum coal, natural gas or certain other organic substances. the term 'asphalt' refers specifically to the black, solid or semi solid bitumens obtained from petroleum. Asphalts occur as natural deposits or are obtained as a residue in the distillation of crude petroleum. This asphaltic residue is called pitch.

Natural deposits of asphalt were first used by ancient civilizations the waterproofing, preservation and cementing properties of asphalt were well known, and asphalt was an important article of commerce in the earliest known civilization that developed in mesopotania, egypt and the Indus valley with the passing of these early civilizations, the use of asphalt tended to diminish. However often 1900, due to the discovery of large amounts of asphalt-base crude petroleum asphalt was obtained as a by-product of petroleum refining.

Most bituminous binders used in the construction of roads are viscous semi solids at normal temperatures. For surface dressing, therefore, they must be brought to a fluid state by heating before being applied in this films to road surfaces.

DIFFERENT FORMULATIONS

Emulsion for Road Making

Formula 1.

	Parts
Spramex bitumen	48.0
Water	49.5
sodium Carbonate (calcined)	0.5
Ollic acid	2.0

The bitumen is warmed at 95 - 98 °C and the oleic acid added. The water is heated separately with the sodium carbonate and the two liquids are introduced into the emulsifier.

Formula 2

	Parts
Spramex bitumen	50.0
Mineral Oil	2-2.5
Resin Soap	1.5 - 2.0
Caustic potash	1.0
Water	45.0

The bitumen is melted and the mineral oil added during afitation. The water is heated to boiling and in it are dissolved the soap and the caustic potash. The liquids are mixed at 95°C with more bitumen, 1-2 % or blue starch, gelation, or sodium silicate must be added during or after emulsification.

PLANT ECONOMICS

Rated Plant Capacity = 4000.00 KGS/day

LAND & BUILDING (Land required 1500 sq.mt) Rs. 10,75,000.00

PLANT & MACHINERY

1. Colloid Mill
2. Baby boiler
3. Dilute emulsifier tank
4. Solvent storage tank.
5. Drums for raw materials and product
6. Pumps
7. Others including piping,conveying
of raw material from storage shed
to production shed.

FIXED CAPITAL

1. Land & Building		Rs.	10,75,000.00
2. Plant & Machinery		Rs.	5,85,000.00
3. Other Fixed Assets		Rs.	1,75,000.00
	TOTAL	Rs.	18,35,000.00

RAW MATERIALS

1. Bitumen (Asphalt)
2. Tannic Acid
3. Boric Acid
4. Oxalic Acid

TOTAL WORKING CAPITAL/MONTH

1. Raw Material	Rs.	5,59,794.56
2. Salary & Wages	Rs.	29,062.50
3. Utilities & Overheads	Rs.	23,200.00
TOTAL	Rs.	6,12,057.06

TOTAL CAPITAL INVESTMENT

Total Fixed Capital	Rs.	18,35,000.00
Total Working Capital for 3 Months	Rs.	18,36,171.18
TOTAL	Rs.	36,71,171.18

TURN OVER/ANNUM

By sale of 12,00,000 kg. Bitumen Road Emulsion	Rs.	1,02,00,000.00

Profit Sales Ratio = Profit / Sales x 100 = 18.04 %

Rate of Return = Operating profit / T.C.I x 100 = 50.12 %

Break Even Point (B.E.P) = 40.76 %

Chapter - 20

CEMENT PAINT

These paints are water base paints and are prepared by a medium miscible with water. Water is used as a thinner. These paints are affected by alkali i.e. resistant to saponification. It is also resistant to water and is low in cost, i.e. it is more economical bearing in mind the large areas that frequently have to be covered.

Such paints may be required for use on various alkaline substrates such as concrete, plasters, massury, slucco, asbestos, cement sheeting and tiles and brick work. The coating are often applied to structures exposed to weather or to humid continous or even immersed in water, such as swimming pools and storage tanks.

It is in these requirements that polystyrene and styrene copolymers with butadiene show to advantage, since they are unaffected by both alkali and water, and whilst the polymers are not unduly costly they have an advantage compared with the vinyl resins as a class, in that they are soluble in relatively cheap solvents, i.e. xylene and naphtha.

Nevertheless, the production of 'masonry' paints is not limited to this class of polymer and good results have been obtained with vinyl chloride-vinyl acetate copolymers, and in some cases with polyvinylacetate.

Using polystyrene or its copolymers, both clear and pigmented finishes can be obtained. As the physical properties of these polymers vary between the hard, brittle nature of polystyrene and the tougher character of the styrene-butadiene copolymer, considerable variation is possible by admixtures of the two types. Further variations may be achieved by the use of modifying resins such as coumarone-indene and by the use of plasticizers. The modifying resins are mainly used with polystyrene in order to produce high gloss pigmented finishes, in which case it preferable to disperse the pigments in the modifying resin.

The main disadvantages of the polystyrenes are that their adhesion to smooth surfaces is not particularly good and their poor wetting properties for pigments complicates the production of high-gloss finishes. Adhesion can be improved by plasticizing the polymers, but care is necessary to prevent the coatings from being too soft thus leading to high dirt retention, and undue flow with uses in temperature.

Styrene-butadiene resins can be used in conjunction with polystyrene. One of their useful properties, is that pigments can be dispersed in them to give gloss coatings where under similar circumstances polystyrene as the grinding medium would yield very dull finishes.

FORMULATIONS FOR DRY CEMENT PAINT

1. Portland Cement	-	65%
Hydrated Lime	-	24.5%
Titanium Di Oxide	-	5.0%
Calcium Stearate	-	1.0%
Calcium Chloride	-	4.0%
Essential Oils like		
Lavender/Jasmine/Rose	-	0.5%
Colours as needed.		

2. Portland Cement	-	65%
Hydrated Lime	-	24.5%
Zinc Sulphide	-	4.0%
Aluminium Stearate	-	1.0%
Calcium Chloride	-	5.0%
Essential Oils like		
Lavender/Jasmine/Rose	-	0.5%
Colours as desired	-	0.5%

MANUFACTURING PROCESS OF CEMENT PAINT

Although the manufacture of cement paint is theoretically quite a simple matter, merely consisting in the thorough incorporation of various ingredients, a great deal of skill has been devoted in recent years to the designing of machinery to accomplish this operation with rapidity, efficiency and economy.

The manufacture is generally divided into 2 stages :

1. Preparation of the paste paint by mixing and grinding.
2. Conversion into finished paint by finishing and refining.

Mixing :

It is originally conducted in an apparatus known as Pug Mill, the general construction of which was that of a cylinder fitted with a vertical shaft carrying arms. Such a simple apparatus in which stirrers continually revolve in one plane is not very efficient, and during the past few years great attention has been paid by makers of such plant to the improvement of the design, with the object of securing more efficient mixing and less power consumption, combined with facilities of easy and rapid cleaning.

Grinding :

The purpose of grinding is to breakdown the aggregates into smaller sized particles. Initially grinding was accomplished by rubbing down the mixed paint with a large 'muller' of glass or granite on a slab of similar material. It was slow and tedius process and except where expensive pigments are employed in small quantity.

Flat stone mills grinds very thoroughly, but are somewhat slow in operation and difficult to clean. In few countries this type of mill is almost exclusively used for paint grinding. Cone mills are modified form of flat stone mill in which the surface of contact is conical instead of flat. Such cone mills are sometimes constructed with grinding surface of stone, but more commonly chilled iron is substituted owing to greater ease of construction and working. A screw arrangement under the cone mill serves to regulate the pressure and consequently the fineness of grinding.

One of defects inherent to both flat stone and cone mills is that, as the movement of grinding surface is concentric, the surfaces gradually wear to fit one another which reduces the output considerably.

Roller grinding mills now-a-days used universally as they combines crushing and shearing effects, on matter, in between the two rollers revolving at different speed. This gives the efficient grinding but by using a third roller with the shaft geared so that it revolves against the second at a different speed again, a thoroughly practically and convenient grinding results.

Roller mills are most efficient for grinding of materials and are conveniently adapted large scale production of cement paints, on account of their rapidity of working and the ease of cleaning.

Ball Mills :

Now-a-days there is growing tendency towards the adaption of the ball mills in the manufacture of cement paints. The raw material enters in the mill from one end and discharged out from the other end in the finished condition. Ball mills consists of number of ball of different diameters enclosed in closed conical cylinder. The Length and Diameter ratio of the mill is selected carefully and cylindrical drum is rotated, with axis in horizontal plane. Speed of rotation is well adjusted. Ball mills are lined internally with the specially constructed materials. Their advantage is simplicity of design and comparative economy of power and labour required for the operation.

PLANT ECONOMICS

Rated Plant Capacity = 2.00 TON/Day

LAND & BUILDING = Rs. 6,40,000.00

PLANT & MACHINERY

1. Paint Mixers
2. Edge Runner Mills
3. Grinding Unit
4. Ball Mills
5. Screening Equipments
6. Weighing Machine
7. Packaging Unit
8. Laboratory and Quality Control Instruments
9. Miscellaneous equipments, conveying unit, pumps, etc.

FIXED CAPITAL

1.	Land & Building	Rs.	6,40,000.00
2.	Plant & Machinery	Rs.	5,55,000.00
3.	Other Fixed Assets	Rs.	1,95,000.00
	TOTAL	Rs.	13,90,000.00

RAW MATERIALS

1. Portland Cement
2. Hydrated Lime
3. Zinc Sulphide
4. Aluminium Stearate
5. Calcium Chloride
6. Essential Oil
7. Packing Charges

TOTAL WORKING CAPITAL/MONTH

1.	Raw Material	Rs.	1,21,900.00
2.	Salary & Wages	Rs.	35,500.00
3.	Utilities & Overheads	Rs.	48,100.00
	TOTAL	Rs.	2,05,500.00

TOTAL CAPITAL INVESTMENT

Total Fixed Capital	Rs.	13,90,000.00
Total Working Capital for 2 Months	Rs.	4,11,000.00
TOTAL	Rs.	18,01,000.00

TURN OVER/ANNUM

By sale of 600 Tonnes of Cement Paint	Rs.	39,00,000.00

Profit Sales Ratio = Profit / Sales x 100 = 22.03 %

Rate of Return = Operating profit / T.C.I x 100 = 47.71 %

Break Even Point (B.E.P) = 53.18 %

Chapter - 21

INSULATING VARNISH

The insulating varnish industry is one of the basic feeder industry which is closely associated with the power development and distribution programs. The electrical equipments based on electro-magnetic induction are fabricated from copper, aluminium and such conducting metals and these are provided with appropriate insulation. These insulation materials are resinous coating compositions protecting the electrical equipments from the environmental factors as well as protecting the human being from the electrical shock. An electrical insulating varnish may be defined as an organic material having film forming properties which gives a smooth, hard, flexible adherent film to the substrate. These organic film forming materials in thin films with as low of 50u film thickness should restrict the leakage of electrical current and possess required mechanical electrical and chemical properties over a prolonged period (about 20 years).

MANUFACTURING PROCESS

An enamel which has become well established in spite of its higher cost because of its toughness, flexibility and high resistance properties, is composed of a bland of poly vinyl butyral with phenol-or cresol formaldehyde resin. This is an example of an application where a non-convertible resin is converted by a cross linking reaction with phenol-or cresol-formaldehyde resin under the action of heat. It is also probable in this particular case that the high performance is in part due to bonding between the metal and the film since high temperatures are used.

Such enamel gives a very high level of performance and is in fact often used as a standard to assess other wire enamels. The phenolic resins used for this purpose are alkali-condensed and have a minimum phenol: formaldehyde molar ratio of 1.0:0.7

A Typical lacquer formulation would contain

FORMULATION - 1

	Parts by weight %
Poly vinyl Butyral resin	16.66
Cresol-formaldehyde resin	8.34
Cresylic acid	25
High-flash Naphtha	50

The method of manufacture is to dissolve the cresol-formaldehyde resin (phenolic resin) in an equal weight of the cresylic acid by stirring in a mixing tank the process is facilitated, by application of gentle heat, which is achieved by employing a mixer or reaction kettle fitted with a steam coil. The remaining cresylic acid is then stirred in with naphtha and poly vinyl butyral/polyvinyl formal, resin is added slowly with efficient stirring. An alternative method which helps to prevent lumping of poly vinyl Butyral resin, is first to make a slurry by stirring it will with some of the naphtha and then to add this slurry to the cresol formaldehyde resin (phenolic resin) solution.

METHOD OF APPLICATION

The means by which the enamels are applied and cursed vary some what, but the general practice is to run the wire through a dip bath containing the enamel and then through a die to remove drip and give a even coating. The wire is then passed through a tunnel oven at elevated temperature to give a cross-linked film coating with excellent electrical physical, and chemical properties (350°C) and at a speed of 17 or more feet per minute depending upon the length and temperature of the oven. Temperature as high as 500°C may be used far very short times i.e., at high through put speeds at in usual to apply several coats to the wire in order to build up film thickness often to 3 mil, although thinner films are used for economic reasons when the required performance permits.

PLANT ECONOMICS

Rated Plant Capacity = 30000 Kg/Year

LAND & BUILDING (Land required 500 sq. mts.) Rs. 7,00,000.00

PLANT & MACHINERY

1. Reaction vessel
2. Boiler
3. Storage tanks
4. Filling & packing M/c.

5. Miscellaneous, viz. pipe, valve, pumps, weighing M/c etc.

FIXED CAPITAL

1. Land & Building	Rs.	7,00,000.00
2. Plant & Machinery	Rs.	5,60,000.00
3. Other Fixed Assets	Rs.	35,000.00
TOTAL	Rs.	12,95,000.00

RAW MATERIALS

1. Poly Vinyl Butyral Resin
2. Cresol-formaldehyde resin
3. Cresylic acid
4. High-flash Naphtha
5. Packaging Material

TOTAL WORKING CAPITAL/MONTH

1. Raw Material	Rs.	1,31,037.50
2. Salary & Wages	Rs.	36,875.00
3. Utilities & Overheads	Rs.	13,740.00
TOTAL	Rs.	1,81,652.50

TOTAL CAPITAL INVESTMENT

Total Fixed Capital	Rs.	12,95,000.00
Total Working Capital for 2 Months	Rs.	3,63,305.00
TOTAL	Rs.	16,58,305.00

TURN OVER/ANNUM

Receipt by sale of 30,000 kgs were Enamel (Poly Vinyl Butyral based)	Rs.	36,00,000.00

Profit Sales Ratio = Profit / Sales x 100 = 24.23 %

Rate of Return = Operating profit / T.C.I x 100 = 52.60 %

Break Even Point (B.E.P) = 47.55 %

Chapter - 22

POWDER COATING

Powder coatings can be described as coatings which are protective or decorative or both, formed by the application of a coating powder on to a substrate using various techniques and fused into a continuous film by the application of heat or radiation energy. The growth of a thermosetting powder coating or various applications has been quite significant in the Eighties. Powder coatings offer several performance advantages over liquid and high material usage efficiency. The formulating considerations for powder coatings are different from those liquid paints and requires careful selection of raw materials. Also, the rheology of powder coating is different from that of a liquid paint.

The flow cure behaviour of thermoset coatings is expected to strongly influence the film formation process, resulting in film properties such as leveling, sagging, gloss, gas release, surface defects, lubricity, toughness and particle sintering. Recent studies show that powder characteristics especially the flow is essentially determined by surface tension, melt viscosity, film thickness and particle shape, size and distribution. Of these much emphasis has been given to the most influencing parameters, surface tension and melt viscosity, Hence the knowledge of rheology helps a paint chemist in formulating powder coatings having desired properties.

In this paper, the work done by various researchers on the rheology of thermosetting powder coatings has been reviewed. The paper also describes the importance of rheology is designing of powder coatings with optimal characteristics.

PROPERTIES OF POWDER COATING

1.This is chemically inset and quite flexible. This flexibility together with good adhesion, allows powder coating to withstand a great deal of physical abuse.

2.This coating may be transparent or coloured.

3.It has higher molecular weight.

PROCESS OF POWDER COATING

Metal articles can be coated with certain resin by applying the powdered resin to the surface followed by heating to melt the resin so that it flow and forms a uniform coating on the article. The method eliminates the fire and toxicity and is associated with the use of solvent based paints and also shows saving in cost.

Here we are discussing about the application of powder to the metallic articles by fluidifed bed system which is chamber type process.

PLANT ECONOMICS

Rated Plant Capacity = 6.00 Nos/Day

LAND & BUILDING (Land 500 sq. mts.) = Rs. 9,75,000.00

PLANT & MACHINERY

1. Fluidised Bed with Electrically heating arrangements
2. Electrostatic Guns
3. Oven
4. Cleaning Tank

FIXED CAPITAL

1. Land & Building		Rs.	9,75,000.00
2. Plant & Machinery		Rs.	15,60,000.00
3. Other Fixed Assets		Rs.	3,60,000.00
	TOTAL	Rs.	28,95,000.00

RAW MATERIALS

1. Epoxide Resin
2. Miscelleneous chemicals

TOTAL WORKING CAPITAL/MONTH

1. Raw Material		Rs.	1,35,000.00
2. Salary & Wages		Rs.	24,480.00
3. Utilities & Overheads		Rs.	85,000.00
	TOTAL	Rs.	2,44,480.00

TOTAL CAPITAL INVESTMENT

Total Fixed Capital	Rs.	28,95,000.00
Total Working Capital for 3 Months	Rs.	7,33,440.00
TOTAL	Rs.	36,28,440.00

TURN OVER/ANNUM

By coating of car 1800 Nos.	TOTAL	Rs.	54,00,000.00

Profit Sales Ratio = Profit / Sales x 100 = 24.70 %

Rate of Return = Operating profit / T.C.I x 100 = 36.76 %

Break Even Point (B.E.P) = 55.42 %

Chapter - 23

PRIMER PAINTS & ENAMEL PAINTS

Priming paints are used for the first coat on previously unpainted surface to provide the foundation on which the durability of the finished painting largely depends; their composition is therefore of fundamental importance.

FORMULATIONS OF PAINT PRIMERS

The priming formulation generally has a higher pigment volume concentration, a higher content of lead pigment and extender, and in some products, zinc in any form is omitted. The higher pigment volume in the priming coat produces a lower gloss, which helps to provide better mechanical adhesion, of the succeeding coat, and also promotes more rapid drying. It is contended by some authorities that zinc in a coating which is in immediate contact with bare wood, increases the tendency to blister under conditions of moisture transmission.

Typical pigment volume concentration for an exterior house paint primer is about 35% and for a finish, coat, 30%

House Paint Under Coater

	% by Wt.
White lead	32
Rutile TiO_2	8
Exterior	23
Raw linseed oil	12
Heat bodied linseed oil	12
Resin	1
Thinner (including drier)	12

Paint Primer :

Formulation:

	Parts by Wt.
White lead	553.7
Rutile non chalking titanium dioxide	74.6
Magnesium silicate	292.1
Litharge	9.2
Raw linseed oil	165.0
Ester gum cold cut (60% non volatile)	37.6
Low-acid heat bodied linseed oil (2-4)	147.8
6% cobalt naphthenate	2.8
Mineral spirits	215.0

FORMULATIONS OF ENAMEL PAINTS

Green Skid Resistant Exterior/Enamel Paint

(Urethane)

Slurry grind method charge to pebble mill	Pounds	Gallons
1. Rutile titanium dioxide	225	6.44
2. Green chromium oxide	100	2.31
3. Carbon black	0.5	0.03
4. Mixture of benzene xylene + Toluene Solvent	230	32.00
5. Toluene diisocyanate Tumble overnight add	30	3.00
6. Urethane resin solution	507	60.00
	1,092.5	103.78

Formulation Notes :

1.This skid-resistant finish can be applied by either brush or roll applicator, provided the wood or concrete surface is clean and dry. A primer is suggested on metal substrates. Convenient size areas are coated and the abrasive material sprinkled on evenly over this area after the coating has set for 15 to 20 minutes. The excess grit is swept off after 24 hours' air dry and a second coat of the skid resistant finish is applied over the grit system.

2.Abrasive material such as aluminium grit, sand, silicone carbide or pumice is used in this type of application.

Physical Constants :

Total solids content	:	70.6% by wt.
Viscosity	:	71 Krebs units
Weight per gallon	:	10.53 pounds
Pigment volume concentration	:	14.8%
Vehicle solids content	:	60.6% by wt.

Key Properties :

Easily applied as two-package mixing is eliminated. Excellent abrasive Zesistance high chemical and corrosion resistance.

PLANT ECONOMICS

Rated Plant Capacity = 4.00 MT/day

PRIMER PAINTS & ENAMEL PAINTS

PRIMER PAINTS = 2 MT/DAY

ENAMEL PAINTS = 2 MT/DAY

LAND & BUILDING (Land area 2000 sq.mts.) Rs. 37,25,000.00

PLANT & MACHINERY

1. Planetary mixer/edge runner
2. Triple roll mill
3. Ball mill
4. Filtration equipment
5. Platform weighing scale
6. Baby boiler
7. Paint storage tanks
8. Lab. equipments
9. Miscellaneous equipments viz. pipe fittings, valves, motors, etc.

FIXED CAPITAL

1. Land & Building	Rs.	37,25,000.00
2. Plant & Machinery	Rs.	20,50,000.00
3. Other Fixed Assets	Rs.	4,85,000.00
TOTAL	Rs.	62,60,000.00

RAW MATERIALS

1. ***FOR PRIMER PAINTS:***
   Medium Quality White lead
2. Rutile non-chalking TiO2
3. Magnesium silicate
4. Litharge
5. Raw linseed oil
6. Ester gum
7. Low acid heat boiled linseed oil
8. Cobalt naphthenate (6%)
9. Mineral spirits
10. B. Exterior house paint primer
    (Alkyd) low quality alkyd resin
11. Lecithin
12. Magnesium aluminium silicate
13. Methyl alcohol
14. Mineral spirits
15. TiO2 Rutile
16. Magnesium silicate
17. Organic mercury compound (mildewci-de/fungicide)
18. Alkyd resin
19. Mineral spirits
20. Cobalt naphthenate (6% cobalt)
21. Zirco catalyst
22. Anti-skinning agent
23. ***FOR ENAMEL PAINTS:*** Interior flat
    white odorless wall enamel paint(Alkyd) (medium quality)
24. Rutile TiO2
25. TiO2 (30%) calcium sulfate (70%) pigment
26. Non-fer-Al Calcium Carbonate
27. Aluminium distearate
28. Alkyd resin solution
29. Alkyd resin solution
30. Mineral spirits
31. High boiling solvent
32. Nuxtra cobalt (6% cobalt)
33. Zirco catalyst (6% zirconium)
34. Anti-skinning agent
35. B. exterior Semigloss white & tint
    base odorless low cost enamel alkyd(low quality) TiO2 Rutile
36. (30%) calcium sulfate (70%) pigment
37. Magnesium silicate
38. Soya lecithin
39. Alkyd resin solution

40. Cobalt drier
41. Zirco catalyst
42. Anti-skinning agent
43. Mineral spirits
44. Packaging materials

TOTAL WORKING CAPITAL/MONTH

1.	Raw Material	Rs.	42,00,880.02
2.	Salary & Wages	Rs.	1,15,045.00
3.	Utilities & Overheads	Rs.	1,28,800.00
	TOTAL	Rs.	44,44,725.02

TOTAL CAPITAL INVESTMENT

Total Fixed Capital	Rs.	62,60,000.00
Total Working Capital for 2 Months	Rs.	88,89,450.04
TOTAL	Rs.	1,51,49,450.04

TURN OVER/ANNUM

1. Primer paint (medium quality) 300 MT
2. Primer paint (low quality)
   (Exterior house paint primer) 300 MT
3. Enamel paint (medium qua.)(interior flat white odorless wall enamel paint) (alkyd) 300 MT
4. Enamel paint(Low qua. ext. semigloss white tint base odorless low cost enamel(alkyd) 300 MT

TOTAL Rs. 6,33,00,000.00

Profit Sales Ratio = Profit / Sales x 100 = 10.67 %

Rate of Return = Operating profit / T.C.I x 100 = 44.58 %

Break Even Point (B.E.P) = 39.34 %

Chapter - 24

PAINT DRIERS

The cobalt (II) salts of a number of organic acids have been used as drying agents for non-saturated oils in paints, varnisher, and inks. The salts used for this purpose include the oleate, ethylhexanoate, naphthenates, soyate, linoleate, varnisher and tallate. These cobalt salts are either soluble in the non saturated oil, or they react with them to from soluble compounds that than act as oxidation accelerators of the oil and as polymerization catalysts, forming a film with increased stability, resistance, and flexibility. The drying action is due entuely to the redox behaviour of the cobalt species present, the carboxylate/moietics simply acts as oleophilic groups to solubilize the cobalt compounds in the oils. The amounts of cobalt added to the oils as drying agents oreas drying agents are in the range of 0.01-0.6%. The salts can be added as solution in organic solvents or as dispersion of ultrafine powder(Drying Agents) cobalt-containing drying agents are also used in law-tempt curing process for silicon resin. The cobalt species promote drying at the surface of the film in contact with atmospheric oxygen .

Its action is so fast that a hard polymeric film can be formed that prevent deep drying. For this reason cobalt is often used in conjunction with other metals viz, Zinc, and Calcium that do not have a drying action but slow down and control the effects of cobalt.

FORMULATION OF PAINT DRIERS

(Drier V75 for the Paint)

The drier is a light coloured naphthenate or lead, manganese and cobalt in the here in after specified proportion, produced by double precipitation, classification & dehydration of the resulting metallic salts from naphthenic acid, & thinning the precipitate to the specified metallic content by addition of a solvent having a pure butanol value of not less then 70.

The thinned drier has the following composition :-

	Percent/wt.
Metallic Lead	16.00
Metallic Manganese	0.16
Metallic Cobalt	0.16
Total Metal	16.32
Other Constituents & Thinner	83.68

The drier remains completely soluble, clear and stable in the container & is satisfactorily reactive without causing cloudiness when used in normal proportion is phenolic resin such as over or V37.25. This drier is specifically designed for the V37.25 varnish vehicle and may not be suitable for other vehicles.

PLANT ECONOMICS

Rated Plant Capacity = 3 Lac Kg./Year

LAND & BUILDING (Land 1500 sq.mts.) Rs. 26,02,000.00

PLANT & MACHINERY

1. Reactor
2. Storage Tanks
3. Evaporator
4. Instrumentation & Process Control Equipments
5. Miscellaneous viz Pipe Fitting Pumps etc.
6. Tank with Steam oil agitator
7. Plate & Frame Filter Press
8. Iron Removal Tank
9. Cobalt Sulphate Solution Storage Tank
10. Soda Soap Kettle Equipped with agitator
11. Precipitation Kettle
12. Cutting Tank
13. Blending Tank
14. Storage Tank
15. Baby Boiler
16. Calcium Sulphate Solution Tank
17. Pipes, fittings, pumps etc.

FIXED CAPITAL

1.	Land & Building	Rs.	26,02,000.00
2.	Plant & Machinery	Rs.	30,80,000.00

3.	Other Fixed Assets	Rs.	2,00,000.00
	TOTAL	Rs.	58,82,000.00

RAW MATERIALS

1. ***(A) COBALT OCTOATE SECTION***
2 ethyl hexoic acid
2. Cobalt Hydroxide
3. White Spirit/Butyl alcohol
4. ***(B) METAL (COBALT) NAPHTHENATES***
Cobalt Hydroxide
5. Sulphuric Acid
6. Caustic Soda
7. Naphthenic Acid
8. Mineral Spirit Solvent
9. Other Chemicals

TOTAL WORKING CAPITAL/MONTH

1. Raw Material	Rs.	19,55,061.00
2. Salary & Wages	Rs.	96,250.00
3. Utilities & Overheads	Rs.	37,600.00
TOTAL	Rs.	20,88,911.00

TOTAL CAPITAL INVESTMENT

Total Fixed Capital	Rs.	58,82,000.00
Total Working Capital for 3 Months	Rs.	62,66,733.00
TOTAL	Rs.	1,21,48,733.00

TURN OVER/ANNUM

1. Cobalt Octoate @ 1,50,000 kgs
2. Cobalt Naphthenate @ 1,50,000 kgs

TOTAL	Rs.	3,45,00,000.00

Profit Sales Ratio = Profit / Sales x 100 = 16.96 %
Rate of Return = Operating profit / T.C.I x 100 = 48.15 %
Break Even Point (B.E.P) = 41.94 %

Chapter - 25

PAINTS AND THINNERS INDUSTRY

The physical property in the paint has very importance to ensure its colour which should not fade and to be discoloured in any case which is a creditable property. It should be empowered to resist heat, water and the other atmospheric conditions. The paint should protect the surface from the above mentioned effects. Its main property should be of high hiding power ensuring the colour durability.

The painted surfaces should be of washable condition. The films which are produced by the painting, when dried when dried well should be of cleaning condition in case of change, the colour and other things extra.

The very important property in the paint in "GLOSS" which is the very must is in paint manufacturing. There are no set methods for the prescribed formulations or recipe balanced for permanent in gloss. Only the trial and errors guide the paint manufacturers through their chemists who have really command to adjust the compound ingredients to obtain the proper gloss.

FORMULATION FOR DRY DISTEMPER:-

General Dry Distemper:

		%
Pigment	:	74.4
Mica	:	10.0
Casein	:	12.0
Borax	:	1.1
Sodium fluoride	:	1.0
Potassium dichromate	:	1.5

For other color distempers different pigments are used in the same proportion. The pigments are the same as mentioned in lime color.

ENAMEL PAINTS

Depending upon their use, the enamel paints are divided into two categories, namely enamels, for interior use and enamels for exterior use. The difference is due to the quality of the vehicle used in each case. The deference is due to the quality of the vehicle used in each case. Enamels are painted on under costs applied first on the surface to be painted.

Formulations :-

Examples of a few types of enamels are given below :

White Alkyd Glass Enamels:

Rutile TiO2	:	29.3%
Coated CaCo3	:	2.8%
Long oil alkyd (70%	:	50.6%
White Spirit	:	13.3%
Dependtene	:	2.1%
Lead Naphthenate (24%)	:	0.4%
Cobalt Naphthenate (6%)	:	0.2%
Calcium Naphthenate (4%)	:	1.2%

RED OXIDE PRIMER

Red oxide paints are used for the first coat on previously impainted surfaces to provide the foundation on which the durability of the finished painting largely depends. Different red oxide primers are used for various surfaces.

For metal work as structural steel practically all the inhibitive pigments give best result in a linseed oil medium red lead paint, and zinc oxide mixture. For non ferrous metals the primers based on zinc chromate are generally employed. Calcium plumbate primers have given good result on galvanized surfaces. Each primers or wash primers are of considerable importance in treatment of of non ferrous metals. These primers consists of essentially of solutions of polyvinyl butyral in mixtures of alcohol and ketones, pigmented with zinc chromate or teroxychromate. Each primers have given very good results on aluminium zinc, lead, copper, cadmium and steel.

Formulation for Red Oxide Primer :-

Manufactured or Natural Red Oxide :-

Red oxide Iron : 57.0% by wt.Oil of turpentine : 5.0 "

"Linseed Oil : 35.0 " "Liquid drier and tinters : 3.0 "

Manufacturing Process is same as in the case of enamel paint.

FORMULATION OF THINNER

FORMULATION

FOR NAPHTHA BASED THINNER

1.	Solvent Naphtha	5%
2.	Butyl acetate	10%
3.	Butanol	10%
4.	Ethyl Acetate	12%
5.	Ethyl Alcohol	13%
6.	Toluene	40%
7.	MTO	7%

PROCESS OF MFG. OF NAPHTHA BASED THINNER FROM CRUDE NAPHTHA

(A) Production of Pure Solvent Naphtha :-

Crude Naphtha is subjected to distillation process for recovery of pure solvent Naphtha to be used for thinner making.

Requisite quantities of crude Naphtha are taken & introduced into distillation column fitted with reboiler and reflux condenser and the contents are distilled at a tempt. 220° to 222° at which pure Naphtha distilled out. Steam is passed through reboiler & the vapours are condensed in the reflux condenser. Recycling process goes on until the desired purity of the distillate is achieved.

Pure solvent Naphtha is then withdrawn from the distillation column & taken to storage rank from where the pure solvent Naphtha is withdrawn to be mixed with other ingredients in the thinner making section.

(B) Blending section for Naphtha Based Thinner Making :-

After the recovery of pure solvent Naphtha from the above Distillation unit, as per the following formulation:

Solvent Naphtha	92 %
Toluene	3 %
Benzene	2 %
White oil	3 %

The above ingredient including pure solvent Naphtha are introduced into a Blender/mixer(ms) fitted with an agitator & the contents are well homogenised to form the Naphtha based thinner.

It is then packed in m.s drums of 100 ltr. cap and dispatched for marketing.

PLANT ECONOMICS

Rated Plant Capacity	= 100.00 Kgs/Day PAINT
LAND & BUILDING (Land 300 sq.mt)	Rs. 2,14,000.00

PLANT & MACHINERY

1. Grinder
2. Ribbon blender
3. Edge Runner
4. OIL DISTEMPER & ENAMEL PAINTS SEC: Edge Runner
5. Ball Mill
6. Mixer
7. Varnish Preparation Reactor
8. Steel Ball Mill
9. *GENERAL EQUIPMENTS :* Weighing Balances platform type
10. Lab. Equipments
11. *ALKYD RESIN* Heating equipment with burner bhatties
12. Stainless steel Reaction vessel

FIXED CAPITAL

1.	Land & Building	Rs.	2,14,000.00
2.	Plant & Machinery	Rs.	3,60,000.00
3.	Other Fixed Assets	Rs.	50,000.00
	TOTAL	Rs.	6,24,000.00

RAW MATERIALS

1. Phthalic Anhyde
2. Glycerine
3. Linseed oil
4. Titanium dioxide
5. White antimony
6. Line seed oil
7. Alkyd Resin

TOTAL WORKING CAPITAL/MONTH

1.	Raw Material	Rs.	1,40,970.00
2.	Salary & Wages	Rs.	7,560.00
3.	Utilities & Overheads	Rs.	9,600.00
	TOTAL	Rs.	1,58,130.00

TOTAL CAPITAL INVESTMENT

Total Fixed Capital	Rs.	6,24,000.00
Total Working Capital for 1 Months	Rs.	1,58,130.00
TOTAL	Rs.	7,82,130.00

TURN OVER/ANNUM

1. Sale of 30,000 kgs enamel paint
2. Sale of 24000 kg oil varnish

TOTAL Rs. 25,80,000.00

Profit Sales Ratio = Profit / Sales x 100 = 17.34 %

Rate of Return = Operating profit / T.C.I x 100 = 57.21 %

Break Even Point (B.E.P) = 41.50 %

Chapter - 26

REFRACTORY PAINT (GRAPHITE BASED)

Refractory paints are one of the important coating material for core coating. It is applicable in both ferrous and non ferrous metal castings.

Cast Iron:- This term is applied to ferrous alloys, which are chiefly composed of iron, carbon, and silicon but also contain manganese, phosphorus, and sulphur as normal elements. The modification of some properties existing in cast iron may be obtained by the addition of other elements, such as chromium, molybdenum, nickel, vanadium, copper, titanium, etc.

Among the ferrous metals, cast iron occupies first position and is recognized as one of the most indispensable materials used in the manufacture of many products necessary in everyday life. Cast iron is not as strong or tough as steel, but it is more economical. From the point of view of processing, cast iron is favoured in many respects above other materials. Its low melting point, low shrinkage, good fluidity, and machinability are the properties that recommend it.

Among the disadvantages of cast iron, the most important are its lack of ductility and low strength, although some progress has been made in recent years in controlling the melting technique and composition of the charge in the plain or unalloyed irons. Considerable progress has been made in improving the properties of alloyed cast irons and malleable cast irons, which fact is greatly responsible for their wide application in industry. The diversity of properties existing in various grades and classes of cast irons makes it possible to choose irons possessing tensile strength of 20,000 to 80,000 pounds per square inch.

RAW MATERIALS

Graphite powder, plastic clay or colloidal china clay, Talcum powder, Bentonite clay, dextrin powder, Tannin (Peptising agent), Carboxy Methyl Cellulose (C.M.C.), Glycerol, Sodium Silicate, Acid Slurry, Hydrochloric Acid.

GRAPHITE PAINT FOR REFRACTORY COATING (DIP COATING)

Formulation

		Parts by wt.
Graphite Powder	-	90
Plastic Clay (Colloidal China Clay)	-	5
Talcum Powder	-	1
Bentonite Powder	-	1
Yellow Dextrin Powder	-	1
Binder*	-	3-5
Tannin (Peptising Agent)	-	0.05
Carboxy Methyl Cellulose (Thickening Agents)	-	0.50
Glycerol (Plasticiser)	-	1.50
Total Quality	=	103 Parts

*Binder System

Sodium Silicate (40°Be')	-	50 Parts
Water	-	150 Parts
Hydrochloric Acid	-	2 Parts
Acid Slurry (Wetting Agent)	-	0.5 Parts

PLANT ECONOMICS

Rated Plant Capacity = 1000.00 LITRES./Day GRAPHITE WASH(FOUNDRY COATING PAINT

LAND & BUILDING (Land 500 Sq.mts.)

PLANT & MACHINERY

1. Powder Sieving Machine
2. Dry Powder Blender
3. Paste Mixing Machine
4. Liquid Mixing Machine with stirrer

FIXED CAPITAL

1. Land & Building		Owned
2. Plant & Machinery		Owned
3. Other Fixed Assets	Rs.	2,75,000.00
TOTAL	Rs.	2,75,000.08

RAW MATERIALS

1. Graphite Powder
2. Plastic Clay
3. Talcum Powder
4. Bentonite Powder
5. Yellow Dextrin Powder
6. Sodium Silicate
7. Hydrochloric Acid
8. Acid Slurry (wetting Agent)

TOTAL WORKING CAPITAL/MONTH

1. Raw Material	Rs.	2,39,400.00
2. Salary & Wages	Rs.	51,870.00
3. Utilities & Overheads	Rs.	67,750.00
TOTAL	Rs.	3,59,020.00

TOTAL CAPITAL INVESTMENT

Total Fixed Capital	Rs.	2,75,000.08
Total Working Capital for 1 Months	Rs.	3,59,020.00
TOTAL	Rs.	6,34,020.08

TURN OVER/ANNUM

By Sale of Graphite Wash or Coating 3,00,000 litres	Rs.	48,00,000.00

Profit Sales Ratio = Profit / Sales x 100 = 7.94 %

Rate of Return = Operating profit / T.C.I x 100 = 60.12 %

Break Even Point (B.E.P) = 64.24 %

Chapter - 27

SOLVENT AND THINNERS

A solvent is a liquid which disperses a solid or semi solid substance so as to yield a useful solution.

The application of a solvent or thinner in the production of paints or varnishes is highly essentials in order to obtain a useful solution. In the solution formation dispersion of solids to liquid phase takes place. Example the addition of linseed oil to hexane, to glycericles present in the oil disperse forming a viscous solution.

A wide range of solvents possessing specific properties are now used in formulations containing synthetic resins. According to their boiling range, solvents are classified as low boilers (B.P.< 100°C) medium boilers (B.P. 100-120°), and high boilers (B.P.) 150°.

Tarpene Hydrocarbons	Boiling Point range
Turpentine	155 -190°
Dipentine	176 - 198°
Pine Oil	190 - 218°
Aliphatic Hydrocarbons:-	
Low and Medium Boiling	
Petroleum Distillate	70 - 150°
Petroleum distillate	140 - 220°
White spirit	
rheumatic Hydrocarbon:-	
Light solvent naphtha	130 - 170°
Heavy " "	160 - 190°
Xylol " "	135 - 140°
Naphthalene derivatives:-	
Tetralene (Tetra Hydronaphthalene)	205°
Decaline. Deca Hydronaphthalene)	190°
Butyl Alcohol	110 - 118°

Solutions of resins, nitrocellulose, etc. are after diluted, in order to adjust their flow, rate of evaporation, cost or other properties, with a liquid which is without solvent action on the dispersed solids. A good example is toluene when added for this purpose to a nitrocellulose lacquer. Such a liquid is termed simply a diluent. With the gradual addition of a diluent to a lacquer, a point s reached at which the dispersed solid is precipitated out. The amount of diluent which can be tolerated before precipitation commences depends on a number of factors, e.g. the solvent power of the solvent, nature of the diluent, and concentration of solids, temperature etc.

Thinners, as the name implies, are added to varnish and lacquers to thin them out usually to brushing consistency. White spirit is the commonest liquid based for this purpose. A thinner differs from a diluent in that it has solvent action on the dispersed resin or other solid and will not as a rule cause precipitation.

Thinners is a hydrocarbon (naphtha) or oleoresinous solvent (turpentine) used to reduce the viscosity of paints to appropriate working consistency usually just this since a thinner is a liquid diluent except that it has active solvent power on the dissolvent resin. Thinners are employed for adjusting the consistency of coating formulations. Turpentine is used as a thinner for resin and oil coatings. It has been replaced by petroleum naphthas (boiling range 300-400°F) and varnish maker's and painter's naphtha. (VM and P naphtha), water is used as a thinner in emulsion paints, water colours and calcimines.

When a varnish or resin has been prepared it is in a hot condition and as such it is at a low handleable viscosity. To keep it thin, thinner are incorporated before it cools too much. In thinning, care must be taken to ensure that the hot varnish or resin is not at a temperature above the auto ignition temperature of the solvent employed. These temperatures are, however, greatly in excess of the normal boiling ranges of the solvents. Thinners may involve mixture comprising xylol, butyl alcohol, and pine oil, and uniform dispersion is obviously important in such cases. Any type of propeller or turbine stirrer will give good results for a small expenditure of power.

FORMULATIONS:

Thinner Formulations for Brushing Lacquers:-

Nitrocellulose brushing lacquers were once popular, but demand for them decreased after introduction of fast-drying alkyd enamels, commonly called 4-hour enamels, or varnishes. the principal limitations of early brushing lacquers were lifting. Pick up on recoating, poor brushability and objectionable odour. after severing all available solvents and diluents in the light of their incluence or these properties chemists of Hercules powder company. arrived at a formulation that second to overcome these objections. The formula was high in alcohols & cellulose acetate, but it contained no aromatic diluents. A typical thinner formula proposed by them is:-

Cellulose	35 %
Ethyl alcohol	10 %
Isopropyl alcohol	10 %
Turpentine	45 %
	100 %

For pigmented brushing enamels, it appears desirable to replace part of the cellosolve acetate with a small proportion of methyl carbitol.

PLANT ECONOMICS

LAND & BUILDING (Land 1000 Sq.Mts.) Rs. 19,57,500.00

PLANT & MACHINERY

1. Mixer (S.S.) fitted with agitator
2. Stainless steel closed tank fitted with agitator
3. Filter
4. Lab apparatus and testing equipments
5. Miscellaneous viz. pipe fittings, pumps, motors, valves, weighing scales etc.

FIXED CAPITAL

1.	Land & Building	Rs.	19,57,500.00
2.	Plant & Machinery	Rs.	19,65,000.00
3.	Other Fixed Assets	Rs.	5,25,000.00
	TOTAL	Rs.	44,47,500.00

RAW MATERIALS

1. *FOR STOVING THINNER* Xylol
2. Hiflash naphtha/white spirit/benzol
3. Butyl cellosolve (ethylene glycol monobutyl ether)
4. Butyl alcohol

5. *FOR NITROCELLULOSE LACQUER THINNER*
   Ethyl acetate
6. n-butyl acetate
7. Methyl ethyl ketone
8. Methyl isobutyl ketone
9. Diacetone alcohol
10. Xylene
11. *FOR ACRYLIC THINNER Cellosolve acetate*
12. Hydrogenated naphtha/benzol/white spirit
13. Xylol
14. *FOR ENAMEL THINNERS Xylene*
15. Toluene
16. 2-Nitropropane
17. Isopropanol
18. VM + P Naphtha/white oil
19. Butanol
20. *FOR GENERAL LACQUER THINNERS Toluene*
21. Benzene
22. Solvent naphtha/benzol/white spirit
23. Special denaturated spirit

TOTAL WORKING CAPITAL/MONTH

1.	Raw Material	Rs.	17,85,252.50
2.	Salary & Wages	Rs.	94,375.00
3.	Utilities & Overheads	Rs.	69,000.00
	TOTAL	Rs.	19,48,627.50

TOTAL CAPITAL INVESTMENT

Total Fixed Capital	Rs.	44,47,500.00
Total Working Capital for 2 Months	Rs.	38,97,255.00
TOTAL	Rs.	83,44,755.00

TURN OVER/ANNUM

1. By sale of stoving thinner 1,50,000 litres
2. Nitrocellulose lacquer thinner 1,50,000 litres
3. Acrylic thinner, 150,000 litres
4. Enamel lacquer, 1,50,000 litres
5. General lacquer thinner 1,50,000 litres

TOTAL	Rs. 3,00,00,000.00

Profit Sales Ratio = Profit / Sales x 100 = 15.04 %

Rate of Return = Operating profit / T.C.I x 100 = 54.07 %

Break Even Point (B.E.P) = 39.03 %

Chapter - 28

TEXTURE PAINTS

WATER REDUCIBLE TEXTURE PAINT

(U. S. PATENT 2,880,104)

Formulation

Ingredients		Parts by wt. (kgs)
Magnesium Silicate	-	68-77
Hydrated Aluminium Silicate	-	66-74
Potassium Aluminium Silicate	-	53-60
Calcium Carbonate	-	30-38
Titanium Dioxide (Rutile)	-	15-20
Water Soluble Cellulose Ether*	-	5-10
Sodium Pentachlorophenate (Fungicide)	-	1-3
Borax	-	1-3
Soybean Meal	-	30-40

*** Water Soluble Cellulose Ether:-**

This consists of following items in % by wt.		**(% by wt.)**
Methyl Cellulose Ether (High Viscosity)	-	55
Sodium Chloride	-	36
Ethylene Glycol (M.E.G.)	-	8
Sodium Carbonate and Bicarbonate	-	1

PLANT ECONOMICS

Rated Plant Capacity = 500 Kg./Day

LAND & BUILDING (Land 200 sq.mt) Rs. 13,00,000.00

PLANT & MACHINERY

1. Weighing balance
2. Ball mill
3. Edge Runner
4. Tripple Roll Mill
5. Laboratory Equipment
6. Water Storage Tank
7. Miscellaneous

FIXED CAPITAL

1.	Land & Building	Rs.	13,00,000.00
2.	Plant & Machinery	Rs.	4,90,000.00
3.	Other Fixed Assets	Rs.	2,25,000.00
	TOTAL	Rs.	20,15,000.00

RAW MATERIALS

1. Talc powder
2. Asbestos fiber
3. Kablinite
4. Feldspar
5. Calcium Carbonate
6. Titanium Dioxide
7. Carboxy Methyl Cellulose
8. Ethylene Glycol
9. Fungicides
10. Borax
11. Soybean meal
12. Packaging Materials
13. Laboratory Chemicals

TOTAL WORKING CAPITAL/MONTH

1.	Raw Material	Rs.	1,71,927.75
2.	Salary & Wages	Rs.	37,240.00
3.	Utilities & Overheads	Rs.	62,000.00
	TOTAL	Rs.	2,71,167.75

TOTAL CAPITAL INVESTMENT

Total Fixed Capital	Rs.	20,15,000.00
Total Working Capital for 1 Months	Rs.	2,71,167.75
TOTAL	Rs.	22,86,167.75

TURN OVER/ANNUM

By Sale of Textured paint (paste form) 1,50,000 kgs	Rs.	46,50,000.00

Profit Sales Ratio = Profit / Sales x 100 = 20.61 %

Rate of Return = Operating profit / T.C.I x 100 = 41.92 %

Break Even Point (B.E.P) = 48.82 %

Chapter - 29

THINNERS/SOLVENTS AND ITS ALLIED PRODUCTS

Solvents or Thinners are used in Paints and lacquers to reduce the viscosity or consistency of the material and facilitate the application of a uniform coating. They must be compatible with the oil or resin present. After application the solvent is no longer required and should evaporate completely from the film.

Another class of organic liquids used in paint industry is plasticizers their function is to remain permanently in the film of paint or varnish after application in order to impart elasticity and proper adhesion to it. In contradistinction to the volatile solvents, plasticizers should be perfectly non-volatile, and should also be chemically stable, and not after in properties on prolonged exposure.

The action of a solvent in the production of a varnish on paint is essentially not different from that takes place when sugar is added to a cup of tea. Water disperses the sugar molecules and a solution is formed. Similarly when linseed oil is added to Lexane, the glyceride of which the oil consists are dispersed or dissolved and a more or less viscous solution results.

A solvent can be defined as a liquid which disperses a solid or semi-solid substance so as to yield a useful solution.

MANUFACTURING PROCESS

The manufacturing process of the thickness and allied solvents are very simple and brief. Only main three number of equipments are required.

A mixer uses and pour the all of the raw materials into it and mix these with the help of agitator rotating at the speed of 1500 rpm with the help of motor. This is the batch process, uniform mixing is the main part of it. From the mixer the solution is outputed and feed to the filtration chamber. The filtrate take to the packing. This material packs in the tin boxes.

Process of Manufacture & Formulation

Thinner Formulations for Brushing Lacquers:-

Nitrocellulose brushing lacquers were once popular, but demand for them decreased after the introduction of fast-drying alkyd enamels, commonly called 4-hour enamels or varnishes. The principal limitations of early brushing lacquers were lifting, pickup on recoating, poor brushability and objectionable odour. After reviewing all available solvents and diluents in the light of their influence on these properties, chemists of Hercules powder company arrived at a formulation that secured to overcome these objection. The formula was high in alcohols and cellusolve acetate, but it contained no aromatic diluents. A typical thinner formula proposed by them is:-

Cellulose acetate	35 %
Ethyl alcohol	10 %
Isopropyl alcohol	10 %
Turpentine	45 %

For pigmented brushing enamels, it appears desirable to replace part of the cellusolve acetate, with a small proportion of methyl carbide.

Thinner Formulations

(All parts by weight)

	Standard, Percent	Hot Spray, Percent
Butyl acetate	35	37.5
Butyl alcohol	15	12.5
Ethyl alcohol	–	10
Toluence	50	---
Xylene	–	40
	100	100

PLANT ECONOMICS

LAND & BUILDING (Land 1000 Sq.Mts.) Rs. 19,57,500.00

PLANT & MACHINERY

1. Mixer (S.S.) fitted with agitator
2. Stainless steel closed tank fitted with agitator
3. Filter
4. Lab apparatus and testing equipments
5. Miscellaneous viz. pipe fittings, pumps, motors, valves, weighing scales etc.

FIXED CAPITAL

1.	Land & Building	Rs.	19,57,500.00
2.	Plant & Machinery	Rs.	19,65,000.00
3.	Other Fixed Assets	Rs.	5,25,000.00
	TOTAL	Rs.	44,47,500.00

RAW MATERIALS

1. *FOR STOVING THINNER* Xylol
2. Hiflash naphtha/white spirit/benzol
3. Butyl cellosolve (ethylene glycol monobutyl ether)
4. Butyl alcohol
5. *FOR NITROCELLULOSE LACQUER THINNER* Ethyl acetate
6. n-butyl acetate
7. Methyl ethyl ketone
8. Methyl isobutyl ketone
9. Diacetone alcohol
10. Xylene
11. *FOR ACRYLIC THINNER* Cellosolve acetate
12. Hydrogenated naphtha/benzol/white spirit
13. Xylol
14. *FOR ENAMEL THINNERS* Xylene
15. Toluene
16. 2-Nitropropane
17. Isopropanol
18. VM + P Naphtha/white oil
19. Butanol
20. *FOR GENERAL LACQUER THINNERS* Toluene
21. Benzene

22. Solvent naphtha/benzol/white spirit
23. Special denaturated spirit

TOTAL WORKING CAPITAL/MONTH

1.	Raw Material	Rs.	17,85,252.50
2.	Salary & Wages	Rs.	94,375.00
3.	Utilities & Overheads	Rs.	69,000.00
	TOTAL	Rs.	19,48,627.50

TOTAL CAPITAL INVESTMENT

Total Fixed Capital	Rs.	44,47,500.00
Total Working Capital for 2 Months	Rs.	38,97,255.00
TOTAL	Rs.	83,44,755.00

TURN OVER/ANNUM

1. By sale of stoving thinner 1,50,000 litres
2. Nitrocellulose lacquer thinner 1,50,000 litres
3. Acrylic thinner, 150,000 litres
4. Enamel lacquer, 1,50,000 litres
5. General lacquer thinner 1,50,000 litres

TOTAL Rs. 3,00,00,000.00

Profit Sales Ratio = Profit / Sales x 100 = 15.04 %
Rate of Return = Operating profit / T.C.I x 100 = 54.07 %
Break Even Point (B.E.P) = 39.03 %

Chapter - 30

VARNISH (CLEAR) FOR WOOD (FLAME-RETARDING TYPE)

The definition of varnish, as given by one of the technical societies is "liquid coating material containing no pigment which flows out to a smooth coat when applied and dries to a smooth, glossy, relatively hard, permanent solid when exposed in a thin film to air".

There can be no doubt that varnishes are a heterogeneous system, consisting of resin and thinners, or resins, oils, thinners, and driers. Some institution consider, varnish a solution, others classify it as a colloid.

In a physical sense varnishes are fluids that can be spread readily to thin smooth films which dry to hard, continuous, permanent, solid coatings when exposed to air or heat. The first step in the drying of varnish films is the evaporation of the volatile portion, which leaves the non-volatile materials to dry by oxidation, and or a combination of polymerization and condensation. Some varnishes dry only by the evaporation, for example, cold-cut resin varnish, and shellac.

In the case of clean wood varnish (fire-retarding type) has the speciality that owing to the fire-retarding constituent viz trichloro-ethyl phosphate or tri-poly phosphate present in the formulation of the varnish, the proneness of combustion or catching fire obviated.

FURNITURE VARNISHES

As for the wooden furniture varnish, in general, the wood is staimed and filled, a sealer coat applied and sanded, and then one or more coats of finishing varnish applied. If more than one coat of varnish is applied. The first coat is sanded lightly.

The finish may be left in its original gloss, but more often it is subdued to a dull or satin finish with pumice and oil. In high-grade work the finish may be polished to a somewhat higher gloss with rotten stone.

It should be apparent that speed and ease of rubbing will depend on hardness of the film. Since short-oil varnisher become day and hard more rapidly than long-oil varnishes and also rub more easily to a better-looking finish, they are used despite their laver flexibility and less resistance to scratching and marring. In addition, furniture is bulky and requires considerable floor space in finishing room and storage. Therefore, the furniture manufacturer wants the fastest possible finishing schedule so that he can ship his stock quickly. Furniture must be packed in paper, burlap, etc., to protect it from damage during shipment, and unless the finish is thoroughly dry and hard material will adhere to it and leave an ugly print mark when removed. This places an additional problem on the varnish formulator to develop rapid drying, print resistant finishes and still retain same degree of toughness and durability.

MANUFACTURING PROCESS OF CLEAR WOOD VARNISH (FLAME RETARDING TYPE)

CONSIDERING, AS PER FORMULATION NO 3
(HIGH GRADE RUBBING VARNISH)

INGREDIENTS	PARTS/WT.	% AGE
1. Alkyd resin/modified phenolic resin (Acid number 100-130 softening Point 150-160°C	100	21.14
2. Tung Oil	60	12.99
3. Linseed Oil	30	6.49
4. Mineral Spirits	250	54.11
5. Plasticizer (Tri-Tolyl Phosphate or Tri Cresyl Phosphate)	15	3.25
6. Drier Cobalt Naphthenate	7	1.52
Total	462	100.00

Therein the following steps are carried out:-

WEIGHING OF THE RAW MATERIALS

The ingredients are first weighted for a given batch, and are storec at the production site.

The resin is broken into very small pieces and cleaned to remove all the impurities present in it.

2. DEPOLYMERIZATION

The alkyd resin or modified phenolic resin as obtained from the market is insoluble in the oil, which is therefore depolymerized first.

Depolymerization is done in a copper kettle with electrically heatinc arrangement, the kettle may also be of aluminium with copper or mone metal bottom the alkyd resin or modified phenolic resin in introduced intc the kettle.

The kettle in then heated slowly so that in 10 minutes a temperature of 350⁰F (168⁰C) is reached. At this temperature the resin begins to melt.

Heat is then applied move slowly, until a thin film of melted resin covers the bottom of the kettle, protecting from charring the remaining unmelted resin.

From this point, the temperature is permitted to rise more rapidly, but greater care is exercised to prevent the blames and sparks from igniting the fumes and other inflammable vapours which are given off at this time, water vapour is also given off.

By the time the temperature of approximately 500⁰F (260⁰C) increached, the resin is completely melted.

The complete melting of the resin takes about 25 to 30 minutes.

The temperature is allowed to rise to 600⁰F (315.6⁰C) and the heating system to the kettle is removed, cooled for a very short time usually 3 to 5 minutes and then again start the heating systems, the temperature is then raised to 635⁰F (335⁰C). At this point, the temperature rises spontaneously by about 20⁰F, and at this the melted therein is processed for about 8 to 10 minutes.

This cooling, reheating and processing are repeated a second time with most resins. With resins of increased hardness, a third and fourth cooling and reheating may be necessary.

An examination of the melted resin should show that it is a homogeneous liquid, free of strings or sponginess.

The cooling period is known as the sweating period. During this time, the solid portion of the resin approaches the liquid state without further heating.

In the above process of resin melting if anything floating therein is removed. The process is known as running. It is done till sufficient foams develop on the upper surface, the resin is then considered depolymerized.

In the above process, resin is heated with chalf the quantity of tung oil at 550⁰F.

This is followed by adding the remaining half of the quantity of tung oil and reheating to 550⁰F.

3. **HEATING OF OIL**

The linseed oil is boiled in a different kettle so as to increase the miscibility of the resin in the oil.

4. MIXING OF DEPOLYMERIZED RESIN WITH LINSEED OIL

The depolymerized resin is then mixed with linseed oil, and is cooled in a kettle.

5. COOLING

The above mass is cooled by switching off the electric heaters and temperature is allowed to fall to about 400°F and reduced with mineral spirits.

6. ADDITION OF OTHER INGREDIENTS

(Cobalt/Lead/Manganese Naphthenate)

Naphthalene driers/may be added to give the following percentages by weight of metal to oil in the varnish. 0.3% Ph, 0.015% Co, 0.015% Mn.

Cobalt-Naphthenate may be preferably added.

Finally, add plasticizer (Tri-Tolyl Phosphate) (flame retardant) with continuous stirring necessary in almost all the operations of varnish making so that proper homogenity can be maintained.

7. FILTRATION

The mass is then further cooled down to room temperature and then passed through a filter press to remove any insoluble mass from the varnish the running varnish as filtrate is collected and stored

8. SETTLING OR AGEING

The varnish is then allowed to settle in any ageing tank where any insoluble gel or gelly formed due to agitation may be removed.

9. FILLING AND PACKING

The aged varnish is finally stored in a varnish storage tank, from here it is filled into tin or plastic containers of different capacities.

These are available in 1/4, 1/2. 1, 2, 5, 10 and 20 litres drums.

PLANT ECONOMICS

Rated Plant Capacity = 500.00 Ltr/Day
CLEAR WOOD VARNISH(FLAME-RETARDING)

LAND & BUILDING (Land reqd. 500 sq.mts) Rs. 11,30,000.00

PLANT & MACHINERY

1. Cooking Kettle of Copper
2. Running kettle with stirrer
3. Filter Press
4. Ageing Tanks
5. Storage Tanks
6. Depolluting Equipment
7. Lab Testing Equipments
8. Miscellaneous viz Pipe fittings, Valves, Motors, etc.

FIXED CAPITAL

1. Land & Building	Rs.	11,30,000.00
2. Plant & Machinery	Rs.	8,20,000.00
3. Other Fixed Assets	Rs.	2,20,000.00
TOTAL	Rs.	21,70,000.00

RAW MATERIALS

1. Alkyd Resin/Modified Phenolic Resin
2. Tung Oil
3. Linseed Oil
4. Mineral Spirits
5. Plasticizer (Tri-Tolyl Phosphate)
6. Drier (Cobalt Naphthenate)
7. Packaging Material viz Tin Cans

TOTAL WORKING CAPITAL/MONTH

1. Raw Material	Rs.	5,16,793.75
2. Salary & Wages	Rs.	68,495.00
3. Utilities & Overheads	Rs.	35,400.00
TOTAL	Rs.	6,20,688.75

TOTAL CAPITAL INVESTMENT

Total Fixed Capital	Rs.	21,70,000.00
Total Working Capital for 2 Months	Rs.	12,41,377.50
TOTAL	Rs.	34,11,377.50

TURN OVER/ANNUM

By sale of 1,50,000 Litres of Clear Wood Varnish (Fire-retarding type)	Rs.	97,50,000.00

Profit Sales Ratio = Profit / Sales x 100 = 15.39 %

Rate of Return = Operating profit / T.C.I x 100 = 43.99 %

Break Even Point (B.E.P) = 46.41 %

Chapter - 31

PRESENT MANUFACTURERS / EXPORTERS

PAINTS

Ahura Paints
G-6, Shalimar Industrial Estate,
Matunga,
Mumbai-400019
Phone : (022)-4090626

A.K.Industries
Plot No. 1315, Phase III,
G.I.D.C. Vatva,
Behind Vijay Transport,
Ahmedabad-382445
Gujarat
Phone : (079)-5836372

Acro Paints Ltd.,
5/3, Kirti Nagar,
Industrial Area,
New Delhi - 110 015
Ph : 5931908
Fax : 5419683
Website :
www.acropaints.com

Almec Paints & Chemical Industries
391/4, Gurjar Estate,
Nagarvel Hanuman Road,
Rakhial,
Ahmedabad-380023
Gujarat
Phone : (079)-2740555

Alpha Paints
C-1/9, G.I.D.C. Estate,
Opp. Ambika Nagar,
2nd Gate, Odhav,
Ahmedabad-382415,
Gujarat
Phone : (079)
2871944,2870043
Fax : (079)-2871587

Ambica Chemical & Industrial Corp.
25, Strand Road,
Room No. 761,
Kolkata - 700001
Phone : (033)-2209488

Amchem Products P. Ltd.
A-79, Sector 58,
Noida-201301,
Uttar Pardesh.
Phone : (0577) 580121,581352
Fax : (0577)-521823
E-Mail :
info@amchemproducts.com.
Website :
www.amchemproducs.com

Asian Paints (India) Ltd.
Nirmal 5th Floor,
Nariman Point,
P.B.No. 11701,
Mumbai-400021
Phone : (022)-2024544,
Fax : (022)-2028993

Auchtel Products Ltd.
142/C, Victor House,
N.M. Joshi Marg,
Lower Parel (w),
Mumbai-400013
Phone : (022)-
4974211,4933975
Fax : (022)-4974211
E-Mail : auchtel@vsnl.com

Automatic Components
A-39, H-Block,
M.I.D.C. Estate,
Pimpri, Pune - 411019
Phone : (020)-772230,
762230

Berger Paints India Ltd.
Berger House,
129, Park Street,
Kolkata - 700017
Phone : (033)-299724-28,
2499754
E-Mail :
berger@giasc101.vsnl.net.in

Bharat Paints Chemicals
Dungarwadi Post,
Atul, Valsad -396020
Gujarat
Phone:(02632)-33648
Fax :(02623)-33165

Bombay Imports Agency
296/31,Samuel Street,
Haveli Buiding
Mumbai-400003
Phone :(022)-
49011448,4012961
Fax : (022)-4013177
E-Mail :
devanshi@giashma.vsnl.nt.ion

Bombay Paints Ltd.
B.D. Patil Marg.
Gavanpada,
Chembur,
Mumbai-400074

B.S. Corp
512, Centre Point,
R.C. Dutt Road,
Vadodara -390007
Gujarat
Phone : (0265)-331063
Fax: (0265)-342937

Century Paints
Opposite Police Station,
Main Road,
Gonida - 441601
Maharashtra,
Phone : (07182)-
22721,21454

Choksey Chemicals P.Ltd.
111, Industrial Area Sion,
Mumbai-400022
Phone : (022)-
4090124,4090127,4090325
Fax: (022)-4072949
E-Mail :
hmp@bom2.vsnl.net.in

Coates of India Ltd.
Transport Depot Road,
P.O. Box 16741,
Kolkata - 700088
Phone : (033)-
4792584,4793311,496591
Fax : (033)-4795267

Deepak Chemicals
2207, Phase IV, G.I.D.C.
Estate,
Vatva, Ahmedabad-382445,
Gujarat
Phone : (079)-5831878
Fax : (079)-5834062,
7419595
E-Mail :
deepakc@ad1.vsnl.net.in
www.deepak chemicals.com

Dekora Pigments and Paints P.Ltd.
A-1/7, Dekora House,
Krishna Nagar,
Delhi-110051
Phone : (011)-2213862
Fax : (011)-2240663

Dilip Brijmohan Marwal
Shelar File,
Marwal Compound,
Akola- 444001
Maharashtra
Phone : (0724)-
436209,440509

Dooall Corpro (India) P.Ltd.
21, Damji Shamji
Industrial Estate,
L.B.S. Marg,
Vikhroli (W),
Mumbai-400083
Phone : (022)-
5781525,5782892
Fax : (022)-5782892
E-Mail :
dooall@bom5.vsnl.net.in

Era Paints & Adhesives (P) Ltd.
17, Chandi Ghosh Road,
Kolkata - 700040
Phone :(033)-
4716702,4715168

FNK Corp
Ahoi Lavate Nagar,
Jai Bhawani Road,
Nashik Road,
Nasik-422102,
Maharashtra
Phone : (0253)-569474
Fax : (0253)-564047
E-Mail : fnkcorp@vsnl.com
www.jainexgroup.com/
fnk.htm

Ganga Rasayanie (P) Ltd.
50-B, Harish Mukherjee
Road,
Kolkata - 700025
Phone : (033)-
485884,482080,483203
Fax : (033)-4731523

Golden Paints Industries
C/7, Jagganath Estate,
Gujarat Bottling Road,
Rakhial,
Ahmedabad-380023
Gujarat
Phone : (079)-2741873

Goodlass Nerolac Paints Ltd.
Nerolac House, Ganpatrao
Kadam Marg,
Lower Parel,
Post Box - 16322,
Mumbai-400013
Phone : (022) 4934001,4934003,
4934007,4934008
Fax : (022)4936296,4973704
www.nerolac.com

Gujarat Metaflux Co
2, Motilal Farm,
Nr. Evergreen Hotel,
Opp. House of Kaydees,
Narol,
Ahmedabad-382405
Gujarat
Phone : (079)- 5354156

Hansa Paints & Chemicals
1/21, Asaf Ali Road,
Atma Rane Singh Mansion,
New Delhi-110002
Phone : (011)-
3236070,3235207
Fax :(011)-3231123

Haryana Chemicals
3816-A, Gali No. 6,
Kanhaiya Nagar
(Tri Nagar)
Delhi-110035
Phone : (011)-7192596,
7195205,7196989
Fax : (011)-7192596,
7195205,7196989

Hem Paints P.Ltd.
Plot No. 302, G.I.D.C.
Estate, Sonala Road,
Morba -363641, Gujarat
Phone : (02822)-24734,
24735

Fax : (02822)-30297
E-Mail :
hem@wilnetonline.net.

Hi-Tech Floorings,
120, Vijay Estate, Odhav,
Ahmedabad-382415,
Gujarat
Phone : (079)-6440531
Fax : (079)-2892535
E-Mail :
jigneshkothari@yahoo.com.
www.acidproof.com.

International Technology Corp
Plot B-31, Near Monginis,
New Link Road,
Andheri West,
Mumbai-400053
Phone : (022)-6324471,6401332
Fax : (022)-6324471

Jayco Paints
22, Comet Estate,
Behind Chakudia Mahadev,
Rakhial, Ahmedabad-380023
Gujarat.
Phone : (079)-2741228

Jenson & Nicholson (I) Ltd.
225, Acharya Jagdish
Chandra Bose Road,
P.Box. No. 50,
Kolkata - 700020
Phone : (033)-2476762,2476764,
6475490,2476553
Fax : (033)-2472632

J.K.Paints
G/1, Khira Industrial Estate,
S.T.Road, Santacruz,
Mumbai-400054
Phone : (022)-6147001,6184217
Fax : (022)-6183332

K.K.Systems
25/1, Keshavkripa,
9th Cross, 7th Main Road,
Malleswaram,
Bangalore-560003
Phone : (080)-3348694
Fax : (080)-5281737

Libra Plastics
No.5 Kalasathamman
Koil Street,
Selavayal, Chennai-600051
Phone : (044)-5930478
Fax : (044)-5930759
E-Mail :
nataraj5@md3.vsnl.net.in

Mallak Adhesives & Polymers
216, Mahavir Industrial
Estate,
Plot No. 32 Off. Mahakali
Caves Road,
Andheri (E)
Mumbai-400093.
Phone : (022)-8384552,8205938
Fax : (022)-8228841
E-Mail : saigroup@vsnl.com
www.saigrp.com

Manjushree Textile Industries P.Ltd.
OS. 11, Municipal
Industrial Estate,
V.P.Road, Vile Parle (W),
Mumbai-400056
Phone : (022)-
6161924,6311414
Fax : (022)-6117049

Mastercot Industries
313/16/7 G.I.D.C. Industrial
Estate,
Near Asian Paint Chokdi,
Ankleshwar - 3932002
Gujarat
Phone : (02646)-24324,23978

MC-Bauchemie (India) P.Ltd.
201, Vardhman Chembers,
2nd Floor, Sector 17,
Vashi, Navi Mumbai-400703
Maharashtra
Phone : (022)-7632627,7618619
Fax : (022)-7633772

Mera Chemicals
74, Shradhanand Marg,
Delhi-110006
Phone : (011)-3951019,3974339
Fax : (011)-2931246
E-Mail :
vispav@nde.vsnl.net.in
www.paintindia.net.

Modern Allied Paints & Chemical Co.
155, Jawahar Nagar,
Goregaon West,
Mumbai-400062
Phone : (022)-8720428,8721132

Modern Metallurgicals
9-130, Poranki,
Vijaywada -521137,
Andhra Pradesh,
Phone : (0866)-583242
Fax : (0866)-540632

Organic Coatings Ltd.
Akal Co-op. Hsg. Society,
Bldg. No. A/2, Flat# 1,
Bamanpuri Village,
J.B.Nagar,
Andheri (E)
Mumbai-400059

Panki Metachem P. Ltd
117/H-2/190 Pandu Nagar,
Kanpur-208005
Uttar Pradesh,
Phone : (0512)-222652,218679
Fax : (0512)-243576

Parimal Industrial Corp
W-60, TTC M.I.D.C. Thane
Belapur Road,
Navi Mumbai - 400701
Maharashtra
Phone : (022)-7692836
Fax : (022)-7692836

Plaza Paints (P) Ltd
Plot No. 47, Sector 27A,
Faridabad -121003
Haryana.
Phone : (0129)-277877
Fax : (0129)-270398

Polymer Casing
301-D, Sahajanand
Shopping Centre,
Shahibaug,

Ahmedabad-380004
Gujarat
Phone : (079)-5624555

Pratik Organics,
A-7, Neelkanth Bhavan,
90 Feet Road,
Ghatkopar (East),
Mumbai-400077
Phone : (022)-5132818

Punjab Paint Colour & Varnish Works P.Ltd.
123/529, Fazalganj,
Kanpur -208012,
Uttar Pradesh
Phone : (0512)-216157,216266
Fax : (0512)-218435

Rako Mercantile Traders
E-12, Industrial Estate,
Talkatora,
Lucknow - 226011
Uttar Pradesh
Phone : (0522)-418842,419768
Fax : (0522)-419768,419735

Remco Products Mfg.Co.
C-1/67/10
G.I.D.C. Industrial Estate,
Vatva Ahmedabad-382445
Gujarat
Phone : (079)-5831162
Fax : (079)-5831528

Resinkoat & Allied Chemicals
Block -4, Plot-10, 2nd Floor,
Above Indian Overseas Bank,
HFS Road,
Jogeshwari (East)
Mumbai-400060
Phone : (022)-8329536

Schenectady-Beck India Ltd.
Arcadia 10th Floor, 195,
Nariman Point,
Mumbai-400021
Phone : (022)-2833224,2833255
Fax :(022)-2829776

Shriji Enterprises,
B-14, Garden Reach Road,
Kolkata - 700024
Phone : (033)-4699856,4696738
Fax : (033)-264024

Sika Qualcrete P. Ltd.
Anuj Chamber,
24 Park Street,
Kolkata - 700016
Phone : (033) 294670,
290329, 290330
Fax : (033)-2498551

Singhal Paints P.Ltd.
1, Aishbagh Road,
Lucknow-226004,
Uttar Pradesh
Phone : (0522)-265061,
265813
Fax : (0522)-265724

S.M.V. Chemicals
Anand Business Centre,
1433A Shukrawar Peth,
Pune-411002
Phone :(020)-4459187
Fax : (020)-4483573

Spraylac Paints Corp
804, Arjun Nagar,
Kotla Mubarakpur,
New Delhi-110003
Phone : (011)-4611594,4611056

Star Paint & Oil Industries
Crescent Chambers,
56, Tamarind Street,
Mumbai-400023
Phone : (022)-
2652243,2652289,2652904
Fax : (022)-2653201
E-Mail :
heatex@bom4.vsnl.net.in

STP Ltd
Shantiniketan,
15th Floor, 8 Camac Street,
Kolkata -700017
Phone : (033)2425420,2425414,
2425426,2425428
Fax : (033)-2423747

Super Paints & Oil Industry
C-1/B-12, G.I.D.C. Antalia,
Billimora - 396325 Gujarat
Phone : (02634)-83730
Fax : (02634)-84730

Tanit Coatings
2, Saurabh Society,
Sanjay Park,
Karlibaug,
Vadodara-390018 Gujarat
Phone : (0265)-424737

Tara Paints & Chemicals
C1/91/20, Phase-I,
G.I.D.C.Estate,
Vatva, Ahmedabad-382445
Gujarat
Phone : (079)-
5830512,5832412,6576679

Umesh Chemicals Industries
203/A7, Kalpak Estate,
5 Mishri Road, Wadala East,
Mumbai - 400037
Phone : 4011448,
4012961,4024036
Fax : (022)-4013177

Universal Paints Corp P. Ltd.
39/41, Nagdevi Street,
Opposite Ram Mandir,
Mumbai-400003
Phone : (022)-3422581,3444996
Fax : (022)-3424160

Usha Paint Industries
Rawatpara, Agra 282003,
Uttar Pradesh
Phone : (0562)-365092

Varna Paints & Allied Products
73/38, Doddanna Industrial Estate,

Near to Peenya 2nd Stage,
Hegganahalli Main Road,
Bangalore- 560091
Phone : (080)-8361181,8362266
Fax : (080)-8362266

VCM Polyurethanes P.Ltd.
329/A-2, Shah & Nahar
Industrial Estate,
Lower Parel (West),
Mumbai-400013,
Phone : (022) 4951967,
4952408, 4960174
Fax : (022)-4974284
E-Mail :
kbc@giasbm01.vsnl.net.in.

Velson Paints
25/6, Phase III,
G.I.D.C. Estate,
Naroda,
Ahmedabad-382325 Gujarat
Phone : (079)-2822280,2842168

Vighy Chemical P.Ltd.
Sector A/80, Scheme 4,
Vijay Nagar, A-B Road,
Indore-452010,
Madhya Pradesh,
Phone : (0731)-552837,574182
Fax : (0731)-552966
E-Mail :
chemjyot@bom4.vsnl.net.in

Amit Traders
59/104B, Canal Road,
2nd Floor,
Kanpur - 208001,
Uttar Pradesh
Phone : (0512)-314931,
313840,296462,296827
Fax : (0512)-355865

Krish Industrial Products P.Ltd.
Padamshri, 710,
Anant Patil Marg,
Shivaji Park, Dadar (West)
Mumbai-400028
Phone : (022)- 4452527, 4468367
Fax : (022)-4452527

L.M.P. Chemicals
4706/6,
Opposite Rallis (I) Ltd.
(Pharma Div).
G.I.D.C. Estate,
Ankleshwar -393002
Gujarat
Phone : (02646)-23269

Malwa General Traders
47, Jawahar Marg,
Indore-542007,
Madhya Pradesh,
Phone : (0731)-474472, 475452
Fax : (0731)-47549
E-Mail :
malwagt@hotmail.com.

M.C.Industries
74, Shradhanand Marg,
Delhi-110006
Phone : (011)-3974339
E-Mail :
vispar@nde.vsnl.net.in
www.paintindia.net.

New Calcutta Paint Stores
42, N.S. Road,
Kolkata - 700001
Phone : (033)-2425065

Padmavati Enterprise
402, Sahjanand Trade
Centre,
Opposite Kothawala Flats,
Pritamnagar,
Ahmedabad-380006
Gujarat
Phone : (079)-6576069,
R-6632862

Premier Sales Agencies
20/E-1, St. John's Road,
Opp. Wesley Girl's College,
Secunderabad-500025,
Andhra Pradesh
Phone : (040)-8152275

Regent Traders
G-L-4 Vijay Plaza,
Opposite Ahmedabad
Dairy, Kankaria Road,
Ahmedabad-380022
Gujarat
Phone : (079)-5327561

Satya Chemicals
74, Shradhanand Marg,
Delhi-110006
Phone : (011)-3951019
Fax : (011)-3931246
E-Mail :
vispar2nde.vsnl.net.in.
www.paintindia.net.

Sterling Salts & Chemicals
20, Aravamudhu Garden
Street,
Egmore, Chennai-600008
Phone : (044)-8258713
Fax : (044)-8226352

Vijay Chemicals Agencies
3/84-A, Kattoor Street,
Pappanaickenpalayam,
Coimbatore - 641037
Tamil Nadu
Phone : (0422)-214935
R-866205

Solutia Chemicals India P.Ltd.
205-207, Midas Sahar
Plaza Complex,
Andheri Kurla Road,
Andheri (E),
Mumbai-400059
Phone : (022)-
8302860,8302862,8302864
Fax : (022)-8302859
E-Mail :
tarun.malkani@solutia.com
www.solutia.com.

VARNISHES

Asian Paints (India) Ltd.
Nirmal 5th Floor,
Nariman Point,
P.B.No. 11701,
Mumbai-400021
Phone : (022)-2024544,
Fax : (022)-2028993

Bakelite Hylam Ltd.
7-2-1669, Sannat Nagar,
P.O.Box No. 1908,
Hyderabad-500018
Phone : (040) 3702641,3702642
3702643,3702644-48
Fax : (040)-3702672

Berger Paints India Ltd.
Berger House,
129, Park Street,
Kolkata - 700017
Phone : (033)-299724-28,
2499754
E-Mail :
berger@giasc101.vsnl.net.in

Bombay Paints Ltd.
B.D. Patil Marg.
Gavanpada,
Chembur,
Mumbai-400074

Chemline India Ltd.
F-1, Sarda Chember I,
Central Market,
Prashant Vihar (Rohini),
Delhi-110085
Phone : (011)-7266965,7864419,
7862992, 7864420
Fax : (011)-7266966
E-Mail : chemline@nda.net.in

Era Paints & Adhesives (P) Ltd.
17, Chandi Ghosh Road,
Kolkata - 700040
Phone : (033)-4716702,4715168

Gayatri Products
Arya Printing Press
Compound,
Maharshi Dayanand Marg,
Ahmedabad-382345
Gujarat
Phone : (079)-2816334
Fax : (079)-2821441
E-Mail :
gayatriproducts@hotmail.com

Goodlass Nerolac Paints Ltd.
Nerolac House, Ganpatrao
Kadam Marg,
Lower Parel,
Post Box - 16322,
Mumbai-400013
Phone : (022)-4934001,4934003,
4934007,4934008
Fax : (022)-4936296, 4973704
www.nerolac.com

Haryana Chemicals
3816-A, Gali No. 6,
JKanhaiya Nagar
(TriNagar)
Delhi-110035
Phone : (011)-7192596,
7195205, 7196989
Fax : (011)-7192596,
7195205, 7196989

Hem Paints P.Ltd.
Plot No. 302, G.I.D.C.
Estate, Sonala Road,
Morba -363641, Gujarat
Phone : (02822)- 24734, 24735
Fax : (02822)-30297
E-Mail :
hem@wilnetonline.net.

International Technology Corp
Plot B-31, Near Monginis,
New Link Road,
Andheri West,
Mumbai-400053
Phone : (022)-6324471, 6401332
Fax : (022)-6324471

Jenson & Nicholson (I) Ltd.
225, Acharya Jagdish
Chandra Bose Road,
P.Box. No. 50,
Kolkata - 700020
Phone : (033)-
2476762,2476764,
6475490,2476553
Fax : (033)-2472632

K.K.Systems
25/1, Keshavkripa,
9th Cross, 7th Main Road,
Malleswaram,
Bangalore-560003
Phone : (080)-3348694
Fax : (080)-5281737

Meenu Petro-chems
S-15, Mahaveer Chamber,
103, Nyniappa Naick Street,
Chennai - 600003
Phone : (044)-5350777,
5343125
Fax : (044)-5356241,

Metroark P. Ltd.
Chatterjee International
Centre,
2nd Floor, 33-A, Jawaharlal
Nehru Road,
Kolkata - 700071
Phone : (033)-2495541,
2262725, 2268872,2268876
Fax : (033)-2268859

Plaza Paints (P) Ltd
Plot No. 47, Sector 27A,
Faridabad -121003
Haryana.
Phone : (0129)-277877
Fax : (0129)-270398

Polymer Casing
301 - D, Sahajanand
Shopping Centre,
Shahibaug,
Ahmedabad-380004
Gujarat
Phone : (079)-5624555

Polymers & Transmission
794, Joshi Path,
Karol Bagh,
New Delhi-110005
Phone : (011)-7778711, 7511183
Fax : (011)-7511069

Polyresin & Chemicals
31, Israil Mohalla,
Bhagwan Bhuvan,
Masjid Bunder Road,
Mumbai-400009
Phone (022)-3720435, 3757009
Fax : (022)-3743931
E-mail :
madhukmar@bom3.vsnl.net.in

Punjab Paint Colour & Varnish Works P.Ltd.
123/529, Fazalganj,
Kanpur -208012,
Uttar Pradesh
Phone : (0512)-216157, 216266
Fax : (0512)-218435

Rako Mercantile Traders
E-12, Industrial Estate,
Talkatora,
Lucknow - 226011
Uttar Pradesh
Phone : (0522)-418842, 419768
Fax : (0522)-419768,419735

Rang Krupa Enterprise
3454 G.I.D.C. Estate,
Ankleshwar -393002
Gujarat
Phone : (02646)-24991

Resin & Pigments
P/4 Ronak Deep
Apartments,
197, Anoop Nagar,
Indore - 452008
Madhya Pradesh
Phone :(0731)-558679
Fax : (0731)-558538
E-mail :
resinan@bom4.vsnl.net.in

Rishabh Resins & Chemicals
15 E & F, Sri Venkateswara
Co-Operative,
Industrial Estate,
Jeedimetla,
Hyderabad-500055
Phone : (040)-3096104, 3092686
Fax : (040)-3097040

Schenectady-Beck India Ltd.
Arcadia 10th Floor, 195,
Nariman Point,
Mumbai-400021
Phone : (022)-2833224, 2833255
Fax :(022)-2829776

Sikane
1216/43, Phase IV, G.I.D.C.
Estate, Naroda,
Ahmedabad-382330
Gujarat
Phone : (079)-2810297
Fax :(079)-2822031

Singhal Paints P.Ltd.
1, Aishbagh Road,
Lucknow 226004,
Uttar Pradesh
Phone : (0522)-265061, 265813
Fax : (0522)-265724

Star Paint & Oil Industries
Crescent Chambers,
56, Tamarind Street,
Mumbai-400023
Phone : (022)-2652243,
2652289, 2652904
Fax : (022)-2653201
E-Mail :
heatex@bom4.vsnl.net.in

Sudes Chemicals
27, Weston Street,
R.No. 226,
Kolkata - 700012
Phone : (033)-2361673
Fax : (033)-2361625

Tara Insulating Products P.Ltd
2, Vikrant Maharashtra
Nagar, L.T.Road,
Borivali (West),
Mumbai-400092
Phone : (022)-8014219
Fax : (022)-8084388

LACQUERS

Ahura Paints
G-6, Shalimar Industrial
Estate, Matunga,
Mumbai-400019
Phone : (022)-4090626

Arihant Paints Manufacturing Co.
485-486/C/3 G.I.D.C.
Estate, Makarpura,
Vadodara-390010
Gujarat
Phone : (0265)-656195,
R-646057
Fax : (0265)-428400

Cookson India Ltd
Developed Plot No. 16,
North Phase,
Sidco Industrial Estate,
Ambattur,
Chennai -600098
Phone : (044)-6258627,
6252666, 6252766, 6248162
Fax : (044)-6258627
E-mail:
cooksonm.india@gems.vsnl.net.in

Fusion Chemicals & Products P.Ltd.
8, I.D.A. Cherlapally,
Hyderabad-500051
Phone : (040)-
7121880,7121509,7121130
Fax : (040)-7122206

Hansa Paints & Chemicals
1/21, Asaf Ali Road,
Atma Rane Singh Mansion,
New Delhi-110002
Phone : (011)-3236070,
3235207
Fax :(011)-3231123

Haryana Leather Chemicals Ltd.
B-316-319 Somdatt
Chambers-1,5,
Bhikaji Cama Place,
New Delhi-110006
Phone : (011)-6106673,
6171967, 6163268
Fax : (011) 6182705, 6160593
E-mail :
manikj@del6.vsnl.net.in
Website : ace101.com/
leatherchem/index.htm.

Matchwell Inks (P) Ltd.
C1-B/320,
G.I.D.C. Industrial Estate,
Chemical Zone,

Behind Lions School,
Naroda,
Ahmedabad-382330
Gujarat
Phone : (079)-2822922,
2822622, 5358450

Plaza Paints (P) Ltd
Plot No. 47, Sector 27A,
Faridabad -121003
Haryana.
Phone : (0129)-277877
Fax : (0129)-270398

Quinn India Ltd
Quinn House,
Road No. 2,
Banjara Hills,
Hyderabad-500034
Phone : (040)-
3743155,3746255
Fax : (040)-3747841
E-mail : info@quinnindia.com.
Website : quinnindia.com

Shri Durga Chemicals Corp.
D-63, Veersandra Industrial
Estate,
Hosur Road,
Bangalore -561229
Phone :(080)-2251246

Spraylac Paints Corp
804, Arjun Nagar,
Kotla Mubarakpur,
New Delhi-110003
Phone : (011)-4611594,
4611056

Standard Polymers P.Ltd
70/2, Rasappa Chetty Street,
Park Town,
Chennai -600003,
Phone : (044)-5356888,
5355481, 5350031
Fax : (044)-5350031

Sudes Chemicals
27, Weston Street,
R.No. 226,
Kolkata - 700012
Phone : (033)-2361673
Fax : (033)-2361625

Universal Paints Corp. P. Ltd.
39/41, Nagdevi Street,
Opposite Ram Mandir,
Mumbai-400003
Phone : (022)-3422581,
3444996
Fax : (022)-3424160

Usha Paint Industries
Rawatpara, Agra 282003,
Uttar Pradesh
Phone : (0562)-365092

Venus Ethoxyethers P.Ltd
109-111,
Bicholim Industrial Estate,
Bicholim -403529,
Goa
Phone : (0832) - 362904,
382898,362337
Fax : (0832)-362257
E-mail :
venus.goa@sma.sprintrpg.ems.vsnl.net.in
Website: www.venus-goa.com

Calcutta Colour Co.
34, Armenian Street,
Ground Floor,
Kolkata-700001
Phone : (033)-2300761

Lakshmi Sales Corp
10489, Sadar Thana Road,
Motia Khan,
New Delhi-110055
Phone : (011)-3540205,
3531267,7518570
Fax : (011)-3540205
E-mail :
1sc@ndc.vsnl.net.in

Madras Polymoulds
7, Sri Ganga Apartments,
108, Royapettah High
Road,
Mylapore,
Chennai - 600004
Phone : (044) - 4994019,
4994065, 4993775,
Fax : (044)-4990908
E-mail :
jswam@md2.vsnl.net.in

Samir Corp
B/2, Sulakshana Society,
Sant Ramdas Road,
Mulund (East),
Mumbai-400081
Phone : (022)-5900505,
5902966,5643562
Fax : (022)-5902966

SOLVENTS

A.H.Chemicals
8, Gulmohar Park,
Near Akote Garden,
Vadodara -390020 Gujarat
Phone : (0265)-341654
Fax : (0265)-341654

Allied Chemicals Corp
658, G.I.D.C. Estate,
Road No. 54,
Makarpura,
Vadodara- 390010
Gujarat
Phone : (0265)-642945
Fax : (0265)-332953

Ankini Petrochem Ltd.
18/2, Shri Krishna Centre,
Near Mithakali Six Road,
Navrangpura,
Ahmedabad-380009
Gujarat
Phone : (079)-401706,
466342
Fax : (079)-6426489
E-mail :
ankpetro@ad1.vsnl.net.in

Avani Petrochem Ltd.
101, Silver Oak,
BPC Road, Akota,
Vadodara - 390020, Gujarat
Phone : (0265)-311317-18
Fax : (0265)-335607

Burgoyne Burbidges & Co. (India) P Ltd.
Devakaran Mansion, 79,

Princess Street,
P.B.No. 2019,
Mumbai-400002
Phone : (022)-2095332, 2013893
Fax : (022)-2010348
E-mail :
burgoyne@bom5.vsnl.net.in

Chemicos Universal P. Ltd.
30, Gazawali Roorkee Road,
Muzzaffarnagar 251002,
Uttar Pradesh
Phone : (0131)-409208
Fax : (0131)-441139

Chemox Industrial Corp
33 A, Vatsa House,
Janmabhoomi Marg,
Fort,
Mumbai-400001
Phone : (022)-2870133, 2874119
Fax : (022)-8574487

Dipti Cellulose P.Ltd
G-27, M.I.D.C. Jalgaon 425003,
Maharashtra
Phone : (0257)-210563, 237292
Fax : (0257)-211838

Ganga Rasayanie (P) LTd.
50-B, Harish Mukherjee Road,
Calcutta-700025
Phone : (033)-485884, 482080,483203
Fax : (033)-4731523

General Chemicals Industries
2285/2, Galittunga Baug,
Tilak Bazar,
Delhi-110006
Phone : (011)-2940375, 3967765

Mahavir Chemicals Industries
Plot No. 313/16/3
G.I.D.C.Estate,
Dist. Bharuch,
Ankleshwar -393002
Gujarat
Phone : (02646)-24575

Maruti Chemical Industries
FF/11, Narshidham Complex,
Opp. Sangam Bus Stand,
Harni Road,
Vadodara - 390022
Gujarat
Phone :(0265)-441721, 445313
Fax : (0265)-441721

Nice Chemicals P.Ltd.
50/221-223, Manimala Road,
Edapally Kochi 682024,
Kerala
Phone : (0484)-344755, 345583
Fax : (0484)-340083
E-mail :
micechem@giasmd01.vsnl.net.in

Philips Paints Pvt. Ltd.
27, Prithvi Raj Market,
New Delhi - 110 003
Ph : 4640599
E-Mail :
philipspaints@hotmail.com

Plaza Paints Pvt. Ltd.,
Plot No. 47, Sector 27 A,
Faridabad (Haryana)
Ph : 915277877
Fax : 91-5270398

Rita Corp
21, Chewool Wadi,
1st Floor,
P.O.Box No. 2722,
Dr. M.B. Velkar's Street,
Kalbadevi Road,
Mumbai-400002
Phone : (022)-2056895
R-8894226
Fax : (022)-8899598

S.D. Fine-Chem Ltd.
315-317, T.V. Industrial Estate,
248, Worli Road,
Mumbai-400025
Phone : (022)-4932429, 4932430, 4932431
Fax :(022)-4937232
E-mail :
sdfc1@giasbm01.vsnl.net.in
Website : www.sdfine.com

Sisco Research Laboratories P.Ltd.
2-F, Satam Industrial Estate,
C Wing 2nd Floor,
Dr. Cardinal Gracious Road,
Chakala, Andheri (E)
Mumbai-400099
Phone : (022)-8203882, 8214005
Fax : (022)-8380998
E-mail :
srl@bom.3.vsnl.net.in
Website : www.srlchem.com

Somu Solvents P.Ltd.
25, S.G.N. Layout
Lalbaugh Road,
Bangalore-560027
Phone : (080)-2222054, 2235756, 2241085
Fax : (080)-2235754

Spectrochem P. Ltd.
1129, Navjivan CHS Ltd.
Dr. Bhadkamkar Marg,
Mumbai-400008
Phone : (022)-3073317, 3072583,2016968
Fax : (022)-2059299

Techno Pharmachem
101-A, Deep Enclave,
Pocket D, Ashok Vihar,
Phase-III,
Delhi-110052
Phone : (011)-7112184, 7226915
Fax : (011)-7226915, 7242427
E-mail :
techno.labchem@axcess.net.in

PAINTS

Saboo-Berlac Ltd.
Plot No. 81,Phase-II
Indl. Area, Chandigarh,
Punjab-160002
India
TEL : +91 (0) 172 652559
FAX : +91 (0) 172 652302
E-mail: sbl@glide.net.in

Andhra Paint & Chemical Industries
C-54, APIE
Balanagar
Hyderabad, Andhra Pradesh-500037
India
TEL : +91 (0) 40 3774401

Corrocoat Industries
Plot No. 8A, Rasool Pura
Secunderabad, Andhra Pradesh-500003
India
TEL : +91 (0) 40 7811196
FAX : +91 (0) 40 6311880
E-mail:
corrocoat@hotmail.com

Graflaks Industries
7-1-27/6, 1st Flr.
Ameerpet, Hyderabad,
Andhra Pradesh-500001
India
TEL : +91 (0) 40 3730430
FAX : +91 (0) 40 3743364
E-mail:
graflaks@hd2.vsnl.net.in

Paint India
1-10-292/2/A
Begumpet, Hyderabad,
Andhra Pradesh-500016
India
TEL : +91 (0) 40 7762175
FAX : +91 (0) 40 7760639

Sridhar Paints Company Pvt. Ltd.
A-4, IDA
Nacharam
Hyderabad, Andhra Pradesh-500076
India
TEL : +91 (0) 40 7173743
E-mail:
rudrasridhar_007@rediff.com

Stucco Textures & Paints Systems Pvt. Ltd.
No. 33
APHB Cmplx.
Vidyanagar
Hyderabad,
Andhra Pradesh-500040
India
TEL : +91 (0) 40 7618208
FAX : +91 (0) 40 7017497

Triton Paints
F-3 & 4
IDA, D Block
Autonagar
Visakhapatnam, Andhra Pradesh-530012
India
TEL : +91 (0) 891 517337
FAX : +91 (0) 891 514675

Universal Paints Co.
Plot No. A-32
Nr. A P Foods
Rd. No. 16
Nacharam
Hyderabad, Andhra Pradesh-500076
India
TEL : +91 (0) 40 7170236

Metro Paints & Chemicals
11/2, Indl. Est.
Patliputra
Patna, Bihar-800013
India
TEL : +91 (0) 612 262281

Mikasu Metreat
B-1, Phase-I, Indl. Area
Adityapur
Jamshedpur, Bihar-832109
India
TEL : +91 (0) 657 408281

Acro Paints Ltd.
1/10-B
Asaf Ali Rd.
New Delhi,
NCT of Delhi-110002
India
TEL : +91 (0) 11 3238013
FAX : +91 (0) 11 3230689
E-mail: acro@del2.vsnl.net.in

Aquolac Group of Companies
70, Najafgarh Rd.
New Delhi,
NCT of Delhi-110015
India
TEL : +91 (0) 11 5467534
FAX : +91 (0) 11 4618606
E-mail: aquolac@vsnl.com

Asia Chemicals Ltd.
3, East Park Rd.
Karol Bagh
New Delhi,
NCT of Delhi-110005
India
TEL : +91 (0) 11 7518670
FAX : +91 (0) 11 7528357
E-mail:
achemlted@ndf.vsnl.net.in

Associated Paints & Allied Products
C-10/1, Mansrover Garden
Ring Rd.
New Delhi,
NCT of Delhi-110015
India
TEL : +91 (0) 11 5437102
FAX : +91 (0) 11 5431373

Bindra Brothers Paints & Chemicals Pvt. Ltd.
404, Faiz Rd.
Karol Bagh
New Delhi,
NCT of Delhi-110005
India
TEL : +91 (0) 11 7770672

Bird Paints India Pvt. Ltd.
301 & 302-B, Arjun Dev
Bhawan Comm Cmplx
Ranjit Ngr.
New Delhi,
NCT of Delhi-110008

India
TEL : +91 (0) 11 5740456
FAX : +91 (0) 11 5740456

Boston Paints (I) Pvt. Ltd.
5433, Katra Baryan
Fatehpuri, Delhi,
NCT of Delhi-110006
India
TEL : +91 (0) 11 3952748
FAX : +91 (0) 11 2946237

Delhi Paints Corp.
A-21, Phase-I
Mayapuri Indl. Area
New Delhi, NCT of Delhi-110064
India
TEL : +91 (0) 11 5138084
FAX : +91 (0) 11 5455587
E-mail: jas_jit@hotmail.com

Dove Industries
Block `R'-76/D
Dilshad Garden
Delhi, NCT of Delhi-110095
India
TEL : +91 (0) 11 2272845
FAX : +91 (0) 11 2110258
E-mail:
doveind@sigmaonline.net

Duro Colours
32/114-A
Bhikam Singh Cly.
Vishwas Ngr.
Delhi, NCT of Delhi-110032
India
TEL : +91 (0) 11 2462431

Embassy Chemical Works
A-20/1, Indl. Area,
Phase-I, Mayapuri
New Delhi,
NCT of Delhi-110064
India
TEL : +91 (0) 11 5130065
E-mail:
motherjyoti@mantraonline.com

Glossy Color & Paints Pvt. Ltd.
50-A & B, Shivaji Marg
New Delhi,
NCT of Delhi-110015
India
TEL : +91 (0) 11 5469932
FAX : +91 (0) 11 5451001
E-mail:
glossy@nds.vsnl.net.in

Hansa Paints & Chemicals Pvt. Ltd.
50/2, 50/3,Okhla Indl. Est.
Phase-II
New Delhi,
NCT of Delhi-110002
India
TEL : +91 (0) 11 6911322
FAX : +91 (0) 11 3231123

Hansflon Plasto Chemical Pvt. Ltd.
B 1/45
Safdarjung Enclave
New Delhi,
NCT of Delhi-110029
India
TEL : +91 (0) 11 6885796
FAX : +91 (0) 11 6888473
E-mail:
hansafln@nda.vsnl.net.in

Indolac Paints
14A, Najafgarh Rd.
New Delhi,
NCT of Delhi-110015
India
TEL : +91 (0) 11 5158231
FAX : +91 (0) 11 5158233
E-mail:
mmcreations@vsnl.com

Jaypee Gold Paints Ltd.
J-A Annexe, 54
Basant Lok, 63, Basement
Vasant Vihar
New Delhi,
NCT of Delhi-110057
India
TEL : +91 (0) 11 6141540
FAX : +91 (0) 11 6143591

Kashmir Minerals & Paint Industries
B-16/3, Jhilmil Indl. Area
G T Rd., Shahdara
Delhi, NCT of Delhi-110095
India
TEL : +91 (0) 11 2272746
FAX : +91 (0) 11 2282365
E-mail:
peterpaints@mantraonline.com

Keshoram Roshanlal Ahuja Pvt. Ltd.
E-48/6, Okhla Indl. Area
Phase-II
New Delhi,
NCT of Delhi-110020
India
TEL : +91 (0) 11 6312523
FAX : +91 (0) 11 6815065

Killick Nixon Ltd.
Killick House, 10
Kailash Cly. Extn.
Zamrudpur Comm. Centre
New Delhi,
NCT of Delhi-110048
India
TEL : +91 (0) 11 6213105
FAX : +91 (0) 11 6222401

Metro Paint (I)
260, Kamla Mkt.
Asaf Ali Rd.
New Delhi,
NCT of Delhi-110002
India
TEL : +91 (0) 11 3235206
FAX : +91 (0) 11 3231383

Neelkanth Paints
A/2, Harbhool Singh Bldg.
Clock Tower
Delhi, NCT of Delhi-110007
India
TEL : +91 (0) 11 2942576

Oracle Chemtech Pvt. Ltd.
F-4 (FF), CSC-II, Blk. G
Preet Vihar
Delhi, NCT of Delhi-110092
India
TEL : +91 (0) 11 2412447
FAX : +91 (0) 11 2453928

Oriental Colour & Paint Ind. Pvt. Ltd.

Phase-I, B-91
Mayapuri Indl. Area
New Delhi,
NCT of Delhi-110064
India
TEL : +91 (0) 11 5133346
FAX : +91 (0) 11 5490052
E-mail:
orientalcolours@hotmail.com

Pagan Paints & Chemicals Pvt. Ltd.
101, Chawla Cmplx.,
911/920
D B Gupta Rd.
Karol Bagh
New Delhi,
NCT of Delhi-110005
India
TEL : +91 (0) 11 5739593
FAX : +91 (0) 11 5737198

Paramount Paints Industries
F-7A, Indl. Area, Phase-I
Okhla
New Delhi,
NCT of Delhi-110020
India
TEL : +91 (0) 11 6818331
FAX : +91 (0) 11 6810731
E-mail:
sharat@del2.vsnl.net.in

Pioneer Paints & Chemical Industries
St. No. 9
Samaipur Indl. Area
Delhi, NCT of Delhi-110042
India
TEL : +91 (0) 11 7292303
FAX : +91 (0) 11 2927328

Print Links International Pvt. Ltd.
213-215, 2nd Flr., Aggarwal Chmbr. IV
27, Veer Savarkar Block
Vikas Marg, Shakarpur
Delhi, NCT of Delhi-110092
India
TEL : +91 (0) 11 2205072
FAX : +91 (0) 11 2242484
E-mail:
akashtuli@hotmail.com

Rajdoot Paints Ltd.
Rajdoot Paint House, 19
DDA Comml. Cmplx.
Kailash Cly. Extn.
New Delhi,
NCT of Delhi-110048
India
TEL : +91 (0) 11 6437449
FAX : +91 (0) 11 6447864
E-mail: rpl@gndel-rajdoot.globalnet.ems.vsnl.net.in

Shrayans Coatings Pvt. Ltd.
Village Prahlad Pur
Bangar, Main Bawana Rd.
Delhi, NCT of Delhi-110042
India
TEL : +91 (0) 11 7891418
FAX : +91 (0) 11 7891418

Standard Scientific Instruments Company (Regd.)
C-122, Phase-I
Ashok Vihar
Delhi, NCT of Delhi-110052
India
TEL : +91 (0) 11 7125213

Super Aquacem (I) Pvt. Ltd.
14-A, Najafgarh Rd.
New Delhi,
NCT of Delhi-110015
India
TEL : +91 (0) 11 5414637
FAX : +91 (0) 11 5158233
E-mail:
dimple@del3.vsnl.net.in

TCC Paints Pvt. Ltd.
110 Suneja Tower Ist
Janakpuri
New Delhi,
NCT of Delhi-110058
India
TEL : +91 (0) 11 5618807
FAX : +91 (0) 11 5509185

U K Paint Industries
Rajoot Paint House, 19
DDA Comml. Cmplx.
Kailash Cly. Extn.
New Delhi,
NCT of Delhi-110048
India
TEL : +91 (0) 11 6437449
FAX : +91 (0) 11 6447864

U K Paints (I) Ltd.
19, DDA Comml. Cmplx.
Kailash Cly. Extn.
New Delhi,
NCT of Delhi-110048
India
TEL : +91 (0) 11 6431573
FAX : +91 (0) 11 6447864

Unitile
Unitile House, 3/35
Punjabi Bagh
New Delhi,
NCT of Delhi-110026
India
TEL : +91 (0) 11 5930518
FAX : +91 (0) 11 5435576

Goa Paints & Allied Products
A Dempo Group Company
Dempo House, Campal
Panaji, Goa-403001
India
TEL : +91 (0) 832 226281
FAX : +91 (0) 832 228588

Anjali Coatings Pvt. Ltd.
19, GIDC Est.,Makarpura
Vadodara, Gujarat-390010
India
TEL : +91 (0) 265 642838
FAX : +91 (0) 265 642698
E-mail:
anjali.asian@rmm.sprintrpg.ems.vsnl.net.in

Arihant Paints Manufacturing Co.
Shed No. 485-486/3/C
GIDC Est., Makarpura
Vadodara, Gujarat-390010
India

TEL : +91 (0) 265 656195

Arkey Paints Pvt. Ltd.
Shed No. J/758/1, 40
Shed Area, GIDC Est.
Vapi, Gujarat-396195
India
TEL : +91 (0) 260 24046

Asian Paints Ltd.
Plot No. 2602
GIDC Est.
Ankleshwar,
Gujarat-393002
India
TEL : +91 (0) 2646 20218

Associated Paints & Polymers Industries
825/4, Village Santej
Kalol, Gujarat-382721
India
TEL : +91 (0) 2764 86550
E-mail:
indotexpaints@hotmail.com

Bharat Paper & Resins Allied Products
4772, GIDC Est.
Ankleshwar,
Gujarat-393002
India
TEL : +91 (0) 2646 25741

C M Coatings
Plot No. 729
Village Rakanpur
Kalol, Gujarat-382721
India
TEL : +91 (0) 2764 86633

Champion Industries
1/29, Phase-IV
GIDC
Vithal Udyognagar,
Gujarat-388121
India
TEL : +91 (0) 2692 36330
FAX : +91 (0) 2692 36085
E-mail:
visionos@wilnetonline.net

Dhara Paints Pvt. Ltd.
411, GIDC Est.
Mansa, Mehsana,
Gujarat-382845
India
TEL : +91 (0) 2762 70122

Grand Polycoats Company Pvt. Ltd.
204, Siddharth Cmplx.
R C Dutt Rd., Alkapuri
Vadodara, Gujarat-390007
India
TEL : +91 (0) 265 336174
FAX : +91 (0) 265 337022
E-mail: gp.brd@smm.sril.in

Gunjan Paints Ltd.
81, 8th Flr.
Newyork Tower `A', Nr.
Thaltej Cross Rds
Opp. Jain Temple
Thaltej
Ahmedabad,
Gujarat-380054
India
TEL : +91 (0) 79 7418881
FAX : +91 (0) 79 7442447
E-mail:
gunjang@ad1.vsnl.net.in

Hem Paints Pvt. Ltd.
Survey No. 62-1
Nr. Crown Ceramics
Hasanpur
Wankaner, Gujarat-363622
India
TEL : +91 (0) 28 2820009
FAX : +91 (0) 28 2820008
E-mail:
hem@wilnetonline.net

Hitesh Polyform Industries
76, GVMM
Odhav
Ahmedabad,
Gujarat-380001
India
TEL : +91 (0) 79 2871497

Jayco Paints
22, Comet Est., B/h
Chakudia Mahadev
Rakhial
Ahmedabad,
Gujarat-380023
India
TEL : +91 (0) 79 2741228

Maruti Paints Pvt. Ltd.
16, Embassy Mkt,
Nr. Dinesh Hall
Ashram Rd.
Ahmedabad,
Gujarat-380009
India
TEL : +91 (0) 79 6583304
FAX : +91 (0) 79 6583304

Omkar Industries Manufacturers
3, Anand Indl. Est.
Opp. Yamuna Mill
Vadodara, Gujarat-390004
India
TEL : +91 (0) 265 462052
FAX : +91 (0) 265 470260

Paints & Chemicals Industries
145, GVMSAV
Odhav
Ahmedabad,
Gujarat-380002
India
TEL : +91 (0) 79 2871517

Ranjit Paint Industries
17-A, Udyognagar
Shanker Tekri
Jamnagar, Gujarat-361004
India
TEL : +91 (0) 288 560982

Rosalee Colours Pvt. Ltd.
1st Flr. Mohan Bldg.
Plot No. C1B/160
L N Rd., GIDC Est.
Vaghodia, Gujarat-390007
India
TEL : +91 (0) 26682 66060

Saraswati Lime
Opp. Girnar Scooter
Nr. GVMM, Odhav
Ahmedabad,

Gujarat-382415
India
TEL : +91 (0) 79 2873327
FAX : +91 (0) 79 2874504

Saurashtra Paints Ltd.
Vatva
Ahmedabad,
Gujarat-382440
India
TEL : +91 (0) 79 5832303
FAX : +91 (0) 79 5832781

Skylab Paints Pvt. Ltd.
Plot No. C1B/33
Phase I, GIDC Est.
Vapi, Gujarat-396195
India
TEL : +91 (0) 260 21146

Sunshine Corp.
35/36, 1st Flr.
Cama Comm. Centre
Mirzapur Rd.
Ahmedabad,
Gujarat-380001
India
TEL : +91 (0) 79 5625525
FAX : +91 (0) 79 5620527

Triveni Colour Industries
Umbergaon,
Gujarat-396171
India
TEL : +91 (0) 260 562791

Usha Paints
C/20, Sardar Est.
Ajwa Rd.
Vadodara, Gujarat-390019
India
TEL : +91 (0) 265 561475

Velson Paints
25/6, Phase-III, GIDC
Naroda
Ahmedabad,
Gujarat-382330
India
TEL : +91 (0) 79 2822415

Vipul Paints Pvt. Ltd.
A/3705, Phase IV
GIDC Est.
Vatva, Gujarat-382445
India
TEL : +91 (0) 79 5830254

Chemitech Industries
14/6, Mathura Rd.
Faridabad,
Haryana-121001
India
TEL : +91 (0) 129 5275440
FAX : +91 (0) 129 5271607
E-mail:
tsindwani@mantraonline.com

Deena Paints Ltd.
57, Indl. Est., Mehrauli Rd.
Gurgaon, Haryana-122001
India
TEL : +91 (0) 124 6320252

ICI India Ltd. Paints
Business
5th Flr.
DLF Plaza Tower
DLF Qutub Enclave 1
Gurgaon, Haryana-122002
India
TEL : +91 (0) 124 6358400
FAX : +91 (0) 124 6359849

Maharani Paints (I) Pvt. Ltd.
Plot No. 344, Sect.-24
Faridabad, Haryana-121005
India
TEL : +91 (0) 129 5233659
FAX : +91 (0) 129 5234559

Pine Forest Prodcuts & Investment Ltd.
Indl. Cmplx.
Bari Brahamana
Jammu,
Jammu & Kashmir-181133
India
TEL : +91 (0) 191 20246
FAX : +91 (0) 191 20617

Agsar Paints Pvt. Ltd.
41/A, Agsar Bhavan
Vanivilas Rd.,Basavangudi
Bangalore,
Karnataka-560001
India
TEL : +91 (0) 80 6611139

Apollo Paints Pvt. Ltd.
Plot No. 51
Indl. Area, Phase-III
4th Main Rd., Peenya
Bangalore,
Karnataka-560058
India
TEL : +91 (0) 80 8394211
FAX : +91 (0) 80 8394396

Betala Associates
85, Stage-II, Phase-II,
West of Chord Rd.
Mahalakshmipuram
Bangalore,
Karnataka-560086
India
TEL : +91 (0) 80 3492033
FAX : +91 (0) 80 3497120
E-mail:
betala@bgl.vsnl.net.in

Courtaulds Coatings & Sealants India Pvt. Ltd.
Plot No. 62P, 62B, 43E
Hoskote Indl. Area,
Pilgumpa, Hoskote Taluk
Bangalore,
Karnataka-562114
India
TEL : +91 (0) 80 5591022
FAX : +91 (0) 80 5598418

Innovative Chemicals & Coatings
144
Lakshmi Malleablenyhalli
Bangalore,
Karnataka-560039
India
TEL : +91 (0) 80 3393722

Media Inks
239/6, 2nd Flr.
Bull Temple Rd.
Bangalore,
Karnataka-560018

India
TEL : +91 (0) 80 6614894
FAX : +91 (0) 80 6677793
E-mail: sansetty@vsnl.com

South Field Prints & Chemicals Pvt. Ltd.
C1/C2, 1st Flr.,
Devatha Plaza
Residency Rd.
Bangalore,
Karnataka-560025
India
TEL : +91 (0) 80 2219019
FAX : +91 (0) 80 2219812

Sree Mukha Paints Pvt. Ltd.
57/5, Panteon Rd.
Basavgudi, Bangalore,
Karnataka-560004
India
TEL : +91 (0) 80 6614645

Sterling Varnishes (Bangalore) Pvt. Ltd.
1140, 4th T-Block
35th 'C' Cross,
Jayanagar,
Bangalore,
Karnataka-560041
India
TEL : +91 (0) 80 6636126
FAX : +91 (0) 80 6640526

Surfa Coats (Bangalore) Ltd.
358, 3rd Block
Rajajinagar, Bangalore,
Karnataka-560010
India
TEL : +91 (0) 80 3353109
FAX : +91 (0) 80 3354718
E-mail: surfa@vsnl.com

Aarkay Paint Industries
Goddev Rd.,
Bhayandar (E)
Thane,
Maharashtra-401105
India
TEL : +91 (0) 22 8196410

Advance Paints Pvt. Ltd.
125, Nagindas
Master Rd. Fort
Mumbai,
Maharashtra-400023
India
TEL : +91 (0) 22 3743305

Amardeep Paint Industries
B/34, Parijat
Bandra Reclamation
Mumbai,
Maharashtra-400050
India
TEL : +91 (0) 22 6458203
FAX : +91 (0) 22 6429633

Ancor Industries
3/15, Mena Chmbrs.,
3rd Flr., Swastik Park
Chembur, Mumbai,
Maharashtra-400071
India
TEL : +91 (0) 22 5229679
FAX : +91 (0) 22 5229679

Asian Paints (I) Ltd.
Nirmal, 5th Flr.,
Nariman Point, Mumbai,
Maharashtra-400021
India
TEL : +91 (0) 22 2024544
FAX : +91 (0) 22 2028993

Asian PPG Industries Ltd.
Dani Wooltex Compound, 158
Vidyanagri Marg, Kalina
Santacruz (E)
Mumbai,
Maharashtra-400098
India
TEL : +91 (0) 22 6526387
FAX : +91 (0) 22 6528044
E-mail:
paritosh@asianppg.com

Asmira Paint Manufacturing Pvt. Ltd.
Asmira House, 2
Stanley Compound
Kherani Rd.
Saki Naka
Mumbai,
Maharashtra-400072
India
TEL : +91 (0) 22 8595023
FAX : +91 (0) 22 8521424

Bombay Paints Ltd.
B D Patil Marg,
Gavanpada Chembur
Mumbai,
Maharashtra-400074
India
TEL : +91 (0) 22 5564016
FAX : +91 (0) 22 5564650
E-mail:
info@bombaypaints.com

Cougar Paints Pvt. Ltd.
1 A, 1 B
Indl. Co-op. Est. Ltd.
Nagargaoan, Lonavala
Pune, Maharashtra-410401
India
TEL : +91 (0) 20 72822
FAX : +91 (0) 20 71352
E-mail:
cougarpaints@vsnl.com

Creative Polymers Pvt. Ltd.
56-A, Giriraj Indl. Est.
Mahakali Caves Rd.
Andheri (E)
Mumbai,
Maharashtra-400093
India
TEL : +91 (0) 22 8221783

Deepika Paints
Plot No.30/17
MIDC, D-2 Block
Chinchwad
Pune, Maharashtra-411019
India
TEL : +91 (0) 20 7474349
FAX : +91 (0) 20 7486881

Delite Paints & Chemicals Pvt. Ltd.
Plot No. 124-A, H-Block
MIDC, Pimpri,

Pune, Maharashtra-411018
India
TEL : +91 (0) 20 772266
FAX : +91 (0) 20 773981

Esdee Paints Ltd.
203, Navketan
Chembur, Mumbai,
Maharashtra-400071
India
TEL : +91 (0) 22 5517982
FAX : +91 (0) 22 5561988

Gardwel Industries
691/A2(6)
Bibwewadi Indl. Est.
Pune-Satara Rd.
Pune, Maharashtra-411037
India
TEL : +91 (0) 20 4218649
FAX : +91 (0) 20 4218649

Gaurav Electronics
H-15, MIDC Indl. Area
Satpur, Nasik,
Maharashtra-422007
India
TEL : +91 (0) 253 350000

Goodlass Nerolac Paints Ltd.
Nerolac House
Ganpatrao Kadam Marg
Lower Parel
Mumbai,
Maharashtra-400013
India
TEL : +91 (0) 22 4934001
FAX : +91 (0) 22 4935743

J K Paints
G-1, Khira Indl. Est.
S T Rd., Santacruz (W)
Mumbai,
Maharashtra-400054
India
TEL : +91 (0) 22 6147001
FAX : +91 (0) 22 6183332

Jayant Color & Chemical Industries
Tulsiram Gupta Mills Est.
Darukhana, Reay Rd.
Mumbai,
Maharashtra-400010
India
TEL : +91 (0) 22 3721249
FAX : +91 (0) 22 3775814
E-mail:
admin@jayantcolor.com

Kankoo Paints Pvt. Ltd.
417, R S Kedari Rd.
Pune, Maharashtra-411001
India
TEL : +91 (0) 20 646180
FAX : +91 (0) 20 643836

Khamir Industries
2, Tirupati
Akurli Cross Rd. 1
Kandivli (E)
Mumbai,
Maharashtra-400101
India
TEL : +91 (0) 22 8877151
FAX : +91 (0) 22 8879212

Kishore Polyurethanes Pvt. Ltd.
X-46, MIDC, Ambad
Nasik, Maharashtra-422010
India
TEL : +91 (0) 253 385820
FAX : +91 (0) 253 383898
E-mail: info@kipol.co.in

Modern Paint & Chemicals
Shop 9, Veena Dalwai
S V Rd., Jogeshwari (W)
Mumbai,
Maharashtra-400102
India
TEL : +91 (0) 22 6780891
FAX : +91 (0) 22 6785455
E-mail: cdee99@vsnl.com

Pidilite Industries Ltd.
Rama Krishna Mandir Rd.
Off Marol Vasanji Rd.
Andheri (E)
Mumbai,
Maharashtra-400059
India
TEL : +91 (0) 22 8387240
FAX : +91 (0) 22 8384989

Poona Paints & Varnishes Pvt. Ltd.
10, Matal Chmbrs., 63
Erandavana
Pune, Maharashtra-411004
India
TEL : +91 (0) 20 5443732
FAX : +91 (0) 20 5410009
E-mail:
floratex@pn2.vsnl.com

Prabhat Paint Industries
2, Mayani Est.
Sonawala Cross Rd. No. 2
Goregaon (E)
Mumbai,
Maharashtra-400063
India
TEL : +91 (0) 22 8748623

Priya Exports
B-22
Satyam Shopping Centre
M G Rd., Ghatkopar (E)
Mumbai,
Maharashtra-400077
India
TEL : +91 (0) 22 5147711
FAX : +91 (0) 22 5164911
E-mail:
priyaexp@bom3.vsnl.net.in

Rainbow Paints
37/38, Govindraoiji Marathe Indl. Est.
Opp. S G Cancer Hospital
Miraj-Sangli Rd.
Miraj, Maharashtra-416410
India
TEL : +91 (0) 23382 211221
FAX : +91 (0) 23382 211270

Resinkoat & Allied Chemicals
B-4, P-10, Above I.O. Bank
HFS Rd., Jogeshwari (E)
Mumbai,
Maharashtra-400060
India
TEL : +91 (0) 22 8329536

FAX : +91 (0) 22 8329536
E-mail: tejas_t@yahoo.com

Sailor Paints
214/4, Rakhangi Mahal
Worli Naka, Mumbai,
Maharashtra-400025
India
TEL : +91 (0) 22 4934412

Sankalp Food Products
3/15, Mena Chmbrs.,
3rd Flr., Swastik Park
Chembur, Mumbai,
Maharashtra-400071
India
TEL : +91 (0) 22 5229679
FAX : +91 (0) 22 5229679

Sansui Paints
J-108, Ansal Indl. Est.
Saki Vihar Rd.
Mumbai,
Maharashtra-400072
India
TEL : +91 (0) 22 8520329
FAX : +91 (0) 22 8590612
E-mail:
sansuipn@bom7.vsnl.net.in

Shree Inks & Coatings Pvt. Ltd.
B-106, Ansa Indl. Est.
Saki Naka, Andheri (E)
Mumbai,
Maharashtra-400072
India
TEL : +91 (0) 22 8523094

Snowchem India
Killick House, Killick Est.
Baji Pasalkar Marg
Chandivli, Mumbai,
Maharashtra-400072
India
TEL : +91 (0) 22 5781482
FAX : +91 (0) 22 5785076

Special Paints Ltd. Formerly Sigma Paints Ltd.
Mogra, Old Nagardas Rd.
Andheri (E), Mumbai,
Maharashtra-400069
India
TEL : +91 (0) 22 8345581

Varunsak Plastic Paints & Chemicals Pvt. Ltd.
11-16, 1st Flr.,
Arannyeshwar Corner
Supreme Indl. Est.
Pune-Satara Rd.
Pune, Maharashtra-411009
India
TEL : +91 (0) 20 4222570
FAX : +91 (0) 20 4225156

Vega Paints Pvt. Ltd.
134, Baner Rd.
Aundh, Pune,
Maharashtra-411007
India
TEL : +91 (0) 20 380573
E-mail: sakirloskar@v-mi.co.in

Saboo-Berlac Ltd.
Plot No. 81, Phase-II
Indl. Area
Chandigarh, Punjab-160002
India
TEL : +91 (0) 172 652559
FAX : +91 (0) 172 652302
E-mail: sbl@glide.net.in

Alliance Paints Pvt. Ltd.
St. No. 12, Suraj Ngr.
Simla Puri, Ludhiana,
Punjab-141003
India
TEL : +91 (0) 161 490989
FAX : +91 (0) 161 456467
E-mail:
alliance@satyam.net.in

Greenlite Pvt. Ltd.
175, Indl. Area, Phase-II
Ramdarbar
Chandigarh, Punjab-160002
India
TEL : +91 (0) 172 652112
FAX : +91 (0) 172 652319

H B Enterprises Pvt. Ltd.
41, Feroze Gandhi Mkt.
Ludhiana, Punjab-141001
India
TEL : +91 (0) 161 401033
FAX : +91 (0) 161 400172

Mahalaxmi Paints
C-40, Indl. Area Phase III
SAS Ngr., Mohali,
Punjab-160057
India
TEL : +91 (0) 172 671057

Radial Paints & Inks Pvt. Ltd.
SCO 51-52
Guru Nanak Engg.
College Mkt., Gill Rd.
Ludhiana, Punjab-141006
India
TEL : +91 (0) 161 491383
FAX : +91 (0) 161 408342

Ram Swarup Dev Raj
Chowk Dholewal
Millar Ganj
Ludhiana,
Punjab-141003
India
TEL : +91 (0) 161 530549
FAX : +91 (0) 161 537513

Sargodha Paints & Chemicals
Shop No. 51-52
GNEC Mkt.
Gill Rd.
Ludhiana, Punjab-141006
India
TEL : +91 (0) 161 491383
FAX : +91 (0) 161 400342
E-mail:
sargodhapaints@hotmail.com

Shivalik Prismo India Ltd.
2nd Flr., SCO 423-424
Sect. 35C
Chandigarh, Punjab-160036
India
TEL : +91 (0) 172 609113

FAX : +91 (0) 172 609112
E-mail: spil@glide.net.in

Sonacem Paints Ltd.
768, Indl. Area, Phase-II
Ramdarbar
Chandigarh, Punjab-160002
India
TEL : +91 (0) 172 652587
FAX : +91 (0) 172 641110

Techno India Paints Pvt. Ltd.
SCO 122-123, Cabin-12
Sect. 8C
Chandigarh, Punjab-160055
India
TEL : +91 (0) 172 402623

Vishal Paints India
7909-B
St. No. 1
Ranjit Ngr.
Ludhiana, Punjab-141003
India
TEL : +91 (0) 161 493070

Mahalaxmi Paints
29, Small Indl. Area
Kota, Rajasthan-321007
India
TEL : +91 (0) 744 361997
FAX : +91 (0) 744 360057
E-mail:
agroengineers@yahoo.com

MRF Ltd.
Speciality Coatings Divn.
Tarapore Towers, 5th Flr.,
826, Anna Salai
Chennai,
Tamil Nadu-600002
India
TEL : +91 (0) 44 8521033
FAX : +91 (0) 44 8520912
E-mail: ho@mrfpaint.co.in

Narrchem Engineers Pvt. Ltd.
Plot No. 344, Nehru Ngr.
4th Link St.
(Off) Old Mahabalipuram Rd.
Chennai,
Tamil Nadu-600096
India
TEL : +91 (0) 44 4925967

Addisons Paints & Chemicals Ltd.
Huzur Gardens
Sembiam, Chennai,
Tamil Nadu-600011
India
TEL : +91 (0) 44 5375887
FAX : +91 (0) 44 5376240
E-mail:
adcolac@md3.vsnl.net.in

Berger Chemicals Pvt. Ltd.
3, Somasundaram St.
T Ngr., Chennai,
Tamil Nadu-600017
India
TEL : +91 (0) 44 8281442
FAX : +91 (0) 44 8256971

Bergo Paints
G-4, Ambattur Indl. Est.
Chennai, Tamil Nadu-600058
India
TEL : +91 (0) 44 6250347
FAX : +91 (0) 44 6250347
E-mail:
berluxe@kmronline.com

Brito Paints
SP-37, 3rd Main Rd.
Ambattur Indl. Est.
Chennai,
Tamil Nadu-600058
India
TEL : +91 (0) 44 6357371

Chemi Organics
10, Badriah Garden St.
Chennai,
Tamil Nadu-600003
India
TEL : +91 (0) 44 5358535
FAX : +91 (0) 44 5359535

Concord Coatings Pvt. Ltd.
52, Sidco Indl. Est.
Thirumazhisai
Chennai, Tamil Nadu-602107
India
TEL : +91 (0) 44 6272531

Continental Coatings Pvt. Ltd.
65, GNT Rd.,
Kanakan Chatram
Ponniamman Medu
Chennai, Tamil Nadu-600110
India
TEL : +91 (0) 44 5375165
FAX : +91 (0) 44 5378421

Corosynth Services Pvt. Ltd.
Flat No. 104, 1st Flr.
Kaveri Cmplx., 96-104
Nungambakkam High Rd.
Nungambakkam
Chennai, Tamil Nadu-600034
India
TEL : +91 (0) 44 8251364
FAX : +91 (0) 44 8252092
E-mail: inarayan@vsnl.com

India Tex Formerly Brilliant Textures Pvt. Ltd.
50/1
Millers Rd.
Kilpauk
Chennai, Tamil Nadu-600010
India
TEL : +91 (0) 44 6422950

Janatha Paint Industries
143, SIDCO Indl. Est.
Ambattur, Chennai,
Tamil Nadu-600098
India
TEL : +91 (0) 44 6251770

Madras Printing Inks
146, Nehru ngr.
Old Mahabalipuram Rd.
Thiruvanmiyur
Chennai,
Tamil Nadu-600041
India
TEL : +91 (0) 44 4482578

Rachana Industries
7, Hunters Rd.
Choolai, Chennai,
Tamil Nadu-600112
India
TEL : +91 (0) 44 5322026
FAX : +91 (0) 44 5324439

Raga Paints & Chemicals
226/6-B
Veeranam Canal St.
Kandanchavadi
Chennai, Tamil Nadu-600096
India
TEL : +91 (0) 44 4961404
FAX : +91 (0) 44 4963206
E-mail:
ragapnt@satyam.net.in

Ravi Paints & Chemicals Ltd.
81, Seshachala Gramani St.
Chennai, Tamil Nadu-600019
India
TEL : +91 (0) 44 5960262
FAX : +91 (0) 44 5962151
E-mail: coating1@vsnl.com

Shenolac Paints Pvt. Ltd.
35-36, 1st Flr.
Anna Ngr. Plaza, C-47
2nd Avenue, Anna Nagar
Chennai,
Tamil Nadu-600040
India
TEL : +91 (0) 44 6284667
FAX : +91 (0) 44 6287494
E-mail: shenolac@vsnl.com

Southern Cements & Engineers Pvt. Ltd.
38, SIDCO Indl. Est.
Ambattur, Chennai,
Tamil Nadu-600098
India
TEL : +91 (0) 44 6252833

Sri Murugan Paint Co.
A-39, Karthikeyom Salai
Periyar Ngr.
Chennai,
Tamil Nadu-600082
India
TEL : +91 (0) 44 5376055
FAX : +91 (0) 44 5370739

Srinath Paints & Chemicals Pvt. Ltd.
7A, New Avadi Rd.
Villivakkam, Chennai,
Tamil Nadu-600049
India
TEL : +91 (0) 44 6286342

Suria Paints & Oil Works
110, Rasappa Chetty St.
Chennai,
Tamil Nadu-600003
India
TEL : +91 (0) 44 5357985

Swaraj Paint Industries
454-A, 1st St.
Gandhipuram
Coimbatore,
Tamil Nadu-641012
India
TEL : +91 (0) 422 491342

Western India Paints & Colour Company Pvt. Ltd.
10/2, Nathamuni St.
T Ngr., Chennai,
Tamil Nadu-600017
India
TEL : +91 (0) 44 8283999
FAX : +91 (0) 44 8240631

Wilson Chemicals
2, Raanathan St., Kilpauk
Chennai, Tamil Nadu-600058
India
TEL : +91 (0) 44 6252111
FAX : +91 (0) 44 6444515

Acee Paints
27, Anand Indl. Est.
Mohan Ngr.
Ghaziabad,
Uttar Pradesh-201007
India
TEL : +91 (0) 120 4737142

Allied Paints
A-2, Govt. Indl. Est.
Talkatora, Lucknow,
Uttar Pradesh-226011
India
TEL : +91 (0) 522 259890
FAX : +91 (0) 522 412417

Balsons Paints Industries
C-226
BSR Indl. Area, Site-1
National Highway 24
Main By-Pass Rd.
Ghaziabad,
Uttar Pradesh-201001
India
TEL : +91 (0) 120 4714257
FAX : +91 (0) 120 4714257

Bharat Petro Chem
C-9, Udyog Puram
Partapur, Meerut,
Uttar Pradesh-250103
India
TEL : +91 (0) 121 515467
FAX : +91 (0) 121 515467

Fine Paints Pvt. Ltd.
S-2, South Side
G T Rd., Ghaziabad,
Uttar Pradesh-201001
India
TEL : +91 (0) 120 742836

Glidden Paints & Chemicals Pvt. Ltd.
F-110, Shastri Ngr.
Meerut,
Uttar Pradesh-250002
India
TEL : +91 (0) 121 761207
E-mail:
bhakti77@hotmail.com

Jainco Paint
C-10, Site-A, Indl. Area
Sikandara
Agra, Uttar Pradesh-282007
India
TEL : +91 (0) 562 350483

JMD Paint Industries
Hindon Vihar, St. No. 2
Delhi-Meerut Rd.
Ghaziabad,
Uttar Pradesh-201003
India

TEL : +91 (0) 120 4747781

Konark Paints Pvt. Ltd.
S-2, Site No. 1, Indl. Area
Bulandshahr Rd.
Ghaziabad,
Uttar Pradesh-201009
India
TEL : +91 (0) 120 4701576
FAX : +91 (0) 120 4700981

Konark Udyog
B-20, Partapur Indl. Area
Meerut,
Uttar Pradesh-250103
India
TEL : +91 (0) 121 514083

Manglam Paints
177, Seva Ngr.,
Hindon Vihar, Meerut Rd.
Ghaziabad,
Uttar Pradesh-201002
India
TEL : +91 (0) 120 4732781

National Paint Industries
D-2
Punjab Expeller Compound
Meerut Rd.
Ghaziabad,
Uttar Pradesh-201001
India
TEL : +91 (0) 120 4790639

Opal Paints Products Pvt. Ltd.
A-48, Sect. 10
Noida,
Uttar Pradesh-201301
India
TEL : +91 (0) 120 4523006
FAX : +91 (0) 120 4555369

Philips Paints Pvt. Ltd.
C-52, Sec. 57
Noida,
Uttar Pradesh-201301
India
TEL : +91 (0) 120 4581322

Ply & Wood
85, Latouche Rd.
Lucknow,
Uttar Pradesh-226018
India
TEL : +91 (0) 522 211682
FAX : +91 (0) 522 213164
E-mail:
ravi2310@hotmail.com

Prem Shanti Paints Pvt. Ltd.
D-115, Site-I, Indl. Area
Bulandshahr Rd.
Ghaziabad, Uttar Pradesh-201001
India
TEL : +91 (0) 120 4701747

Rajeev Paints & Chemicals
P-136, BHIG Flat
Sanjay Ngr.
Ghaziabad,
Uttar Pradesh-201001
India
TEL : +91 (0) 120 4716684

S G Paints
E-6, 7, Udyog Puram
Partapur Meerut,
Uttar Pradesh-250103
India
TEL : +91 (0) 121 531948

Sarvottam Paints & Chemicals
Krishna Ngr.
Meerut Rd.
Ghaziabad,
Uttar Pradesh-201001
India
TEL : +91 (0) 120 4780007

Shivalik Paints Pvt. Ltd.
A-2, Kailashjyoti
Krishnalok
Lucknow,
Uttar Pradesh-226008
India
TEL : +91 (0) 522 242653

Shree Balaji Industries
Sewa Vihar, Hindon Vihar
Ghaziabad,
Uttar Pradesh-201002
India
TEL : +91 (0) 120 4790115

Sundeep Paint & Chemical Industries
431, Sewa Ngr.
Meerut Rd., Ghaziabad,
Uttar Pradesh-201003
India
TEL : +91 (0) 120 4734035

Superlac Paints Pvt. Ltd.
D-100, Indl. Area
Bulandshahr Rd.
Ghaziabad,
Uttar Pradesh-201009
India
TEL : +91 (0) 120 4700135

Su.ana Paints & Chemical
85, Indl. Est.
Nunhai, Agra, Uttar Pradesh-282006
India
TEL : +91 (0) 562 344916

Universal Chemical Industries
B-31, Indl. Est.
Partapur, Meerut,
Uttar Pradesh-250103
India
TEL : +91 (0) 121 510168

Utkal Paint Industries
4, Pandav Ngr. Indl. Area
Bulandshahr Rd.
Ghaziabad,
Uttar Pradesh-201009
India
TEL : +91 (0) 120 4703558

Weldon Paint & Chemical Pvt. Ltd.
Handloom Cmplx., Indl. Area
Bulandshahr Rd.
Ghaziabad,
Uttar Pradesh-201001
India
TEL : +91 (0) 120 4701936

Anupam Enterprises
208, 1st Flr., M G Rd.
Kolkata,
West Bengal-700007
India
TEL : +91 (0) 33 2381587
FAX : +91 (0) 33 2389823

Berger Paints India Ltd.
Berger House,
129, Park St., Kolkata,
West Bengal-700017
India
TEL : +91 (0) 33 2299724
FAX : +91 (0) 33 2499009
E-mail:
berger@giascl01.vsnl.net.in

Hardsol Paints
91R, B L Saha Rd.
Kolkata,
West Bengal-700041
India
TEL : +91 (0) 33 4687086
FAX : +91 (0) 33 4778195

Harekrishna Paints
P O Box 176, 93
Beliaghata Main Rd.
Kolkata,
West Bengal-700010
India
TEL : +91 (0) 33 3530885
E-mail:
hkpaints@sataym.net.in

Kothari Paint Industries
92, Jamuna Lal Bazaz St.
Kolkata,
West Bengal-700007
India
TEL : +91 (0) 33 2301034

Piyanshu Chemicals Pvt. Ltd.
40, Room.No.1, 3rd Flr.
Strand Rd.
Kolkata,
West Bengal-700001
India
TEL : +91 (0) 33 2431584
FAX : +91 (0) 33 4645670
E-mail:
ishaan@cal.vsnl.net.in

Shalimar Paints Ltd.
13, Camac St.
Kolkata,
West Bengal-700017
India
TEL : +91 (0) 33 2472341
FAX : +91 (0) 33 2404191
E-mail:
shalimar@cal2.vsnl.net.in

Shiva Paint & Ink Works
32, Foreshore Rd.
Botanical Garden
Howrah,
West Bengal-711103
India
TEL : +91 (0) 33 6682584

United Paint Industries
8/1, Gurudas Dutta
Garden Lane
Kolkata,
West Bengal-700067
India
TEL : +91 (0) 33 3565217
FAX : +91 (0) 33 2433904

Chapter - 32

SUPPLIERS OF PLANT & MACHINERY

STORAGE/MIXING TANKS

Adam Fabriwerk (P) Ltd.
203, Rajguru Apts.
New Nagardas Road,
Andheri (E),
Mumbai-400069
Phones : 8380548,8384173,
Telefax : 022-8390195,
E-Mail: adamfab@vsnl.com

Alankar Industries
Post Box : 27371,
Andheri (West)
Mumbai-400058

Anup Engineering Limited
Behind 66 Kv Electric
Sub -Station, Odhav Road,
Ahmedabad-382415
(Gujarat)
Phones: 2870622,2872823,
Gram. ANUPAM.
Telex : 121-6327
ANUP IN.
Fax : 079-2870642

Atomplant Industries
52, Angol Road,
Tilakwadi,
Belgaum-590006
(Karnataka)
Phone : 22024, 22910
Gram. ATOMPLANT

Bhuvaneswari & Co.,
13,Old Trunk Road,
Pallavaram,
Chennai-600043

Burman Plant & Machinery Co (P) Ltd.
36, Sarkar Lane.
Kolkata-700007
Phone : 2411340,
Fax : (91)(33) 296077

Chemitex Engineering Enterprises
Plot 277-278, GIDC
Odhav-382415 (Gujarat)
Phone : 2871180,2871280

Cosywo Engg. Co.
15, Laxmi Co-op,Industrial
Estate Ltd.
Amraiwadi Road, Near
Nagarvel Hanuman Mandir,
Ahmedabad-380026
Telefax :
2748168,2748001,
E-Mail: cosywo@usa.net,
Website:
www.indianic.com/cosywo

Eureka Engineering
E-13,14, Industrial Area,
Site No. 1, Bulandshahar
Road,
Ghaziabad -201001 (U.P)
Phone :
722712,711916,713905
Gram. EUREKA
Fax : 0575-712136

Filiopack Industries
Unit No.2,
Vijay Industrial Estate
I.B.Patel Road.
Goregaon (E)
Mumbai-400063
Phones : 6122399

Gopinath Engg.Co.
9/C, Archana Industrial
Estate,
No.2 Beside Anil
Synthetic,
Behind Rakhial P.O.
Rakhial,
Ahmedabad-380023
Phones : 362711,367080,
Gram. EMBEETRUCK
Telex : 121-7002
EMBE IN .

Hospital Supply Company
111, Chittranjan Avenue,
Kolkata-700012

Iadlab Equipment Corporation.
403, 4th Floor,
Binu Aptt, Section 25,
Behind Venus,
Ulhasnagar-421004.
Phones : 0251-534246
Fax : 0251-530254

BALL MILL

Kumar Sales Corporation,
10, Santok House, Dady
Santok Lane,
2nd Floor, Dhobi Talco,
Mumbai-400002

Phone : 2062776,2084749
Fax : 022-8873345

L & M Automatics,
60/7, Old Dal Mandi,
Kanpur-400098
Phone : 6122928,6127440
Gram. LANAFLOR.

Rank & Co.
A-95/3, Wazirpur Industrial Estate,
Delhi-110052
Phone : 7456101-2-3-4,7441958,
Garm. MIXKING
Fax : 7234126,7471905

Saran Brothers,
87/362, Jarib Ki Chowki,
G.T.Road, Kanpur-208003 (U.P)
Phone : 246790,220180

S.S. Engineering
Plot. No.C-2/8,
Mayapuri Industrial Area,
Phase II ,
New Delhi-110064.

REACTION VESSELS

Burman Plant Machinery Co. (P) Ltd.
36, Sarkar Lane,
Kolkata-700007
Phone : 2411340,
Fax : (91)(33) 296077

Dalal Engineering Pvt. Ltd.
Post Box No. 63,
Thane-400061 (Maharashtra)
Phone : 022-5343577,5343528,
Fax: 022-5345570
E-Mail: dalalfac@vsnl.com.

Machino Medicinia Pvt. Ltd.
WZ-12, Phool Bagh,
Rampur More,
Delhi-110035
Phone : 91-11 5447399,5430672
Gram. ASIAN SALES
Fax : 91-11-5156151

Neomachine Mfg.Co. Pvt. Ltd.
39/2A, Purna Das Road,
Kolkata-700029
Phones : 4644568,4640457,4647253
Gram. TECHPHARMA
Fax : 91-33-4643473,4647254

Rank & Co.
A-95/3, Wazipur Industrial Estate,
Delhi-110052
Phone : 7456101-2-3-4,7441958
Gram. MIXKING
Fax :7234126,7471905

Sainath Boilers & Pneumatics,
18-A, Minerva Industrial Estate,
Mulund (West)
Mumbai-400080
Phones : 5613239

Sehgal Industrial Works
T-1698, Malka Ganj Road,
Subzi Mandi, Delhi-110007
Phone : 3953823,3970381,
Fax : 011-3970381

Textiles Art Machinery
Unit No. 145, Adarsh Industrial Estate,
Sahar Road, Chakala,
Andheri (E),
Mumbai-400093
Phone : 8322721,8325957
Gram. TAMHYDRO
Telex. 011-71933 TAM IN.

BOILERS

Chem Engineering Co.
Plot 517, Sector 25, Nigdi,
Pune 411044.
Phone :(020)-784792, 782605
Fax : (020)-782605,789822

Chemtex Engineering Enterprises,
Plot No. 277-278.,
Opp. Shed No- L-1, G.I.D.C. Industrial Estate,
Odhav,
Ahmedabad-382415,
Gujarat.
Phone : (079)-2871180,2871280,
Email : chemtex@vsnl.net.in

Fluidtech Boilers P.Ltd.
2703, Phase-IV, G.I.D.C. Vatva,
Ahmedabad-382445
Gujarat
Phone - (079)-5830105, 5830106
Fax : (079)-5830041.
Email : fluidltd@vsnl.com
Website : http://www.infoquestindia.com/fluidtech.

Double Ace Engineers
1/3, Siddharth Nagar-3,
Next to Siddhi Vinayak Temple,
S.V.Road, Goregaon (West),
Mumbai-104.
Tel : 91-22-8728436, 8771948
Fac : 91-22-8740466
Website : www.doubleaceboiler.com
Email : dblace@bom5.vsnl.net.in

Maxima Boilers Pvt. Ltd.
G-14, Meghal Service Industrial Estate
Devidayal Road,
Mulund (W),
Mumbai - 400080
Tel : 5646815,5612759

Fax : 5670030
Email :
maxima@bom8.vsnl.net.in

Indcon Boilers Ltd.
D-170, Okhla Indl.Area,
Phase-1,
New Delhi - 110020
Ph.
6811440,6811441,6811442
Fax : 011-6812425
Email :
pnmpsa@del2.vsnl.net.in

Lal Sons Boilers
A-45, Maya Puri Indl. Area,
Phase-1
New Delhi-110064
Phone : 5138121-5143223
Fax : 5147483

POWDER FILLING MACHINE

Amba Engineers
6, Laxmi Industrial Estate,
Navnit Prakashan Compound,
Ajod Dairy Road, Rakhial,
Ahmedabad-380023
Phone : (079) 2743948,
Gram. AMBAFILL
Fax : (079) 2743948

EEE CEE & Co.
1, Anant Estate,
Opp. Comet Estate,
Rakhial,
Ahmedabad-380023
(Gujarat)
Phone : 079-2743075
Fax : 079-2743075

Machino Medicinia Pvt. Ltd.
WZ-12, Phool Bagh,
Rampur More,
Delhi-110035
Phone: 91-11-5447399,5430672
Gram. ASIAN SALE
Fax: 91-11-5156151

N.K.Engineering Co.
Plot No. 1808
Phase-III, GIDC,
Vatva,
Ahmedabad-382445
Telefax. 91-79-5891746

Supar Seals Company
WZ-12, Phool Bagh,
Rampura More,
Delhi-110035
Phones : 91-11-5447399,
5430672,
Gram. ASIAN SALE
Fax: 91-11-5156151

Virajka Machinery Mfg. Co.
5, Shrine Industrial Estate,
Rakhial,
Ahmedabad-380023

WEIGHING BALANCES

Anamed Instrument Pvt. Ltd.
7 Sita Estate, First Floor,
133/136, Mahul Road,
Chembur,
Mumbai - 400074
Phones :
5516908,5555137,
Fax:022-5563356.

Bombay Burmah Trading Corpn. Ltd.
334, A-Z, Industrial Estate,
G. Kadam Marg.
Lower Parel,
Mumbai - 400013.
Phones : 4938218/19.
Fax :4951384.

Instrument & Equipment
35, Chittaranjan Avenue,
Kolkata - 700012.

Labman Industries
24/1 B, Manmath Nath
Ganguly Road,
Kolkata - 700002.

Modern Scientific Instruments Co.
48/A, 48/B, Sadashiv Cross
Lane,
Shri Girdhari Bhavan,
Kandewadi,
Mumbai - 400004.

Zenith Surgical Co.
Central Building No.1
1st Floor,
Bomaji Master Road,
(New Silk Bazar),
Opp. Kalbadevi Post Office.
Mumbai - 400002.
Phones : 259526/310157

EXPERIMENTAL TESTING EQUIPMENTS

Armstrong Smith Ltd.
Brady House, 12/14,
Veer Nariman Road,
Mumbai - 400023

Instruments & Chemical Pvt. Ltd.
Modal Town.
Ambala City - 134
(Haryana)
Phones : 56079,56690,
Gram. INCO

Jayron Electronics
7, Mihir Park Society,
Near Dollars Avenue,
Old Padra Road,
Baroda - 390020 (Gujarat)
Phones : 342487,
Fax : 340850

LABELLING AND GUMMING MACHINE

Adrian Engineering Works
11-A, Nirmala Colony,
St. John Baptist Road,
Bandra, Mumbai - 400050
Phones : 6824783

Beekay Pharma Mach Industries
Plot No. 11, Bldg. No. A-41,

Sector No.3 Shantinagar,
Mira Road - 401107
(W.Rly) Dist. Thane
(Maharastra).
Phones : (Off) 022-8105686, 8116416
(Fact) 022-8521608
Fax : (91-22) 8113673

Chemtronick Enterprises
16-11-20/4/1/2, Saleem Nagar Colony,
St. Domnic's School Lane,
New Malakpet,
Hyderabad-500036
Phones : 548461.

Hemson Private Limited
60, Mistry Ind, Complex,
M.I.D.C. Cross Road, A
Andheri (E), P.B.No. 9409,
Mumbai - 400093
Phones :
8321820,8325841,8326148
Gram. HEMSEAL

Indo-German Pharma Pvt. Ltd.
Kothari House,
Plot No. A-13,
Off. Cross Road B,
Street No.5
MIDC, Andheri (E),
Mumbai - 400093
Phones : 8342338,8323615, 8372500,8387411,8219251
Fax : 91-22-8374426
E-Mail :indogmbh@bom3.vsnl.net.in.

Kailas Machine Tools
12, Harshad Estate,
(Margha Farm),
Mamtanagar,
Near Viratnagar Char Rasta,
Rakhial (Bapunagar),
Ahmedabad-380024.
Phones : 2744697,
Fax : (079) 2744394

KNK Engineering Works
A/135, Ghatakopar
Industrial Estate,
L.B.Shastri Marg,
Ghatkopar,
Mumbai - 400086

Mahdav Machinery
B-22, Rajbaug Society,
Canal Road, Ghodasar,
Ahmedabad-380008
(Gujarat)
Phone: 079-2772431

LABORATORY EQUIPMENTS

Astronix Enterprises
199-A, Sake,
Meerut,
(U.P)

D.R. Surgicals
A-56, Gandhi Nagar,
Moradabad
(U.P)

Electronic Instrumentation
12, Mahesh Nagar,
Ambala Cantt. 133001
(Haryana)
Phone : 171-643087, 641797,643057
Telex: 392-214 MIT IN.
Fax. 91-171-6425595

Gordhandas Desai Pvt. Ltd.
Court Chambers,
35 Sir V. Thackersey Marg,
Mumbai - 400020
Phone: (022)-2004208,2001418,
Telex: 011-83065,
Fax. (91-22) 2000581.

Indequip Scientific Enterprises
10/12, Jamboolwadi,
Kalbadevi Road,
Mumbai - 400002

Instruments & Chemical Pvt. Ltd.
Model Town,
Ambala City-134003
(Haryana)
Phone : 56079,56690
Gram. INCO

Lawrence & Mayo
Instruments Division,
274, D.N.Road,
Mumbai - 400001

Santosh Medical & Surgical Centre
Opp. B.L.D.E. Hospital,
Bijapur-586101
(Karnataka)

MIXERS/BLENDERS

Accumax Engineering
C-5A/184, Janakpuri,
New Delhi-110058,
Telefax. 5501092

Alliance Engineering Co.
Trisandhya Building,
97, D. Phalke Road,
Dadar CR,
Mumbai-400014,
Phones : 4112461,4156510
Gram. QUICKMIX.
Fax: (022) 4138307,4137648,

Amit Trading Co.
21, Chewool Wadi,
Dr. M.B.Velkar Street
(Kolbhat Lane),
Kalbadevi Road,
Post Box No. 2691,
Mumbai-400002
Phone : 2056895

Bectochem Engineers,
B-202, Rising Sun
Apartment,

Juhu Tara Road,
Opp.Palmgrove
Hotal, Santa Cruz.
Mumbai-400009
Phones :
8500300,8500057,8502400
Gram. BECENG
Fax: 022-8506785

Burman Plant & Machinery Co.(P) Ltd.
36, Sarkar Lane,
Kolkata-700007
Phone : 2411340
Fax : (91) (33) 296077

Dalal Engineering Pvt. Ltd.
Post Box. No. 63,
Thane-400601
(Maharashtra)
Phones : 022-5343577,5343528
Fax. 022-5345570,
E-Mail: dalalfac@vsnl.com.

Flora Engineering Corporation,
28-A, Phool Bag.
Rampura (Near Railway Crossing)
Delhi-110035

Gem Pharma Machineries,
Plot No. A/82, Road No.16,
Towards Kisan Nagar,
Wagle Estate,
Thane-400604
(Maharashtra)
Phones : 022-5820257,5814158
Telex : 91-022-5826387
E-Mail :
Gemmumbai@hotmail.com.

OVER-PRINTING MACHINE

Amar Engineering Works
B-6, Gupta Palace,
A-2/42, Opp. M.C.D. Office,
Rajouri Garden,
New Delhi-110027
Phone : 5431105,5938670
Fax: 55469291.

Gowtham Pharma Distributors,
1st Floor, 111, Nyniappa
Naicken Street,
Chennai-600003,
Phone : 5357700,5352400
Gram. GOWTHAM CAPS,
Telex : 41-5189 SPSI IN,
Fax : 91-44-5352401

L & M Aotomatics,
60/7, Old Dal Mandi,m
Kanpur-208001 (U.P),
Phone : 352367,352570
Fax : 91-512-316788.

Mixo Fill (India)
1351, Street No. 45,
Jafrabad, New Seelampur,
Shahdara, Delhi-110053
Phones : (Fact)
2263446,2263362,
(Off) 327460,3270735
Fax : 011-3265278

Patel Engineering Works
Bhajiwala Chawl, Ram Nagar
Chincholi Bunder Road,
Malad (West)
Mumbai-400058
Phone : 8815065

Push Pack Industries,
J-149, GIDC,
Killa-Pardi-396125,
Valsad (Gujarat)
Phone : 026352-680,
Gram. PUSHPACK

Techno-Blist,
65/5, F Road, GIDC
Phase-I Vatva
Ahmedabad-382445
(Gujarat)
Phone : 5834253
Fax : 91-079-5834253.

FILLING MACHINES

Armstrong Smith Ltd.
Brady House, 12/14,
Veer Nariman Road,
Mumbai-400023

Frederick Herbert
10, Second Pasta Lane,
Colaba,
Mumbai-400005

Gowthem Pharma Distributors,
1st Floor, 111, Nyniappa
Naicken Street,
Chennai-600003.
Phones : 5357700,5352400,
Gram. GOWTHAM CAPS
Telex. 41-5189 SPSI IN
Fax : 91-44-5352401
Pagar No. 9610-107700

Square Pharma Machineries,
Gala No. 30/31
Arihant Industrial Estate,
Off. Saki Vihar Road,
Saki Naka,
Mumbai-400072
Phone: 8528306,8500201,
Fax : 022-8378552

Sreeniwas Engineering Works
2-1-460/1, Nallakunta,
Hyderabad-500044,
Phone : Off. 7662606
Fact . 7619475
Gram. SREENEX

Supar Pharma Indl. Severice
20, Mahalaxmi Industrial Estate,
Near Bombay Conductor,
GIDC, Vatva,
Ahmedabad-382445
(Gujarat)
Phone : 079-5833849,
390407

United Engineering Co. (The)
35-A, Hazra Road,
Kolkata-700029
Phones : 4759744
Gram. UNIENGCO
Fax : 91-033-4757727

AGITATOR

Adam Fabriwerk Pvt. Ltd.
203, Rajguru Apts.
New Nagardas Road,
Andheri (E),
Mumbai-400069.
Phones : 83 80548,
8384173,
Telefax: 022-8390105,
E-Mail:adamfab@vsnl.com

Burman Plant & Machinery Co (P) Ltd.
36, Sarkar Lane,
Kolkata-700007.
Phones : 2411340.
Fax : (91)(33) 296077.

Instruments & Equipments,
35, Chittaranaj Avenue,
Kolkata-700012.

Modern Scientific Industries,
199-A, Saket,
Meerut-250001 (U.P).
Phone-(0121) 644086,
Gram:INDUSTRIES.

Multitech Services,
221-226, Gala Complex,
2nd Floor,
D. Upadhyaya Marg,.
Mulund (W),
Mumbai-400080.
Phones :
5613136,5611291,5650593,
Fax- (91) 022-5646325.

Pharma Machinery (The),
1092, M.B.Road, Mahajati
Nagar,
Kolkata-700051.
Phones : 5513779.

CRUSHING & GRINDING MACHINES

(Disintegrators)

Adair Dutt & Co. (I) Pvt. Ltd.
5,B.B.D. Bagh East.
Kolkata-700001

Frederick Herbert,
10, Second Pasta Lane,
Colaba,
Mumbai-400005

Ganesh Engineering Works
1507, Ganesh Pura,
Main Market, Tri Nagar,
Delhi-110035
Phones : 7117972

Industrial Scientific Corporation,
BA-148B, Janakpuri
New Delhi-110058.

Metrex Scientific Instruments Pvt. Ltd.
WH-20, Mayapuri Industrial
Area, Phase-I,
New Delhi-110064
Phones : 5130702,5138271

Monarch Engineering Works.
13, Kharwa Gali,
6th Kumbharwada,
Mumbai-400004

Raman & Well Pvt. Ltd.
Chateau MArine,
3rd Floor, 133, Netaji
Sabhash Road,
Mumbai-400020
Phones :
2049164,2049527,2856397
Gram. RAMANWELL.
Fax : 2023042

Talson Industries (India)
Shed No. 128, Block B,
Sector II, Noida,
Ghaziabad-201207 (U.P)

Toshniwal Brothers Pvt. Ltd.
Industrial Estate,
Makhupura,
Ajmer-305002 (Rajasthan).

DRYERS & DRYING OVENS

Adair Dutt & Co. (I) Pvt. Ltd.
5, B.B.D. Bagh East.
Kolkata-700001

Alpha Scientific & Surgical Co.
18, St. John's Church Road,
Bangalore-560005
(Karnataka)
Phones : 5565945

Andhra Scientific Co. Ltd.
3rd Floor, Janambhoomi
Chambers.
Fort Street, Ballard Estate,
Mumbai-400001

Associated Instrument Manufacturers (India) Pvt.Ltd.
India House, Fort Street,
P.O.Box 119,
Mumbai-400001

Altanto Enterprises,
Gala No. 15, 3rd Floor,
Jogani Estate, J.Ramji
Boricha Marg.
Opp. Kasturba Hospital.
Mahalaxami,
Mumbai-400001
Phones : 3096098
Fax : 91-22-3073537

Bhuvaneswari & Co.
4-3-314, (3464) 1st Floor,
Dundoho Vihar,
Rashtrapathi Road.
Secunderabad-500003
(A.P)
Phones : 7713632,
Gram. TRADEBOOM.

Telex. 0425-6333
PCO IN-TMB
237,
Fax : 7713632

B.P. Industries
B-103, G.T.Karnal Road
Industrial Area.
Delhi - 110033
Phones :
7125184,7115196,7123501

Create Industries
C/7, Anup Estate,
N.H.8, Near Bharat Party
Plot,
Amraiwadi,
Ahmedabad-380026
Phones : 2874085
Fax : (790) 6302607

K. Scientific Industries,
4,5, Ashoka Chember.
Rasala Marg.
Near Lions Hall, Ellisbridge.
Ahmedabad-380006
(Gujarat)
Phones : 079-6469471 to 74
Fax : 6469471
E-Mail :dksipttd@icenet.net

Eastern Scientific Machinery Corp.
12-A, Peermohamed Manzil,
Colaba,
Mumbai-400005

BALL MILLS

Ashoka Technologies
A-15, Phase-I
Mayapuri Indl. Area
New Delhi,
NCT of Delhi-110064
India
TEL : +91 (0) 11 5135308
FAX : +91 (0) 11 5138250
E-mail:
amtc@ndb.vsnl.net.in

Jindal Scientific Industries
14-UA
Opp. Milier Ganj Crossing
Jawahar Ngr.
Delhi,
NCT of Delhi-110007
India
TEL : +91 (0) 11 2919408
FAX : +91 (0) 11 2166039

Karamson Engg. Corp.
3/24, Kirti Ngr. Indl. Area
New Delhi,
NCT of Delhi-110015
India
TEL : +91 (0) 11 5417621
FAX : +91 (0) 11 5433577
E-mail: kencor@usa.net

NMF Equipments & Plants Pvt. Ltd.
A-146, Kalkaji
New Delhi,
NCT of Delhi-110019
India
TEL : +91 (0) 11 6410340
FAX : +91 (0) 11 6436639
E-mail:
nmfeqpts@ndf.vsnl.ne.tin

Premier Engg. Works
7/23, Gali 7
Anand Parbat Indl. Area
New Delhi,
NCT of Delhi-110005
India
TEL : +91 (0) 11 5730730

T R Sharma Engg. Works
A-156, Hari Ngr.
New Delhi,
NCT of Delhi-110064
India
TEL : +91 (0) 11 5405328
FAX : +91 (0) 11 5403754
E-mail:
paintmachinery@yahoo.com

Ahura Power Equipments Pvt. Ltd.
2/A, 'B' Block
Goldcoin Cmplx.
Satellite Rd.
Ahmedabad,
Gujarat-380015
India
TEL : +91 (0) 79 5830219
FAX : +91 (0) 79 6763997
E-mail:
power_engn@hotmail.com

Airtech Engineers
32, P D Corporation Est.
Nr. Revabhai Est.
CTM, Ahmedabad,
Gujarat-380026
India
TEL : +91 (0) 79 5854303

Alfa Engineers
862/7/B, GIDC
Makarpura
Vadodara, Gujarat-390010
India
TEL : +91 (0) 265 652245
FAX : +91 (0) 265 652245
E-mail:
alfaengineers@rediffmail.com

Amar Fabricators & Engineers A Unit of Power Engg. Works
C1/B, 4305, Phase-IV
GIDC, Vatva,
Gujarat-382445
India
TEL : +91 (0) 79 5830219
FAX : +91 (0) 79 6745567

Atin Industries
C 1/4412, Phase-IV
GIDC, Vatva
Ahmedabad,
Gujarat-382445
India
TEL : +91 (0) 79 5830714

Chemitex Engineers
13, Laxmi Co-op. Indl. Est.
Nr. Nagarvel Hanuman
Mandir
Amraiwadi Rd.
Ahmedabad,
Gujarat-380026
India
TEL : +91 (0) 79 2748001
FAX : +91 (0) 79 2748001

Fab Consultants & Engineers Pvt. Ltd.
D-30, Sect. 17
Kavi Ngr. Indl Area

Ghaziabad,
Uttar Pradesh-201002
India
TEL : +91 (0) 120 4702065
FAX : +91 (0) 120 4702751
E-mail: fabcon30@usa.net

International Combustion (I) Ltd.
107/1, Park St.
Kolkata,
West Bengal-700016
India
TEL : +91 (0) 33 2457524
FAX : +91 (0) 33 2493713
E-mail:
intcomc2@giascl01.vsnl.net.in

Mcnally Bharat Engg. Company Ltd.
44, Park St.
Kolkata,
West Bengal-700016
India
TEL : +91 (0) 33 2478611
FAX : +91 (0) 33 2402086
E-mail:
mbe.cal@smy.sprintrpg.ems.vsnl.net.in

TRF Ltd. Formerly Tata Robins Fraser Ltd.
43, Chowringhee Rd.
Kolkata,
West Bengal-700071
India
TEL : +91 (0) 33 2881117
FAX : +91 (0) 33 2881143

COLLOID MILLS

Cadmach Machinery Company Pvt. Ltd.
3604 & 3605
GIDC Indl. Est., Phase-IV
Vatva, Ahmedabad,
Gujarat-382445
India
TEL : +91 (0) 79 5831491
FAX : +91 (0) 79 5832602
E-mail:
cadmach@ndl.vsnl.net.in

Reva Pharma Machinery
Plot No. 492/4
GIDC, Makarpura
Vadodara, Gujarat-390010
India
TEL : +91 (0) 265 640082

Chemech Engg.
106, Udyog Bhawan
Sharma Indl. Est.
Wallahat Rd.
Goregaon (E)
Mumbai,
Maharashtra-400063
India
TEL : +91 (0) 22 8731941
FAX : +91 (0) 22 8731941

Chhaya Enterprises
C-14, Mohammed Ali Est.
Salim Compound,
Chimatpada, Marol Naka
Andheri (E)
Mumbai,
Maharashtra-400059
India
TEL : +91 (0) 22 8329259

Frigmaires Engineers
Janata Indl. Est.
Gala No. 8,
Opp. Phoenix Mill
Senapati Bapat Marg
Lower Parel
Mumbai,
Maharashtra-400013
India
TEL : +91 (0) 22 4944108
FAX : +91 (0) 22 4968371
E-mail: fe@vsnl.com

Kamal (E) Industries
Datta Bhavan
Kashinath Dhuru Rd.
Dadar (W)
Mumbai,
Maharashtra-400028
India
TEL : +91 (0) 22 4221555
FAX : +91 (0) 22 4373474
E-mail: kei@vsnl.com

Ravikiran Industries
213, Mittal Indl. Est., No-2,
Marol, Andheri (E)
Mumbai,
Maharashtra-400059
India
TEL : +91 (0) 22 8506569
FAX : +91 (0) 22 8506135
E-mail: ravikiran@vsnl.com

Sams Machines Pvt. Ltd.
C/12, Nand Dham Indl. Est.
Andheri (E)
Mumbai,
Maharashtra-400059
India
TEL : +91 (0) 22 8500906
FAX : +91 (0) 22 8371968

Vinayak Exports
Gokul Arcade, 302- 'B'
Bldg., Subhash Rd.
Vile Parle (W)
Mumbai,
Maharashtra-400057
India
TEL : +91 (0) 22 8323264
FAX : +91 (0) 22 8371460
E-mail: krish.v@usa.net

Intel Systems
5-234/2, H P Rd.
Moosapet
Hyderabad, Andhra Pradesh-500018
India
TEL : +91 (0) 40 3711379
FAX : +91 (0) 40 3713567
E-mail:
intelarch@mantraonline.com

LABORATORIES TESTING

AES Testing & Research Lab
1304/1405, Nirmal Tower,
26, Barakhamba Rd.
New Delhi,
NCT of Delhi-110001
India
TEL : +91 (0) 11 3323156
FAX : +91 (0) 11 3357481
E-mail:
aesrt@ndb.vsnl.net.in

Analytical Testing Services Pvt. Ltd.
E-47/9, 1st Flr.
Phase-II
Okhla Indl. Area
New Delhi,
NCT of Delhi-110020
India
TEL : +91 (0) 11 6310306
FAX : +91 (0) 11 6822361

Dodel Analytical Laboratories
Plot No. 120
Phase-II, GIDC
Vapi, Gujarat-396195
India
TEL : +91 (0) 260 32542

Electrical Research & Development Association
ERDA Rd., GIDC
Makarpura
Vadodara, Gujarat-390010
India
TEL : +91 (0) 265 642942
FAX : +91 (0) 265 643182
E-mail:
erda@wilnetonline.net

Asia Inspection & Testing Pvt. Ltd.
87B, Phase-I
Udyog Vihar
Gurgaon, Haryana-122015
India
TEL : +91 (0) 124 6348811
FAX : +91 (0) 124 6398353
E-mail: asianinspection@mantraonline.com

Bhartiya Enterprises
Plot No. 254
Sect. 24
Faridabad,
Haryana-121005
India
TEL : +91 (0) 129 5232462
FAX : +91 (0) 129 5237464
E-mail:
sarvo@del2.vsnl.net.in

Choksi Laboratories Ltd.
6/3, Manormaganj
Indore,
Madhya Pradesh-452001
India
TEL : +91 (0) 731 490592
FAX : +91 (0) 731 490593
E-mail:
info@choksilab.com

A to Z Pharmaceuticals Pvt. Ltd.
12, Balaji Ngr.
Ambattur,
Chennai,
Tamil Nadu-600053
India
TEL : +91 (0) 44 6376811
E-mail:
omsoc@md2.vsnl.net.in

Cement & Allied Material Testing Laboratory
21, 17th St., Mosque Cly.
Guindy
Chennai,
Tamil Nadu-600032
India
TEL : +91 (0) 44 2455672
FAX : +91 (0) 44 6264271
E-mail:
thamilakharanr@hotmail.com

Askib Engineers Pvt. Ltd.
2nd Flr., 47
Lenin Sarani
Kolkata,
West Bengal-700013
India
TEL : +91 (0) 33 2456271
FAX : +91 (0) 33 2449664
E-mail: askib@usa.net

AES Testing & Research Lab
1304/1405, Nirmal Tower,
26, Barakhamba Rd.
New Delhi,
NCT of Delhi-110001
India
TEL : +91 (0) 11 3323156
FAX : +91 (0) 11 3357481
E-mail:
aesrt@ndb.vsnl.net.in

Analytical Testing Services Pvt. Ltd.
E-47/9, 1st Flr.
Phase-II, Okhla Indl. Area
New Delhi,
NCT of Delhi-110020
India
TEL : +91 (0) 11 6310306
FAX : +91 (0) 11 6822361

Dodel Analytical Laboratories
Plot No. 120, Phase-II

GIDC, Vapi,
Gujarat-396195
India
TEL : +91 (0) 260 32542

Electrical Research & Development Association
ERDA Rd., GIDC
Makarpura
Vadodara, Gujarat-390010
India
TEL : +91 (0) 265 642942
FAX : +91 (0) 265 643182
E-mail:
erda@wilnetonline.net

Asia Inspection & Testing Pvt. Ltd.
87B, Phase-I
Udyog Vihar
Gurgaon, Haryana-122015
India
TEL : +91 (0) 124 6348811
FAX : +91 (0) 124 6398353
E-mail: asianinspection@mantraonline.com

Bhartiya Enterprises
Plot No. 254, Sect. 24
Faridabad,
Haryana-121005
India
TEL : +91 (0) 129 5232462
FAX : +91 (0) 129 5237464
E-mail:
sarvo@del2.vsnl.net.in

Electronics Regional Test Laboratory (East)
DN Block, Sect. V
Salt Lake City
Bidhannagar
Kolkata,
West Bengal-700091
India
TEL : +91 (0) 33 3343662
FAX : +91 (0) 33 3349472
E-mail:
ertleast@ertie.ernet.in

Eskaps (I) Pvt. Ltd.
Chowringhee Mansion, 30
J L Nehru Rd.
Kolkata,
West Bengal-700016
India
TEL : +91 (0) 33 2299682
FAX : +91 (0) 33 2265917
E-mail:
eskaps@cal2.vsnl.net.in

Inspection Survey & Surveillance (I) Pvt. Ltd.
21, Park Lane
Kolkata,
West Bengal-700016
India
TEL : +91 (0) 33 2293651
FAX : +91 (0) 33 2297658
E-mail:
insurvey@cal2.vsnl.net.in

PAINT DRYING APPARATUS

Bry-Air (Asia) Pvt. Ltd.
20, Rajpur Rd.
Delhi,
NCT of Delhi-110054
India
TEL : +91 (0) 11 3912800
FAX : +91 (0) 11 3915127
E-mail:
enquire@pahwa.com
www.bryair.com

J S Engg. Enterprises
40, B/h Union Bank
Yusuf Sarai
New Delhi,
NCT of Delhi-110016
India
TEL : +91 (0) 11 6560657

Techmac Engg. Works
325, Usha Kiran Bldg.
Azadpur
Delhi,
NCT of Delhi-110033
India
TEL : +91 (0) 11 7137027
FAX : +91 (0) 11 7137027

Welkin Engg. Co.
255-256
GIDC Est.
Ankleshwar,
Gujarat-393002
India
TEL : +91 (0) 2646 52185
FAX : +91 (0) 2646 52423

NSW India Ltd.
Plot No. 43-44, Sect. 34
EHTP
Gurgaon, Haryana-122001
India
TEL : +91 (0) 124 6371106
FAX : +91 (0) 124 6372859
E-mail:
pnarang@del2.vsnl.net.in

Bhagwati Allied Products
K-216, MIDC
Waluj, Maharashtra-431136
India
TEL : +91 (0) 240 554727

PAINT GUNS

Rdevis Engineers Pvt. Ltd.
1, Vikram Vihar Extn.
Lajpat Ngr. IV
New Delhi,
NCT of Delhi-110024
India
TEL : +91 (0) 11 6480741
FAX : +91 (0) 11 6423862
E-mail: rdevis@vsnl.com

USA Spray Gun Corporation (Regd.)
263, Onkar Ngr. B
Nr. DMS Milk Booth
Tri Ngr.
Delhi,
NCT of Delhi-110035
India
TEL : +91 (0) 11 7108391

Wilhelm Wagner GmbH & Company KG
208/9, 5th Main Rd.
OMBR Layout

Banaswadi
Bangalore,
Karnataka-560043
India
TEL : +91 (0) 80 5450213
FAX : +91 (0) 80 5452461
E-mail:
sales@prismsurface.com

Manik Machinery Manufacturers Pvt. Ltd.
8/4, Sona Udyog
Parsi Panchayat Rd.
Andheri (E)
Mumbai,
Maharashtrà-400069
India
TEL : +91 (0) 22 8341233
FAX : +91 (0) 22 8365104
E-mail:
spraygun@pilotindia.com

Ronuplate Pvt. Ltd.
Kishori Court, 11 A
Abdul Gaffar Khan Rd.
Worli Seaface
Worli, Mumbai,
Maharashtra-400025
India
TEL : +91 (0) 22 4921107
FAX : +91 (0) 22 4930147

Statfield Systems
(Coating) Pvt. Ltd.
132/B, Opp. Hotel Vaibhav
Ganeshkhind Rd.
Pune,
Maharashtra-411007
India
TEL : +91 (0) 20 5537284
FAX : +91 (0) 20 5535320
E-mail:
surcoat@giaspn01.vsnl.net.in

Thermax Surface Coatings Ltd.
A Thermax Group Co.
Plot No. 38 & 39
Block No. D-II
MIDC Indl. Area
Chinchwad, Pune,
Maharashtra-411019
India
TEL : +91 (0) 20 778884
FAX : +91 (0) 20 754622
E-mail:
tscl@globalnet.ems.vsnl.net.in

V R Coatings
J-138, Bhosari Indl. Area
Bhosari, Pune,
Maharashtra-411026
India
TEL : +91 (0) 20 7122331
FAX : +91 (0) 20 7121891
E-mail:
vfdsouza@vsnl.com

Metallizing Wires & Conductors
C-433, Phase-II
MIA, Basni
Jodhpur, Rajasthan-342005
India
TEL : +91 (0) 291 741011
FAX : +91 (0) 291 741014
E-mail:
metallizing@vsnl.com

Foretek Engineers Pvt. Ltd.
Flat E-4, 3rd Flr.,
Chathura, 6
Dr. Nair Rd., T Ngr.
Chennai,
Tamil Nadu-600017
India
TEL : +91 (0) 44 8278374
FAX : +91 (0) 44 8263615
E-mail:
foretek@md3.vsnl.net.in

PAINT KETTLES

Dipesh Engg. Works
3, Sheroo Villa
87, J P Rd.
Andheri (W)
Mumbai,
Maharashtra-400053
India
TEL : +91 (0) 22 6336729
FAX : +91 (0) 22 6315507
E-mail:
kjpatel_71@hotmail.com

Fluidtech Engineers
10/8, Race View Cly.
Chakrapani Rd.
Guindy, Chennai,
Tamil Nadu-600032
India
TEL : +91 (0) 44 2453952
FAX : +91 (0) 44 2452440
E-mail:
beadmill@md3.vsnl.net.in

PAINT MFRS. MACHINERY

Coromandel Paints & Chemicals Ltd.
Opp. Junior College
Pendurthy
Visakhapatnam, Andhra Pradesh-531173
India
TEL : +91 (0) 891 824218
FAX : +91 (0) 891 824065

Intel Systems
5-234/2, H P Rd.
Moosapet
Hyderabad, Andhra Pradesh-500018
India
TEL : +91 (0) 40 3711379
FAX : +91 (0) 40 3713567
E-mail:
intelarch@mantraonline.com

T R Sharma Engg. Works
A-156, Hari Ngr.
New Delhi,
NCT of Delhi-110064
India
TEL : +91 (0) 11 5405328
FAX : +91 (0) 11 5403754
E-mail:
paintmachinery@yahoo.com

Marshal Fab Industries
Plot No. 4B
Nr. Shri Narayan Textile Mill
CTM Cross Rd.
Amraiwadi, Ahmedabad,
Gujarat-380026
India
TEL : +91 (0) 79 5854027

FAX : +91 (0) 79 5851380

Radhe Marketing Pvt. Ltd.
211, VIP View
VIP Rd., Karelibaug
Vadodara, Gujarat-390018
India
TEL : +91 (0) 265 447296
FAX : +91 (0) 265 447296
E-mail:
sales@safetycaps.com

Wel-Fab & Engineers
1009, Phase-IV
GIDC Est.
Vithal Udyognagar,
Gujarat-388121
India
TEL : +91 (0) 2692 35496
FAX : +91 (0) 2692 37371

Pharmaceutical Machinery Manufacturing Works
47/B, Laxmibai Ngr.
Indore,
Madhya Pradesh-452006
India
TEL : +91 (0) 731 410963
FAX : +91 (0) 731 410071
E-mail:
pharmamach@satyam.net.in

Hindustan Glass Beads
B-9/10, Vinochem Indl.
Est. Goddeo Rd.
Bhayander (E)
Mumbai,
Maharashtra-401105
India
TEL : +91 (0) 22 8192473
FAX : +91 (0) 22 8188576

Indo-German Engineers
302, Sanjiv Apts.
Sion Chunabhatti Rd.,
Vrindavan Chowk
Sion, Mumbai,
Maharashtra-400022
India
TEL : +91 (0) 22 4070527
FAX : +91 (0) 22 4091399
E-mail:
sanjiv@bom7.vsnl.net.in

Micromill Technologies Pvt. Ltd.
Warden House, 1st Flr.
P M Rd., Fort
Mumbai,
Maharashtra-400001
India
TEL : +91 (0) 22 2872295
FAX : +91 (0) 22 2873475
E-mail: milltech@vsnl.net

Raymer Engg. Corp.
20, Thakkar Indl. Est.
Chapsi, Bhimji Rd.
Mazgao, Mumbai,
Maharashtra-400010
India
TEL : +91 (0) 22 3774333
FAX : +91 (0) 22 3729904
E-mail:
rayomundeng@mailcity.lycos.com

Technica Engineers
Opp. Paper Products
Majiwada, Thane,
Maharashtra-400601
India
TEL : +91 (0) 22 5342580
E-mail: technicaengrs@
maharashtradirectory.com

Soti Engg. Industries
D-115, Sect. 10
Noida,
Uttar Pradesh-201301
India
TEL : +91 (0) 120
4443198

Sonder-Technologie Pvt. Ltd.
Plot No. F/1 & F/2
Behala Indl. Est., 620
Diamond Harbour Rd.
Kolkata,
West Bengal-700034
India
TEL : +91 (0) 33 4686497
FAX : +91 (0) 33 4686496
E-mail:
welding@technologist.com

PAINT MIXERS

Jogindra Engg. Works
70, Rama Rd.
New Delhi,
NCT of Delhi-110015
India
TEL : +91 (0) 11 5442112
FAX : +91 (0) 11 5453836
E-mail:
jogindra@ndf.vsnl.net.in

Cosywo Engg. Co.
15, Laxmi Co-op. Indl. Est.
Nr. Nagarvel Hanuman
Mandir, Amraiwadi Rd.
Ahmedabad,
Gujarat-380026
India
TEL : +91 (0) 79 2748168
FAX : +91 (0) 79 2748001
E-mail: cosywo@usa.net

Marshal Fab Industries
Plot No. 4B
Nr. Shri Narayan Textile Mill
CTM Cross Rd.
Amraiwadi
Ahmedabad,
Gujarat-380026
India
TEL : +91 (0) 79 5854027
FAX : +91 (0) 79 5851380

Febchem Engg. Works
A/2, Sect. A, Indl. Area
Sanwer Rd., Indore,
Madhya Pradesh-452015
India
TEL : +91 (0) 731 720467
FAX : +91 (0) 731 723087

Suresh Engg. Works
14B, Kalyan Vishranti Grah
South Tukoganj
Indore,
Madhya Pradesh-452001
India
TEL : +91 (0) 731 529155
FAX : +91 (0) 731 527872
E-mail:
suresen@bom4.vsnl.net.in

Chemac Equipments Pvt. Ltd.
M J D'Souza Compound
Safed Pool, Sakinaka
Mumbai,
Maharashtra-400072
India
TEL : +91 (0) 22 8510777
FAX : +91 (0) 22 8516986
E-mail:
chemac@bom4.vsnl.net.in

Filtromix
Krishna Metal Compd.
Opp. Laghu Udyog Kendra
I B Patel Rd.
Goregaon (E)
Mumbai,
Maharashtra-400063
India
TEL : +91 (0) 22 8756411
FAX : +91 (0) 22 6253969
E-mail:
filtromix@hotmail.com

Frigmaires Engineers
Janata Indl. Est.
Gala No. 8,
Opp. Phoenix Mill
Senapati Bapat Marg
Lower Parel, Mumbai,
Maharashtra-400013
India
TEL : +91 (0) 22 4944108
FAX : +91 (0) 22 4968371
E-mail: fe@vsnl.com

Glow Industries
32, B/h Automatic Co.
Wagle Indl. Est.
Thane,
Maharashtra-400604
India
TEL : +91 (0) 22 5328511
FAX : +91 (0) 22 5327660
E-mail: info@glowplast.com

Pimco Machines Pvt. Ltd.
A/28, Nanddham Est.
Marol Maroshi Rd.
Andheri (E), Mumbai,
Maharashtra-400059
India
TEL : +91 (0) 22 8597175
FAX : +91 (0) 22 8500351
E-mail:
pimco@bom5.vsnl.net.in

Pioneer Manufacturing Corp.
A/28, Nanddham Est.
Marol-Maroshi Rd., Marol
Andheri (E), Mumbai,
Maharashtra-400059
India
TEL : +91 (0) 22 8597175
FAX : +91 (0) 22 8500351
E-mail:
pimco@bom5.vsl.net.in

Pooja Engg. Works
Gala No. 20/21
Shukla Compound
New Link Rd., Osiwara
Jogeshwari
Mumbai,
Maharashtra-400102
India
TEL : +91 (0) 22 6789050

Valsons
Plot No. 15
St. No. 10, MIDC,
Phase-II
Andheri (E), Mumbai,
Maharashtra-400093
India
TEL : +91 (0) 22 8221663
FAX : +91 (0) 22 8323849
E-mail: skp@bom7

Great Cheran Engg.
482-A, Palghat Rd.
Coimbatore,
Tamil Nadu-641008
India
TEL : +91 (0) 422 822492
FAX : +91 (0) 422 823459

Intel Systems
5-234/2, H P Rd.
Moosapet
Hyderabad,
Andhra Pradesh-500018
India
TEL : +91 (0) 40 3711379
FAX : +91 (0) 40 3713567
E-mail:
intelarch@mantraonline.com

PAINT OVENS

Chass Engineers Pvt. Ltd.
Plot No. 1603
Phase-III, GIDC
Vatva
Ahmedabad,
Gujarat-382445
India
TEL : +91 (0) 79 5833374
FAX : +91 (0) 79 5893395

Shivang Furnance & Ovens Pvt. Ltd.
Himja
Nr. Gandhinagar Soc.
Maninagar (E)
Ahmedabad,
Gujarat-380008
India
TEL : +91 (0) 79 2774741
FAX : +91 (0) 79 2772031
E-mail: furnace@email.com

Kelleys Engg. Works
24-B/6, Indl. Area
Faridabad,
Haryana-121001
India
TEL : +91 (0) 129 5233251
FAX : +91 (0) 129 5233251
E-mail: kelleysvib@usa.net

NSW India Ltd.
Plot No. 43-44, Sect. 34
EHTP, Gurgaon,
Haryana-122001
India
TEL : +91 (0) 124 6371106
FAX : +91 (0) 124 6372859
E-mail:
pnarang@del2.vsnl.net.in

Thermotherm Engineers
455, 12th Cross, Phase-IV
Peenya Indl. Area
Bangalore,
Karnataka-560058
India

TEL : +91 (0) 80 8362507
FAX : +91 (0) 80 8362919

AMI Industries
8, Surve Indl. Est.
1st Sonawala Cross Rd.
Goregaon (E)
Mumbai,
Maharashtra-400063
India
TEL : +91 (0) 22 8727120
FAX : +91 (0) 22 8734753
E-mail:
oven@bom5.vsnl.net.in

Apte Amalgamations Ltd.
Airlines Bldg.
Opp. Eros Cinema
Mumbai,
Maharashtra-400020
India
TEL : +91 (0) 22 2852639
FAX : +91 (0) 22 2871405

Bharat Engg. Industries
Chitalsar Manpada
Ghodbunder Rd.
Thane,
Maharashtra-400607
India
TEL : +91 (0) 22 5346098
FAX : +91 (0) 22 5346098

Gel Consultants Pvt. Ltd.
16, Vishal Indl. Est.
Opp. Ceat Tyres,
Village Rd.
Bhandup (W)
Mumbai,
Maharashtra-400078
India
TEL : +91 (0) 22 5610334
FAX : +91 (0) 22 5902771
E-mail: gel@vsnl.net

Tata Automation Ltd.
C/O Tata Engineering
Chinchwad, Pune,
Maharashtra-411033
India
TEL : +91 (0) 20 7405530
FAX : +91 (0) 20 7476318
E-mail: ynath@telco.co.in

Pollution Control Equipments
C-433, MIA
Phase-II, Basni
Jodhpur,
Rajasthan-342005
India
TEL : +91 (0) 291 741011

Vitech Enviro Systems Pvt. Ltd.
AP-123, AF Block,
6th St., 11th Main Rd.
Anna Ngr.
Chennai,
Tamil Nadu-600040
India
TEL : +91 (0) 44 6220115
FAX : +91 (0) 44 6280288
E-mail:
vfs@md4.vsnl.net.in

Vitech Finishing Systems
AP-123, AF Block, 6th St.
11th Main Rd.
Anna Ngr., Chennai,
Tamil Nadu-600040
India
TEL : +91 (0) 44 6220115
FAX : +91 (0) 44 6280288
E-mail:
vfs@md4.vsnl.net.in

Caltherm Engineers & Consultants
6, Andul Raj Rd.
Kolkata,
West Bengal-700026
India
TEL : +91 (0) 33 4749240
FAX : +91 (0) 33 4754903
E-mail: caltherm@vsnl.net

The Wesman Engg. Company Pvt. Ltd.
"Wesman Center", 8
Mayfair Rd.
Kolkata,
West Bengal-700019
India
TEL : +91 (0) 33 2405320
FAX : +91 (0) 33 2478050
E-mail:
mailbox@wesman.com

Unifire
4th Flr., 16-B
Shakespeare Sarani
Kolkata,
West Bengal-700071
India
TEL : +91 (0) 33 2829621
FAX : +91 (0) 33 2829624
E-mail:
unifire@cal.vsnl.net.in

A G Industries
A-108
Lok Vihar
Pitampura
New Delhi,
NCT of Delhi-110034
India
TEL : +91 (0) 11 7103194
FAX : +91 (0) 11 2113355

Krishna Scientific Works
WZ 436-B
Nangal Raya
New Delhi,
NCT of Delhi-110046
India
TEL : +91 (0) 11 5613539
FAX : +91 (0) 11 5613539
E-mail: ksw@satyam.net.in

Rdevis Engineers Pvt. Ltd.
1, Vikram Vihar Extn.
Lajpat Ngr. IV
New Delhi,
NCT of Delhi-110024
India
TEL : +91 (0) 11 6480741
FAX : +91 (0) 11 6423862
E-mail: rdevis@vsnl.com

SPRAYERS

Rdevis Engineers Pvt. Ltd.
1, Vikram Vihar Extn.
Lajpat Ngr. IV
New Delhi,
NCT of Delhi-110024

India
TEL : +91 (0) 11 6480741
FAX : +91 (0) 11 6423862
E-mail: rdevis@vsnl.com

USA Spray Gun Corporation (Regd.)
263, Onkar Ngr. B
Nr. DMS Milk Booth
Tri Ngr.
Delhi, NCT of Delhi-110035
India
TEL : +91 (0) 11 7108391

Wilhelm Wagner GmbH & Company KG
208/9, 5th Main Rd.
OMBR Layout
Banaswadi
Bangalore,
Karnataka-560043
India
TEL : +91 (0) 80 5450213
FAX : +91 (0) 80 5452461
E-mail:
sales@prismsurface.com

Manik Machinery Manufacturers Pvt. Ltd.
8/4, Sona Udyog
Parsi Panchayat Rd.
Andheri (E)
Mumbai,
Maharashtra-400069
India
TEL : +91 (0) 22 8341233
FAX : +91 (0) 22 8365104
E-mail:
spraygun@pilotindia.com

Ronuplate Pvt. Ltd.
Kishori Court, 11 A
Abdul Gaffar Khan Rd.
Worli Seaface
Worli, Mumbai,
Maharashtra-400025
India
TEL : +91 (0) 22 4921107
FAX : +91 (0) 22 4930147

Statfield Systems
(Coating) Pvt. Ltd.
132/B, Opp. Hotel Vaibhav
Ganeshkhind Rd.
Pune,
Maharashtra-411007
India
TEL : +91 (0) 20 5537284
FAX : +91 (0) 20 5535320
E-mail:
surcoat@giaspn01.vsnl.net.in

Thermax Surface
Coatings Ltd. A Thermax
Group Co.
Plot No. 38 & 39
Block No. D-II
MIDC Indl. Area
Chinchwad
Pune,
Maharashtra-411019
India
TEL : +91 (0) 20 778884
FAX : +91 (0) 20 754622
E-mail:
tscl@globalnet.ems.vsnl.net.in

V R Coatings
J-138, Bhosari Indl. Area
Bhosari, Pune,
Maharashtra-411026
India
TEL : +91 (0) 20 7122331
FAX : +91 (0) 20 7121891
E-mail:
vfdsouza@vsnl.com

Metallizing Wires & Conductors
C-433, Phase-II
MIA, Basni
Jodhpur,
Rajasthan-342005
India
TEL : +91 (0) 291 741011
FAX : +91 (0) 291 741014
E-mail:
metallizing@vsnl.com

Foretek Engineers Pvt. Ltd.
Flat E-4, 3rd Flr.,
Chathura, 6, Dr. Nair Rd.
T Ngr., Chennai,
Tamil Nadu-600017
India
TEL : +91 (0) 44 8278374
FAX : +91 (0) 44 8263615
E-mail:
foretek@md3.vsnl.net.in

STORAGE TANKS

Air Flow Pvt. Ltd.
13/1090, Naiwalan
Karol Bagh
New Delhi,
NCT of Delhi-110005
India
TEL : +91 (0) 11 5721236
FAX : +91 (0) 11 5752267
E-mail:
airflow@del3.vsnl.net.in

Alpha Process Vessels Pvt. Ltd.
A-90, 1st Flr., Amar Cly.
New Delhi,
NCT of Delhi-110024
India
TEL : +91 (0) 11 6427087
FAX : +91 (0) 11 6467084

Ark Industrial Products Pvt. Ltd.
S-255, Greater Kailash-II
New Delhi,
NCT of Delhi-110048
India
TEL : +91 (0) 11 6236892
FAX : +91 (0) 11 6236898
E-mail:
akashyap@ndb.vsnl.net.in

Aero Engineers
Plot No. 3419
Phase-IV, GIDC
Vatva, Gujarat-382445
India
TEL : +91 (0) 79 5831556
FAX : +91 (0) 79 5891041
E-mail: aero@icenet.net

Airtech Engineers
32, P D Corporation Est.
Nr. Revabhai Est.
CTM, Ahmedabad,
Gujarat-380026
India
TEL : +91 (0) 79 5854303

Annapurna Fabricators
312, Ananamangal-II
C G Rd., Navrangpura
Ahmedabad,
Gujarat-380009
India
TEL : +91 (0) 79 6566709
FAX : +91 (0) 79 6462268
E-mail:
atrivedi@ad1.vsnl.net.in

Adarsh Fabricators
Plot No. 212, Sect. 24
NIT, Faridabad,
Haryana-121005
India
TEL : +91 (0) 129 5234689
FAX : +91 (0) 129 5233028

Amrapali Structurals Pvt. Ltd.
14/7 Mill Stone
Delhi-Mathura Rd.
Faridabad, Haryana-121003
India
TEL : +91 (0) 129 5275552
FAX : +91 (0) 129 6524172
E-mail:
khannav@123india.com

Galaxy (FRP) Pvt. Ltd.
183, Phase-I
Udyog Vihar
Gurgaon, Haryana-122000
India
TEL : +91 (0) 124 6341725
FAX : +91 (0) 124 6340294
E-mail: galaxyfrp@id.eth.net

Alfa Fluid Piping Systems Pvt. Ltd.
E-27, Phase-VII
SIDCO Indl. Est.
Hosur, Karnataka-635109
India
TEL : +91 (0) 4344 76417
FAX : +91 (0) 4344 76417
E-mail: alfafluid@eth.net

Air Flow Pvt. Ltd.
13/1090, Naiwalan
Karol Bagh
New Delhi,
NCT of Delhi-110005
India
TEL : +91 (0) 11 5721236
FAX : +91 (0) 11 5752267
E-mail:
airflow@del3.vsnl.net.in

Arul Rubbers Pvt. Ltd.
B-5, SIDCO Indl. Est.
Hosur, Karnataka-635126
India
TEL : +91 (0) 4344 76650
FAX : +91 (0) 4344 77504
E-mail:
aspl@bgl.vsnl.net.in

Fibreglass Moulding Co.
No. 5, 3rd Flr., Narang
Chmbrs., N R Rd.
Bangalore,
Karnataka-560002
India
TEL : +91 (0) 80 2236923
FAX : +91 (0) 80 2217920
E-mail:
fmcbangalore@hotmail.com

Electro Mechanicals
31, Sect. E, Indl. Area
Govindpura, Bhopal,
Madhya Pradesh-462023
India
TEL : +91 (0) 755 589338
FAX : +91 (0) 755 581041
E-mail:
electromechanicals@vsnl.com

Febchem Engg. Works
A/2, Sect. A, Indl. Area
Sanwer Rd., Indore,
Madhya Pradesh-452015
India
TEL : +91 (0) 731 720467
FAX : +91 (0) 731 723087

Indore Petrocon Industries
24/1, B/h Narayan Kothi
Race Course Rd.
Indore,
Madhya Pradesh-452003
India
TEL : +91 (0) 731 433488
FAX : +91 (0) 731 434254
E-mail:
petrocon@bom4.vsnl.net.in

Abros Enterprises
12/8, D-1
MIDC, Chinchwad
Pune, Maharashtra-411019
India
TEL : +91 (0) 20 7475687
FAX : +91 (0) 20 7470678

Albaj Engg. Corp.
340, Clover Centre
Moledina Rd.
Pune, Maharashtra-411001
India
TEL : +91 (0) 20 631511
FAX : +91 (0) 20 6137255
E-mail: albaj@vsnl.com

Alpha Beta Engg. Construction Pvt. Ltd.
222, Swastik Chmbrs.
CST Rd., Chembur
Mumbai,
Maharashtra-400071
India
TEL : +91 (0) 22 5224527
FAX : +91 (0) 22 5224237
E-mail:
alpha.beta@lwbbs.net

Mech Engineers
920-A, Phase-II, Indl. Area
Ramdarbar
Chandigarh, Punjab-160002
India
TEL : +91 (0) 172 652417
FAX : +91 (0) 172 652417

Air Flow Pvt. Ltd.
13/1090, Naiwalan
Karol Bagh
New Delhi,
NCT of Delhi-110005
India
TEL : +91 (0) 11 5721236
FAX : +91 (0) 11 5752267
E-mail:
airflow@del3.vsnl.net.in

Raj Machines
263, Indl. Area A
Ludhiana, Punjab-141003
India
TEL : +91 (0) 161 608152
FAX : +91 (0) 161 405680

Ananda Fabrications (CBE) Pvt. Ltd.
"Anand Nilayam", 70,
Bharathi Park
Rd. No. 2
S B Mission P. O.
Coimbatore,
Tamil Nadu-641011
India
TEL : +91 (0) 422 866034
FAX : +91 (0) 422 455990

Anandha Fabrications (Cbe) Pvt. Ltd.
Nr. Sankara Polytechnic
Chinnavadampatti (Post)
Coimbatore,
Tamil Nadu-641006
India
TEL : +91 (0) 422 446213
FAX : +91 (0) 422 866634
E-mail:
anandhafabrications@usa.net

Baalu Fabrication Works
K-15, Indl. Est.
Ambattur
Chennai,
Tamil Nadu-600058
India
TEL : +91 (0) 44 6252685

Campion Plastic Industries Pvt. Ltd.
37, Postal Cly.
3rd St., West Mambalam
Chennai,
Tamil Nadu-600033
India
TEL : +91 (0) 44 4853173

Cope Industries
TS-73, SIDCO Tiny Sect.
Thiru-Vi-Ka Indl. Sect.
Ekkattuthangal
Chennai,
Tamil Nadu-600097
India
TEL : +91 (0) 44 2323787
E-mail: copeex@usa.net

A K Tech Engg. Works
B-24, Sect. 10
Noida,
Uttar Pradesh-201301
India
TEL : +91 (0) 120 543863

Abdul Karim & Co.
D-21, Indl. Area,
Sect. 17, Kavi Ngr.
Ghaziabad,
Uttar Pradesh-201003
India
TEL : +91 (0) 120
4702282

Anand Dis-Brew Engg. Works
5, Rajinder Ngr. Indl. Area
Mohan Ngr.
Ghaziabad, Uttar
Pradesh-201007
India
TEL : +91(0)120 4627318
FAX : +91(0)120 4721508

TESTERS

Elmech Pneumatic Industries Pvt. Ltd.
DDA Sheds, 103 Type-A
Phase-II
Okhla Indl. Area
New Delhi,
NCT of Delhi-110020
India
TEL : +91 (0) 11 6841320
FAX : +91 (0) 11 6841369
E-mail:
elemech@ndf.vsnl.net.in

Hydraulic & Engg. Instruments
P. O. Box 10215, A-13,
Phase-II
Naraina Indl. Area
New Delhi,
NCT of Delhi-110028
India
TEL : +91 (0) 11 5701151
FAX : +91 (0) 11 5700237
E-mail:
heico@del2.vsnl.net.in

Precision Standard Testing Equipment Corp.
C-117, FF Cmplx.,
Phase-III
Okhla Indl. Area
New Delhi,
NCT of Delhi-110020
India
TEL : +91 (0) 11 6915846
FAX : +91 (0) 11 6834850
E-mail: presto@vsnl.com

Prolific Engineers
D-91, Sect. 2
Noida,
Uttar Pradesh-201301
India
TEL : +91 (0) 120 4524251
FAX : +91 (0) 120 4522648
E-mail:
gkedia@ndf.vsnl.net.in

Test Master
C.No. 3, 1st Flr., 46
B B Ganguly St.
Kolkata,
West Bengal-700012
India
TEL : +91 (0) 33 2379836
FAX : +91 (0) 33 2379836

Specific Instruments
SNR Cmplx.
Neredmet X Rds.
Sainkpuri
Hyderabad, Andhra
Pradesh-500094
India
TEL : +91 (0) 40 7115275
FAX : +91 (0) 40 7116418
E-mail:
dattank@hd1.vsnl.net.in

LIQUID FILLING MACHINE

Delhi Packaging Services
B-1/160A
Vishnu Garden Extn.

New Delhi,
NCT of Delhi-110018
India
TEL : +91 (0) 11 5155295
FAX : +91 (0) 11 5557292
E-mail:
packode@delhipackaging.com

Join Pack India Pvt. Ltd.
19/21, Shakti Ngr.
Delhi, NCT of Delhi-110007
India
TEL : +91 (0) 11 7436892
FAX : +91 (0) 11 7125360
E-mail:
pack_mach@satyam.net.in

R D Singal & Co
A-81/2
Wazirpur Indl. Area
Delhi, NCT of Delhi-110052
India
TEL : +91 (0) 11 7242692
FAX : +91 (0) 11 7187224

Rajat Electronics
3704, Charkhewalan
St. Lohe Wali
Chawri Bazar
Delhi, NCT of Delhi-110006
India
TEL : +91 (0) 11 3913742
FAX : +91 (0) 11 3915525

Mamata Machinery Pvt. Ltd.
5/1/1A, Phase-I
GIDC, Ahmedabad,
Gujarat-382445
India
TEL : +91 (0) 79 5832023
FAX : +91 (0) 79 5832026
E-mail:
mmpl@ad1.vsnl.net.in
www.mamata.com

Bharati Trade & Engg. Enterprise
16, Gayatri Chmbrs.
Nr. GD High School
Krishnanagar Rd.
Saijpur Bogha
Ahmedabad,
Gujarat-382345
India
TEL : +91 (0) 79 2812291
FAX : +91 (0) 79 2823201

Maruti Auto-Mac Engineers
3, Lilabhai Est.
B/h Matru Chhaya
Vidhyalaya
Rajendra Park
Odhav, Gujarat-382415
India
TEL : +91 (0) 79 2975760
FAX : +91 (0) 79 2975760
E-mail:
maruti_123@yahoo.com

Precision Machine Tools
136, Vikas Indl. Est.
Opp. Anil Starch
Bapunagar
Ahmedabad, Gujarat-380024
India
TEL : +91 (0) 79 2123342
FAX : +91 (0) 79 2125754
E-mail:
precisionmachine@yahoo.com

Protech Engineers (I)
884/3-4, GIDC
Makarpura
Vadodara, Gujarat-390010
India
TEL : +91 (0) 265 641478
FAX : +91 (0) 265 641478
E-mail:
protech_in@yahoo.com

Radhe Marketing Pvt. Ltd
211, VIP View
VIP Rd., Karelibaug
Vadodara, Gujarat-390018
India
TEL : +91 (0) 265 447296
FAX : +91 (0) 265 447296
E-mail:
sales@safetycaps.com

RCS Engg. Works
22, Ajay Est.,
Opp. Dena Bank
Uttam Dairy Rd.
Rakhial
Ahmedabad,
Gujarat-380023
India
TEL : +91 (0) 79 2740022

Aprotech Engineers Pvt. Ltd.
1573, Sect. 7E
Faridabad,
Haryana-121006
India
TEL : +91 (0) 129 5242140
FAX : +91 (0) 129 5243452
E-mail: aprotech@vsnl.com

Baba Packaging
14, Krishna Palace
Neelam Flyover
Faridabad,
Haryana-121007
India
TEL : +91 (0) 129 5291107
FAX : +91 (0) 129 5240741
E-mail:
baba@ndb.vsnl.net.in

E C Packaging Pvt. Ltd.
14/7, Mile Stone
Mathura Rd.
Faridabad,
Haryana-121003
India
TEL : +91 (0) 129 5277796
FAX : +91 (0) 129 5255602
E-mail:
ecppl@del3.vsnl.net.in

Ganga Packaging
279-C, Sect. 59
HSIDC Indl. Est.
Faridabad,
Haryana-121004
India
TEL : +91 (0) 129 5441224
FAX : +91 (0) 129 5440063
E-mail:
gangapac@mantraonline.com

Glaxy Packaging Machines
Nr. Novelty Cinema
Circular Rd.
Ambala City,
Haryana-134002
India
TEL : +91 (0) 171 518515
FAX : +91 (0) 171 518517

Sevana Electrical Appliances Pvt. Ltd.
X/106, P.O. Box 2
Kizhakkambalam,
Kerala-683562
India
TEL : +91 (0) 484 680780
FAX : +91 (0) 484 680680
E-mail: seal@sevana.com

Limco
1426, Kasba Peth
Phadke Haud Chowk
Pune, Maharashtra-411011
India
TEL : +91 (0) 20 4454306

Accurate Weighing Machines Co.
139, Motishah lane
Prabhatwadi, Byculla
Mumbai,
Maharashtra-400001
India
TEL : +91 (0) 22 3774308
FAX : +91 (0) 22 3732091
E-mail: acuweigh@vsnl.com

Apollo Glass Containers
7, J K Indl. Est.
Off Mahakali Caves Rd.
Andheri (E), Mumbai,
Maharashtra-400093
India
TEL : +91 (0) 22 8329530
FAX : +91 (0) 22 8363208

Automatic Devices
105 A, Hind Saurashtra
Indl. Est., Marol
Andheri-Kurla Rd.
Andheri (E), Mumbai,
Maharashtra-400059
India
TEL : +91 (0) 22 8501376
FAX : +91 (0) 22 8593042
E-mail:
autodevices@vsnl.com

Autopack Machines Pvt. Ltd.
101-C, Poonam Chmbrs.
Dr. Annie Besant Rd.
Worli, Mumbai,
Maharashtra-400018
India
TEL : +91 (0) 22 4924806
FAX : +91 (0) 22 4964926
E-mail:
autopack@bom3.vsnl.net.in

Bectochem Engineers
5C/204, Sanjay Bldg.
Mittal Indl. Est.
Andheri (E), Mumbai,
Maharashtra-400059
India
TEL : +91 (0) 22 8500008
FAX : +91 (0) 22 8506785
E-mail:
bectochem@vsnl.com

Arunatts Industries
60,SIDCO Indl. Est.
Chennai,
Tamil Nadu-600098
India
TEL : +91 (0) 44 6252683

Kanchana Pack Machins
No. 213, New Tiny Sect.,
Indl. Est., Ambattur
Chennai,
Tamil Nadu-600058
India
TEL : +91 (0) 44 6256005

M G Industries
9/A/1, Avinashi Rd.
Aerodrome Post
Coimbatore,
Tamil Nadu-641014
India
TEL : +91 (0) 422 571235
FAX : +91 (0) 422 235297
E-mail: mgi@vsnl.com

Plastopack Machineries (I) Pvt. Ltd.
B-15, Mugappair Indl.
Est. (W)
Chennai,
Tamil Nadu-600058
India
TEL : +91 (0) 44 6246283

Shivsu Watek Pvt. Ltd.
14, Spurtank Rd.
Chetput, Chennai,
Tamil Nadu-600031
India
TEL : +91 (0) 44 8266075
FAX : +91 (0) 44 8256606

Authentic Designer's
C-112, Sect. 10
Noida,
Uttar Pradesh-201301
India
TEL : +91 (0) 120 4540451
FAX : +91 (0) 120 4543233
E-mail:
authdesi@nda.vsnl.net.in

B R Pouch Packing
Machines Pvt. Ltd.
C-22/15, Sect.-57
Noida,
Uttar Pradesh-201301
India
TEL : +91 (0) 120 4580829
FAX : +91 (0) 120 4584930

Cannon Engg. Industries
7-152/7, G-21, Ravi Cmplx.
Fathenagar
Hyderabad,
Andhra Pradesh-500018
India
TEL : +91 (0) 40 3774967
FAX : +91 (0) 40 3779156
E-mail:
info@cannonindia.com

Eclat Auto Packs Pvt. Ltd.
No. 2-4-82, 301, 3rd Flr.
Misha Gardens, Shamalal
Est., Sikh Rd.
Secunderabad, Andhra

Pradesh-500009
India
TEL : +91 (0) 40 7818896
FAX : +91 (0) 40 7729132
E-mail:
eclatap@satyam.net.in

Kavacha Engg.
Plot No. D-45
Electronic Cmplx.
Kushaiguda
Hyderabad,
Andhra Pradesh-500062
India
TEL : +91 (0) 40 7123665
FAX : +91 (0) 40 7120892

Pack-Tech Engg. Industries
Plot No. 25
E C Extn., Phase-II
Kushaiguda
Hyderabad,
Andhra Pradesh-500062
India
TEL : +91 (0) 40 7125029

Automatic Devices
105 A
Hind Saurashtra Indl. Est.,
Marol
Andheri-Kurla Rd.
Andheri (E), Mumbai,
Maharashtra-400059
India
TEL : +91 (0) 22 8501376
FAX : +91 (0) 22 8593042
E-mail:
autodevices@vsnl.com

Autopack Machines Pvt. Ltd.
101-C, Poonam Chmbrs.
Dr. Annie Besant Rd.
Worli, Mumbai,
Maharashtra-400018
India
TEL : +91 (0) 22 4924806
FAX : +91 (0) 22 4964926
E-mail:
autopack@bom3.vsnl.net.in

Bectochem Engineers
5C/204, Sanjay Bldg.
Mittal Indl. Est.
Andheri (E), Mumbai,
Maharashtra-400059
India
TEL : +91 (0) 22 8500008
FAX : +91 (0) 22 8506785
E-mail:
bectochem@vsnl.com

Elegant Engineers
D-352, Sect. 10
Noida,
Uttar Pradesh-201301
India
TEL : +91 (0) 120 4525503
FAX : +91 (0) 120 4444892
E-mail:
elegant11@satyam.net.in

KBK Plascon Pvt. Ltd.
24/168, P.O.Box 158
Birhana Rd., Kanpur,
Uttar Pradesh-208001
India
TEL : +91 (0) 512 369353
FAX : +91 (0) 512 352058
E-mail: kbk@sancharnet.in

Rado Packaging Machines Pvt. Ltd.
A-41, Sect. 10
Noida,
Uttar Pradesh-201301
India
TEL : +91 (0) 120 4555190
FAX : +91 (0) 120 4525699

Chapter - 33

SUPPLIERS OF PACKAGING MATERIALS

CONTAINERS

Agra Bottle Stores
17/37, Prayag Market,
Old Banaras Bank,
Phulatti Bazar,
Agara-282003 (U.P)
Phone : 367158,368116

Anand Timber Traders
170, Reay Road,
Mumbai-400010
Phones :
8725768,8121224,
8514650,8512098

Arora Metal Industry,
Ist Floor, 66,Ezra Street,
(G.P.O Box No. 2289),
Kolkata-700001
Phone : (033)
2254367,2254170
Gram. Metal Seal

Bajaj Glass Enterprises,
B-5/10, Mahesh Nagar,
Goregaon (w),
Mumbai-400062
Phones : 6723867

Bharat Associated Industries
P-5, B.R.B. Basu Road,
2nd Floor,
Kolkata-700001
Phones : 317470

LABLES

Agra Bottle Stores,
17/37, Prayag Market,
Old Banaras Bank
Phulatti Bazar,
Agra-282003
(U.P)
Phone : 367158,368116

Divya
25, Band Street,
Fort, Mumbai-400023
Phone : 2664396

Kiv Group Industries,
Sunmill Compound,
Lower Parel,
Mumbai-400003

Open Foils Enterprises,
Plot No. 403/1,
Opposite Gurukul,
Sector 22, Gandhinagar-382022
(Gujarat)
Phone : 91-0-2712-24422

Reliable Printers
170, Mahatma Gandhi Road,
Kolkata-700007

PAPER WAXED

Aryan Chemicals
Maharshi Dayanand Marg,
Near Railway Line,
Saijpur Bogha,
Ahmedabad-382345
Phone : 2816331-32-2822933
Fax : 91-79-2821441

Arya Printing Press,
Maharshi Dayanand Marg,
Nr Rly. Line, Saijpur Bogha,
Ahmedabad-382345
Phone :2816331-32-2822333,
Gram. ARYAPRESS,
Fax : 91-79-2821441
E-Mail :
aryanChemicals@hotmail.com.

Manish Printing & Packaging,
Maharshi Dayanand Marg.
Saijpur Bogha,
Ahmedabad-382345
(Gujarat)
Phones : 816331-32-33-34,
Fax : 91-79-8515441,

WRAPPERS

Paper Products Ltd.
120, Dinshaw Wacha Road,
Mumbai-400001

Subnil Packing Machines Pvt. Ltd
Shed No.37, Road, No.1,
IDA Mallapur, Nacharam,
Hyderabad-500076 (A.P.)
Phone : 91-40-7176810,
Fax : 91-40-7176841
E-Mail : works@subnil.com

Chapter - 34

SUPPLIERS OF RAW MATERIALS

Gayatri Starchkem Ltd.
6-3-1090, T S R Towers
Rajbhavan Rd.
Somajiguda
Hyderabad, Andhra
Pradesh-500082
India
TEL : +91 (0) 40 3324444
FAX : +91 (0) 40 3321424

Pumax Chemicals Pvt. Ltd.
50, Ground Flr.
Opp. Vikrampuri
HACP Cly.,Secunderabad,
Andhra Pradesh-500009
India
TEL : +91 (0) 40 7810247
FAX : +91 (0) 40 7848157
E-mail:
pumax@satyam.net.in

Sree Rama Resins & Chemicals
7-21/1, IDA, Subhash Ngr.
Jeedimetla
Hyderabad, Andhra
Pradesh-500055
India
TEL : +91 (0) 40 3079302

Sri Annapurna Chemical Industries
Flat-71, Block-12
Municipal Cly., Malakpet
Hyderabad, Andhra
Pradesh-500036
India
TEL : +91 (0) 40 4548600
FAX : +91 (0) 40 4548605
E-mail: gudisrr@hd1.vsnl.net.in

Aerotech India Pvt. Ltd.
202, Shivam House
Karampura Comml. Cmplx.
New Delhi,
NCT of Delhi-110015
India
TEL : +91 (0) 11 5433375

FAX : +91 (0) 11 5459768
E-mail:
headoffice@aerotech.
wipro.net.in

Carbon India
152-153, Ajmeri Gate
Delhi,
NCT of Delhi-110006
India
TEL : +91 (0) 11 3236666
FAX : +91 (0) 11 3237383

Chowdhry Rubber & Chemical Co.
1403, Pan Mandi
Sadar Bazar
Delhi,
NCT of Delhi-110006
India
TEL : +91 (0) 11 3673373
FAX : +91 (0) 11 7534153

Hindustan Rasayan Pvt. Ltd.
705, Vikram Towers
Rajendra Palace
New Delhi,
NCT of Delhi-110008
India
TEL : +91 (0) 11 5750215
FAX : +91 (0) 11 5789698

Industrial Coatings & Adhesives
A-679/A, Shastri Ngr.
Delhi,
NCT of Delhi-110052
India
TEL : +91 (0) 11 3551487

Kansal Chemicals Pvt. Ltd.
26, St. No. 3
Friends Cly. Indl. Area
Shahdara
Delhi, NCT of Delhi-110095
India
TEL : +91 (0) 11 2113488
FAX : +91 (0) 11 2293488

Rastogi Shell Oils Pvt. Ltd.
5A/14, Ansari Rd.
Daryaganj
New Delhi,
NCT of Delhi-110002
India
TEL : +91 (0) 11 3276075
E-mail:
ggsons@mantraonline.com

Sandvik Chemicals & Plasticizers Pvt. Ltd.
C 15/2
Mansarovar Garden
New Delhi,
NCT of Delhi-110015
India
TEL : +91 (0) 11 5191958
FAX : +91 (0) 11 5191958

Shakti Minerals & Chemicals
1/2222, Ram Ngr.
Mandoli Rd.
Shahdara
Delhi, NCT of Delhi-
110032
India
TEL : +91 (0) 11 2283065
FAX : +91 (0) 11 2297381

Cosmos Chemicals
760, GIDC Est.
Makarpura
Vadodara, Gujarat-390010
India
TEL : +91 (0) 265 642064

Gujarat State Fertilizers & Chemicals Ltd.
Polymers Unit
P.O. Petrofils
Vadodara, Gujarat-391347
India
TEL : +91 (0) 265 373341
FAX : +91 (0) 265 372794
E-mail:
gafcpu@gsfcho.xeebdq.
xeemail.com

Precious Chemicals
88, Gandhinagar Cly.
Karelibaug
Vadodara, Gujarat-390001
India
TEL : +91 (0) 265 422716
FAX : +91 (0) 265 270373
E-mail:
sureshapatel@icent.com

Samkap Chemicals Ltd.
9th Flr.
Ramkrishna Chmbrs.
Productivity Rd.
Alkapuri
Vadodara, Gujarat-390005
India
TEL : +91 (0) 265 331917
FAX : +91 (0) 265 331917

Shreeji Chem
Plot No. 2210
Nr. Post Office
GIDC Est.
Ankleshwar,
Gujarat-393002
India
TEL : +91 (0) 2646 52476

Sree Guru Enterprises
18,Ibrahim Shah Cmplx.
Godown St.
S P Rd.
Bangalore,
Karnataka-560002
India
TEL : +91 (0) 80 6614645

A & M Group
P.O. Box 5653
Dadar, Mumbai,
Maharashtra-400014
India
TEL : +91 (0) 22 4142634
FAX : +91 (0) 22 4135638

Alginates Allied Chemicals Pvt. Ltd.
Plot A-41, MIDC
Badlapur
Thane,
Maharashtra-421503
India
TEL : +91 (0) 251 690224
FAX : +91 (0) 251 557434
E-mail:
gosain@bom5.vsnl.net.in

Ashok Alco-Chem Ltd.
406, Sharda Chmbrs.,
33, New Marine Lines
Mumbai,
Maharashtra-400020
India
TEL : +91 (0) 22 2056410
FAX : +91 (0) 22 2089456

Auchtel Products Ltd.
142/C, 2nd Flr.,
Victor House
N M Joshi Marg
Lower Parel
Mumbai,
Maharashtra-400013
India
TEL : +91 (0) 22 4933975
FAX : +91 (0) 22 4939755

Bentec Organoclays Pvt. Ltd.
204, Madhu Indl. Est.
Mogra Village Rd.
Andheri (E)
Mumbai,
Maharashtra-400069
India
TEL : +91 (0) 22 8215381
FAX : +91 (0) 22 8201750
E-mail:
bentec@bom3vsnl.net.in

Coatwell Paints
6/19
Tardeo Air Conditioned Mkt.
Tardeo, Mumbai,
Maharashtra-400034
India
TEL : +91 (0) 22 4941271
FAX : +91 (0) 22 4971533
E-mail: coatwell@vsnl.net

Dura Chemical Corporation Pvt. Ltd.
11, Sprott Rd.
Ballard Est.
Mumbai,
Maharashtra-400038
India
TEL : +91 (0) 22 2610264
FAX : +91 (0) 22 2617352

Eon Chemicals Pvt. Ltd.
15/20, Loha Bhavan
P D Mello Rd.
Masjid Bunder,
Mumbai,
Maharashtra-400009
India
TEL : +91 (0) 22 3448625
FAX : +91 (0) 22 3401619
E-mail: eonchem@giasbm01.vsnl.net.in

Fine Organics
Fine House
Anandji St., Off M G Rd.
Ghatkopar (E)
Mumbai,
Maharashtra-400077
India
TEL : +91 (0) 22 5148101
FAX : +91 (0) 22 5153215
E-mail: fine@vsnl.com

Gomati Chemicals Pvt. Ltd.
Bhagwat, 1st Flr.
N S Rd., 2
Vile Parle (W)
Mumbai,
Maharashtra-400056
India
TEL : +91 (0) 22 6183623
FAX : +91 (0) 22 6147720

Jain & Jain
21, Shamsheth St.
Mumbai,
Maharashtra-400002
India
TEL : +91 (0) 22 3423097
FAX : +91 (0) 22 3434898
E-mail: jain-rk@vsnl.com

Jaya Non Ionics Pvt. Ltd.
Jaya Est.,
Jaya Talkies Bldg.
S V Rd., Borivili (W)
Mumbai,
Maharashtra-400001
India
TEL : +91 (0) 22 8981134
FAX : +91 (0) 22 8985708
E-mail: viren@vsnl.com

Jayant Oil Mills
13, Sitafalwadi
Dr. Mascarenhas Rd., P.O. Box 6209
Mazgaon, Mumbai,
Maharashtra-400010
India
TEL : +91 (0) 22 3738810
FAX : +91 (0) 22 3738107
E-mail:
udeshi@giasbmo1.vsnl.net.in

L N Chemical Industries
150,Adarsh Indl. Est.
Sahar Rd., Chakala
Andheri (E), Mumbai,
Maharashtra-400099
India
TEL : +91 (0) 22 8225719
FAX : +91 (0) 22 8366434
E-mail: inchem@vsnl.com

Laffans Petrochemicals Ltd.
10, Luthra Indl. Est.
Safed Pool
Saki Naka, Andheri
Mumbai,
Maharashtra-400072
India
TEL : +91 (0) 22 8511919
FAX : +91 (0) 22 8513186

Mehta Petro Refineries Ltd.
50 Raja Bahadur Bldg.
128/132, Kazi Syed St.
Masjid Bunder
Mumbai,
Maharashtra-400003
India
TEL : +91 (0) 22 3415266
FAX : +91 (0) 22 8980360
E-mail: calichem@bol.net.in

Modhera Chemicals Pvt. Ltd.
101-A
Sanjay Bldg. No. 2
Mittal Indl. Est., Andheri
Kurla Rd., Andheri (E)
Mumbai,
Maharashtra-400059
India

TEL : +91 (0) 22 8500179
FAX : +91 (0) 22 8503534
E-mail: modhera@vsnl.com

Pidilite Industries Ltd.
Rama Krishna Mandir Rd.
Off Marol Vasanji Rd.
Andheri (E), Mumbai,
Maharashtra-400059
India
TEL : +91 (0) 22 8387240
FAX : +91 (0) 22 8384989

RSB Chemical Industries
T-136, MIDC
Bhosari
Pune, Maharashtra-411026
India
TEL : +91 (0) 20 7120805
FAX : +91 (0) 20 7122516
E-mail: rsbchem@vsnl.com

Rupani Chemical Industries Pvt. Ltd.
35/36
Sidhpura Indl. Est.
Masrani Lane
Kurla, Mumbai,
Maharashtra-400070
India
TEL : +91 (0) 22 5145455
FAX : +91 (0) 22 5145455

Selective Minerals & Color Inds Pvt. Ltd.
1, Sonu Bldg.
28th Rd.
Off Waterfield Rd.
Mumbai,
Maharashtra-400050
India
TEL : +91 (0) 22 6431789
FAX : +91 (0) 22 6437732

Sunshield Chemicals Ltd.
Janki Niwas
N C Kelkar Rd., Dadar
Mumbai,
Maharashtra-400028
India
TEL : +91 (0) 22 4313265
FAX : +91 (0) 22 4307094
E-mail:
sunshild@bom4.vsnl.net.in

Eddy Chemical Pvt. Ltd.
F 43-44, Phase-VII
Focal Point
Ludhiana, Punjab-141010
India
TEL : +91 (0) 161 674963
FAX : +91 (0) 161 675307

Anabond Ltd.
Functional Chemicals Divn.
3rd Flr., No. 3-A
Adyar Bridge Rd.
Adyar, Chennai,
Tamil Nadu-600020
India
TEL : +91 (0) 44 4900728
FAX : +91 (0) 44 4919105
E-mail:
anamarke@vsnl.com

Karmen International Pvt. Ltd.
Developed Plot No. 31A/20
North Phase,
SIDCO Indl. Est.
Ambattur, Chennai,
Tamil Nadu-600098
India
TEL : +91 (0) 44 6251831
FAX : +91 (0) 44 6251831
E-mail: karmen@vsnl.com

Malpro Silica Pvt. Ltd.
400
Bhavani Main Rd.
Ashokapuram
Erode, Tamil Nadu-638004
India
TEL : +91 (0) 424 293474
FAX : +91 (0) 424 293894
E-mail: malpro@vsnl.com

Pneumatic Atomising Mills Pvt. Ltd.
29/2, Sembhudoss St.
Chennai,
Tamil Nadu-600001
India
TEL : +91 (0) 44 5226831
FAX : +91 (0) 44 5224087
E-mail:
pamltd@rediffmail.com

Tetrahedron Ltd.
17/A, SIDCO Indl. Est.
Chennai,
Tamil Nadu-600098
India
TEL : +91 (0) 44 652973
FAX : +91 (0) 44 6257220
E-mail:
sales@tetrahedronltd.com

Thirumalai Chemicals Ltd.
Lakshmi Towers, 1st Flr.
48, N Usman Rd.
T Ngr., Chennai,
Tamil Nadu-600017
India
TEL : +91 (0) 44 8255289
FAX : +91 (0) 44 8257637

Trichy Distilleries & Chemicals Ltd.
14, Mahalakshmi Mansion
Gandhi Ngr.
1st Main Rd., Adyar
Chennai,
Tamil Nadu-600020
India
TEL : +91 (0) 44 4417791
FAX : +91 (0) 44 4917796
E-mail:
tdc@md3.vsnl.net.in

Atoot Udyog Samuha
2(A)/113
Azadnagar
Nawabganj, Kanpur,
Uttar Pradesh-208002
India
TEL : +91 (0) 512 560244
FAX : +91 (0) 512 692578
E-mail:
nssathe@rediffmail.com

Paswara Petrochem Ltd.
Paswara House
Baghpat Rd.
Meerut,
Uttar Pradesh-250001
India

TEL : +91 (0) 121 510015
FAX : +91 (0) 121 526873
E-mail:
paswara@ndf.vsnl.net.in

Ambe Sneyo Oxides Ltd.
Central Plaza, 2/6
Sarat Bose Rd.
Kolkata,
West Bengal-700020
India
TEL : +91 (0) 33 4745234

Gem Chemicals Industries
Suite F, 4th Flr., 25
R N Mukherjee Rd.
Kolkata,
West Bengal-700001
India
TEL : +91 (0) 33 2483650

Golchha Pigments Pvt. Ltd.
Suite No. 406, 6
Brabourne Rd.
Kolkata,
West Bengal-700001
India
TEL : +91 (0) 33 2254690
FAX : +91 (0) 33 2250072
E-mail:
gp@golchhapigments.com

Kolmak Chemicals Ltd.
21-A
Shakespeare Sarani
Kolkata,
West Bengal-700017
India
TEL : +91 (0) 33 2477512
FAX : +91 (0) 33 2406476
E-mail:
tioxide@cal2.vsnl.net.in

Kumar Chemical Industries
78, Bentinck St.
Kolkata,
West Bengal-700001
India
TEL : +91 (0) 33 2362368
FAX : +91 (0) 33 2363278
E-mail:
kci@cal3.vsnl.net.in

Nirkon International Ltd.
3rd Flr., 11
Pollock St.
Kolkata,
West Bengal-700001
India
TEL : +91 (0) 33 2352188

Passari Cellulose Ltd.
4, Ho Chi Minh Sarani
Kolkata,
West Bengal-700071
India
TEL : +91 (0) 33 2824868
FAX : +91 (0) 33 2824451
E-mail: popl@caltiger.com

Pinkto Chemicals
48/3P, B T Rd.
P.O. Sinthee
Kolkata,
West Bengal-700050
India
TEL : +91 (0) 33 5531256
FAX : +91 (0) 33 5578137
E-mail: pinkto@vsnl.com

Precision Balance (I)
6, Wood St.
Kolkata,
West Bengal-700016
India
TEL : +91 (0) 33 2403476
FAX : +91 (0) 33 2400168

Seth Chemical Works Pvt. Ltd.
13, Camac St.
Kolkata,
West Bengal-700017
India
TEL : +91 (0) 33 2476562
FAX : +91 (0) 33 2401736

W B Chemical Industries Ltd.
Powertool Bhavan, 3rd
Flr., 2, BBD Bag (E)
Kolkata,
West Bengal-700001
India
TEL : +91 (0) 33 2481340
FAX : +91 (0) 33 2430571

PAINT COLOURS

20 Microns Ltd.
307-308
Arundeep Cmplx.
Race Course (S)
Vadodara, Gujarat-390007
India
TEL : +91 (0) 265 330714
FAX : +91 (0) 265 335755
E-mail:
20microns@pi.zaverchand.coin

Alpanil Industries
81, Phase II
GIDC Est. (Vatva)
Ahmedabad,
Gujarat-382445
India
TEL : +91 (0) 79 5833940
FAX : +91 (0) 79 5833403
E-mail: alpanil@vsnl.com

AMI Pigments Pvt. Ltd.
Plot No.627
Nr. Mardia Steel
GIDC, Phase-IV
Vatva, Ahmedabad,
Gujarat-382445
India
TEL : +91 (0) 79 5830235
FAX : +91 (0) 79 5836462

Asahi Songwon Colors Ltd.
30, Ambica Society,
Usmanpura, Ahmedabad,
Gujarat-380013
India
TEL : +91 (0) 79 7550044
FAX : +91 (0) 79 7551255
E-mail:
ali.ahm@audichem.sril.in

Atlanta Pigments Pvt. Ltd.
C1-89/12
Phase-I, GIDC, Vatva
Ahmedabad,

Gujarat-382445
India
TEL : +91 (0) 79 5893344
FAX : +91 (0) 79 5831134

Avee Rang Rasayan
1/B, Krupasagar Soc.
Shantivan Narayan Ngr.
Paldi
Ahmedabad,
Gujarat-380007
India
TEL : +91 (0) 79 5834748
FAX : +91 (0) 79 6633113

Devarsons Industries Ltd.
443, GIDC Indl. Est.
Nr. Water Tank
Odhav, Gujarat-382415
India
TEL : +91 (0) 79 2871092
E-mail:
devarson.coldyes@gnahd.global.net.in

Mira Chemicals
Plot No. 618, GIDC
Panoli, Gujarat-394116
India
TEL : +91 (0) 2646 72573
FAX : +91 (0) 2646 72513

Pratiksha Chemicals Ltd.
3rd Flr.
H K Cmplx., Nr. Dharnidhar
Derasar, Paldi
Ahmedabad,
Gujarat-380007
India
TEL : +91 (0) 79 6632265
FAX : +91 (0) 79 6612843
E-mail: exports@dhara-pratiksha.com

ABC Chemical Exports Pvt. Ltd.
104/105
Dhamji Shamji Udyog
Bhawan
Veera Desai Rd.
Andheri (W), Mumbai,
Maharashtra-400053
India
TEL : +91 (0) 22 6325545
FAX : +91 (0) 22 6321557
E-mail:
abc@bom3.vsnl.net.in

Bagadia Colourchem Ltd.
Bagadia House, 23-B
Kasba Peth
Pune,
Maharashtra-411011
India
TEL : +91 (0) 20 4455443
FAX : +91 (0) 20 4459972

Colour-Chem Ltd.
Ravindra Annexe, 194
Churchgate Reclamation
Mumbai,
Maharashtra-400020
India
TEL : +91 (0) 22 2022161
FAX : +91 (0) 22 2029781
E-mail:
colrchem@bom3.vsnl.net.in

Diamond Chemicals
S-66, MIDC
Bhosari
Pune, Maharashtra-411026
India
TEL : +91 (0) 20 623230

Ducol Organic & Colours Pvt. Ltd.
15
Old Bangalipura
Mumbai,
Maharashtra-400003
India
TEL : +91 (0) 22 3429601
FAX : +91 (0) 22 3429601

Dwarkesh Organics Pvt. Ltd.
43, 3rd Flr., Off. No. 27
Veer Vithaldas Chandan
St.
Masjid Bunder Rd.
Mumbai,
Maharashtra-400003
India
TEL : +91 (0) 22 3429373
FAX : +91 (0) 22 3433798

Highland Organic Pigments Ltd.
25, Kembros Indl. Est.
Off LBS Marg, Sonapur
Lane
Bhandup, Mumbai,
Maharashtra-400078
India
TEL : +91 (0) 22 5670346
FAX : +91 (0) 22 5670346
E-mail: pigment@vsnl.com

Imperial Pigments
M B House, 1st Flr., 79
Janmabhoomi Marg
Fort, Mumbai,
Maharashtra-400001
India
TEL : +91 (0) 22 2870675
FAX : +91 (0) 22 2870801
E-mail:
kotwal@bom3.vsnl.net.in

Jayant Color & Chemical Industries
Tulsiram Gupta Mills Est.
Darukhana, Reay Rd.
Mumbai,
Maharashtra-400010
India
TEL : +91 (0) 22 3721249
FAX : +91 (0) 22 3775814
E-mail:
admin@jayantcolor.com

Jaysynth Dyechem Ltd.
301, 3rd Flr., Sumer Kendra
P B Marg, Worli
Mumbai,
Maharashtra-400018
India
TEL : +91 (0) 22 4937291
FAX : +91 (0) 22 4950489
E-mail:
jaysynth@bom3.vsnl.net.in

Kanak Pigments Pvt. Ltd.
3, Akshay, 95/2
Rly. Lines
Solapur,
Maharashtra-413001

India
TEL : +91 (0) 217 620376
FAX : +91 (0) 217 315280
E-mail: dawda@vsnl.com

Pidilite Industries Ltd.
Rama Krishna Mandir Rd.
Off Marol Vasanji Rd.
Andheri (E)
Mumbai,
Maharashtra-400059
India
TEL : +91 (0) 22 8387240
FAX : +91 (0) 22 8384989

Shiva Dyestuff Pvt. Ltd.
6, Hari Nivas, 2nd Flr.
Carter Rd.No. 4
Borivali (E), Mumbai,
Maharashtra-400066
India
TEL : +91 (0) 22 8625555
FAX : +91 (0) 22 8060801

Shiva Pigments Pvt. Ltd.
6, Hari Nivas
Carter Rd. No. 4
Borivli (E), Mumbai,
Maharashtra-400066
India
TEL : +91 (0) 22 8625555
FAX : +91 (0) 22 8060801

Solar Dye Chem Pvt. Ltd.
112/3, Naran Baug
Senapati Bapat Marg
Mahim, Mumbai,
Maharashtra-400016
India
TEL : +91 (0) 22 4372021
FAX : +91 (0) 22 3737887
E-mail:
bhushan@hotmail.com

Soujanya Enterprises
103, 'D', Wing Sita Vihar,
Damani Est., LBS Marg
Naupada, Thane,
Maharashtra-400602
India
TEL : +91 (0) 22 5426756
FAX : +91 (0) 22 5408182
E-mail: jashan@vsnl.com

Sudarshan Chemical Industries Ltd.
162, Wellesley Rd.
Pune,
Maharashtra-411001
India
TEL : +91 (0) 20 6127334
FAX : +91 (0) 20 6125900
E-mail:
scil@giaspn01.vsnl.net.in

Ultramarine & Pigments Ltd.
Plot No. 101-102, Ston
Matunga Est.
Scheme No. 6, Nr. Sion
Fort, Rd. No. 29, Sion (E)
Mumbai,
Maharashtra-400021
India
TEL : +91 (0) 22 7017834
FAX : +91 (0) 22 2042162
E-mail:
thiraomalai@gnbom/
tcl.global.net.in

Vardhaman Dyestuff Industries Pvt. Ltd.
Vardhman Mansion, 110
Keshavji Naik Rd.
Chinch Bunder
Mumbai,
Maharashtra-400009
India
TEL : +91 (0) 22 3747074
FAX : +91 (0) 22 3737887
E-mail:
green@giasbm01.vsnl.net.in

Tamilnad Pigments Pvt. Ltd.
A-6/3, SIPCOT Indl.
Cmplx., Cuddalore,
Tamil Nadu-607005
India
TEL :+91(0)4142 339525
FAX :+91(0)4142 339525

Tamilnadu Pigments Pvt. Ltd.
A-6/3, SIPCOT Indl.
Cmplx., Cuddalore,
Tamil Nadu-607005
India
TEL : +91 (0) 4142 39565
FAX : +91 (0) 4142 39525
E-mail:
tnblue@md3.vsnl.net.in

The Tata Pigments Ltd.
`Tata Centre', 43
Chowringhee Rd.
Kolkata,
West Bengal-700071
India
TEL : +91(0)33 2403783
FAX : +91(0)33 2403783

Alishan Paints (I)
47/2, Hastsal Village
Uttam Ngr., New Delhi,
NCT of Delhi-110059
India
TEL : +91(0)11 5648218
FAX : +91(0)11 5635908

Mayur Paints (I) Pvt. Ltd.
74, Shardhanand Marg
Delhi,
NCT of Delhi-110006
India
TEL : +91 (0) 11 3963128
FAX : +91 (0) 11 3986561
E-mail:
paints@nda.vsnl.net.in

Orient Paint Industries
Plot No. 4
St. No. 4, New Rohtak Rd.
Anand Parbat Indl. Area
New Delhi,
NCT of Delhi-110005
India
TEL : +91 (0) 11 5725526

Shree Nathji Dyestuffs
R-60/1, Model Town-III
Delhi, NCT of Delhi-110009
India
TEL : +91 (0) 11 7133896
FAX : +91 (0) 11 7444651
E-mail: jatin@satyam.net.in

Shankar Dyes and Chemicals
1209, Shankar Building,
Gali No. 11, Sadar Bazar,
Delhi - 110 006
Ph : 3673462, 3558239, 3616830
E-Mail : djeswani@sattiya.net.in
Website : www.shankardyesandchemicals.com

Chowdhry Rubber & Chemical Co.
1403, Pan Mandi, Sadar Bazar, Delhi - 110 006
Ph : 3634153, 3634380
Fax : 91-11-3634153

Advance Petrochemicals Ltd.
93, New Cloth Market,
Ahmedabad-380002
Gujarat
Phone : (079)-2124097, 2164795.
Fax : (079)-2165386, 5322219
E-Mail : goenka@wilnetonline.net.

Indokem Ltd.
Khatau House,
Plot No.410/411,
Mogul Lane, Mahim,
Mumbai-400016.
Phone : (022)-4461975, 4450050,
Fax : (022)-4458139
E-Mail : bombay@indokem.2.indokem.gems.vsnl.net.in
Website : www.indokem.com

Paras Minerals & Alloys
N-1A/27, Kirti Nagar,
New Delhi - 110 015
Ph : 5434766, 5414322, 5122484
Fax : 91-11-5121874

Pidilite Industries Ltd
Ramkrishna Mandir Road,
M.Vasanji Road, Andheri (E)
P.Bcx- 17411,
Mumbai - 400059
Phone : (022)-8387240, 41,42,
Fax : (022)-8384989, 8367241
E-Mail : pil@pidilite.com.
Website : www.pidilite.com.

AKD Polymers Pvt. Ltd.,
N-1A, Ist Floor, Kirti Complex,
Kirti Nagar, New Delhi - 110 015
Ph : 5105010, 5467322
Fax : 5448553
E-Mail : akdpoly@del3.vsnl.net.in

Virgo Pharma Chem
C-14, Gita Park,
Narayan Nagar,
N.H.8, P.O.Khodiyar Nagar,
Ahmedabad-3823352
Gujarat
Phone : (079)-2893215
Fax : (079)-2745841

All Chem Agencies
9, 1st Floor,
Janpath Commercial Complex,
Ellishridge, Ashram Road,
Ahmedabad-380006
Gujarat
Phone : (079)-6587067, 6580291
Fax : (079)-6587031

Amjay Impex P.Ltd
Anand Bldg. Suit No. 308,
3rd Floor, 62/84,
Kazi Sayed Street,
Mumbai-400003
Phone : (022)-3435906, 3432280
Fax : (022)-3434686

Byramjee Framjee & Co.
63/3, Mahatma Gandhi Road, Kanpur-208004,
Uttar Pradesh,
Phone : (0512)-369876, 300302,
Fax : (0512)-362270

Chemico International P.Ltd
A-75, Madhuban,
Vikas Marg, Delhi-110092
Phone : (011)-2230125, 2463154
Fax : (011)-2413155

Dhaval Industries
16/18, Garibdas Street,
8, Madiar Mansion,
Vadgadi - 400003
Phone : (022)-3437069, 3438556
Fax :(022)-3413783

General Traders
29 & 97, N.R.K. Rajarathinam Street,
Sivakasi - 626123
Tamil Nadu.
Phone : (04562)-74014, 74310,75310
Fax : (04562)-72810

Indian Overseas Corp
29, Abhechand Gandhi Marg,
Masjid Bunder (West)
P.O. Box-3445
Mumbai-400003
Phone : (022)-3420848, 3424222
Fax : (022)-3449490
E-Mail : ioc@vsnl.com
Website : http://www.ioconline.net.

Jeykey Chemicals
308, Anand Building,
82/84, Kazi Sayed Street,
Mumbai-400003
Phone : (022)-3432280, 3433357, 3435906
Fax : (022)-3434686

Kalpesh Industrial Corp
8, Mahavir Apartments,
S.L. Road,
Mulund, Mumbai-400080

Phone : (022)-5650888
Fax : (022)-3729051

Kamal Agencies
12, Badshah Ka Zanda,
Pali -306401, Rajasthan.
Phone : (02142)-22415, 23449, 25304,
Res-22455,26608
Fax : (02142)-23449

Manas Chemicals
Plot No. 257,
Aditi 101,
Sher-E-Punjab Society,
Andheri (E),
Mumbai-400093
Phone : (022)-8300556,
Fax : (022)-8312167

Mineral & Chemical Corp
4, Synagogue Street,
6th Floor, Room 605,
Kolkata - 700001
Phone : (033)-2424006, 2422167
Fax : (033)-2426685
Email : hiralal@cal.vsnl.net.in

Punam Enterprise
8, Sambhu Mullick Lane,
Singhania House,
Kolkata-700007
Phone :(033)-2331758, 2302585

Sagar Trading Co.
D/4, Sarvoday Estate,
B/h. Anand Hotel,
Near Shakti Estate,
Isanpur, Narol Road,
Ahmedabad-382443
Gujarat
Phone : (079)-5322096, 6740337

Tide Sales Corp
4, Ganesh Chandra Avenue,
5th Floor, Kolkata-700013
Phone- (033)-277699
Fax : (033)-273365

Chemet
Span Centre, 2nd Floor,
P.B.No. 26933,556
Ramkrishna Mission Road,
Santacruz (West),
Mumbai-400054
Phone : (022)-6045601
Fax : (022)-6484049
E-Mail : chemet.com@rme. sprintrp g.ems.vsnl.net.in

Degussa-Hills India P.Ltd.
12 A/A, Bakhtawar, 229,
Nariman Point,
Mumbai-400021
Phone : (022)-2307070
Fax : (022)-2307071
E-Mail : dhi@vsnl.com
Web : http://www.degussa-huels.com

Fortuna Marketing
5B/9, Sangeeta,
P.O.Box no. 18267,
Juhu Road,
Mumbai-400049

Solutia Chemicals India P.Ltd.
205-207, Midas Sahar
Plaza Complex.
Andheri (E)
Mumbai-400059
Phone : (022)-8302860, 8302864,
Fax : (022)-8302859
E-Mail : tarun.malkani@solutia.com.
Website : http:// www.solutia.com

CALCIUM CARBONATE

Akay Chemicals
5-J.V.Chotai Complex,
Vazari Chowk,
M.G.Road,
Junagarh 362001,
Gujarat
Phone : (0285)-625922, 651921,651990,625925, 650930,6223340.
Fax : (0285)-650930.

Chowdhry Rubber & Chemical Co.,
1403, Pan Mandi, Sadar
Bazar, Delhi - 110 006
Ph : 3634153, 3634380
Fax : 91-11-3634153

Gujarat Clay Mills P.Ltd.
Microfine House,
Qureshi Nagar,
Kurla (East),
Mumbai-400070.
Phone : (022)-5228688, 5228689
Fax : (022)-5230932

Gumpro Chem
56, C.P.Tank Road,
Mumbai-400004.
Phone : (022)-3827671, 3827672.
Fax : (022)-3804564.
Email : gumpro@vsnl.com.

Oswal Cable Products
A-93/1, Wazirpur Group
Ind. Area,
Delhi - 110 052
Ph : 7211108, 7228845
Fax : 91-11-7246570
E-Mail : ocp@mantraonline.com

K.Mohan & Co.
12/14, Moores Road,
Moores Garden,
Chennai 600006.
Phone : (044)-8271320, 8277704
Fax : (044)-8572388.
Email : kaymohan@vsnl.com.
Web:http// www.metroindia.com/ kaymohan.

Paras Minerals & Alloys
N-1A/27, Kirti Nagar, New
Delhi - 110 015
Ph : 5434766, 5414322, 5122484
Fax : 91-11-5121874

Lime Chemicals Ltd.
Prem Estate, 2nd Floor,
Near Sant Savater,
Cross Road No. 1,
Mustafa Bazar,
Mazgaon,Mumbai- 400010.
Phone : (022)-3714083,
3714151,
Fax : (022)3775647.
Email : info@limechem.com.
Web: http://
www.limechem.com.

Margee Minerals (P) Ltd.
711, Saffron Complex,
Fatehgunj,
Vadodara -390002,
Gujarat.
Phone : (0265)-786770.
Fax : (0265)-445103.

DRIER

AKD Polymers Pvt. Ltd.,
N-1A, Ist Floor,
Kirti Complex, Kirti Nagar,
New Delhi - 110 015
Ph : 5105010, 5467322
Fax : 5448553
E-Mail :
akdpoly@del3.vsnl.net.in

Arihant Dye-Stuffs (India)
6, Tripathi Sadan, 110,
S.V. Road, Jogeshwari (w),
Mumbai-400102.
Phone : (022)-6790450,
Fax : (022)-6797299.
Email :
ramesh@bom4.vsnl.net.in

Nixon Chemical P.Ltd.
Copper Roller's Premises,
2nd Floor, L.B.S. Marg,
Bhandup (West),
Mumbai-4000078.
Phone : (022)-5679134,
5679135.
Fax : (022)-5676519.
Email : lumipon@bom4.net.in

Dhaval Industries,
16/18, Garibdas Street 8,
Madiar Mansion, Vadgadi,
Mumbai-400 003.

General Traders.
29 & 97, N.R.K.
Rajarahinam Street,
Sivakasi -626123,
Tamil Nadu
Phone : (04562)-74014,
74310,
Fax : (04562)- 72810.

OMG Asia Pacific Co. Ltd.
208, Anand Estate,
189/A,
Sane Guruji Marg,
Mumbai-400011.
Phone : (022)-3010740.
Fax : (022)-3015106.
Email :
vsamir@bom5.vsnl.net.in.
Web : http://www.omgi.com.

TOLUENE

Allied Chemicals Corp.
658,G.I.D.C.Estate,
Road No. 54.
Makarpura,
Vadodara -390010,
Gujarat.
Phone : (0265)-642945
Fax : (0265)-332953

Ases Chemicals Works
Brahm Bagh, Jalori Gate,
Jodhpur -342001,
Rajasthan
Phone (0291)-30437,37882
Fax : (0291)-38266

LINSEED OIL

M.P.Dyechem Industries
59 & 63, Sector A,
Sanwer Road Industrial
Area,
Indore -452003,
Madhya Pradesh,
Phone : (0731)-
420325,420775
Fax : (0731)-420136

Viscus Oils P.Ltd.
55/1/2C, New Palasia,
Indore-452001,
Madhya Pradesh,
Phone : (0731)-533710,
432205
Fax : (0731)-431168,
538226
Telex : 0735-6313

TITANIUM DIOXIDE

Associated Cement Companies Ltd.
CRS Complex, LBS Marg,
Thane-400604.
Phone : (022)-5323631,
5320962
Fax : (022)-5320962
E-Mail :
rcd@giasbm01.vsnl.net.in

Bajaj Rubber Co.
15, Khurshid Market,
Sadar Bazar,
Delhi - 110 006
Ph : 3626038, 3535592
Fax : 011- 3612498
E-Mail :
anilchemical@yahoo.com

Cochin Minerals And Rutile Ltd
P.B.No. 73, XVIII/219,
Market Road,
Alwaye-683101
Kerala
Ph:.0484-626789,
Fax: 0484-625674
E-Mail :
sachexim@vsnl.com

METHYL ETHYL KETONE

Cetex Petrochemicals,
Manali, Chennai -600068.
Phone : (044)-5941358,
5941359
Fax : (044)-5941835.
Email :
cetex.fac@cetex.sprintrpg.
cms.vsnl.net.in
Web : http://
www.cetexpetro.com.

Chemilite Industries
42/14, Babu Genu Road,
Mumbai-400002.
Phone : (022)-2050805,
Fax : (022)-2061582.

Gujarat Carbon & Industries Ltd.
Offtel Towers. 6th Floor,
R.C.Dutt Road,
Vadodara - 390007.
Gujarat

XYLENE MIXED

Ases Chemicals Works
Brahm Bagh, Jalori Gate,
Jodhpur -342001, Rajasthan
Phone (0291)-30437,37882
Fax : (0291)-38266

Reliance Industries Ltd.
Maker Chambers IV,
3rd Floor,
222, Nariman Point,
P.B.No. 11717,
Mumbai 400021.
Phone : (022)-2842384,
2842331,
Fax : (022)-2042268,288
Telex : 86542,82950
Web:http://www.ril.com.

ZINC OXIDE

A. Kumar & Co
30/2, Ellisbridge Shopping Centre,
Opp Town Hall Ashram
Road, Ahmedabad-380006
Gujarat
Phone : (079)-6578457, (R)
6440733
Fax : (079)-6577585

Amvee Chemicals
Saket, Baptista Road.
Vile-Parale(west)
Mumbai-400056.
Phone -(022)-
6161504,6141485
Fax: (022)-6117049,

Bajaj Rubber Co.
15, Khurshid Market,
Sadar Bazar,
Delhi - 110 006
Ph : 3626038, 3535592
Fax : 011- 3612498
E-Mail :
anilchemical@yahoo.com

NITRO CELLULOSE

Amrut Chemicals,
31, Old Bardan Lane,
Above Somiya Transports,
Vadgadi,
Mumbai-400003.
Phone: (022)-3441951.
Fax : (022)-345221.
Br.Office: B/102,
Avanti Building No.2,
Haridas Nagar,
Shimpoli Road,
Borivali (West),
Mumbai-4000092.
Phone : (022)-8189807,
8997177.
Estd.1990

Kunal Petrochemicals,
18, Saptashrungi,
Pestom Sagar, Road No.5,
Tilak Nagar P.O.,
Mumbai - 400089.
Phone : (022)-5229255.
Br. Office : 2,
Saurabh Society,
Sanjay Park, Karelibag,
Vadodara 390018,
Gujarat.
Phone : (0265)-424737.
Fax : (0265)-424737.
Estd. 1984 (Proprietary Firm).

Jaichem
301, Madhav Kunj,
South Pond Roa,
Vile Parle (West),
Mumbai-400056,
Phone : (022)-612894.
Fax : (022)-6124814.
Estd. 1998
(Proprietary Firm)

PIGMENTS

Bajaj Rubber Co.
15, Khurshid Market,
Sadar Bazar,
Delhi - 110 006
Ph : 3626038, 3535592
Fax : 011- 3612498
E-Mail :
anilchemical@yahoo.com

Oswal Cable Products
A-93/1, Wazirpur Group
Ind. Area,
Delhi - 110 052
Ph : 7211108, 7228845
Fax : 91-11-7246570
E-Mail :
ocp@mantraonline.com

STABILIZERS

AKD Polymers Pvt. Ltd.,
N-1A, Ist Floor,
Kirti Complex,
Kirti Nagar,
New Delhi - 110 015
Ph : 5105010, 5467322
Fax : 5448553
E-Mail :
akdpoly@del3.vsnl.net.in

Oswal Cable Products
A-93/1, Wazirpur Group
Ind. Area,
Delhi - 110 052
Ph : 7211108, 7228845
Fax : 91-11-7246570
E-Mail :
ocp@mantraonline.com

POWDER FOR POWDER COATING

Ameetuff Technical Paints Industry
1-8, DLF Ind. Area,
Phase-1,
Faridabad (Haryana)
Ph : 6942208

ALL FOLLOWING PROJECT REPORTS ARE READILY AVAILABLE

- Integerated Complex Of Easter & Allied Products (D.O.P, D.B.P, Ethyl Acetate Wire Enamel & Cable Jelly)
- Insta Whitening System (Ujala Type)
- Imfl (Whisky) & Country Liquor
- Imfl (Whiskey) From Potato
- Iron Oxide For Making Feritte
- Iron Sulphide
- Jatropha (Biodiesel) Cultivation And Extraction
- J. Acid
- Jute Batching Oil
- Kesh Kala Tel (Hair Dye Lotion) (Vasmol 33, Black Nite Type)
- L-Lysine Monohydrochloride
- Lactic Acid From White Sugar By Fermentation Process
- Ldpe Granules From Virgin (Ldpe Resin)
- Lead Extraction From Battery Scrap
- Lead Oxide
  (A) Lead Monoxide
  (B) Lead Tetra Oxide
  (C) Greylead Oxide
- Liquid Glucose & Its By Products
- Liquid Gold (In Paste Form)
- Lemon Oil From Lemon
- Liquid Oxygen Bottling Plant
- Liquid Shoe Polish
- Liquid Floor Polish
- Lithium Based Grease
- Linear Alkyl Benzene Sulphonate
- Lube Oil Viscosity Improved For P.P.G/P.E.G.
- Lube Oil And Greases
- Lube Oil From Cnsl To Reduce Friction
- Lubricants Ashless 100% Combustion
- Maize Oil
- Magnesium Carbonate And Magnesium Bicarmonate
- Magnesium Hydroxide Powder
- Magnesium Silicate
- Magnesium Sulphate
- Malachite Green
- Maleic Acid
- Maleic Anhydride
- Manganese Sulphate
- Manufacturing Of Carbon Mono-Oxide Water Gas
- Menthol Bold Crystals From Flakes
- Menthol Crystal & Mentha Oil
- Mercuric Oxide
- Metal Pre-Treatment Chemicals
- Methyl Chloride
- Methyl Cinnamate
- Methane Gas By Sodium Acetate & Soda Lime
- Methyl Acetyl Ricinolate
- Methyl Parathion 2% Dust Powder
- Methyl Stearate
- Metol
- Metol From Hydroqui-None & Methylamine
- Micanite
- Micro Crystalline Wax
- Micro Nutrient Mixture
- Mineral Water
- Mineral Water And Pet Bottilng Plant
- Mineral Water In Bottles, Glass And Pouches
- Mini Cement Plant (By Rotary Kiln Process)
- Mixed Fertilizer
- Mosquito Repellent Vaporiser (Liquid Mosquito Destroyer)
- Mosquito & Flies Repellent Agarbatti (Incense Sticks)
- Monochloro Acetic Acid
- Monocrotophos (Technical)
- Mosquito Coil
- Mosquito Coil & Mat
- Mosquito Mat
- Mosquito Net
- Mosquito Coil Agarbatti
- Mother Tincture & Bio Chemic Medicines
- Naphthalene & Phenyl (Integrated Unit)
- Natural Mineral Water By Reverse Osmosis Process
- Nickel Plating Brightner (Primary Or Carrier Brightner & Secondary Brightner)
- Nickel Sulphate
- Nicotine From Tobacco Waste
- Nicotine Sulphate From Tobacco Waste
- Nitro Benzene
- Nitro Cellulose Sanding Sealer/Lacquer
- Nitro Musk
- Nitrogen & Oxygen Gas Plant
- Non-Ionic Surfactant (Wetting Agent)
- No-Carb Paste
- Npk Mixed Fertilizer (Molasses Based)
- N.P.K Fertilizer
- Octanol
- Oleoresin From Chilly And Ginger (Extraction)
- Oleoresins From Marigold Petals (Extraction)
- Organic Fertiliser
- Ortho Nitro Phenol
- Ortho Phthalic Polyester
- Oxalic Acid From Molasses
- Oxalic Acid From Rice Husk
- Oxalic Acid From Tree Bark
- Oxalic Acid From Waste Vegetables
- Oxygen Gas Plant
- Oxygen And Nitrogen Gas Plant
- Oxygen Gas Plant (Air Seperation Method)
- Para-Amino Benzoic Acid
- Para-Amino Phenol
- Para Toluene Sulphonic Acid
- Pectin From Raw Papaya
- Pectin From Apple Pomace
- Pectin From Mango Peel
- Pectin From Oranges
- Pectin From Citrus/Lemon
- Perfume (Lemon & Others)
- Perfume Spray Deodorant (Non-Alcoholic)
- Pest Control
- Pesticide Preparation Using Neem Fruit & Seeds (Margosa)
- Pet Bottles From Pre-Form
- Pet Granules (Dana)
- Pet Preform From Resin For Pet Bottles
- Petroleum Jelly
- Phenol
- Phenyl Acetic Acid
- Phenyl
- Phenyl (Black) In Liquid Form
- Phthalic Anhydride
- Phosphoric Acid From Rock Phosphate
- Phosphorus By Chemical Process
- Photo Emulsion For Rotary Screen Printing
- Phthalocyanine Blue
- Pigment Emulsion For Textile
- Pigment Gum
- Plant Growth Reagen Based Chlorothyltrimethyl Ammonium Chloride
- Plant Harmones Based On 2,4-Dichlorphenoxy
- Acentic Acid & Naphthalene
- Plastazote Polythylene Foam Used For Fibre Cable Joint
- Plasticine (Modelling Clay)
- Plastic Waste Reprocessing
- Plaster Of Paris Bandages
- Polyester Resin (G.P. Grade Laminate Grade, Electrical Grade)
- Polyol From Propylene Oxide
- Poly Vinyl Acetate
- Polyvinyl Acetate Emulsion
- Polyvinyl Alcohol
- Polyurethene Foam
- Potassium Dichromate/Bichromate
- Potassium Iodate
- Potassium Nitrate
- Potassium Permagnate
- Potassium Per Sulphate
- Potassium Sulphate (Fertilizer Grade)
- Potassium Per Oxy Di-Sulphide
- Potassium Silicate By Ion Exchange Process
- Potassium Silicate
- Potassium Stearate
- Processing Of Datura Stramonium Into Hyosyamina And Atropin
- Power Alcohol
- Pvc Resin From Ethyl Alcohol
- Pyridine & Its Derivatives
- Rapid Fast Dyes (Only Process)
- Reactor (Chemical)
- Resorcinol
- Reclamation Of Used Engine Oil (By Clay & Vacuum Distillation Process)
- Refinery Petrol/Diesel Etc.
- Reclamation Of Spent Bleaching Earth
- Reclamation Of Nickel Spent Catalyst From Vanaspati Industry
- Rectified Spirit From Molasses & Mahua Flowers
- Rectified Spirit From Rice Straw
- Red Oxide Paint/Primer (Anti Corrosive) Based Organic Red Pigments
- Refinery Petrol/Diesel Etc.
- Removal Of Antimony From Lead Scrap
- Resorcinol
- Rice Bran Oil (Rbo)
- Rosin Sizing Agent

PAINT, ENAMEL, SOLVENTS, THINNERS, INKS & VARNISHMEDICINES, HOMOEOPATHIC MEDICINES, DISPOSABLE SYRINGE, DENTAL COLLEGE & FINE CHEMICALS ETC.

ALL FOLLOWING PROJECT REPORTS ARE READILY AVAILABLE

- Polyester Resin
- Polyester Yarn From Waste
Polyester Zip Fasteners
- Power Loom
- Printing On Saree
- Readymade Garments & Hosiery
- Readymade Garments Merchandise
- Readymade Garments & Covers
- Readymade Garments & Embroidery Of Gowns, Shirts, Blouses, T-Shirts Etc. (Only Ladies)
- Readymade Salwar Suit
- Ready Made Garments
- Recovery Of Nylon From Nylon Waste
- Rotary Printing And Dyeing On Cotton, Synthetic Textile
- Sanitary Napkins
- Screen Printing On Cotton Cloth
- Sewing Thread Reels & Balls Making Industries
- Screen Printing On Cotton, Polyester & Acrylic
- Shawls (Woollen)
- Shoe Laces
- Silk Fabrics On Handloom
- Socks Knitting
- Spinning, Doubling Dyeing, Mercerising & Bleaching Of Cotton Yarn
- Spinning & Carding Of Wool Into Yarns
- Starch Book Binding Cloth
- Surat Jari
- Surgical Cotton & Bandage
- Synthetic Textile Industry (Suiting, Shirting, Sarees) Terry Cloth
- T-Shirts
- Towels, Bed Sheet Covers
- Terry Towel
- Terry Fabrics Weaving Unit
- Textile Auxilliaries & Chemicals
- Textile Bleaching, Dyeing & Finishing & Printing Of Cotton Fabrics
- Textile And Finishing Agent
- Textile (Hosiery)
- Textile Mill
- Textile Dyeing & Printing
- Textile Printing (Job Work)
- Textile Pigment Printing Binder
- Towel (Terry)
- Velvet Cloth By Flocking Process
- Viscose Staple Fibre
- Wadding Oil (100%) For Wadding Of Cotton Hosiery Cloth In The Dyeing Process
- Weaving Of Dasuti Cloth With Printing, Dyeing, Embroidery & Finishing
- Washing Of Jeans & Other Garments
- Worsted Woollen Yarn Cloth
- Zari Glitter Salma Sitara Of Plastic Film

INFOTECH/IT, HOSPITALITY, HOSPITAL, COLLEGE, SCHOOL, MEDICAL, ENTERTAINMENT, CLUB, WARE HOUSING & REAL ESTATE PROJECTS.

- Amusement Park
- Aided School
- Amusement Park Cum Water Park
- Banquet Hall
- B.Ed And Law College
- Business Process Outsourcing (Bpo)
- Call Center (Domestic)
- Call Center (International)
- Children Recreation Centre
- Cold Storage
- Community Hall
- Community Centre
- Computer Education Institute
- Computer Software
- College
- Club
- Cyber Café
- Data Processing Centre
- Dental Clinic
- Dental College
- Diagonostic Centre
- E-Commerce/Business
- E-School (Rs. 10,000/-)
- Engineering College
- Entertainment Club
- Entertainment Club, Holiday Resort, 4 Star Hotel, Amusement Park Cum Water Park, Mushroom & Its Products, Fish Farming, Lake For Boating, Deer Park
- Fashion Technology Institute
- Fast Food Parlour
- Five Star Hotel
- Food Parlour
- Franchise Training Programme For Iit & Engineering Entrance Exams.
- Golf Course
- Health Club, Beauty Parlour
- Health Club And Fitness Center
- Health Resorts
- Holiday Resorts
- Holiday Resort Cum Entertainment Club With 4 Star Hotel
- Hospitals
- Hospital Cum Research Centre
- Hospital (400 Beds)
- Ice Cream Parlour
- Internet Service Provider (I.S.P.)
- I.T. Park (Infotech Park)
- Maternity Nursing Home
- Medical College
- Medical College, Hospital & Research Institute
- Medical Transcription Centre
- Mental Retardation Hospital & Cerebral Palsy
- Motel/Small Hotel
- Multistorey Commercial Complex

- Multistorey Residential Complex
- Multiplex Cum Entertainment Centre
- Nursery School
- Nursing School/College
- Nature Care Centre
- Nursing Home
- Old Age Home
- Online Shopping Mall (Rs. 10,000/- Report)
- Portal
- Pre-Fabricated Building
- Prenursery School
- Rehabilitation Centre For Aged & Needy Persons
- Residential Cum Commercial Complex
- Restaurant
- Restaurant With Pub
- Senior Secondary School
- Special Economic Zone (Sez)/Industrial Park
- School (Primary)
- School (Higher Secondary)
- School With Hostel
- School Of Nursing
- Three Star Hotel
- Township
- Tourist Club
- Training Institute For Medical Transcription
- Video Film Studio
- Vetenary College With Hospital
- Ware House
- Website Design & E-Mail Registering

POTATO AND POTATO BASED PRODUCTS

- Alcohol From Potatoes
- Dextrose Powder From Potatoes
- Frozen Finger Chips
- I M F L (Whisky) From Potatoes
- Liquid Glucose From Potato
- Potato Chips/Waffers
- Potato Powder (Automatic Plant)
- Potato Starch
- Potato Chips (Automatic Plant)
- Potato And Onion Flakes
- Potable Beer (Alcoholic) Based On Potato & Barley/Malt
- Potato Powder
- Sago Seeds (Saboo Dana)
- Vodka From Potatoes

Market Survey Cum Detailed Techno Economic Feasibility Report on all Projects are available Contact.
"ENGINEERS INDIA RESEARCH INSTITUTE", 4449, Nai Sarak (D), Main Road, Delhi-110006 (India)
Ph. : 09811437895, 91-11-23918117, 23916431, 45626431, 64727385 Fax : 91-11-23916431
E-mail : eiriprojects@gmail.com, eiribooks@yahoo.com • website: www.eiri.in, www.eiriindia.org

ALL FOLLOWING PROJECT REPORTS ARE READILY AVAILABLE

- Alluminium Printing Plate For Offset Printing Machine
- Aluminium Foils
- Aluminium Wire And Rods
- Brass And Aluminium Hinges
- Hard Anodizing On Aluminium
- Pilfer Proof Caps
- Piston Assembly (Aluminium Alloy)
- Pressure Die Casting (Aluminium)
- Paper Coated Aluminium Wire
- Pressure Cooker

FISH FARMING AND FISHERY PRODUCTS

- Aquaculture Prawn Farming (Fresh Water)
- Chitin & Chitosan From Prawn Shell Waste
- Chemicals From Prawn Fish Head
- Developing Trout Fish Preservation & Storage And Marketing Infrastructure
- Fish Farming
- Fish Canning And Pouching
- Fish Processing (Blast Freezing Process)
- Fish Net
- Fish Oil Soap
- Fish Meal
- Hdpe Fishing Net
- Plastic Milk Crate And Plastic Fish Crate
- Trout Fish Farming, Canning & Preservation With Aqua Feed Manufacturing (Integrated Complex)

SURGICAL AND DISPOSABLE MEDICAL PRODUCTS

- Ayurvedic/Herbal Pharmacy
- Blood Bags
- Bandage Cloth Weaving On Power Loom
- Crepe Bandage
- Disposable Surgical Caps & Masks
- Dextrose Saline (I.V.Fluid) In Plastic Bottle
- Dextrose Saline (I.V.Fluid)
- Disposable Needles For Syringes
- Disposable Plastic Syringes
- Diagnostic Centre
- Electronics Blood Pressure Measuring Instument
- Hospital Cum Nursing Home
- Homeopathic Medicines
- I. V. Fluids (Ffs Technology)
- I.V. Set-Cannula
- Intravenous
- Medical College
- Plastic I.V. Bottles

- Plaster Of Paris Bandages
- Pharmaceuticals (Tablet, Capsule, Syrups And Ointments)
- Repacking Of Medicines
- Surgical Cotton & Bandage
- Surgical Examination Gloves
- Surgical Bandage
- Surgical Adhesive Tape On Cloth Surface
- Surgical Methylated Spirit
- Sodium Phosphate Enema
- Vetenary Medicines

ALCOHOL, BEER, IMFL, COUNTRY LIQUOR, WINE & OTHER RELATED PROJECTS

- Alcohol From Rice Straw
- Alcohol From Molasses
- Alcohol From Potatoes
- Alcoholic Beverages And Vinegar From Coconut Water
- Alcoholic Drinks From Ethyl Alcohol
  By Mixing Of Various Flavours (Flavoured Alcoholic Beverages)
- Beer Plant (E.O.U.)
- Country Liquor
- Cider Plant
- Ethanol (Biofuel)
- Grape Wine
- Herbal Beer
- Mineral Water (Packed In Bottles, Glasses, Jars)
- Rectified Spirit For Potable Alcohol
- Industrial Alcohol & Medical Alcohol
- Rectified Spirit From Rice/Paddy Straw
- Indian Made Foreign Liquor
- Imfl (Whisky) From Potatoes
- Octalol (Octyl Alcohol) From Molasses
- Potable Beer (Alcoholic) Based On Potato & Barley/Malt
- Vodka From Potatoes
- Whisky
- Wine From Dates

PULP, PAPER, STRAW/GREY BOARD, KRAFT PAPER,PACKAGING, PAPER CARRY BAG, PAPER FROM AGRO WASTE & STATIONERY ETC.

- Ammonia Paper
- Automatic Book Binding
- Adhesive (Fevicol Type)
- All Pin & Gem Clips
- Ball Pen
- Ball Pen Refill Ink
- Ball Pen Ink Remover
- Carbon Paper
- Card Board
- Carbon Less Paper
- Cellphane Paper
- Computer Continuous Stationery
- Computer Forms & Security Printing Press
- Corrugated Board & Box (Printed & Laminated)
- Corrugated Board And Boxes From From Card Boards
- Corrugated Cartons From Plain Papers
- Corrugated Paper
- Corrugatred Packing & Material (Bulb & Tubes Packing)
- Desk Top Publishing
- Defoaming Agent For Paper Plant
- Drinking Straw Paper
- D.T.P Cum Offset Press
- Egg Trays From Pulp
- Ecg Paper
- Exercise Note Book, Register And Pad
- Flexographic Ink
- Greeting Card By Offset Press
- Hand Made Paper Filter Paper
- Hard Board
- Hard Board From Bagasse
- Injection Ampoules Packaging Boxes
- Insulatiing Paper
- Kraft Paper
- Kraft Paper From Bagasse
- Laminated Packaging Paper With Printing
- Lamination & Coating On Paper
- M.G. Paper From Waste Paper
- Mill Paper From Waste Paper
- Mill Board From Rice & Wheat Straws
- Mill Board From Waste Paper
- Mini Paper Plant From Sisal
- Mini Paper Plant
- Multi Wall Paper Sacks
- News Paper For Children
- News Print Paper From Rice Straw/Bagasse
- News Paper Childrens
- News Print Paper

Market Survey Cum Detailed Techno Economic Feasibility Report on all Projects are available Contact.
"ENGINEERS INDIA RESEARCH INSTITUTE". 4449, Nai Sarak (D), Main Road, Delhi-110006 (India)
Ph. : 09811437895, 91-11-23918117, 23916431, 45626431, 64727385 Fax : 91-11-23916431
E-mail : eiriprojects@gmail.com, eiribooks@yahoo.com • website: www.eiri.in, www.eiriindia.org